Contents

Sport Development in Action

This practical textbook explains the sport development process from a practitioner's viewpoint, showing what actually works, how, and why. Focusing on the development of sport, the book considers the efforts of sport organisations to revitalise their sports at a community level to ensure their future relevance, growth, and sustainability.

Full of real-world cases and data, as well as the voices and reflections of a wide range of practitioners, *Sport Development in Action* explains how to research and draw up a development plan, how to design and implement programmes and establish delivery networks, and how to monitor and evaluate initiatives.

This is essential reading for any sport development course, and useful reading for courses in sport management, sports coaching, or sports studies. It is also an indispensable reference book for practitioners.

Alec Astle is an Independent Researcher and Level III Cricket Coach with lifelong experiences of sport as a player, coach, and administrator; he previously held roles as New Zealand Cricket's National Development Manager and SPARC's Manager, Community Sport. In 2014, he received the Sutcliffe Medal from New Zealand Cricket for outstanding services to cricket.

Sarah Leberman is Professor of Leadership and Dean Academic at Massey University, New Zealand. Her research focus is on women in leadership within sport and academia. She co-founded Women in Sport Aotearoa, an organisation providing leadership, research, and advocacy to ensure women and girls are valued, visible, and influential in sport. Sarah has had over 30 years' experience in sport at all levels, as an athlete, coach, administrator, board member, and manager.

Geoff Watson is Senior Lecturer in History at Massey University, New Zealand. He has written and contributed to many books and articles on sport in New Zealand, and has been actively involved in playing and coaching sport.

Sport Development in Action

Plan, Programme and Practice

Alec Astle, Sarah Leberman and Geoff Watson

Routledge
Taylor & Francis Group

LONDON AND NEW YORK

First published 2019
by Routledge
2 Park Square, Milton Park, Abingdon, Oxon OX14 4RN

and by Routledge
52 Vanderbilt Avenue, New York, NY 10017

Routledge is an imprint of the Taylor & Francis Group, an informa business

British Library Cataloguing-in-Publication Data
A catalogue record for this book is available from the British Library

Library of Congress Cataloging-in-Publication Data
A catalog record has been requested for this book

ISBN: 978-1-138-89581-2 (hbk)
ISBN: 978-1-138-89582-9 (pbk)
ISBN: 978-1-315-17932-2 (ebk)

Typeset in Berling and Futura
by Swales & Willis Ltd, Exeter, Devon, UK

Illustrations

FIGURES

TABLES

Appendices

Pause and ponders

Facts and figures

Case studies

Acknowledgements

We would like to acknowledge the following practitioners for sharing their first-hand, practical sport development knowledge and experiences within Chapters 8, 9 and 10, and case studies throughout the book.

Ryan Astle	Digital Marketing Specialist, Jade Logistics Group; and Vice President, Old Boys' Collegians Cricket Club, Christchurch, New Zealand.
Brent Anderson	Head of Community Rugby, New Zealand Rugby, Wellington, New Zealand.
Nigel Brooke	Manager, Community Cricket, Central Districts' Cricket Association, New Zealand.
Lindsay Calton	Sports Coordinator and Coach, Palmerston North Boys' High School, Palmerston North, New Zealand.
Emma Campbell	Cricket Development Officer, Otago Country Cricket Association; Club Manager, Queenstown Cricket Club; and Programme Coordinator, Sports Coaching Solutions Ltd, Queenstown, New Zealand.
Mark Cameron	Former Chief Executive Officer, Auckland Cricket Association, current Chief Executive Officer, Bowls New Zealand, Auckland, New Zealand.
James Carr	Former part-time Learning Difficulty/Physical Disability Cricket Development Officer, Lancashire Cricket Board, England, current Cricket Development Officer, Southland Cricket Association, Invercargill, New Zealand.
Jack Clayton	Community Hockey Manager, Young People, Hockey New Zealand, Auckland, New Zealand.
Peter Clinton	Former Cricket Development Manager, Auckland Cricket Association, former Chief Executive, Cricket Wellington, Wellington, New Zealand.
Adrian Dale	Former Cricket Development Manager. Auckland Cricket Association, current General Manager Community Cricket, New Zealand Cricket, Auckland, New Zealand.
Rob Dearing	Head of Tennis Delivery and Innovation, Lawn Tennis Association, London, UK.
Ige Egal	Executive Director, Toronto Inner-City Rugby Foundation, Toronto, Canada.
Blair Franklin	Former Community Cricket Coordinator, Canterbury Country, current Account Manager, Kookaburra Sport, New Zealand.

Ian Francis   Former National Game Development Manager, Tennis New Zealand, current Chief Executive Officer, Hockey New Zealand, Auckland, New Zealand.

Tony Gill   National Grants Manager, New Zealand Community Trust, 2004–2015, New Zealand.

Mike Harvey   General Manager, Christchurch Metropolitan Cricket Association, Christchurch, New Zealand.

John Herdman   Former Director of Football, Football New Zealand, Auckland, New Zealand, current National Men's Team Head Coach and Men's National EXCEL Director, Soccer Canada, Vancouver, Canada.

Neil Hood   Hood Consulting, Levin, New Zealand.

Stuart Leighton   Teacher and Coach, Palmerston North Boys' High School, Palmerston North, New Zealand.

Andy Martin   Professor in Sport and Physical Activity, School of Exercise, Sport and Nutrition, College of Health, Massey University, Palmerston North, New Zealand.

Craig MacFarlane   Investment Coordinator, Planning, Investment and Performance, Sport New Zealand, Wellington; and Junior Convenor/Chairperson, Upper Hutt Rams Junior Rugby Football Club, Upper Hutt, New Zealand.

Kieran McMillan   Former Community Cricket Coordinator, Auckland Cricket Association, New Zealand, former East Asia Pacific Development Manager, International Cricket Council, current Community Development Manager, Cricket Australia, Melbourne, Australia.

Cameron Mitchell   Former Community Football Director, Football New Zealand, current Chief Executive, Cricket Wellington, Wellington, New Zealand.

Peter Miskimmin   Chief Executive, Sport New Zealand, Wellington, New Zealand.

Craig Morris   General Manager, Community Tennis and Youth Tennis, United States Tennis Association, Orlando, Florida, USA.

Rohan Obst   National Program Manager, Cricket Australia, Melbourne, Australia.

Michael Peacock   Cricket Australia Junior Participation Specialist, New South Wales, Sydney, Australia.

Alex Reese   Chairman and Founder, Cricket Live Foundation, Christchurch, New Zealand.

John Reid   Former General Manager Community Sport, Sport New Zealand, current Major Projects Property Manager, Selwyn District Council, Rolleston, New Zealand.

Ian Sandbrook   Head of Participation, Cricket Scotland, Edinburgh, Scotland, UK.

Lauren Shaw   Secretary/Treasurer, Maniototo Cricket Club, Ranfurly, Otago Country Cricket Association, New Zealand.

Martin Snedden   Former Chief Executive Officer, New Zealand Cricket; current Board Member and Project Lead, One Cricket Review, New Zealand Cricket, Auckland, New Zealand.

Neil Snowling   Senior Advisor – Monitoring and Performance, Sport New Zealand, Wellington, New Zealand.

Jamie Tong   Former National Game Development Manager, Tennis New Zealand, current Chief Executive, Squash New Zealand, Auckland, New Zealand.

Anna Walker   Former Sport Participation Consultant, Byron Bay, Australia, current Sport Development Manager, Surfing Australia, Coolangatta, Australia.

Scott Walker   Director of Rugby Development, Irish Rugby Football Union, Dublin, Ireland.

Trafford Wilson   Former Chief Executive, Wellington Hockey Association, Wellington, New Zealand, current Chief Executive, Snowsport Scotland, Edinburgh, Scotland, UK.

Abbreviations

BBL	Big Bash League
CA	Cricket Australia
CC	cricket club
CCC	community cricket coordinator
CDM	cricket development manager
CDO	cricket development officer
CE	chief executive
CEO	chief executive officer
DA	district association
DM	development manager
DMSP	development model of sport participation
ECB	England and Wales Cricket Board
FIFA	Fédération Internationale de Football Association
FDM	football development manager
FDO	football development officer
FMS	fundamental movement skills
HNZ	Hockey New Zealand
ICC	International Cricket Council
IGO	international governing organization
ILTF	International Lawn Tennis Federation
IOC	International Olympic Committee
IPL	Indian Premier League
ITF	International Tennis Federation
KPI	key performance indicator
LTA	Lawn Tennis Association
LTAD	long term athlete development
MA	major association
M&E	monitoring and evaluation
MSS	MILO Summer Squad
NDM	national development manager
NDP	national development programme
NFDU	national football development unit
NGB	national governing body

NGDM	national game development manager
NGO	non-governmental organisation
NSO	national sport organisation
NZ	New Zealand
NZC	New Zealand Cricket
NZCT	New Zealand Community Trust
NZF	New Zealand Football
NZFA	New Zealand Football Association
NZLTA	New Zealand Lawn Tennis Association
NZS	New Zealand Soccer
PA	provincial association
RDM	regional development manager
RDO	regional development officer
RFDU	regional football development unit
RSO	regional sport organisation
RST	regional sports trust
SCC	school cricket coordinator
SDM	sport development manager
SDO	sport development officer
SLA	service level agreement
SMART	specific, measurable, achievable, realistic, time-bound
SPARC	Sport and Recreation New Zealand
Sport NZ	Sport New Zealand
SWOT	strengths, weaknesses, opportunities, threats
TA	Tennis Australia
TNZ	Tennis New Zealand
T20	Twenty 20 cricket
UK	United Kingdom
UN	United Nations
USA	United States of America
USTA	United States Tennis Association
WBBL	Women's Big Bash League
WOFP	whole of football plan
WSP	whole sport plan

Introduction
Opening the innings

Millions of children and adults play sport in schools and clubs on a daily basis across the globe. With the increasing focus on healthy lifestyles and lifelong involvement, it's more important than ever to understand how to develop and provide the best sporting opportunities and experience within community sport.

For this reason, sport development has become increasingly important both as an emerging field of academic interest, and an expanding opportunity for employment of graduates in the sport industry. Sport development, for the purpose of this book, focuses on the 'development of sport', where community sport is valued and developed for its own sake, and increasingly also for the sake of its participants. Community sport is defined as organised sport within clubs and schools. This is where most people access and play sport (Doherty and Rich 2015) and is recognised as the foundation for high-performance sport (Nicholson, Hoye, and Houlihan 2011). But for many, the latter is of limited significance. As Prodger (quoted in Walker 2017: 60) claims with reference to community cricket in England:

> 99.98% of participation in this country plays recreational, not elite, cricket, yet 95% of all money goes to the elite game. To me, the recreational game needs to be celebrated in its own right, not with the pretence that it's a pathway to becoming a professional cricketer.

Since the 1990s, organised community sport, and its predominantly volunteer-based club and school structure, has been challenged by social, economic, and technological change. This includes: pressure from other entertainment and leisure options, and the diversification, commercialisation, and professionalisation of sport, with consumer-driven demands for choice and convenience affecting community sport attractiveness and participation rates. As Hulse (2017: 16) claims, "the world of sport is changing, and traditional sports are increasingly realising they have to adapt to keep up with an increasingly fickle audience". In the last two decades, a number of national sport organisations (NSOs) (termed national governing bodies (NGBs) in some countries) have intervened in community sport to assist adapting to these challenges.

Unfortunately, some sports and their NSOs have not adjusted to change, either ignoring the warning signs, lacking the foresight and resources to respond, or having slow-moving, complicated delivery networks without the flexibility or capability to adapt, as the following comments from athletics and lawn bowls in New Zealand (NZ) attest:

> Some athletics clubs are running towards oblivion as they fail to attract new members and suffer from the growing commercialisation of large-scale social running events.
>
> (Thomas 2017: A5)

> We still haven't got enough commitment within our own community that the world
> has changed from the good old 70s when everyone had the whole weekend to play
> sport. . . . If we don't adapt, we could continue to see a decline in some clubs.
>
> (Chief Executive, Bowls NZ,
> quoted in Smith 2016: D5)

To achieve this, some NSOs have designed holistic plans and innovative programmes, supported by professional delivery networks of sport development officers (SDOs), to work with volunteers, to revitalise, grow, and sustain their sports at a community level. These have helped meet increasingly diverse participant needs and expectations, by creating multiple pathways of competitive and social community sporting opportunities, especially for children and young people, catering for all ages, abilities, interests, and genders.

The focus for examining the 'development of sport' is organised community sport in NZ, in particular, cricket and New Zealand Cricket's (NZC) sport development plan, programme, and practice, which unapologetically have been the main source of the sporting knowledge, experiences, and research of the lead author, Alec Astle. His perspectives are complemented by the views of over 35 other practitioners representing various sports, sports partners, and countries, whose insights are interspersed throughout the book.

The book's uniqueness is in offering a practitioner's first-hand knowledge and experience of the 'development of sport' process, to explain and illustrate 'what actually works', 'how it works', and 'why it works'. Unlike the more abstract views of other books on the subject, *Sport Development in Action* gives an applied perspective on the 'development of sport'. It provides guidelines and exemplars for sports organisations and their practitioners on defining development and its scope, researching plans, designing programmes, devising initiatives, and establishing delivery networks to implement these to grow and sustain community sport.

REASONS FOR WRITING

There are two compelling reasons to write this book. The first is to fill a gap identified in the existing scholarship on the 'development of sport'. The second is to provide a 'how-to-guide' from a practitioner on planning, designing, implementing, and monitoring a 'development of sport' programme to increase and enhance participation in community sport.

Filling the gap in 'development of sport' research

Since Houlihan and White (2002) identified their broad interpretation of the 'development of sport', there have been limited studies of this process and its role and impact within community sport, despite a growing interest in the latter (Doherty and Cousens 2013). Most recent sport development books (Collins 2010; Girginov 2008; Houlihan and Green 2011; Sherry, Schulenkorf, and Phillips 2016), while making reference to the 'development of sport', tend to concentrate on sport as a vehicle to derive an array of non-sporting personal, community, or international development outcomes.

An excellent account of the 'development of sport' is that compiled by Eady in the United Kingdom (UK) titled *Practical Sport Development* (Eady 1993). It covers both the theory and practice of the 'development of sport' and provides an insightful guide for practitioners about the process and its application within community sport. This work, however, was published more than 20 years ago, and since then the field has evolved considerably.

Most 'development of sport' research has comprised:

- specific projects in a sport, club or community (Green 2005; Sport England 2007; Vail 2007), but often for the purpose of achieving non-sporting 'development through sport' outcomes, which are discussed in Chapter 1;
- external 'helicopter' studies using evidence derived from NSO strategic plans and annual reports (Sotiriadou, Shilbury, and Quick 2008); or
- surveys of SDO views of various aspects of the sport development process (Bloyce and Green 2011; Bloyce, Smith, Mead, and Morris 2008).

While Van Bottenburg and De Bosscher (2011) assessed the broad impact of sport development on sports participation, until the longitudinal study by Astle (2014) of the impact of the planned intervention by NZC into community cricket in NZ, there appeared to be no rigorous studies evaluating the effects of NSO interventions into community sport to specifically increase participation (Priest, Armstrong, Doyle, and Waters 2009). This paucity of research with reference to the 'development of sport', had previously been recognised by Shilbury, Sotiriadou, and Green (2008: 219), who identified in a special issue of *Sport Management Review* on sport development the need for research around this theme, "as clearly, from the perspective of the traditional NSO, there is much to be studied in relation to the systems and pathways designed by sports to attract, maintain and nurture participants".

The lack of investigations into the 'development of sport' is reflective of a combination of factors:

- The relative newness of the concept of sport development
- The lack of consistency and commitment to developing community sport by NSOs and national sport agencies fixated with high performance
- The preoccupation by most practitioners with designing and implementing plans and programmes rather than documenting and sharing their knowledge and experiences
- The dearth of long-term sport development data
- The limited emphasis on sport development in many tertiary institutions, where the focus is more on sport management and coaching, despite it "being an area of exponential growth in the international sport industry" (Schulenkorf, Sherry, and Phillips 2016: 3).

Sport Development in Action seeks to fill this void in the literature by examining the process, and using case studies of NSO interventions, to provide evidence of its long-term impact on community sport, particularly in three universally recognised sports: cricket, tennis, and football.

A practical guide to the 'development of sport' from a practitioner's perspective

Sport development, for Astle, has been a 'learn by doing' exercise. Starting as a practitioner-manager in the 1990s, he was charged with planning, designing, and implementing a national development programme (NDP) for NZC. He had, like his few contemporaries, no specific sport development training, and limited access to either practical examples of planned interventions by NSOs or academic literature on the subject. His early years in the field, therefore, were preoccupied with consultation, collecting information, and relying on his lifelong involvement in sport and unique combination of past lived experiences and roles as an academic; sportsman, coach and administrator; educator, both teacher and senior manager; and parent to understand the 'development of sport' process. This is not the case, however, with many younger sport development practitioners, who may have the advantage of a tertiary sport development or similar qualification, but still find there is much to be learned and experienced to fill the "gap between knowing and doing" (Lussier and Kimball 2014: 211), as they attempt to translate their academic theory into practice in the field – a field dominated by passionate and committed volunteers, with their own ideas and attitudes to their sport and its traditions, and not always receptive to innovation and change. *Sport Development in Action* is about closing this gap, with practical information and solutions from lessons learned, which can be applied and adapted in the field by practitioners working in community sport.

More lately, as an insider-researcher, it was necessary to sift through the now burgeoning literature on sport development, to understand and differentiate the various interpretations of sport development, in order to define and describe the 'development of sport' and its importance to community sport. In doing so, it revealed the previously mentioned lack of research into this growing area of interest for NSOs and national sport agencies. This provided the catalyst for contributing to both the theory and practice of sport development and extending a bridge across the so-called 'knowing–doing' divide between academics and practitioners, or as Emery (2011: 1) described it the "gap between classroom teaching and workplace needs".

Longitudinal research was undertaken to document NZC's plan, programme, and practice between 1998 and 2008; assess its impact on community cricket in NZ; and consider the applicability of the lessons learned by NZC to other NSOs looking to intervene into their sports (Astle 2014). This provided the inspiration and realisation of the need for a book to disseminate the knowledge and experience acquired to a wider sport development audience.

Sport Development in Action draws on Astle's more than 50 years of involvement in community sport at all levels in NZ, including being NZC's inaugural national development manager (NDM), and later the foundation Manager, Community Sport for New Zealand's national sport agency, Sport and Recreation New Zealand (SPARC), to share his rich insights and know-how about the 'development of sport' process. These are supported by a cross-section of community sport views and experiences from practitioners working for sports and sports partners in various countries, including: NZ, Australia, England, Scotland, Wales, Ireland, Sri Lanka, Canada, and United States of America (USA). The intention is to transfer this practical knowledge and experience into this format to provide other practitioners, academics, and students with a valuable, theoretically informed, reference about sport development, the practicalities of the 'development of sport' process in a community sport setting, and best practice solutions adopted in the field.

BOOK STRUCTURE AND CONTENT

The book is divided into four parts comprising 11 chapters. These follow a conceptual and theoretical pathway through to the practical application of the 'development of sport' process. They conclude with a summary of the 'planning to practice' steps which are key to its success.

The chapters are interspersed with useful facts and figures, pause and ponder observations, insightful case studies by practitioners active in developing community sport, and review questions to stimulate thinking.

Part I Sport development in theory and practice

The two introductory chapters provide a conceptual and theoretical background for the subsequent practical chapters. They examine sport development as a concept and outline a classification of its different interpretations. One interpretation – the 'development of sport' and its applicability to NSO interventions into community sport to ensure growth and future sustainability, is explored in more detail.

Part II Getting started in sport development

Chapters 3–7 each deal with a different step in the 'development of sport' process that need to be addressed by NSOs intervening to revitalise and grow community sport. These include: formulating a plan, designing a programme with a framework of pathways and meaningful initiatives, establishing a delivery network, implementing the programme and managing change, and monitoring and evaluating the practice.

Part III Sport development in practice

Chapters 8 and 9 examine the development of two organised sports in NZ: tennis and football. These provide insights from practitioners in these sports into their planning, programme design, implementation process, and challenges of 'doing' sport development. The NSOs of both sports were initially targeted by NZ's national sport agencies to improve their organisational structures, leadership, and capability, before specialist assistance and investment were provided to assist them create sport development plans, pathways, programmes, and regional SDO networks to increase community sport participation.

Part IV Reflections on sport development in practice

The final two chapters reflect on the views of a range of practitioners on the 'development of sport' process, its purpose, importance, and changing emphasis within community sport. From the lessons learned about the planning, design, and real-world application of NSO plans and programmes, a sequence of steps is identified for sport organisations and their sport development practitioners seeking to initiate the process of development in their own sports, and/or improve their own professional practice.

CONCLUSION

Sport Development in Action provides sport development practitioners and scholars with an in-depth account of the theory of the 'development of sport' process, and its practical application in different sports. The book draws on the experiences of a diversity of practitioners associated with the 'development of sport' at a community level and provides practical guidance on 'what to do' and 'how to do it'.

REFERENCES

Astle, A. M. (2014). *Sport development – Plan, programme and practice: A case study of the planned intervention by New Zealand Cricket into cricket in New Zealand.* PhD, Massey University, Palmerston North, New Zealand.

Bloyce, D., & Green, K. (2011). Sports development officers on sport development. In B. Houlihan & M. Green (Eds.), *Routledge handbook of sports development* (pp. 477–486). London and New York: Routledge.

Bloyce, D., Smith, A., Mead, R., & Morris, J. (2008). 'Playing the game (plan)': A figurational analysis of organisational change in sports development in England. *European Sport Management Quarterly, 8*(4), 359–378.

Collins, M. (Ed.). (2010). *Examining sports development.* London and New York: Routledge.

Doherty, A., & Cousens, L. (2013). Introduction to the special issue on community sport. *Journal of Sport Management, 27,* 419–421.

Doherty, A., & Rich, K. (2015). Sport for community development. In M. T. Bowers & M. A. Dixon (Eds.), *Sport management: An exploration of the field and its value* (pp. 124–145). Urbana, IL: Sagamore Publishing.

Eady, J. (1993). *Practical sports development.* Harlow: Longman.

Emery, P. (2011). *The sports management toolkit.* London: Routledge.

Girginov, V. (Ed.). (2008). *Management of sports development.* Oxford: Elsevier/Butterworth-Heinemann.

Green, B. C. (2005). Building sport programs to optimise athlete recruitment, retention, and transition: Toward a normative theory of sport development. *Journal of Sport Management, 19,* 233–253.

Houlihan, B., & Green, M. (Eds.). (2011). *Routledge handbook of sports development.* London and New York: Routledge.

Houlihan, B., & White, A. (2002). *The politics of sports development: Development of sport or development through sport?* London: Routledge.

Hulse, T. (2017, May). Disrupting sport. *Business Life,* 14–20.

Lussier, R. N., & Kimball, D. C. (2014). *Applied sport management skills* (2nd ed.). Champaign, IL: Human Kinetics.

Nicholson, M., Hoye, R., & Houlihan, B. (2011). Introduction. In M. Nicholson, R. Hoye, & B. Houlihan (Eds.), *Participation in sport: International policy perspectives* (pp. 1–9). London and New York: Routledge.

Priest, N., Armstrong, R., Doyle, J., & Waters, E. (2009). Interventions implemented through sporting organisations for increasing participation in sport (Review). *The Cochrane Library* (4), 1–15.

Schulenkorf, N., Sherry, E., & Phillips, P. (2016). What is sport development? In E. Sherry, N. Schulenkorf, & P. Phillips (Eds.), *Managing sport development: An international approach* (pp. 3–11). London and New York: Routledge.

Sherry, E., Schulenkorf, N., & Phillips, P. (Eds.). (2016). *Managing sport development: An international approach.* London and New York: Routledge.

Shilbury, D., Sotiriadou, K., & Green, B. C. (2008). Sport development. Systems, policies and pathways: An introduction to the special issue. *Sport Management Review, 11*(3), 217–223.

Smith, T. (2016, Saturday, November 5). CEO Clark quits NZ bowls after 20 years. *The Press,* p. D5.

Sotiriadou, K., Shilbury, D., & Quick, S. (2008). The attraction, retention/transition, and nurturing process of sport development: Some Australian evidence. *Journal of Sport Management, 22,* 247–272.

Sport England. (2007). *Impact in 3D: A learning guide for practitioners in community sport.* Retrieved from http://www.sportengland.org/research/evaluating_impact.aspx website.

Thomas, J. (2017, Sunday, October 1). Running clubs puff to their finish line. *Sunday Star Times,* p. A5.

Vail, S. E. (2007). Community development and sport participation. *Journal of Sport Management, 21,* 571–596.

Van Bottenburg, M., & De Bosscher, V. (2011). An assessment of the impact of sports development on sports participation. In B. Houlihan & M. Green (Eds.), *Routledge handbook of sports development* (pp. 600–614). London and New York: Routledge.

Walker, P. (2017). Cricket's battle for the working classes: Breaking the grass ceiling. In L. Booth (Ed.), *Wisden cricketers' almanack* (154th ed., pp. 55–61). London: John Wisden & Co.

PART I

Sport development in theory and practice

CHAPTER 1

Sport development
The concept and a model of interpretations

The first challenge for sport development practitioners and scholars is to define sport development. This is essential to comprehending and executing their role or scoping their research. However, to articulate a definition is not straightforward, as the academic literature reveals, and many authors steer clear of committing to a definition. This is because the purpose and focus of the concept have changed over time and place, according to the agendas of the increasing diversity of agencies involved in sport development, and whether their prime interest is on 'sport' or on 'development'.

While simply sport development is about "getting more people to play more sport" (Houlihan 2011b: 3), this definition is frequently complicated by the ambiguity arising from the competing interests of 'who' is involved in sport development (i.e. agency), 'where' they operate (i.e. setting), and 'what' they expect to accomplish (i.e. objectives and outcomes), such as increasing participation, developing talent, and/or tackling non-sporting, societal issues. To explain how the interplay of these interests influences the purpose and focus of sport development, and how it is defined, several interpretations of the concept have been articulated. The terminology assigned to these interpretations juxtaposes the terms 'sport' and 'development', and separates them with different conjunctions, making the concept complex and highly contested.

The extant literature on sport development does not accurately capture this complexity as it is experienced by practitioners dealing with different agencies and expectations (Bloyce, Smith, Mead, and Morris 2008). To better understand sport development, and clarify the confusion of definitions and terminologies associated with it, this chapter will:

1. Discuss the terms 'sport' and 'development', and the applicability of 'development' to sport in understanding the concept.
2. Consider the difficulties in formulating a definition of the concept, before presenting a practical description of sport development.
3. Examine the existing classifications of sport development, then outline a more differentiated model that identifies and describes the variances in interpretation of how sport develops, grows, changes over time, and increasingly is used to contribute to the development of non-sporting outcomes.

DEVELOPMENT AND ITS APPLICABILITY TO SPORT

Sport development appears to be a 'catch-all' concept that is applied to everything, from developing sport to assure its participatory appeal and future growth, to using sport as a vehicle for personal, political, or socio-economic improvements that benefit the development of individuals, groups, communities, and/or nations (Eady 1993; Hylton and Bramham 2008).

Because sport development means different things to different agencies, it is difficult to interpret and define.

Sport is interpreted here as a competitive, formal, and rule-bound activity that requires physical and sport-specific skills and takes place in an organised setting (Nicholson, Hoye, and Houlihan 2011a). In this book, the organised setting is primarily clubs and schools who deliver 'community sport'. Community sport is what most participants experience. It is essentially amateur sport, played competitively, mainly for enjoyment and recreational purposes. It is "the grassroots foundation of a country's sport system. . . where most people engage in organised sport" (Doherty and Cousens 2013: 419) (see Facts and figures 1.1). In Australia, Canada, and England, community sport is organised mainly through volunteer-led clubs (Doherty and Rich 2015), while in NZ it is provided by both schools and clubs (see Case studies 1.1 and 1.2).

FACTS and FIGURES 1.1

Importance of community sport

Just 3% of all community sport participants graduate into representative or high-performance sport. From these, just a fraction, 0.001–0.002%, become elite performers (Walker 2017). This is illustrated by the few elite athletes who represented their countries across numerous sports in the 2016 Rio De Janeiro Olympic Games.

Country	Elite athletes	Number of sports
Australia	418	23
Great Britain	372	25
New Zealand	199	20

Source: www.mapsofworld.com/sports/olympics/athletes.

Question

Calculate the percentage of players in a sport within a club or school you are familiar with that are currently in representative teams? Is this more or less than 3%?

CASE STUDY 1.1

Contribution of secondary schools to community sport in New Zealand

Stuart Leighton, Teacher/Coach, and Lindsay Calton, Sport Coordinator/Coach, Palmerston North Boys' High School, Palmerston North, New Zealand

Schools, to varying degrees, contribute to providing organised community sport for children and young people. In NZ, both primary (5–12 years) and secondary (13–17 years) schools offer opportunities for students to play sport.

In 2017, of the 2,531 schools in NZ, 374 were secondary schools. The contribution of secondary schools to community sport varies with their understanding of the value of sport, role in encouraging lifelong participation, and number of teachers committed to delivering sport. The latter have declined with increasing numbers of female teachers, less emphasis on physical education, and greater assessment and reporting demands placed on teachers. At the same time, the demands and expectations of young people (and their parents) to participate in the diversity of sports now available is challenging the capability, capacity, and resources of many schools. Schools have variously responded by: reducing their commitment to sport; relying on local sports clubs; paying external coaches; and forming internal 'closed' clubs in different sports to involve parents and qualify for community funding to assist deliver sport. A small number of schools, have created individual sport academies within their schools, and offered sport scholarships to recruit talented players.

Schools such as Palmerston North Boys' High School (PNBHS), a single-sex, state secondary school located in Palmerston North, a city of 80,000 people, have embraced sport as an integral part of their curriculum. PNBHS currently has a roll of 1,849 boys, of whom 72% regularly participate in one or more of 32 sports the school offers, and unlike many state schools, 73% of its 131 full-time teachers are involved as coaches and managers of these sports.

Sport and the intrinsic values it instils (e.g. loyalty, discipline, teamwork), and the experiential mix of fun, friendship, skill development, and competitive challenges it offers, are integral to PNBHS's philosophy of producing well-rounded young men. Sport is not only character-building for students, but has created a special rapport between students and staff, and a positive, supportive environment within the school.

While the most popular sports are basketball, cricket, football, and rugby, each with over 200 participants, the diversity of sports now available include golf croquet, canoe polo, and motocross. Competitive and social pathways of opportunities cater for all students, irrespective of age, ability, or interest. To support this, PNBHS has fundraised to construct and improve its sport facilities, funded staff to attend coach education courses, established a 'Sports Develop' curriculum option for Years 9/10 sportsmen, and regularly acknowledges and celebrates its students' sporting achievements.

PNBHS's commitment to sport is not without challenges. Among these are the need to: balance academic, sporting, and cultural objectives; provide sporting opportunities for all not just the most talented; try and cater for the increasing demands of students to participate in the widening diversity of sports; encourage teachers to continue to commit their time to sport; maintain the number and quality of coaches; collaborate rather than compete with local clubs for student players; and provide sufficient facilities and manage their effective use.

Questions

1. How important are secondary schools in the provision of sport in your country? What challenges do they face?
2. How does PNBHS believe sport contributes to its students, and what has it done to ensure all students can play sport? Do schools you are familiar with have a similar understanding of the value of sport? If not, why?

CASE STUDY 1.2
Community cricket clubs in New Zealand

Neil Hood, Hood Consulting, Levin, New Zealand

In NZ, among the estimated 15,000 community sport clubs, there are over 300 cricket clubs who play a significant role in developing community cricket, providing opportunities and experiences for local cricketers, and encouraging the involvement of volunteers as administrators and coaches. The role clubs play varies depending upon their size, services, and location (e.g. rural community or metropolitan area). They range from small, one-team, mainly rural clubs, whose survival often depends upon one committed volunteer, who is frequently still an active player; to very large metropolitan clubs with over 1,500 participants, overseen by professional administrators and a mix of paid and volunteer coaching and development personnel.

The success and sustainability of many small and medium-size clubs is often reliant upon the leadership of an enthusiastic, hard-working individual capable of motivating others; a membership willing to share the workload; a functional strategic plan focused on providing quality player experiences; sound financial management with an efficient system to collect membership levies and generate income from external funding sources; active player recruitment through a junior club or strong links with local schools; and effective player communication.

Cricket clubs face numerous challenges; among these, funding and player numbers are usually on their agendas. Funding is difficult because subscriptions and clubroom bar takings often fail to cover the ongoing costs of affiliation fees, pitch and ground preparation, facility and clubroom maintenance, and equipment purchase. Few clubs, however, undertake traditional fundraising; most are over-reliant on unsecured Gaming Trust funding. Player numbers are also a perennial issue. An increasingly time-poor society, exacerbated by seven-day trading and longer working hours, has seen players prioritise their weekends for family and friends, with their availability to play dependent upon family and social events. Cricket faces more difficulties than in the past attracting and retaining players; to do this it must adapt and offer more flexible, less time-consuming, playing options.

Since 2000, the introduction of NZC's NDP has provided playing, coaching, and management initiatives and resources to assist clubs recruit and develop players, and improve their own capability, infrastructure, and services to retain them. While these initially challenged the status quo, they have assisted clubs increasingly realise the importance and benefits of responding to players' changing needs and experiences through shorter version formats, quality services, especially coaching, and more organised club environments.

Questions

1. Are player numbers a major challenge for clubs in a sport of your choice? If so, list three reasons for this. Are these similar or different from NZ's cricket clubs?
2. Has the NSO of your chosen sport implemented strategies to assist clubs increase player numbers? If so, what are they and how effective have they been?

Sport is acknowledged as a social construct, subject to social, political, economic, and technological change. This requires sport organisations to be flexible and adaptable in developing their sports to ensure they remain contemporary and sustainable. 'Development', however, has many different meanings (Girginov 2008; Hartmann and Kwauk 2011). In different contexts, development can be applied to changes at individual, community, or national levels that produce sustainable growth and/or improvement. Development is defined here, following Girginov (2008) and Black (2010), as actions that are 'interventive and intentional' in nature; 'top-down' or 'bottom-up' in conception and implementation; and 'progressive' in philosophy, that is, they aim to produce an improvement on the status quo. To accomplish this often requires sports organisations to work with multiple agencies and long- established hierarchies which may not be receptive to such change; hence buy-in is needed from the outset, because the delivery of community sport is still largely reliant on volunteers.

In its sporting manifestation, 'development' usually involves the design of policies and programmes by different agencies to provide meaningful and accessible opportunities to participate in sport for either people generally, or specifically targeted groups based on factors such as location, age, ability, inactivity, gender, socio-economic status, and/or ethnicity. The objectives of creating these opportunities, and potential outcomes they expect from individuals participating in sport, vary with the agendas of these agencies and the settings in which they operate. While a key objective for most is to increase participation, the outcomes they seek from this are diverse (see Pause and ponder 1.1).

PAUSE and PONDER 1.1

Sport development outcomes

Sport development outcomes tend to focus on the betterment of one or more of the following:

- Sports themselves (sustainable growth).
- Individuals for the sporting (skill development, pursuit of excellence, lifelong involvement); personal (educational performance, self-esteem); health (fitness, nutrition, disease prevention, mental state); and social (enjoyment, friendship, inclusion) experiences and benefits to be derived from their involvement in sport.
- Communities and nations (volunteering, social capital, integration, crime reduction, removal of inequalities); and their infrastructures (urban and regional regeneration); economies (events, tourism); and identity (pride, status).

Question

With reference to your own involvement in community sport, consider which, if any, of the above apply to you and how they have influenced your practice?

TOWARDS A DEFINITION OF SPORT DEVELOPMENT

The most significant transition in the changing definition of sport development has been the shift in emphasis from sport development being primarily about 'sport for sport's sake' to it being more about 'sport for good' (Houlihan 2011b). Scholars such as Eady (1993: 1) emphasised the former, characterising sport development as a "process which enhances opportunities for people of all ages, degrees of interest and levels of ability to take part, get better and excel in their chosen sporting activities". This aspirational definition emphasises the role of sport in creating opportunities to increase participation and improve performance.

More recent definitions, such as Cryer's (2009: 1), define sport development in a broader sense as a "social intervention. . . to provide opportunities designed to motivate and encourage people to take part in sport and physical activity at all levels of ability and through all stages of the life cycle for a variety of personal and societal rationales". This introduces "the utilitarian and instrumental notion" of sport (Houlihan 2011c: 4) and extends sport development to encompass the use of sport to address wider societal issues. This has been influenced, especially in developed countries (e.g. Australia, Canada, NZ, UK), by the interventionist attitudes of central governments and their national sport agencies, increasingly seeking to harness the potential of sport for social, economic, and political purposes (Collins, M. 2010; Green, M. 2009).

This book is written from a practitioner's perspective and focuses on the development of 'sport for sport's sake'. For this process, to have a meaningful and ongoing impact, any definition of sport development needs to incorporate two key objectives: first, growth, to increase participation, and second, sustainability, to maintain this increase over time. To achieve this, sport organisations, whether national, regional, or local, must plan their approach; identify pathways for participants, volunteers, and administrators; design flexible programmes; and implement these through integrated organisational structures with the capability to deliver meaningful participatory opportunities and experiences (Astle 2011, 2014). In this context, sport development is defined as:

> The sustainable provision of, and access to, integrated pathways of relevant, appealing and affordable sporting opportunities for individuals, irrespective of age, ability, interest or gender, to participate, enjoy and progress in a supportive environment that has the infrastructure and services, capable of offering high quality experiences, that satisfy their diverse and changing needs, motivations and expectations, and ensure their continued involvement in sport.
>
> (Astle 2014: 15)

Sport development is foremost about participants, and creation of opportunities for them to engage in sport. "Participants must be at the centre of the process; opportunities provided by the organisation which supports, coordinates and then manages participants should always start with the participants' needs and be sufficiently flexible to meet these" (Watt 2003: 66). This requires volunteer-led clubs and schools to have the capability, services, and facilities to understand and deliver opportunities that are relevant, accessible, and afford participants the quality of experience that satisfies their needs. In this sense, sport development "is about developing not just sport but also the individual within sport, the sports organisation to better provide for the sport, sport within the community and sport for its own sake" (Watt 2003: 66).

REVIEW QUESTIONS

1. Why is 'sport development' such a contested concept?
2. What is community sport and how important is it for (a) participants and (b) sport organisations?
3. What does 'sport for sport's sake' mean?
4. What are the key objectives of the development of 'sport for sport's sake'? What measures have sport organisations put in place to achieve these?

PROBLEMS WITH EXISTING INTERPRETATIONS OF SPORT DEVELOPMENT

In the academic literature, sport development is presented as a contested, multifaceted concept that is interpreted in various ways by different agencies (Bramham and Hylton 2008; Houlihan 2011b). A number of scholars have previously posited classifications of sport development to encapsulate these interpretations. These include: Houlihan and White's (2002) schema of 'development in sport' and 'development through sport', and Coalter's (2008) categorisation of sport development into 'sport', 'sport plus', and 'plus sport'. We contend these existing interpretations are too broad, and the existing terminology too confusing, so a more differentiated model is necessary for practitioners and scholars to better comprehend the complexities of the field.

Within sport development, Houlihan and White (2002) determined that while not mutually exclusive, there were significant differences in emphasis between 'development of sport' to enhance participation and performance in sport as an end in itself, and 'development through sport' which uses sport as a vehicle to achieve a range of social, economic, and political objectives. Schulenkorf, Sherry, and Phillips (2016: 6) describe these as "the two arms of sport development".

Coalter's (2008) three-fold classification of sport development interpretations is based on the relative emphasis given to sport to achieve certain objectives and outcomes. He identified three classes: 'sport', 'sport plus', and 'plus sport'. In examining the role of sport, he focused on the 'plus' value of sport as a legitimate social intervention, and in doing so acknowledged that sport was also an effective setting for the delivery of non-sporting benefits to participants. He recognised the major objective of 'sport' was "to develop sustainable sporting organisations in order to remove barriers to sports participation, train and support leaders and coaches, develop basic sporting skills and provide opportunities to develop and progress" (Coalter 2008: 47), that is, deliver sporting outcomes. However, achieving this objective is seldom the only reason. Sport is also used by various agencies, because of its perceived inherent developmental qualities for participants, to promote social good ('sport plus'), such as social inclusion. While the delivery of sport and increased participation were the main concern, these development outcomes were a by-product of participation in sport. 'Plus sport', on the other hand, is the use of sport as a means to achieve primarily non-sporting outcomes: it places "much more emphasis on sport as a means to an end. . . Non-sporting outcomes (e.g. HIV/AIDS education and behaviour change) are more important than the longer-term sustainable development of sport" (Coalter 2008: 48).

TOWARDS A MORE NUANCED MODEL OF SPORT DEVELOPMENT INTERPRETATIONS

While Coalter's (2008) classification separates Houlihan and White's (2002) 'development through sport' into 'sport plus' and 'plus sport', it still does not differentiate the full range of interpretations evident in the literature. These interpretations arise from the subtleties in the combination of how the juxtaposition of the two words 'sport' and 'development', and their linkage by various conjunctions, shift the primary emphasis:

- from '**sport**', where development is '**IN**', '**OF**', or '**FOR**' sport, and is primarily about the improvement of sport for sport-specific objectives and outcomes;
- to '**development**', where sport is used as a vehicle to achieve a range of non-sporting objectives and outcomes from development '**THROUGH**' sport; or a combination of sport '**AS**', '**FOR**', '**IN**', or '**AND**' development.

All these terminological permutations are evident in the literature. For practitioners and scholars this creates confusion, especially when different terminologies are often used interchangeably as synonyms to describe the same interpretation of sport development (Kay 2011).

While the shift in primary emphasis creates a distinction between 'sport' and 'development' similar to that noted by Houlihan and White (2002) and Coalter (2008), after examining the existing academic literature, Astle (2014) further refined these classifications into a more differentiated model of sport development interpretations (see Table 1.1).

TABLE 1.1 Different classifications of sport development interpretations

Houlihan and White differentiation	Coalter classification	Astle model
		Development IN sport
Development OF sport	Sport	Development OF sport
	Sport PLUS	Development FOR sport
Development THROUGH sport		Development THROUGH sport
	PLUS sport	Sport FOR development
		Sport AND development

Source: Houlihan and White (2002); Coalter (2008); Astle (2014).

Six interpretations are identified which span the spectrum of expectations of sport development, which frequently are bundled together under the concept (see Figure 1.1 and Table 1.2). These interpretations include:

1. Development **IN** sport
2. Development **OF** sport
3. Development **FOR** sport
4. Development **THROUGH** sport
5. Sport **FOR** development
6. Sport **AND** development

Each interpretation in the model is defined by the setting in which it occurs, and the agencies' expectations of sport development involved with respect to their objectives and outcomes (see Table 1.2). The settings distinguished include: within a sport per se; within specifically community sport or elite sport; and/or within sports in developed or developing countries. These settings are "related to the many different contexts in which these programmes take place, which in turn have an effect on the type of outcomes" (Coalter 2006: 2). In other words, while sport development is about creating opportunities for individuals to participate, the objectives and outcomes of that participation vary according to each of the model's interpretations.

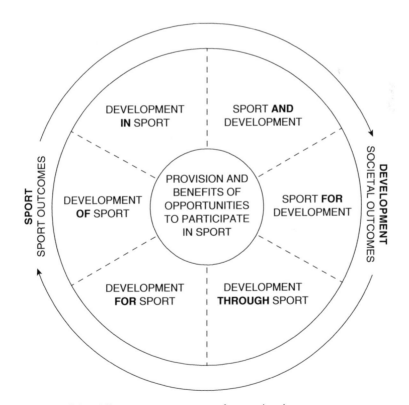

FIGURE 1.1 A model of the different interpretations of sport development

Source: © Astle.

TABLE 1.2 Determinants of the different interpretations of sport development

Interpretation	Development IN Sport	Development OF Sport	Development FOR Sport	Development THROUGH Sport	Sport FOR Development	Sport AND Development
Setting	Sport, especially traditional organised team games	Community or grassroots sport, especially traditional organised team games in clubs and schools	Elite sport and elite sport events in mainly developed countries, such as in Europe, Canada, Australia and NZ	Community sport in developed countries, such as the UK, Canada, Australia and NZ	Community sport in developing countries, especially in Africa, Asia and Latin America	Sport, originally in developed countries, particularly Victorian England and later its colonies, but now more in developing countries, especially in Africa, Asia and Latin America
Organisations	Clubs, schools, regional sport organisations (RSOs), NSOs, international governing organisations (IGOs), media, especially television	Clubs, schools, RSOs, NSOs, central governments, national sports agencies, local authorities	Central governments, national sports agencies, NSOs, IGOs, transnational corporations, media, especially television	Central governments, national sports agencies, NSOs, local authorities, domestic NGOs	Central governments from developed countries, especially Western Europe and North America, UN, domestic and international NGOs, IGOs, transnational corporations	Originally Victorian Britain public schools, churches, and the military, later the administrations in British colonies, now central governments from developed countries, especially Western Europe and North America, UN, international NGOs
Objectives	To adapt the content and form of a sport to change and innovation over time	To maintain the relevance, availability, accessibility and appeal of a sport to ensure its future growth and sustainability	To create facilities, support systems and services to enhance the development and delivery of elite sport and hosting of large-scale sporting events	To immerse sport into 'physical activity' and social marketing programmes, to target specific population groups, as a means of addressing a mix of social welfare issues and costs	To use sport in international development to spread social and humanitarian messages and tackle social, health, educational and economic issues	To access the inherent values of sport for its moral, social and physical benefits
Outcomes	Transform the content and form of a sport to its current stage of evolution and codification	Grow and sustain a sport, especially at a community level in clubs and schools, by increasing participation and contribution, and improving capability, infrastructure, and services	Win medals and titles in Olympic Games and world championships, and benefit from the global exposure of hosting international events	Improve health and fitness, education and economic prospects, and reduce medical costs, social exclusion and anti-social behaviour, especially crime	Realise the Sustainable Development Goals (SDGs) to tackle poverty, famine, and disease, especially HIV/AIDS	Recognise the right of individuals and communities to participate in sport, experience its opportunities and acquire its perceived inherent values

Source: Astle (2014: 20).

The six interpretations, while different in purpose and focus, are not mutually exclusive – they are interconnected and share much in common (Schulenkorf et al. 2016). They represent a continuum of emphasis from sport as an end in itself to sport as a means to achieve a range of non-sporting outcomes. The boundaries between the interpretations are not impervious – overlaps occur between them. Each interpretation represents a different perspective of sport development, delineated by core characteristics that reflect the interests and expectations of the different agencies involved, and the setting in which they operate. The model's purpose is to clarify the concept, distinguishing between these interpretations for ease of understanding, explanation, and practical use.

REVIEW QUESTIONS

1. What are the main differences between the classifications of sport development discussed in this chapter?
2. How are the interpretations in the Astle model differentiated?

A MODEL OF INTERPRETATIONS

Each of the six interpretations in the model (see Figure 1.1), identified on the basis of the criteria (setting, agency, objectives, and outcomes) established in Table 1.2, is discussed below.

Development IN sport

Development IN sport is about sport per se and its historical evolution. It focuses on the emergence, codification, diffusion, and adaptation to change of different sports. It considers how sports over time have innovated and adapted their content (i.e. rules, formats) and appearance (i.e. equipment, facilities) for the benefit of the sports themselves, their participants, and increasingly their appeal to spectators, television audiences, and commercial sponsors (Hopwood and Edwards 2008).

This process, which can be 'bottom up' and/or 'top-down', occurs within all sports. It reflects the adaptation of sports to changes arising from influences such as: experimentation and innovation, application of science and technology (Wilson 2015), need to reduce injury (Woolmer, Noakes, and Moffett 2008), and impact of television and its associated media rights (Cashman 2011; Majumdar 2011) (see Pause and ponder 1.2). McGarry (2015: 1) summarises the impact of such influences, with reference to cricket:

> while the aim of the game – to score runs and take wickets – is still the same, the way it is played, the format, the equipment, the way it is officiated and even the ball that is used have all changed.

PAUSE and PONDER 1.2

Development in sport: impact of technology

The impact of advances in technology, through the use of new, advanced materials and manufacturing processes, has led to changes in the appearance of most sports. Such changes are evident in the design of sport-specific clothing, footwear, and equipment currently used by participants. Examples of this include:

- Durable lycra clothing (athletics, cycling, rowing, swimming, triathlon, volleyball)
- Lightweight, cushioned shoes (athletics, triathlon)
- Moulded synthetic boots (football, rugby union, rugby league)
- Titanium clubs (golf)
- Carbon fibre racquets (tennis)
- Protective helmets (baseball, cricket, hockey)
- Heavier, better balanced bats (cricket)
- Derailleurs on bikes (cycling)
- Synthetic, waterproof balls (football, netball, rugby union, rugby league)

In tennis, all aspects of the game, racquets, balls, and surfaces, have been influenced by science and technology. For example, racquets have undergone continual innovation. The original wooden racquets, which had become slimmer and more symmetrical in shape in the 1930s, prevailed until the 1970s, despite brief experiments with steel and aluminium racquets in the 1920s and 1960s respectively. By the mid-1970s these were replaced by new lighter, stronger graphite racquets with a larger head, and more recently, carbon fibre racquets. Similarly, racquet strings made from natural animal gut were replaced in the 1950s with artificial nylon strings, although today top players use a mix of both.

Questions

1. How have technological changes affected sport(s) you are involved in? What impact has it had on how your sport(s) is now played?
2. To what extent have these changes affected the cost of equipment and/or facilities, and how has this influenced who can play your sport(s)? What measures can be taken to address this?

Since the mid-1980s a major 'development in sport' trend influencing the content of sport has been game modification (see Chapter 4). This has witnessed the conventional version of sports being adapted to formats that better suit the age, ability, needs, and/or interests of players, and time, space, and equipment available with which to play. This trend is evident in the design of specific junior formats for children, and their inclusion as the introductory steps in the player development pathways of sports; and for adult sport where shorter version, reduced player number options have been adopted and marketed as a showpiece at the elite level (e.g. T20 cricket, Sevens rugby) (Astle 2014). The refashioning of these sports has often been accelerated by securing lucrative television rights and creation of elite international leagues, such as the Indian Premier League (IPL) (Hopwood and Edwards 2008; Majumdar 2011) and Big Bash League (BBL) in Australia (see Case study 5.3).

Development OF sport

Development OF sport is the ongoing need of community sport to remain relevant and contemporary by providing flexible pathways of opportunities and experiences that attract and retain participants to ensure its future growth and sustainability. This requires sport organisations to understand the changing needs and expectations of current and prospective participants and create pathways of appealing and accessible sporting opportunities and experiences. These need to cater for participants of all ages, abilities, and interests, and be delivered in supportive environments (e.g. clubs and schools) that have the appropriate infrastructure (e.g. facilities) and services (e.g. coaching).

In NZ and other countries, historically the 'development of sport' has been an uncoordinated, small-scale, 'bottom-up' process driven by enthusiastic and influential volunteers within regions, clubs, and schools. It originated in Britain during the eighteenth and nineteenth centuries, and later transferred to British colonies, such as NZ, when nineteenth-century settlers brought team games (e.g. cricket, rugby) from Victorian Britain. Their voluntary efforts were responsible for the gradual emergence of initially teams, then clubs, and later Regional Sport Organisations (RSOs) and NSOs, each of whom provided opportunities for participants to partake in regular local, regional, and national competitions. From the start of the twentieth century, primary schools, and later secondary schools, also began to offer opportunities to experience sport and a pool of participants to feed into the sport system.

This volunteer-led 'development of sport' dominated until the 1990s, when participation in many traditional, organised sports began to decline under pressure from a variety of socio-economic and political changes (Nicholson, Hoye, and Houlihan 2011b) (see Chapter 2). Some NSOs, to counter these changes, adopted more holistic approaches to their sports, and intervened at the community level to grow participation, not just to identify talent, but encourage lifelong involvement. To accomplish this, NSOs strengthened their vertical integration with their RSOs, clubs, and schools, and partnered with them, and increasingly corporate sponsors and community funders, to fund planned, large-scale, 'top-down' interventions into their sports (Astle 2014). This involved the formulation of development plans, and design and implementation of innovative programmes, often by sport-specific SDOs, to revitalise and grow community sport. These programmes, comprising integrated sets of pathways and flexible initiatives, provide participants with a range of opportunities and are delivered in clubs and schools with the requisite capability, services, and facilities.

In the last decade, many NSO programmes have been supported by central government funding and the assistance of national sport agencies in countries such as Australia, Canada, NZ, and the UK, themselves concerned with increasing national participation rates (Doherty and Rich 2015; Green, M. 2009; SPARC 2009).

REVIEW QUESTIONS

1. Select one sport, then use the internet to identify three 'development in sport' changes in the way it is played, or the equipment it uses.
2. Since the 1990s sports organisations have planned 'development of sport' interventions into their sports. What is their purpose and focus?

Development FOR sport

Development FOR sport is the provision of quality systems, infrastructure, and events within countries to enhance elite sport to achieve international success. Although most NSOs prioritise elite sport and winning, since the 1960s the sport policies of central governments and their national sport agencies (e.g. Australian Sports Commission, Sport Canada, Sport NZ, UK Sport), have intensified this interest by intervening in elite sport to 'cash-in' on the benefits of its success, and those of hosting major elite sporting events (e.g. Olympic Games, Commonwealth Games, and World Championships). They have targeted significant investment into select NSOs to professionalise their organisation and elite sport systems in order to enhance the preparation and chances of their athletes winning medals or titles on the global stage, especially in major events. Recently, this public and national lotteries investment has been boosted by substantial private investment from corporate sponsors keen to profile their business activities through elite sport events and success.

This intense interest in elite sport was originally the domain of developed countries, particularly in Europe (McDonald 2011; Van Bottenburg 2011), but also Australia (Stewart 2011), Canada (Slack and Hinings 1992), and NZ (Collins, S. 2008). Many of these countries have adopted sport policies that duplicate strategies associated with elite sporting success, namely: substantial financial support; talent identification and development, including support for 'full-time' athletes; specialist coaching, sports science, and medicine; high-quality training facilities; and hierarchical competition structures, which have shaped the 'pathways to the podium' constructed by their NSOs (De Bosscher, De Knop, Van Bottenburg, and Shibli 2006). Although these elite sport systems are very similar (Green and Houlihan 2008), they do not guarantee elite success (Sotiriadou, Brouwers, and De Bosscher 2016).

The justification by central governments for their substantial investment in elite sport and hosting of major international sport events has been threefold. The provision of international opportunities for their elite athletes to compete at 'home'; the globally symbolic status, national prestige, and commercial opportunities of staging such events; and the potential of successful elite performances and events to excite and inspire their population, especially young people, to participate in grassroots sport. The impact of the latter 'legacy' effects are strongly contested, as are the narrowly focused policies of governments seeking international glory through elite sport and events (see Facts and figures 1.2).

FACTS and FIGURES 1.2

Impact of major events on community sport participation

While major sports events provide a short-term period of intense excitement for residents of host cities and countries, it is difficult to justify their immense expense on the basis they produce long-term benefits for sport participation. Evidence from both hosting major events, such as the Olympic/Paralympic Games (Green, K. 2012; Green, M. 2009), and achievement of elite success in this international arena (Grix and Carmichael 2012; Hanstad and Skille 2010) indicate that neither produces an enduring 'legacy', through either 'role model' or 'trickledown' effects, of increases in sport participation (Macrae 2017; Mutter and Pawlowski 2014).

Despite this evidence, recent events like the 2012 London Olympic Games show these lessons have not been learned. This is a consequence of the: absence of coordinated NSO sport development strategies and initiatives to capitalise on these events; legacy efforts being short-term 'one-off' projects, not integrated into long-term NSO development programmes and pathways which are necessary to convert people's enthusiasm into opportunities to stay in community sport (UK Sport 2011); and/or lack of capability, capacity, infrastructure, and services in volunteer-run clubs and schools to sustain any positive impact of participation. Macrae (2017), in a survey of 39 voluntary sports clubs in Glasgow following the 2014 Glasgow Commonwealth Games, found that 64% indicated a lack of capacity (e.g. coaching, facilities, volunteers) to sustain any influx in participation after the event.

Question

To what extent has participation in a sport you are familiar with been influenced by 'mega-events', such as the Olympic Games or a World Championship?

Development THROUGH sport

Development THROUGH sport is the instrumental use of sport by central governments, particularly in developed countries, arising from their increasing interest in the extrinsic benefits, especially the valuable social experiences that individuals and communities can derive from their involvement in community sport (Doherty and Rich 2015). This practice, which challenged traditional ways of providing access to sport, originated in the 1970s in the UK in response to concerns about health and urban unrest. Since then central governments, through their national sport agencies, have introduced sport policies and programmes, and invested in NSOs and local authorities as the key drivers of sport participation, primarily for the purposes of social marketing and achieving a range of social, economic, cultural, and political outcomes. This emphasis on the utility value of sport reflects its adaptability, its capacity to bring people together, and the fact that it is seen as "a relatively low cost, high visibility and malleable response to a wide range of social policy issues" (Houlihan 2011a: 3).

While this objective is mostly secondary to elite sport outcomes for both governments and NSOs (Green, M. 2007), the universal appeal of sport and its inherent values has been used, particularly by local authorities, to achieve various social welfare outcomes, such as improving health, combating social exclusion, increasing educational and economic prospects, and reducing anti-social behaviours, especially crime. Initially, such policies focused on providing community facilities to create more opportunities for participation (Bloyce et al. 2008). More recently, this focus shifted to renewing and strengthening communities, particularly those in deprived inner-city areas (McCormack 2010) (see Case study 10.2), and/or immersing sport into broader 'physical activity' programmes to target specific, often inactive, groups such as youth, women, disabled, indigenous, ethnic minorities, and elderly, to address a mix of social welfare issues and costs as a by-product of participation in sport (Coalter 2007; Green, M. 2009). For example, in NZ the 'Push Play' programme run between 2004 and 2009 was an advertising campaign targeting groups such as Māori, Pacific Islanders, and women to become more physically active (www.sportnz.org.nz/en-nz/communities-and-clubs/Push-Play/).

Research suggests such policies have generally not increased sport participation because they are seldom a priority for central governments (Green, M. 2009; Nicholson et al. 2011b). Evidence is also inconclusive about their societal impacts, apart from those related to preventative health (Coalter 2007; Sport England 2011), and facilitation of positive change in sport-specific communities, such as generating social capital, fostering social inclusion, and promoting a sense of community identity and cohesion, especially through sports clubs (Auld 2008; Doherty and Rich 2015).

'Development through sport' policies have challenged NSOs, because they tend to be short-term, and expect NSOs, who are reliant on arm's-length volunteer networks, to satisfy the needs of both their sport and those of the government (Green, M. 2009). The lack of tangible success of such policies saw a number of central governments (e.g. Australia, NZ, UK) in the first decade of the twenty-first century shift their policies and investment in NSOs to the 'development of sport', to grow community sport (SPARC 2009). Although this focus in NZ subsequently drifted back to 'development through sport' projects, targeting specific groups (e.g. secondary school students, women) to become more physically active, Sport NZ has recently again shown interest in 'development of sport' because of declining participation in the competitive pathways of community sport, and the need to improve the quality of this experience to retain participants (Sport NZ 2017).

REVIEW QUESTIONS

1. List the reasons central governments invested heavily in 'development for sport' policies? How successful have these been in creating a 'legacy' for community sport?
2. Why have central governments invested in 'development through sport' programmes? Has the impact of these justified this investment?

Sport FOR development

Sport FOR development applies to the intentional use of sport as a simple, practical, cost-effective, and cross-cutting instrument to facilitate social, health, educational, and/or economic improvement in countries targeted for development. This interpretation includes synonymous terminologies, namely: 'sport as development', 'sport in development', 'international sport development', 'sport in international development', and 'sport for development and peace' (Kidd 2008; Levermore 2011; Schulenkorf et al. 2016).

Since the 1990s an expanding number of development agencies, mainly from developed countries in North America and Europe, have implemented a myriad of sport-related development programmes in developing nations, principally Africa, Asia, and Latin America (Kidd 2008; Levermore 2011) (see Case study 10.3). These programmes have used the popularity and appeal of sport to communicate socio-economic development and humanitarian messages and/or assist tackle issues such as poverty, disease, gender inequality, and conflict in disadvantaged and/or disenfranchised communities and divided countries (Kidd 2008, 2011; Levermore 2008, 2011).

Non-governmental organisations (NGOs) (e.g. Right to Play) have played a major role in this arena (Beacom and Read 2011; www.righttoplay.com). They have lobbied the United Nations (UN) to recognise the potential of sport as a powerful tool for international development. This prompted the UN to establish eight Millennium Development Goals (MDGs) in 2000 to coordinate and focus the development efforts of the numerous agencies operating in this field (Kay 2011; Levermore 2011). Foremost among the MDGs were the need to combat extreme poverty, halt the spread of HIV/AIDS, and ensure the provision of universal primary education. The MDGs era ended in 2015 (www.un.org/millenniumgoals/news.shtml) and have been succeeded by a broader agenda comprising 17 Sustainable Development Goals (SDGs) that seek to address a raft of humanitarian and environmental issues by 2030 (www.un.org/sustainabledevelopment/; www.unchronicle.un.org/article/role-sport-achieving-sustainable-development-goals).

Initially, sport was used in international development to provide opportunities to marginalised groups, often through the provision of sporting infrastructure (e.g. equipment, facilities) (Burnett 2010). Since 2000, sport and sports events have been used to achieve wider development outcomes in hundreds of international development projects (Kay 2011; Levermore 2011) (see Facts and figures 1.3).

FACTS and FIGURES 1.3

Myriad of 'sport for development' organisations

In 2018, the International Platform on Sport and Development website (www.sportanddev.org), listed 964 'sport for development' organisations which use sport as a vehicle to make personal, political, or socio-economic improvements, benefiting the development of individuals, groups, and communities, particularly in less developed countries.

Question

In your experience, does sport play a useful role in addressing social issues? If so, identify a sport and indicate where and how it has achieved this.

Where these sport-based projects have been designed in consultation with local communities and employed as a practical form of guided self-help (Schulenkorf 2010), they have often been effective in achieving their specific development objectives (Coalter 2010; Hartmann and Kwauk 2011; Kidd 2008). Many projects, however, have been imposed 'top-down' by development agencies with their own non-accountable agendas, which has created problems about ownership, sustainability, and relevance (Kidd 2008; Levermore 2011; Misener and Wasser 2016). Questions have been raised about whether the intent of such projects is one of interference and dependency, or as some suggest 'neo-colonialism' (Levermore 2011), with the paternalistic attitudes of NGOs undervaluing local engagement, input, and empowerment, and prohibiting communities realising their own potential (Schulenkorf 2010).

Concerns have also been raised about the benefits and returns on investment of such sport-related development programmes and lack of evidence to justify their use. This witnessed a rise in research-based monitoring and evaluation, particularly by governments and academics, seeking evidence to account for their investment and/or justify the benefits of sport, its value in development work in terms of how projects have been set up and why they work (Coalter 2013; Kay 2009), and its potential impact on disadvantaged communities (Kidd 2011; Levermore 2008; Levermore and Beacom 2009). Increasingly, evidence-based participatory research is drawing on community decisions, local knowledge, and lived experiences of those involved in, or affected by, the projects to demonstrate their effectiveness (Schulenkorf, Sugden, and Burdsey 2014).

Sport AND development

Sport AND development is applied to the capacity of sport to contribute to personal and social development. It is contended sport has inherent physical, social, and moral qualities, and the experience of participating in sport, particularly team sports, provides opportunities for individuals to develop these intrinsic qualities, such as confidence, learning to accept winning and losing, developing a strong work ethic and team spirit.

Historically, in nineteenth-century Victorian Britain the emergence of modern, codified sport and its culture became synonymous with civilised behaviour. It was believed that sport was much more than a mere game. Participation in sport, especially team games, by boys in public schools, was seen to provide important lessons for life and developed people into good citizens (Polley 2011). Sport built character, discipline, self-sacrifice, and a sense of loyalty, and was the perfect medium to teach about ethics, morals, justice, religion, and life itself (Sandiford 1983). This blending of values, known as 'Muscular Christianity', inculcated through sport in public schools, had an influential role in the spread of such civilised behaviour within British society (Mangan 2000).

Subsequently, the international transmission of sport and its values became inextricably linked with colonisation. The British saw sport as an important civilising influence (Levermore and Beacom 2009) and used it to extend the benefits of civilisation throughout its empire (Allen 2009). Sport intertwined with education was taken by the British to its colonies, where it has been adopted and adapted. Opinion is divided about the extent of the contribution of this early exporting of sport and its values (Allen 2009), and the role of indigenous peoples in translating these (MacAloon 2006). Nevertheless, for some former colonies (e.g. Australia, NZ), sport and its values have not only helped define their own distinctive national culture, identity, and pride, but also provided insights into the character of their people (Cashman 2002; Ministerial Taskforce 2001).

Since the mid-1970s, the main 'sport and development' focus has been on sport's perceived ability to transcend national and cultural differences, in particular, for marginalised communities in developing countries to access and participate in sporting opportunities, so they can benefit from the wider individual and collective benefits presumed to be associated with sport (Coalter 2010). Initially this was from a human rights perspective (Coalter 2010), as international organisations, NGOs, and governments, mainly from developed countries, recognising the value of sport and participation in it, launched projects to support the principle of the 'right to participate' in sport in developing countries, mainly in Africa and the Middle East. These projects focused on the removal of barriers to participation, creating physical and organisational infrastructures, to allow sport to be accessed and played (Van Eekeren 2006).

In the last decade, the 'sport and development' agenda has widened to provide humanitarian assistance to divided societies and seriously disadvantaged communities. This has seen this interpretation of sport development subsumed within the broader international 'sport for development' practices of governments, NGOs, and the UN, as they have embraced the utilitarian contributions sport can make to a wide range of development and peace issues (Coalter 2010; Kidd 2008; Van Eekeren 2006).

The six different interpretations of sport development identified in this chapter have emerged over time and place influencing the policies, programmes and practices, particularly those of NSOs and their SDOs (see Case studies 1.3 and 1.4).

CASE STUDY 1.3
Changing sport development interpretations in New Zealand

Alec Astle

In NZ, three phases of sport development are discernible.

Phase 1: 1850–1970. Here, the focus was on the 'development of sport' as an organic, 'bottom-up', volunteer-driven process that introduced team games (e.g. cricket, rugby) to NZ from Victorian Britain, and subsequently established local, regional, and national structures and competitions to sustain their provision. This process was frequently intertwined with 'sport and development', as many early volunteers, influenced by their British public school experiences, advocated the physical, social, and moral values of participating in sport.

Phase 2: 1970–2009. During this phase, central government became increasingly involved in sport. Sport and recreation legislation established a series of national sport agencies to oversee government policies and the investment of public and lotteries funding into sport. Their main priority was investing in 'development for sport' to professionalise and create elite sport systems within select NSOs to achieve Olympic success and world titles. Secondary to this, a range of 'development through sport' physical activity programmes were implemented to address fitness and health issues in the community, in conjunction with regional sports trusts (RSTs, a network of 17 autonomous organisations set up across NZ in the 1990s, but which receive considerable central government funding to deliver national programmes in their regions). Central government showed limited interest in the 'development of sport', as community sport was considered the responsibility of individuals and volunteer groups. They did, however, provide NSOs with modest sport development funding, fostered coach education, and introduced Ki-wiSport, a primary school-based, modified sport programme.

Phase 3: 2009–current day. Central government continues to subscribe to 'development for sport' by prioritising elite sport, but for community sport their attention shifted to the 'development of sport'. This came over a decade after several NSOs (e.g. rugby, cricket, netball) had already commenced 'top-down' 'development of sport' interventions to revitalise their sports at a community level. Since 2009, central government through successive national sport agencies (SPARC and Sport NZ), has endorsed these efforts, by formulating a national community sport strategy (SPARC 2010), providing NSOs with community sport investment, and fostering collaborative partnerships between targeted NSOs and RSTs to grow community sport (SPARC 2009). Since 2014, however, Sport NZ's intent has drifted back towards 'development through sport' and a targeted physical activity approach. Although its recent consultation on improving the experience of competitive community sport to meet participants needs indicates a renewed interest in the 'development of sport' (Sport NZ 2017).

Question

1. In your country, identify which interpretation of sport development is currently prevalent and what is its purpose?

CASE STUDY 1.4

Sport development: contrasting perspectives

Anna Walker, Sport Participation Consultant, Byron Bay, Australia

Over 14 years as a practitioner working in community sport, I have participated in the evolution of 'sport development' in different settings. I joined the Australian sporting system through a NSO in 2002 as a SDO. My role encompassed everything outside high performance. I wrote and delivered coaching courses; created grassroots-to-national competition pathways; and developed coaching programmes for children. Working within 'emerging sports' (skateboarding and inline skating), however, I had the opportunity to step outside the typical club delivery model, engage with private coaches and develop 'hubs' around popular skate shops, a new concept at the time. I relished 'pushing the boundaries' of the typical sport delivery model.

In 2006, I commenced a 16-month contract with Sport England, where my team's purpose was to entice private investors to partner with grassroots sport projects. I worked alongside sport projects of greater resource levels than I have ever experienced. Leveraging sport as a recipient of corporate social responsibility programmes forced a more specific articulation of the impact of sport participation on society. Thus, unknowingly, I began working within 'development through sport'. I observed new and emerging projects, such as Doorstep clubs, which took sports from the confines of traditional providers (i.e. clubs and schools) and, as described, 'to the people' within disadvantaged communities. This removed cost and transport barriers and positioned sport as a tool for youth leadership development and diversion from lesser entertainment and lifestyle choices.

Meanwhile in England, traditional sports were beginning to think more strategically about reaching new markets in challenging circumstances. Traditional sports, such as cricket, through the support of private investors and the 'Chance to Shine' programme, were addressing the lack of playing facilities in high-density urban environments through placing cricket fields on roof tops and small parks. Sport development fuelled by significant investment was getting creative.

During my five years at Sport NZ (2010–2014), in a new, dedicated 'Community Sport' team, we injected a new level of sophistication to the way we thought about, invested in, and strategised for grassroots sport in NZ. On the back of a three-year stint back in the Australian system, the nimbleness and pace of evolution surprised and delighted me. NSOs, backed by evidence-based insights, were thinking creatively about what a great 'sporting' experience looked like and how to change people's behaviour in relation to sport participation. The emphasis, however, was still on the 'development of sport'. The merits of participating in sport, other than 'for sport's sake', remained largely unharnessed.

In some ways, my most meaningful experiences occurred volunteering in the Pacific Islands as a member of an Oceania National Olympic Committee sport education project. It is my observation that 'sport for development' in the context of poorer communities is an incredibly valued instrument because of its impact on cohesion, the opportunities it presents young athletes, and its importance to health promotion. Sport is able to tap into a breadth of agendas and investment sources. Its broader impact on lives and communities is so apparent when strolling through Fijian villages.

In summary, my thoughts on sport development are that sport should not be, and is not, the realm of the talented. Our sporting systems require rapid readjustment to open their minds and doors, and move beyond the confines of traditional sport. My business motto is 'believing in the potential of sport to be more' as I push and evolve the boundaries of what is possible. My definition of sport development remains fluid and adaptable to whatever our society needs!

Questions

1. From a NSO's perspective, what did sport development initially encompass? What is the current perspective of a NSO you are familiar with?
2. How has the practitioner's perspective of sport development evolved over time and place? What is it now?

REVIEW QUESTIONS

1. Search the www.sportanddev.org website, select two 'sport for development' organisations, and for each identify the sport used for development, its setting, target audience, and objectives.
2. Historically, why was sport believed to be 'more than a mere game'? How is this 'sport and development' belief reflected in recent demands for the 'right to participate' in sport?
3. Why have different interpretations of sport development emerged over time and place?
4. Why is it essential as a practitioner in the field, or a scholar undertaking research, to appropriately define sport development?

CONCLUSION

From a practitioner's perspective one of the most problematic issues in sport development is that it is a highly contested, multifaceted concept that is complicated by an ambiguity of definitions, terminology, and interpretations. For this reason, many academics have avoided formulating an inclusive definition of sport development; instead they present a number of definitions ranging from aspirational to utilitarian versions of the concept. This chapter offers a definition of the sport development process based on research and practice.

Fundamental to this is recognising the core of the concept, which requires sports to create and deliver a choice and flexibility of relevant sporting opportunities and experiences, and support these within an environment that has the appropriate infrastructure and services, if they are to attract, develop, and retain participants of all ages, abilities, and interests. This is a prerequisite for all development agencies, including those trying to derive extrinsic, non-sporting benefits from sport. In fact, in well organised community sport programmes, participants derive both the intrinsic and extrinsic benefits from their involvement (Bowers and Green 2016: 15) (see Chapter 10). Unfortunately, many programmes are short-term, standalone, often 'one-off' projects that fail to transition participants into organised community sport programmes; and/or recognise "that social benefits which may accrue from sport participation cannot simply be imposed artificially by political decree or through social engineering" (Spaaij 2009: 1111).

To classify the different interpretations of sport development, and clarify their terminologies, the model in this chapter provides a more nuanced explanation and understanding of sport development than the existing models of Houlihan and White (2002) and Coalter (2008). Six interpretations of sport development are identified, each delineated by its core characteristics, with reference to its setting, the main development organisations involved, and their objectives and outcomes. These interpretations are not perceived as discrete, yet represent six different, but interconnected perspectives of the concept, emanating from the diverse expectations of sport and its potential. The benefit of further differentiating the interpretations of previous classifications is that it allows practitioners and scholars to understand the different terminology and subtleties of sport development, and tailor their planning to the particular objectives and outcomes they seek to achieve.

REFERENCES

Allen, D. (2009). South African cricket and British imperialism, 1870–1910. *Sport in Society, 12*(4/5), 464–481.

Astle, A. M. (2011). *Community sport implementation plan: Collaborative delivery and outcomes.* Planning document. Sport and Recreation New Zealand, Wellington.

Astle, A. M. (2014). *Sport development – Plan, programme and practice: A case study of the planned intervention by New Zealand Cricket into cricket in New Zealand.* Unpublished PhD thesis, Massey University, Palmerston North, New Zealand.

Auld, C. (2008). Voluntary sport clubs: The potential for the development of social capital. In M. Nicholson & R. Hoye (Eds.), *Sport and social capital* (pp. 143–164). London: Butterworth-Heinemann.

Beacom, A., & Read, L. (2011). Right to play: Sustaining development through sport. In B. Houlihan & M. Green (Eds.), *Routledge handbook of sports development* (pp. 337–352). London and New York: Routledge.

Black, D. R. (2010). The ambiguities of development: Implications for 'development through sport'. *Sport in Society, 13*(1), 121–129.

Bloyce, D., Smith, A., Mead, R., & Morris, J. (2008). 'Playing the game (plan)': A figurational analysis of organisational change in sports development in England. *European Sport Management Quarterly, 8*(4), 359–378.

Bowers, M. T., & Green, B. C. (2016). Theory of development of and through sport. In E. Sherry, N. Schulenkorf, & P. Phillips (Eds.), *Managing sport development: An international approach* (pp. 12–27). London and New York: Routledge.

Bramham, P., & Hylton, K. (2008). Introduction. In K. Hylton & P. Bramham (Eds.), *Sports development: Policy, process and practice* (2nd ed., pp. 1–9). London: Routledge.

Burnett, C. (2010). Sport-for-development approaches in the South African context: A case study analysis. *South African Journal for Research in Sport, Physical Education and Recreation, 32*(1), 29–42.

Cashman, R. (2002). *Sport in the national imagination: Australian sport in the federation decades.* Sydney: Walla Walla Press.

Cashman, R. (2011). The Packer cricket war. In A. Bateman & J. Hill (Eds.), *The Cambridge companion to cricket* (pp. 100–115). Cambridge: Cambridge University Press.

Coalter, F. (2006). *Sport in development monitoring and evaluation manual.* London: UK Sport.

Coalter, F. (2007). *A wider social role for sport: Who's keeping the score?* London and New York: Routledge.

Coalter, F. (2008). Sport-in-development: Development for and through sport? In M. Nicholson & R. Hoye (Eds.), *Sport and social capital* (pp. 39–67). Oxford: Elsevier/Butterworth-Heinemann.

Coalter, F. (2010). The politics of sport-for-development: Limited focus programmes and broad gauge problems? *International Review for the Sociology of Sport, 45*(3), 295–314.

Coalter, F. (2013). *Sport for development: What game are we playing?* London: Routledge.

Collins, M. (2010). The development of sports development. In M. Collins (Ed.), *Examining sports development* (pp. 14–41). London and New York: Routledge.

Collins, S. (2008). New Zealand. In B. Houlihan & M. Green (Eds.), *Comparative elite sport development: Systems, structures and public policy* (pp. 218–241). Oxford: Elsevier/Butterworth-Heinemann.

Cryer, J. (2009). *Teaching sports development.* Retrieved from http://www.sportdevelopment.info/index.php?option=com_content&view=article&id=495:definitions&catid=54:introsv&Itemid=74 website.

De Bosscher, V., De Knop, P., Van Bottenburg, M., & Shibli, S. (2006). A conceptual framework for analysing sports policy factors leading to international sporting success. *European Sport Management Quarterly, 6*(2), 185–215.

Doherty, A., & Cousens, L. (2013). Introduction to the special issue on community sport. *Journal of Sport Management, 27*(4), 419–421.

Doherty, A., & Rich, K. (2015). Sport for community development. In M. T. Bowers & M. A. Dixon (Eds.), *Sport management: An exploration of the field and its value* (pp. 124–145). Urbana, IL: Sagamore Publishing.

Eady, J. (1993). *Practical sports development.* Harlow: Longman.

Girginov, V. (2008). Management of sports development as an emerging field and profession. In V. Girginov (Ed.), *Management of sports development* (pp. 3–37). Oxford: Elsevier/Butterworth-Heinemann.

Green, K. (2012). London 2012 and sports participation: The myths of legacy. *Significance, 9*(3), 13–16.

Green, M. (2007). Olympic glory or grassroots development? Sport policy priorities in Australia, Canada and the United Kingdom, 1960–2006. *The International Journal of the History of Sport, 24*(7), 921–953.

Green, M. (2009). Podium or participation? Analysing policy priorities under changing modes of sport governance in the United Kingdom. *International Journal of Sport Policy, 1*(2), 121–144.

Green, M., & Houlihan, B. (2008). Conclusion. In B. Houlihan & M. Green (Eds.), *Comparative elite sport development: Systems, structures and public policy* (pp. 272–293). Oxford: Elsevier/Butterworth-Heinemann.

Grix, J., & Carmichael, F. (2012). Why do governments invest in elite sport? A polemic. *International Journal of Sports Policy and Politics, 4*(1), 73–90.

Hanstad, D. V., & Skille, E. A. (2010). Does elite sport develop mass sport? A Norwegian case study. *Scandinavian Sport Studies Forum, 1*, 51–68.

Hartmann, D., & Kwauk, C. (2011). Sport and development: An overview, critique, and reconstruction. *Journal of Sport and Social Issues, 35*(3), 284–305.

Hopwood, M., & Edwards, A. (2008). 'The game we love. Evolved.': Cricket in the 21st century. In S. Chadwick & D. Arthur (Eds.), *International cases in the business of sport* (pp. 255–269). Oxford: Butterworth-Heinemann.

Houlihan, B. (2011a). Defining sports development. 1–3. Retrieved from www.sportdevelopment.info/index. php?option=com_content&view=article&id=265:definition&catid=54:introsv&Itemid=74 website.

Houlihan, B. (2011b). Introduction. In B. Houlihan & M. Green (Eds.), *Routledge handbook of sport development* (pp. 1–4). London and New York: Routledge.

Houlihan, B. (2011c). Sports development and adult mass participation. Introduction: The neglect of adult participation. In B. Houlihan & M. Green (Eds.), *Routledge handbook of sports development* (pp. 213–215). London and New York: Routledge.

Houlihan, B., & White, A. (2002). *The politics of sports development: Development of sport or development through sport?* London: Routledge.

Hylton, K., & Bramham, P. (2008). Models of sport development. In V. Girginov (Ed.), *Management of sports development* (pp. 41–58). Oxford: Elsevier/Butterworth-Heinemann.

Kay, T. (2009). Developing through sport: Evidencing sport impacts on young people. *Sport in Society, 12*(9), 1177–1191.

Kay, T. (2011). Sport and international development. Introduction: The unproven remedy. In B. Houlihan & M. Green (Eds.), *Routledge handbook of sports development* (pp. 281–284). London and New York: Routledge.

Kidd, B. (2008). A new social movement: Sport for development and peace. *Sport in Society, 11*(4), 370–380.

Kidd, B. (2011). Epilogue: Cautions, questions and opportunities in sport for development and peace. *Third World Quarterly, 32*(3), 603–609.

Levermore, R. (2008). Sport: A new engine of development? *Progress in Development Studies, 8*(2), 183–190.

Levermore, R. (2011). Sport in international development: Facilitating improved standard of living? In B. Houlihan & M. Green (Eds.), *Routledge handbook of sports development* (pp. 285–307). London and New York: Routledge.

Levermore, R., & Beacom, A. (2009). Sport and development: Mapping the field. In R. Levermore & A. Beacom (Eds.), *Sport and international development* (pp. 1–25). Basingstoke: Palgrave Macmillan.

MacAloon, J. (2006). Muscular Christianity after 150 years. *The International Journal of the History of Sport, 23*(5), 687–700.

Macrae, E. (2017). Delivering sports participation legacies at the grassroots level: The voluntary sports clubs of Glasgow 2014. *Journal of Sport Management, 31*(1), 15–26.

Majumdar, B. (2011). The Indian Premier League and world cricket. In A. Bateman & J. Hill (Eds.), *The Cambridge companion to cricket* (pp. 173–186). Cambridge: Cambridge: Cambridge University Press.

Mangan, J. A. (2000). *Athleticism in the Victorian and Edwardian public school: The emergence and consolidation of an educational ideology*. London: Frank Cass.

McCormack, F. (2010). 'Sport for good'? Streetsport in Stoke-on-Trent. In M. Collins (Ed.), *Examining sports development* (pp. 211–224). London and New York: Routledge.

McDonald, I. (2011). High-performance sport policy in the UK: An outline and critique. In B. Houlihan & M. Green (Eds.), *Routledge handbook of sports development* (pp. 371–385). London and New York: Routledge.

McGarry, A. (2015). *Innovations that changed the game of cricket.* Retrieved from www.abc.net.au/news/2015-11-26/innovations-that-changed-cricket/6977816 website.

Ministerial Taskforce. (2001). *Getting set for an active nation: Report of the sport, fitness and leisure ministerial taskforce ('Graham Report').* Wellington: The Taskforce.

Misener, L., & Wasser, K. (2016). International sport development. In E. Sherry, N. Schulenkorf, & P. Phillips (Eds.), *Managing sport development: An international approach* (pp. 31–44). London and New York: Routledge.

Mutter, F., & Pawlowski, T. (2014). Role models in sports – Can success in professional sports increase the demand for amateur sport participation? *Sport Management Review, 17*(3), 324–336.

Nicholson, M., Hoye, R., & Houlihan, B. (2011a). Introduction. In M. Nicholson, R. Hoye, & B. Houlihan (Eds.), *Participation in sport: International policy perspectives* (pp. 1–9). London and New York: Routledge.

Nicholson, M., Hoye, R., & Houlihan, B. (2011b). Conclusion. In M. Nicholson, R. Hoye, & B. Houlihan (Eds.), *Participation in sport: International policy perspectives* (pp. 294–308). London and New York: Routledge.

Polley, M. (2011). Sports development in the nineteenth-century British public schools. In B. Houlihan & M. Green (Eds.), *Routledge handbook of sports development* (pp. 9–19). London and New York: Routledge.

Sandiford, K. A. P. (1983). Cricket and the Victorian society. *Journal of Social History, 17*(2), 303–317.

Schulenkorf, N. (2010). The roles and responsibilities of a change agent in sport event development projects. *Sport Management Review, 13*(2), 118–128.

Schulenkorf, N., Sherry, E., & Phillips, P. (2016). What is sport development? In E. Sherry, N. Schulenkorf, & P. Phillips (Eds.), *Managing sport development: An international approach* (pp. 3–11). London and New York: Routledge.

Schulenkorf, N., Sugden, J., & Burdsey, D. (2014). Sport for development and peace as contested terrain: Place, community, ownership. *International Journal of Sport Policy and Politics, 6*(3), 371–387.

Slack, T., & Hinings, B. (1992). Understanding change in national sport organisations: An integration of theoretical perspectives. *Journal of Sport Management, 6*, 114–132.

Sotiriadou, P., Brouwers, J., & De Bosscher, V. (2016). High performance development pathways. In E. Sherry, N. Schulenkorf, & P. Phillips (Eds.), *Managing sport development: An international approach* (pp. 63–76). London and New York: Routledge.

Spaaij, R. (2009). The social impact of sport: Diversities, complexities and contexts. *Sport in Society, 12*(9), 1109–1117.

SPARC. (2009). *Sport and recreation – Everyone. Everyday. Sport and Recreation New Zealand's strategic plan 2009–2015.* Wellington: Sport and Recreation New Zealand.

SPARC. (2010). *Community sport strategy: 2010–2015.* Planning document. Wellington: Sport and Recreation New Zealand.

Sport England. (2011). *The value of sport monitor.* Retrieved from http://www.sportengland.org/research/value_of_sport_monitor.aspx website:

Sport New Zealand. (2017). *Competitive sport transition.* NSO Consultation Paper. Sport New Zealand. Wellington.

Stewart, B. (2011). Sports development and elite athletes: The Australian experience. In B. Houlihan & M. Green (Eds.), *Routledge handbook of sports development* (pp. 418–432). London and New York: Routledge.

UK Sport. (2011). *The inspirational effect of major sporting events.* Retrieved from www.eventimpacts.com/pdfs/the_inspirational_impact_of_major_sporting_events.pdf. website.

Van Bottenburg, M. (2011). The Netherlands. In M. Nicholson, R. Hoye, & B. Houlihan (Eds.), *Participation in sport: International policy perspectives* (pp. 25–41). London and New York: Routledge.

Van Eekeren, F. (2006). *Sport and development: Challenges in a new arena.* 1–13. Retrieved from www.
toolkitsportdevelopment.org/html/resources/88/88A6D715-4E19-46ED-9226-0B47DC30A580/Van%20
Eekereneng.doc website.

Walker, P. (2017). Cricket's battle for the working classes: Breaking the grass ceiling. In L. Booth (Ed.), *Wisden cricketers' almanack* (154th ed., pp. 55–61). London: John Wisden & Co.

Watt, D. C. (2003). *Sports management and administration* (2nd ed.). London: Routledge.

Wilson, E. (2015). *Love game: A history of tennis, from Victorian pastime to global phenomenon.* Chicago, IL:
The University of Chicago Press.

Woolmer, B., Noakes, T., & Moffett, H. (2008). *Bob Woolmer's art and science of cricket.* London: New Holland Publishers (UK).

Websites

www.mapsofworld.com/sports/olympics/athletes

www.righttoplay.com.

www.sportanddev.org.

www.sportnz.org.nz/en-nz/communities-and-clubs/Push-Play/

www.unchronicle.un.org/article/role-sport-achieving-sustainable-development-goals

www.un.org/millenniumgoals/news.shtml

www.un.org/sustainabledevelopment/

CHAPTER 2

Development of sport

Its relevance to community sport

The 'development of sport', as explained in Chapter 1, is one interpretation of sport development, where sport is valued and developed for its own sake (Shilbury and Kellett 2011). It's a process whereby the benefits of, and opportunities to, participate in community sport, are provided to attract, develop, and retain participants. Historically, the 'development of sport' has been an uncoordinated, 'bottom-up' process, orchestrated by influential volunteers keen to grow their particular sports within their communities. In the last two decades, confronted by social, economic, and political changes and declining participation, a number of NSOs of traditional, organised sports, have intervened to ensure the growth and sustainability of their sports at a community level. It is this interventionist role of NSOs to influence the development and delivery of their sports in clubs and schools that is the focus of this book.

Some question the limitations of NSOs in this respect, because of their high-performance prioritisation, and lack of capability, resources, and connection with clubs and schools to effectively develop their own sports (Charlton 2010). However, in Australia, England, and NZ, central government sport agencies have invested in NSOs because they provide access to the largest captive audience of sport participants with their: national to local reach; existing structures within regions, clubs, and schools to deliver sport and service participants; pathways of opportunities for participants; existing networks of relationships that support community sport; and increasingly their realisation of the need to change and innovate to remain relevant and thrive. There also still exists a strong belief that 'sport owns sport'. For national sport agencies to successfully influence the development and delivery of sport in clubs and schools requires the agreement and support of the sport's NSO.

This chapter will:

1. Discuss the 'development of sport' as an uncoordinated, 'bottom-up', volunteer-led process.
2. Explore change in the process in response to recent challenges confronting community sport.
3. Evaluate various sport and participant development theories to explain the process, and their influence on recent NSO approaches.
4. Examine recent planned, 'top-down' interventions by NSOs, the accompanying change, and community partnerships and delivery systems necessary to facilitate growth in participation and future sustainability of their sports in clubs and schools.
5. Consider the growing involvement of central government sport agencies in the process, and their attempts to create collaborative partnerships to maximise benefits for the sake of community sport.

AN UNCOORDINATED 'BOTTOM-UP' PROCESS

Participation in community sport has traditionally been a naturally occurring process, facilitated through the 'bottom-up' efforts of dedicated voluntary followers of a particular sport from within communities (Shilbury and Kellett 2011). This process created a succession of playing opportunities from club participation to national representation. It was accompanied by the establishment of a hierarchical organisational structure to provide this diversity of opportunities and represented a conscious decision to organise sport on a more permanent and continuing basis (see Case study 2.1). In countries such as Australia, Canada, NZ, and the UK, this 'bottom-up' process is still predominant today, especially in many medium- and small-sized sports, which remain dependent upon volunteer organisation to deliver their sports at local, and often, regional levels (see Case study 2.2). Volunteers continue to provide the backbone for both the administration of community sport, and its delivery through clubs and schools, which are the centrepiece of most people's sporting experiences.

CASE STUDY 2.1
Origins of cricket in New Zealand

Alec Astle

As a British colony, NZ inherited many team games, such as cricket, from Victorian Britain. First introduced by missionaries in the Bay of Islands in 1825, cricket spread slowly because of: harsh conditions in the frontier environment, the dominance of work, restrictions imposed by the church, and geographical challenges of travel. For these reasons, matches were limited to enthusiasts arranging teams on an ad hoc basis for one-off fixtures.

By the 1840s and 1850s, as the number of players and frequency of matches increased, the first cricket clubs began to appear in urban centres. These had little formal structure, matches tended to be sporadic, and rules flexible.

Cricket's expansion was facilitated in the 1860s by improvements in transport, making travel easier, so teams started to play inter-regional contests. New waves of immigration also swelled population, especially within the main settlements of Auckland, Wellington, Christchurch, and Dunedin, providing the numbers to form teams, clubs, and sustain regular competitions.

By the mid-1870s these changes prompted the rise of RSOs in these settlements to organise cricket on behalf of their clubs, standardise playing conditions, administer local inter-club competitions, arrange representative teams for inter-regional matches and negotiate with local councils about facilities. Wellington (1875), Otago (Dunedin, 1876), Canterbury (Christchurch, 1877) and Auckland (1883) were cricket's first RSOs. They were later joined by Central Districts (1950) and Northern Districts (1956) to form its six Major Associations (MAs), the basis of cricket's current organisational structure, inter-provincial identities, and rivalries.

While smaller towns and rural areas initially lacked the population to arrange regular competitions, by the 1880s and 1890s the proliferation of clubs, desire for more organised fixtures, and need to secure facilities prompted them to form 28 minor associations. Today, these have reduced to 22, and are known as District Associations (DAs).

The expansion of inter-regional cricket and possibilities of international competition saw the formation of cricket's NSO in 1894 – the New Zealand Cricket Council. It was a voluntary, administrative body, and although responsible for overseeing cricket in NZ, its prime focus was inter-provincial and international cricket. In 1992, it was replaced by a new entity, New Zealand Cricket (NZC), which combined the administration of both men's and women's cricket.

Questions

1. Construct a flow diagram identifying the steps in the emergence of the organisational structure of cricket in NZ?
2. Did the steps emerge 'bottom-up' or 'top-down'? What role did volunteers play in this process?
3. What is the organisational structure of a sport you are familiar with? How similar or different were its origins to those of cricket?

CASE STUDY 2.2

Manawatu Triathlon Club: volunteer-led, 'bottom-up' development of community sport participation

Andy Martin, Professor in Sport and Physical Activity, School of Exercise, Sport and Nutrition, College of Health, Massey University, Palmerston North, New Zealand

Triathlon (swim, bike, run) is a popular, multidiscipline sport in NZ, with strong elite representation and success in world series and Olympic Games. While the sport's NSO, Triathlon New Zealand, is involved with this elite programme, it lacks the capability and resources to influence its community sport, where events are mainly organised by corporate sponsors or local authorities (e.g. Sanitarium Weet-Bix Kids TRYathlon).

The Manawatu Triathlon Club (MTC), based in Palmerston North, is its RSO in NZ's Manawatu region. Established in 1997, the club is volunteer-led. In 2001, in response to fluctuating participation levels, the club's leadership group set about strengthening the club and revitalising its sport. A review of the club and state of its sport was conducted using a self-administered, organisational development tool health check designed by SPARC. This systematic audit allowed the club to identify its priorities for future improvement.

The club adopted a number of the review's recommendations to improve its capability and planning, modify its event infrastructure, and increase the relevance and sustainability of its sport. The club itself became more efficient, financially viable and appealing to community partnerships and investment, and consequently in a better position to launch measures to grow its participation base.

Two major measures were introduced that have significantly increased and sustained participation: diversifying its events to target the needs, interests, and demands of a wide range of participants of differing ages, abilities, and genders; and selecting new event locations, such as local parks, to provide safe environments for races, minimising the risks of using public roads and need for traffic management.

Although club events have been well supported by males, female numbers fluctuated, and attempts to stabilise these had limited success. More effective in influencing both female and overall participation, has been the club hosting throughout the year not only its competitive series of triathlons, duathlons, and kids' triathlons, but also introducing a range of whole family-related, recreational events, such as ladies' triathlon, a team relay challenge event, family triathlons, and off-road duathlons. These highlighted the importance of the family's role in increasing and sustaining community participation.

The overall impact of expanding the number and type of events the club offered, and running these in safe locations, has seen a substantial increase in club participants, both adults from 300 (1999) to 1,200 (2013), and children from 300 (2004) to 3,400 (2013).

The MTC provides an excellent example of a community club, where the efforts of its committed volunteers have instigated a 'bottom-up' 'development of sport' process to ensure their club's future sustainability and that of its sport.

Source: Martin, Eagleman, and Pancoska (2014).

Questions

1. List two reasons the MTC took a 'bottom-up' approach to review and improve the club and sport.
2. Why did they conduct a review, and what improvements were made to increase participation and the club's sustainability?
3. In a sport of your choice, what approach is evident in the development of the sport? How effective has it been in growing the sport?

The development and delivery of many traditional team sports has been characterised by its spontaneity and lack of coordination. It was small-scale and reliant upon key influential individuals with the vision to set up and administer teams and clubs in their own communities, and to ensure the existence and quality of regional competitions.

In NZ, these clubs and competitions, initially catered for adult males. By the First World War they had expanded to include children and young people, and by the 1930s, women (Ryan 2007). Both world wars and the intervening Great Depression impacted community-based, volunteer-run club and school programmes. Following the Second World War, men returning home stimulated sport participation across a range of codes. Industrial growth, economic prosperity, increasing mobility, and urban growth, saw the provision of local council sports grounds and facilities. This increased access for many to community sport and offered individuals of all ages and genders opportunities to participate, primarily through clubs and schools.

Although local councils provided basic facilities to foster participation in organised community sport, central government was noticeable by its absence, and NSOs, with their elite sport focus, lacked the capability and resources to provide support. Therefore, most sports were administered by dedicated volunteers "who gave time and expertise to the tasks associated with sustaining a sport" (Stothart 2000: 89).

Even today, most clubs are still volunteer-based, administered by enthusiastic amateurs, and function with little planning, few organisational systems, and limited resources (Astle, Dellaca, and Pithey 2013). This makes it difficult to draw them into a coherent structure, constraining the development and delivery of consistent community programmes across many sports.

REVIEW QUESTIONS

1. What is the focus and purpose of the 'development of sport'?
2. How did volunteers contribute to the early 'bottom-up' 'development of sport' process?

CHANGE OF EMPHASIS: A PLANNED 'TOP-DOWN' PROCESS

Historically, while sports at a community level have been volunteer-run and grew organically, little consideration was given to why and how this occurred, and what impact it had on future sustainability. The popularity of traditional, organised sports, such as cricket, netball, rugby, and their volunteer-led club and school structures, however, have been challenged since the 1990s by a number of social, economic, and political changes, reducing their participation levels (Nicholson, Hoye, and Houlihan 2011). These include:

- The professionalisation of sport, including greater commercialisation and overemphasis on elite and professional sport.
- The growth of broadcast coverage of elite and professional sport and penetration of pay digital television networks.
- The repackaging of elite and professional sport as entertainment focusing on growing spectator interest rather than promoting participation.
- An increase in the number of available sports, especially individual sports (e.g. martial arts), new sports (e.g. touch rugby), and multi-sports (e.g. triathlon).
- An increase in individual recreational pursuits (e.g. jogging, biking) and community recreational sporting events (e.g. fun runs).
- An increase in alternative physical activities (e.g. fitness centres) and pay-for-play options (e.g. indoor sports – cricket, futsal), with greater time and service flexibility, and not requiring traditional club structures or regional organisations, as these are often owned by private providers.
- The growing competition from other sports for participants, but also volunteers and facilities, as some sports have abandoned traditional seasons to provide year-round opportunities (e.g. football, hockey).

- The failure of sports to remain contemporary and provide relevant sporting opportunities which result in participants starting and staying in sport.
- Less physical education within schools.
- A dwindling number of teachers prepared to coach and manage sports.
- Pressure on voluntary sport clubs, particularly as NSOs, governments, and other third parties have introduced more stringent compliance requirements (e.g. smokefree, health and safety legislation).
- Lifestyle changes, such as:
  o An increase in the number of families in which both parents work and the pressure this places on available leisure time for adults and children.
  o Urban design trends and increasing population density, resulting in smaller property sizes and more pressure on less open space and public facilities.
  o The growth of other leisure options (e.g. television, e-sports, shopping malls).
  o Casualised labour market, longer working hours (e.g. seven-day working week), and extended shopping hours which have impacted on traditional weekend sporting options.
  o Greater affluence and mobility allowing greater choice of sport and leisure options.

This multitude of changes confronting organised sports has contributed to a rise in expectations by individuals about not only 'what' they want to play, but increasingly 'when', 'where', and 'how' they want to play, and an increase in competition between sports for these more discerning participants. This prompted Sam (2011: 240) to warn NSOs that they:

> must not assume they have a captive market. They have to earn people's commitment of interest, time and money with service and attention to fulfilling needs. People. . . expect professional level services, even from volunteers. Meeting this standard requires a different mindset and skill set.

This implied NSOs, like business organisations, need to respond to changing circumstances, by considering "how to provide high-quality products or services to customers who have increasing choices, and how to innovate constantly to stay ahead of the competitors" (Inkson and Kolb 1998: 5).

These changes, and the challenges they presented organised community sport, prompted a number of progressive NSOs in Australia (Gilson, Pratt, Roberts, and Weymes 2000), NZ (Astle 1999), and the UK (Houlihan and White 2002) to shift their attention and resources from solely elite sport development, and balance these with developing their sports at a community level. Their efforts have involved large-scale, 'top-down' interventions to integrate, revitalise, and strengthen the community base of their sports within regions, clubs, and schools. This has required NSOs to have the leadership, vision, capability, and resources to think and act holistically about their sport and be prepared to change the way they did things.

INCREASING OPPORTUNITIES TO PARTICIPATE

This 'top-down' NSO approach to the 'development of sport' sought to increase the range of community sport opportunities to ensure the types, relevance, appeal, and accessibility of these opportunities contributed to sustained participation growth. To achieve this, and continue their focus on elite sport development, NSOs have needed to adopt a more proactive and innovative role in diversifying their sporting opportunities and experiences available at a community level. This has produced a more sustainable balance between establishing a strong participatory base to engender lifelong interest and involvement in the game for most participants, providing opportunities for a minority to progress into regional high-performance programmes, and a select few, into elite national programmes focused on winning on the international stage (Shilbury and Kellett 2011). Increasing the number of participants through sport development programmes also has the potential to expand the "consumption of sport via attendance at sporting events, television and other forms of media and the purchase of memberships, merchandise and other related products" (Shilbury, Sotiriadou and Green 2008: 218–219), as well as generate commercial sponsorship opportunities.

The type and availability of participatory opportunities within a sport is often determined by RSOs. They provide both a high-performance programme for a minority of talented participants, which often stretches their limited resources; and a hierarchy of competitions, offering a progression of challenges, for most participants involved in community sport through clubs and schools. The latter participants range from children to adults and are spread across three broad levels: primary/junior (5–12 years), secondary/youth (13–17 years), and club/adult (18 years and over), each with its own set of competitions that are structured according to age, ability, weight, height, interest, and gender. While there is similarity in the provision of community sporting opportunities between regions, there is often local variability in its structure and delivery within many sports, because of the lack of standardised NSO playing pathways. These variations reflect a combination of: participant numbers; their needs and expectations; local and regional interpretations of game development trends; practices of local and regional volunteers and administrators; and degree of influence of NSOs on the development of their sports.

Participants therefore entering a sport are usually offered a predetermined progression of formats and competitions that suit the sport, rather than a smorgasbord of options that cater for participants' needs. For this reason, adult versions of a sport have often been the only option for children, rather than more appropriate modified formats. Likewise, performance-orientated formats at the secondary/youth and club/adult levels frequently do not meet the recreational needs of most school and club participants. This lack of understanding and/or accommodation of the needs of mainstream participants has significantly contributed to participation decline in many traditional sports, who have failed "to adapt their offerings to cater to changing needs in the marketplace, especially in relation to the young" (Nicholson et al. 2011: 298).

Some NSOs have responded to this challenge, through planned interventions, modifying their programmes to create meaningful opportunities for all their participants. There are few studies of such interventions by NSOs. In the UK, Houlihan and White (2002) analysed the approaches of four NSOs – rowing, hockey, tennis, and rugby. Rowing, hockey, and tennis concentrated on designing talent systems as part of their elite sport development strategies. Rugby adopted more of a community perspective and focused on youth development, which included appointing SDOs, introducing new competition formats, and placing greater emphasis on coaching to counter "the changes in schools and the physical education curriculum and the challenges the sport was facing in recruiting young people and teaching them the basics of the game" (Houlihan and White 2002: 181). In Australia, the Australian Cricket Board (ACB) began its sport development programme in 1983, and soon found it necessary to rethink and restructure the game to ensure the retention of children and young people. This was a consequence of realising that "we've got to play when they want to play, not when we think they should play and, more importantly, we have to take into account what they want to play" (Gilson et al. 2000: 77).

These changes in emphasis and approach have arisen from an increasing NSO understanding of the importance and value of community sport in the lives of individuals for fun, fitness, camaraderie, skill development, and competitive challenge. This understanding is evident in Cricket Wellington's decision that senior cricket be limited to just Saturdays, because the competition's prime function was not preparing first-class cricketers but providing opportunities for cricketers who "play for the love of the game as their weekend's recreation" (Geenty 2011: C10).

REVIEW QUESTIONS

1. Identify three differences between 'bottom-up' and 'top-down' approaches to the 'development of sport'?
2. Why did some NSOs intervene in the development and delivery of their sports at a community level?

THEORIES AND THEIR INFLUENCE ON COMMUNITY SPORT PLANS, PATHWAYS, AND PROGRAMMES

These major shifts in thinking have had a strong impact on the 'development of sport' at a community level. In NZ, similar to Australia and England, this has involved the direct intervention of NSOs, designing national 'development of sport' plans and programmes, and implementing these at a regional level through delivery networks of SDOs in conjunction with community volunteers. Such plans, and their long-term programmes integrate concurrently and collaboratively, the development of the game, and its players, providers (clubs and schools, including administrators), coaches (including officials), and facilities – these are the five key elements of sport development necessary to achieve the sustainable growth of a sport (see Figure 2.1). This integration has been woven through sports, using aligned 'whole-of-sport' pathways that identify the types and progressions of game development opportunities for players, and prerequisite development for coaches, providers, and facilities to supply the infrastructure and services to support and sustain these opportunities (see Figure 2.2). These sequential and interconnecting pathways underpin this approach to the 'development of sport'.

These sport development plans have drawn on various game and player development models to create a framework for the provision of sporting opportunities. There are two main types of models. First are the more generic, diagrammatic game development models, such as the sport pyramid (see Figure 2.3) and its derivative, the sport development pathway continuum, that depict the levels of competition and types of opportunities within a sport and the implied interdependence of participation and performance (Eady 1993). Second are the stage-based, individual participant development models proposed by Côté (1999) and Balyi (2001, 2002). Although there is considerable variation between these models, all have a central focus around the concept of sport pathways (Bowers and Green 2016).

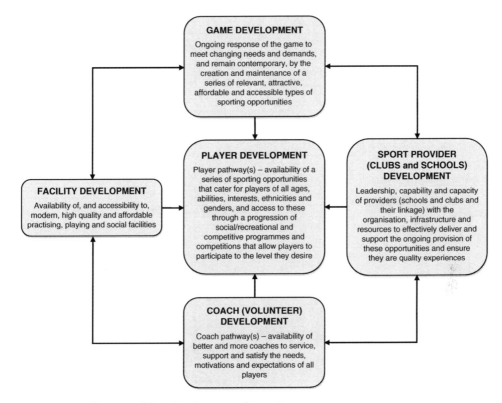

FIGURE 2.1 Key elements of the 'development of sport'

Source: Astle (2014: 33).

While it is acknowledged the earlier game development models are descriptive and schematic simplifications of programme delivery reality, they do provide practitioners and policymakers with an easy representation of sport development and set of key concepts to describe and promote 'development of sport' programmes and policies. They offer "an idea of how things 'ought to be' in a perfect world rather than how things necessarily operate in each situation" (Bramham and Hylton 2008: 5). Such models, however, have not found favour with academics who have criticised them for focusing on establishing a talent identification and development system to deliver elite excellence (Bailey, Collins, Ford, MacNamara, Toms, and Pearce 2010; Bailey, Toms, Collins, Ford, MacNamara, and Pearce 2011). Considerable debate has also centred on the two ends of the pyramid, in particular, the strength of the relationship between the two; the extent of high-performance benefits from a broad sport participation base (De Bosscher and van Bottenburg 2011); and the base of the pyramid being the only entry point, with participants either moving up towards the apex or dropping out (Bowers and Green 2016).

Sport pyramid model

Initially, the simple sport pyramid model was used to familiarise community stakeholders with the 'development of sport' process. Although not an empirically derived model (Sotiriadou, Shilbury, and Quick 2008), it is a practical construct that is easy to understand and describe, and as such has been used by many countries and their NSOs in formulating

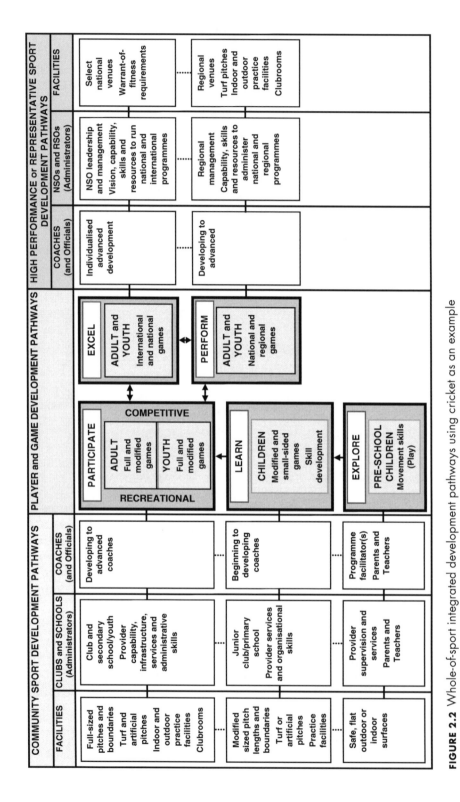

FIGURE 2.2 Whole-of-sport integrated development pathways using cricket as an example

Source: Astle (2011: 9, based on a concept by Paul Ackerley).

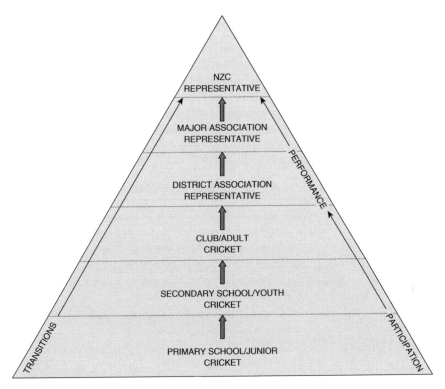

FIGURE 2.3 Sport pyramid model of cricket in New Zealand

NB: The pyramid model in cricket is paralleled by a similar hierarchical, organisational structure within the sport – schools, clubs, DAs, MAs, NZC – each providing an increasing capability and professionalism of leadership and management to organise, administer, and service the game.

Source: Astle (2014: 103).

sport development policies and programmes (Houlihan 2000). Despite its limitations, this descriptive model continues to have a powerful residual influence on thinking about sport development and the creation of sporting opportunities (Bailey et al. 2010). The sport pyramid analogy depicts sport with a broad base of participation converging upwards through increasing levels of performance to a narrow apex of elite sport (Bramham and Hylton 2008). "The goal is to increase the number of participants at each level so as to increase the number of potential athletes who will reach the apex of the pyramid" (Shilbury and Kellett 2011: 244). It is assumed the wider the participatory base, the greater the likelihood of a larger pool of talent to select from to achieve more consistent elite sporting success and raise the profile and appeal of the sport (Sotiriadou and Shilbury 2009).

Eady (1993: 14) maintains the perceived levels of participation/performance in the sport pyramid actually represent a pathway continuum "for individuals to progress to the level of performance which is appropriate/available to them". Houlihan and White (2002) identify four hierarchical levels in this continuum within the pyramid – foundation, participation, performance, and excellence. As participants progress upwards through each level, their number decreases as the skill and competitive requirements intensify. The use of such a pathway continuum by UK NSOs has provided a logical coherence for their plans, policies, and strategies (Bramham and Hylton 2008).

Stage-based, participant development models

Since 2000, many UK NSOs, and more recently those in Australia, Canada, and NZ, have been influenced by the concepts emanating from the stage-based, participant development models formulated by Côté (1999) and Balyi (2001, 2002). Shaped by sport science and Bloom's (1956) work on child development, both Côté's development model of sport participation (DMSP), and Balyi's long term athlete development (LTAD) model identify a sequence of stages in the psychological (Côté) or physiological (Balyi) maturational readiness of participants to progress from one sport stage to the next. Côté's model defines three stages of sport participation based on age, beginning with young children being socialised into sport through sampling a range of sports. Balyi's model comprises four training stages, based on age and gender, for early specialisation sports (e.g. gymnastics), and five for late specialisation team sports, with an emphasis in the early stages of children acquiring fundamental movement skills (Bailey et al. 2010). Unlike the previous game development models, which present sport development as a linear progression of opportunities and competitive challenges from childhood to retirement, those concerned with player developmental pathways focus on idiosyncratic stages as they develop from novice to expert (Bailey et al. 2010). The LTAD model, in particular, has supplanted the pathway continuum in the UK, where it has been widely adopted by NSOs in their sport development plans and programmes (Bailey et al. 2010) (see Case study 2.3). Like the more traditional sports pyramid and pathway continuum models, these stage-based models, especially the LTAD model, are also predicated on talent development for elite performance, rather than sports participation per se (Bailey et al. 2010).

CASE STUDY 2.3
'Top-down' rugby development in Ireland

Scott Walker, Director of Rugby Development, Irish Rugby Football Union, Dublin, Ireland

> Each of you [in relation to Ireland's Six Nations Grand Slam team] in turn reminded us of where it all begins – in the heart of community with people who introduce youngsters to sport in schools and clubs week in and week out.
>
> (President Mary McAleese's address to the victorious Irish team, 20 April 2009)

The Irish Rugby Football Union (IRFU) is the governing body for rugby in Ireland. It has four autonomous provinces to whom clubs are affiliated, and has jurisdiction for the game in both the Republic of Ireland and Northern Ireland.

The IRFU is responsible for the national team and professional game down to community rugby in clubs and schools. Rugby has over 186,000 participants spread across 226 clubs and 830 secondary schools, and is serviced by approximately 3,600 volunteers. Participation has been boosted by significant increases in the number of women and girls playing rugby (4,560), with 49% of clubs having women's sections, and through summer, social tag and touch rugby programmes that cater for 25,000 participants.

Significant national and media attention on the performances and success of the national and provincial teams has generated an income surplus, with the IRFU investing around 18% of its turnover into developing rugby in clubs and schools. Most is allocated to funding national and provincial development officers, assisting clubs and schools, and providing training programmes for referees, coaches, and volunteers.

Independent research shows participation in rugby declines from 15% of children, to 7% of youth, down to 1% adults. Although this attrition is not new, it is exacerbated in Ireland by its unique demography, particularly its emigration patterns, population shifts, and changing birth rates. The challenge this presents rugby is not recruiting players, but ensuring there are appropriate volunteers, coaches, and facilities to retain them.

While 15-a-side is the core game in clubs and schools, several small-sided games have been introduced to address the above demographic challenges. Aldi Play Rugby, a sponsored primary school initiative, is delivered to 75,000 boys and girls annually, and tag and touch programmes are run in clubs during the summer. The IRFU has also moved away from a conventional junior pathway to a philosophy of 'opportunity and access' for people to play rugby – similar to rocks across a stream which allow progression, but are not always linear.

The IRFU coaching and development programmes are guided by LTAD principles. The coaching programme is delivered through workshops, in-club visits and online resources by a network of coach development officers. Because a good coaching experience is critical to player retention, this programme provides support for increasingly time-limited, volunteer coaches, and guidance for those at a junior level managing parental expectations.

Several programmes are also run to support and recognise volunteers, whose contribution is critical to rugby's future; and to develop community clubs that promote a lifelong involvement in rugby. These clubs provide playing opportunities for players of all ages, abilities, and genders; engage and deploy volunteers in coaching, officiating, and administration; and promote community cohesion and social values. To foster the latter, the IRFU has launched a 'Spirit of Rugby' programme, with a team of 'spirit officers' to demonstrate rugby's values and the positive impact sport can have on communities.

Questions

1. How much does the IRFU invest in developing community rugby? From your knowledge, how does this figure compare to other sports?
2. Are the declines in Irish rugby similar to most other organised sports? If so, what strategy other than recruitment might reduce this?
3. How important are coaches to this strategy and why?
4. How has the IRFU extended their development programme beyond rugby and why?

Sport and Recreation Pathway

Although many UK NSOs have followed the LTAD model, in NZ these models do not underpin most NSOs sport development plans and programmes. New Zealand Football's national player development framework is an exception (Meylan, Koutstaal, Priestman, Eaddy, Rumpf, and Herdman 2011) (see Chapter 9). Instead, they reflect a combination of three main factors. First is the expertise of their sport development managers (SDMs), many of whom have backgrounds in teaching, playing, and coaching (Astle 1999, 2009). Second is their awareness of the broad generic game development models, especially the sport pyramid, and its focus on the upward progression of competitive challenges spanning the participation/ performance continuum and its implied interrelationship. Third, their increasing appreciation of the need for sports to offer a wider range of different types of opportunities to meet player needs. This has been influenced by both central government driven modified sport programmes to increase children's physical literacy (see Chapter 4); and the stage-based participant development models, and/or in NZ's case, a recent derivative of these formulated by the national sport agency, Sport and Recreation New Zealand (SPARC), known as the Sport and Recreation Pathway (SPARC 2009b, 2009c) (see Figure 2.4).

The Sport and Recreation Pathway has been used to underpin the whole-of-sport overviews and community sport development plans and programmes of several NZ sports targeted by SPARC, including football, hockey, and tennis (Astle 2011). It represents the sequential development of participants in a five-stage (Explore, Learn, Participate, Perform, Excel), three-phase (Foundation, Participation, Talented) model, and identifies both lifelong participation and talent identification and development as outcomes that can be achieved as part of one integrated sport development system (see Figure 2.4). The first three stages characterise community sport and include the Foundation phase (Explore and Learn) where fundamental movement and basic sports skills are developed in a playful and supportive environment, and the Participation phase (Participate) in which social and competitive opportunities are

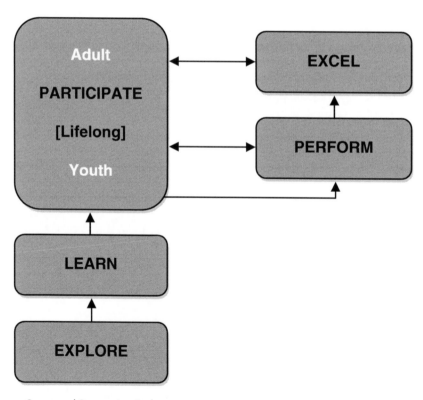

FIGURE 2.4 Sport and Recreation Pathway
Source: SPARC (2009a: 17).

offered in community sport through multiple formats and options to cater for participants' diverse needs. The Talented phase (Perform and Excel) is limited to a select few individuals.

The Sport and Recreation Pathway has provided a framework for NSOs to design participant-centred development pathways spanning community and high-performance sport, and surround these with similar development pathways for their coaches/officials, providers/administrators, and facilities. Along these pathways, NSOs have devised progressions of opportunities for participants to learn, enjoy, and/or excel in their code, and coaches, officials, and administrators to acquire the requisite knowledge and skills to support these participants at a level appropriate to their age, ability, and interest. Such integrated pathways of opportunities and support, especially at a community level, enrich participants' experience, develop their sporting competence and confidence, and are likely to foster their long-term love of, and involvement in, sport.

Key concepts derived from the modified sports programmes and stage-based participant models in NSO 'development of sport' plans include:

- An increasing awareness of the importance of participant-centric development, rather than the previous sport or game-centric approach.
- The creation of a progression of initiatives offering relevant, but challenging opportunities that meet the competitive and social/recreational expectations of participants.
- The linking of these initiatives into an integrated player development pathway, with multiple strands catering for their age, ability, interest, gender, and/or re-entry options, and offering flexibility of choice as they progress and develop in a sport (see Figure 3.2).
- An understanding of the need to modify initiatives, especially for children, so they are age and stage appropriate, enable sport to be experienced as a source of fun and enjoyment, and allow the development of fundamental movement and sports skills as a foundation for future participation.
- The importance of involving parents (and teachers), through an aligned coach development pathway, training them as introductory coaches to support their children's sporting activities and ensure the quality of their first sport experiences.
- The importance of 'informal sport' or participant-led activities in backyards, parks, and school playgrounds in the development of children and young people's sporting skills.

Implications for coach development

The concepts from the stage-based models also have implications for coach development. The increased understanding of the specific participant characteristics and expectations at each stage of their development has influenced the design of national coach development frameworks (e.g. NZ – SPARC 2006; UK – Sports Coach UK 2008, 2009), and NSO coach development programmes (e.g. cricket – Astle 2006), and alignment of these with their participant development pathways (see Chapter 4). This has seen new learning opportunities devised for coaches to develop the requisite expertise to ensure their coaching is appropriate to meet their participants' needs, and a shift in their approach to coaching (Astle 2006). Instead of primarily concentrating on the 'what' of coaching (i.e. the technical skills of a sport), coaches have begun to focus more on the 'who' and the 'how' of coaching (i.e. the participants they are coaching and their age/stage of development, and the appropriateness of the way they coach them so they address their diverse needs) (Astle 2006).

Participant development pathways

Today practitioners use an amalgam of concepts drawn from the various sport development models to describe the progression of opportunities available to participants, and the staged-based pathways to explain the requirements of participants at different stages in their maturation. This has witnessed the provision of a greater range of sporting opportunities and an understanding that instead of one mainstream pathway, there are multi-strands of opportunities which allow participants to "enter, exit or re-enter at various levels of participation" depending upon their personal choice, sporting skills and availability of opportunities (Sotiriadou, Brouwers and De Bosscher 2016: 65). Such pathways are non-linear and flexible, and cater for participants at different stages of their playing cycle to ensure lifelong involvement, possible re-entry options, and for a few, the chance to excel (Bailey et al. 2010).

The provision of opportunities is just one part of the sport development equation. Equally important is how participants access these opportunities and what strategies and processes sports have devised to facilitate this. Researchers studying NSOs in the USA (Green, B.C. 2005) and Australia (Sotiriadou et al. 2008) have identified a series of interrelated processes, pathways, and strategies, related to what practitioners may refer to as the recognition (awareness), recruitment, and retention sequence (see Chapter 3). Sotiriadou et al. (2008) suggest this comprises three interrelated dynamic pathway processes for participants, namely, their initial attraction to a sport, their subsequent retention/transition, and finally their nurturing.

These pathways and the importance of transition from one stage to the next provide useful insights for SDMs and SDOs. As Bailey et al. (2010) note individuals must employ a variety of skills to optimise development opportunities, adapt to setbacks and effectively negotiate key transitions along the way. NSOs also must address these transitions in their pathways (e.g. school–club links). For this reason, pathways need to offer flexibility, individual choice, and re-entry options if participants are to remain in the sports system and realise their potential (Bailey et al. 2010).

The models by Sotiriadou et al. (2008) and B. C. Green (2005) emphasise the 'development of sport' process as being a progression for participants from participation, through the development of talent, to high performance. Most participate in sport, however, without any desire or expectation of progressing to a higher level of performance (De Bosscher and van Bottenburg 2011). As Baker (2002: 10) indicates, with reference to sport in Australia, "less than three per cent of children who play competitive sport will ever reach the elite level. But 100 per cent can have a chance to enjoy their sport, if we let them."

The 'development of sport' then, is more about satisfying the needs, expectations, and motivations of these community level participants, than it is about the 3% of those with talent seeking to reach the top, which only around 0.001–0.002% attain (see Facts and figures 1.1).

For NSOs to facilitate the 'development of sport' requires a significant long-term change process within their sports (Eady 1993) (see Chapter 6). Before they proceed, NSOs need to be clear on 'why' and 'how' they intend to do this. The 'why' is related to the purpose and objectives of change, which primarily are to increase participation, strengthen volunteer services, and improve the capability and infrastructure of clubs and schools, and frequently their RSOs, as prerequisites to ensuring the future sustainability of their sports; while the 'how' is about the nature of the intervention which is largely dependent upon the structure, capability, and mindsets within their sporting organisations. Frequently, the latter all need to be changed for an intervention to be effective.

Indeed, the ability of many NSOs to intervene and affect change in their sports is often constrained by their lack of vision, capability, internal alignment as a sport, and financial resources. Although most have a strategic plan that focuses on their key goals as a national body, few have a plan that encompasses their whole sport and its organisation. Furthermore, in these strategic plans they tend to prioritise financial viability and elite sport development, giving limited attention to revitalising and growing their sport at a community level (Green, M. 2007). According to Shilbury and Kellett (2011: 347) this focus on elite sport "is tantamount to self-destruction".

REVIEW QUESTION

1. What two types of models have influenced the design of NSO 'development of sport' plans? How do they differ? How have they affected their design?

THE INFLUENCE OF CENTRAL GOVERNMENT ON PLANNED 'TOP-DOWN' INTERVENTIONS

Since the mid-2000s, central government sports agencies have encouraged NSOs to undertake 'whole-of-sport planning' in Australia and NZ (Astle 2011; Shilbury and Kellett 2011; SPARC 2010), or 'whole sport planning' in England (Green, M. 2009; Sport England 2008), to expand their visions and create a more balanced view of high-performance and community sport (see Facts and figures 2.1). In NZ, NSOs designed 'big picture', whole-of-sport overviews (see Figure 2.2) to provide an integrated framework of pathways between community participation and elite sport performance, weigh up their relative importance, and consider how they can most effectively impact each (Astle 2011). This allows NSOs then to delineate the role and responsibility of community sport in these pathways, begin to design coordinated community sport development plans and programmes, and subsequently, implement these through a regional delivery structure (see Chapter 3).

FACTS and FIGURES 2.1

Whole sport plans

In 2004, Sport England through its 'Framework for Sport in England' recognised NSOs as key agents to deliver development opportunities in England. A number of these NSOs were prioritised for investment and required to create whole sport plans (WSPs) identifying strategies and initiatives to achieve mutually agreeable participation outcomes. To measure and monitor these participation outcomes Sport England initiated its Active People Survey.

In 2009, the England and Wales Cricket Board (ECB), who manage grassroots to elite cricket in England and Wales, formulated its WSP. This required them to negotiate individual participation targets with their 39 constituent county cricket boards (CCBs), then collate and submit these in their WSP to Sport England. They subsequently funded the ECB to design appropriate national development initiatives to achieve these targets. For example, in 2017 the ECB launched its entry-level participation programme, 'All Stars Cricket', with the initial target to attract 50,000 5–8-year-old boys and girls into cricket. To achieve this, the ECB apportioned the Sport England funding to its CCBs to assist them implement this initiative in their clubs and schools.

The WSP process, inclusive of establishing and monitoring mutually agreeable targets, provided greater accountability for Sport England's investment in the development of community sport to increase national participation rates.

Question

Why have national sport agencies invested in NSOs to achieve community sport outcomes?

To successfully intervene and influence the nature and delivery of their sports at a community level has often required NSOs to address one or more of the following:

- Their governance, leadership, and management competencies and skills at multi-levels from national to local.
- Their ability to understand and be prepared to initiate change in their sport.
- Their organisational capability, in terms of the appointment of a SDM to design and implement the change through a national development plan.
- Their formation of viable partnerships to generate sufficient resources to fund SDOs to translate the plan into a coordinated programme and facilitate the change through its implementation.
- Their vertical alignment and collaboration with RSOs, clubs and schools, and the personnel at each of these levels – administrators, SDOs, and volunteers, to work together to accept and adopt change to improve, revitalise, strengthen, and grow their sport at a community level to ensure its sustainable future.

Many of these improvements have been prompted by central government investment requirements for NSOs to modernise and represent the professionalisation of the organisational and personnel structures that underpin their community sport delivery systems (Gryphon Governance Consultants 2011).

This tendency for NSOs to professionalise and expect their RSOs, clubs, and schools to adopt businesslike practices has challenged the skills and efforts of volunteers on which these organisations are heavily reliant (Harris, Mori, and Collins 2009). Tensions exist when paid staff have been employed with specific expertise, to support these volunteers with administration, coaching and development tasks, but without necessarily understanding the role and importance of these volunteers (Gryphon Governance Consultants 2011). These growing pains are symptomatic of the community sport sector being in transition as sports, reliant on clubs and schools "are evolving through former volunteer-only delivery models to hybrid models in which both volunteers and professionals must work with each other to develop a sport to its full potential" (Shilbury and Kellett 2011: 78).

NSOs interventions have usually involved major long-term structural, organisational, and cultural change not just for the NSO, but also for its RSOs, clubs, and schools and their volunteers, in terms of what and how they deliver sporting opportunities and experiences to cater for participants. Such change needs to add value, if it is going to be accepted by volunteers, and have an ongoing impact on community sport. For this to occur, a significant degree of integration, communication, and collaboration within sporting organisations is required (Astle 2011; SPARC 2010).

These 'top-down' NSO interventions have been criticised. Charlton (2010) claims UK NSOs lack the capability, planning, and resources to be effective agents of managing and delivering these policies, while Harris et al. (2009) assert these policies are founded on the debatable expectation by governments and NSOs that volunteers, who are mostly amateurs primarily motivated by their willingness to contribute to their sport, will deliver them unquestioningly to increase participation in clubs and schools. Instead of 'top-down' interventions, Charlton (2010) supports a more collaborative, community-based organisation and delivery of locally derived initiatives and sporting opportunities, through clubs and schools with the necessary infrastructure and volunteer support services, similar to the community sport development practice instigated by tennis in Canada (Vail 2007).

An understanding of these views in NZ has seen SPARC initially target and provide additional community sport support to only those NSOs with existing, or SPARC-improved, capability to intervene in their sports at a community level (Astle 2011; SPARC 2009a). It is important to note that while NSOs with leadership and vision can influence community sport development, only those NSOs also with capability and resources can influence both development and delivery through a structured change process that permeates their entire organisation. This process is nationally (NSO) led and enabled, regionally (RSO) facilitated, and locally (clubs and schools) delivered. Where this process has been stimulated by central governments to increase sports participation for 'social good', it has had limited success (e.g. UK – Charlton 2010). Where it has been undertaken in partnership with sports to achieve agreed community 'sport for sport's sake' outcomes, it has proved beneficial to both (e.g. NZ – Astle 2011).

REVIEW QUESTIONS

1. What has motivated the interest and involvement of central governments in community sport?
   - How have they influenced the approach of NSOs to the 'development of sport' process?
   - What have been the pros and cons of this influence for NSOs throughout their sport organisation?
2. What is a 'whole-of-sport' plan?
   - What benefits does creating such a plan have for NSOs in their approach to the 'development of sport' process?

IMPORTANCE OF SPORT-SPECIFIC SPORT DEVELOPMENT OFFICERS

Central to the community delivery systems in the NSOs of many of the larger traditional sports has been the establishment of regional networks of sport-specific SDOs, who have facilitated the implementation of their national development programmes in conjunction with volunteers in clubs and schools (see Chapter 5). To engage and motivate this volunteer base to change from the status quo has required NSOs to have a credible value proposition before they can intervene with any degree of confidence to change the delivery and structure of their sport at a community level. This necessitates research into trends and participant needs, the identification of aligned player and coach development pathways, and design of a progression of attractive initiatives, competition tiers, and format options to provide a range of relevant opportunities and quality experiences within an overall programme.

To translate a national sport development plan into a community programme, be responsible for its promotion, and facilitate its regional delivery requires SDOs with a special mix of skills to support and foster the provision of sport within schools and clubs (Astle 1999; Bloyce and Green 2011). At the forefront of these skills is the ability to market the community programme; educate volunteers in clubs and schools to react positively to the change and seize the opportunities that arise from the programme; and attract participants to access these opportunities. Their "interventionist and proactive" role (Eady 1993: 1) in promoting these sporting possibilities, however, is frequently compromised by SDOs being drawn into administration, coaching, and talent development, and as the 'paid person' overloaded with tasks (Astle et al. 2013). To cope with the latter, SDOs need to ensure that their professional preparation includes not just academic study, but also in-field practical experience, on how to work with volunteers (Shilbury and Kellett 2011).

COMMUNITY SPORT PARTNERSHIPS

SDOs are also constrained by the impact of partnerships, especially those with local authorities and central governments, which require sport to be used to achieve wider social and economic goals. These have placed increasing demands on SDOs and created conflicting pressures within their role of developing sport for its own sake (Bloyce and Green 2011; Bloyce, Smith, Mead, and Morris 2008; Harris et al. 2009). Over the past two decades, partnerships have become increasingly important for NSOs and RSOs to assist fund their SDO networks.

These partnerships vary considerably. They can exist at all levels across a sporting organisation – local, regional, national, and in some cases international – and have usually been formed to maximise available resources and ensure their effective use to improve the quality and delivery of their sport (Lindsey 2011). Many NSOs in Australia, Canada, England, and NZ have benefited from significant partnerships with central governments and their sporting agencies (e.g. Australian Sports Commission, Sport Canada, Sport England, Sport NZ); corporate sponsors (see Case study 2.4); media networks; local authorities (see Case study 2.5); national philanthropic, gaming, and community trusts (see Case study 2.6); and in some cases, international sporting bodies (e.g. IOC, FIFA, ICC) (see Case study 4.4). Collins (2010) suggests such partnerships are justified if they increase the budget, add value through the more effective use of resources, increase efficiency or effectiveness, and/or if they benefit from the legitimacy and/or synergy that bringing together a diverse group of stakeholders can generate.

CASE STUDY 2.4
Cricket Australia and the MILO partnership

Rohan Obst, National Program Manager, Cricket Australia, Melbourne, Australia

Cricket Australia's (CA) junior development programme has been supported for 25 years by a mutually beneficial sponsorship partnership with Nestlé Australia, through its MILO brand. This alliance emerged from the desire by CA, then the ACB, to underwrite its junior programme designed to attract 5–12-year-old boys and girls into cricket, and MILO's keenness to access this target audience to positively promote their brand through fostering grassroots sport and healthy and active lifestyles. The longevity and success of this relationship has seen CA's junior programme become synonymous with the MILO brand.

The MILO sponsorship has assisted in funding the branded clothing, support resources, equipment, and salaries of the cricket development officers (CDOs) engaged throughout Australia to initially deliver MILO Kanga Cricket and MILO Super 8s, both modified games, in primary schools; and MILO Have-a-Go Cricket, an entry-level skill development initiative, within clubs. Subsequently, as CA's MILO branded pathway of junior cricket has evolved, so too have the initiatives comprising its junior programme. These continue to focus on primary schools, clubs, and also the broader community through the MILO in2CRICKET skill development programme, MILO T20 Blast School Cup competition in primary schools, and MILO T20 Blast modified game programme in clubs and the community (see Case study 5.3).

For Nestlé Australia, such a long-standing partnership has provided the opportunity to not only connect the MILO brand with grassroots sport and physical activity, but also leverage the relationship with naming rights of all CA's junior cricket development programme initiatives, and see its logo appearing on all the programme's communications, support resources, CDO uniforms, ground signage, t-shirts of children playing on grounds at lunch breaks at international and Big Bash League (BBL) matches, CA's website (where it headlines the 'Play Cricket' campaign), and through television and digital endorsements.

Accountability for Nestlé Australia of the effectiveness of this partnership with CA is monitored by brand awareness tracking and media exposure, and the impact of CA's junior cricket development programme through its school visits and overall participation results.

Questions

1. List the benefits of a long-term partnership for a sport and its corporate sponsor.
2. What level of cricket is the MILO sponsorship focused on and why?
3. Select two other sports, and from your own knowledge, identify their main corporate sponsors. What is their target audience and why?

CASE STUDY 2.5

Local councils' contribution to community sport in New Zealand

John Reid, Major Projects Property Manager, Selwyn District Council, Rolleston, New Zealand

Councils are vital to community sport. Traditionally, their primary role has been to provide facilities (e.g. playing fields, indoor and outdoor courts, and aquatic centres). In NZ, over NZ$1b per year is invested by councils in community sport. Without council support, the cost of facility provision for clubs would severely restrict participant access to community sport, through both a shortage of facilities and cost of participation. The high levels of sport participation in NZ are in large part due to local council support, who invest considerable time and resources creating long-term plans to provide and predict future demand for sports facilities.

The role of councils, beyond facility provision, is becoming increasingly extensive. They have started to take strategic leadership roles across sports to facilitate discussions around the best way to invest their resources in community sport. Other initiatives include: promoting and investing in the development of shared facilities, providing contestable sport support funds, offering advisory services and shared equipment to clubs, and conducting sports events.

Local councils invest in community sport as one means of improving the quality of life for people in the community. Councils have an inherent belief that participation in sport provides a number of benefits to both individual participants (e.g. experiencing fun and enjoyment; improving health and well-being; and having opportunities to realise their sporting potential), and the wider community (e.g. heightening the sense of community, responsibility to others, and the collective good (social capital); reducing the cost of health and anti-social behaviour issues; and attracting people and economic activity through community sport events).

Local councils in supporting community sport, however, face a number of challenges:

1. **Keeping the costs of development and operation of facilities and personnel costs at a level acceptable to the community.** Rising community expectation around the standard of facilities, has increased demands for facilities like 'they see on television', which are often not required for community sport. Managing this expectation creep is critical to keeping costs of developing and operating facilities at manageable levels.
2. **Dealing with shifting demographic patterns**, such as fluctuations in population numbers requiring more or fewer facilities, and composition (e.g. age, ethnicity) necessitating different types of facilities. Both capital and operational costs associated with facilities have an impact on property rates and maintaining optimal levels of provision in a changing demographic is demanding.
3. **Sharing facilities across codes and seasons** is becoming increasingly difficult as sports move away from distinct summer and winter seasons. This trend requires the

development of more facilities to serve a similar number of participants and is exacerbated by sports developing high-performance programmes for younger participants and their 'need' for more and better facilities.

4. **Coping with the recent rapid growth in the number of sporting options** has required councils to constantly develop new facilities or reconfigure old ones. This, and the need to maintain these, often stretches their capability, capacity, and resources.

5. **Managing communities' expectations** that they should have their 'own' facilities instead of subscribing to a wider regional facility vision. These expectations frequently result in an oversupply and overexpenditure on local facilities.

Questions

1. How important is council support for the delivery of community sport? What is the main focus of their support?
2. Identify three non-sporting reasons local councils support community sport.
3. Select a community sport club you are familiar with and identify the type of support it receives from its council. Does this present any challenges to your club? If so, how do these align with the challenges facing councils?

CASE STUDY 2.6

Community sport and Gaming Trust partnerships in New Zealand

Tony Gill, National Grants Manager, New Zealand Community Trust, 2004–2015, New Zealand

In NZ, many clubs and schools are reliant on forming funding partnerships with Charitable Gaming or Community Gaming Trusts to underwrite their delivery of community sport. These trusts, who operate gambling machines in hotels and taverns in NZ, are required to distribute 40% of their revenue to community groups. Currently, $NZ120m per annum of this funding is distributed to support the betterment and sustainability of community sport.

Gaming Trusts generate their income from within individual communities across NZ. As the industry has evolved, trusts are increasingly contributing to community-based organisations that make a real difference. Well organised sport, such as community cricket, that delivers opportunities and experiences to meet the changing needs of players, and engages officials and volunteers, especially coaches, is an obvious target for Gaming Trust investment.

Practically all levels within a sport organisation (schools, clubs, regions, and national bodies, but not individual teams and players) can apply to most Gaming Trusts for funding. Schools and cricket clubs receive funding for equipment and balls, hiring grounds, and indoor training facilities, travel and accommodation to tournaments, and coaching. At regional association level, Gaming Trusts have funded facility development (e.g. training centres), council ground leases, and the salaries and vehicle leases of cricket development and management staff. While NZC receives funding towards salaries and vehicle leases for the amateur, community sport side of the sport, and staging age-group tournaments.

To offset the more harmful aspects of gaming on some people, Gaming Trusts are keen to make a positive difference and know their funding has contributed to the well-being of communities. Schools and clubs are close to the heart of communities, so investing in their cricket programmes provides an opportunity to achieve this objective. The ability of Gaming Trusts to provide funding, however, is dependent on their retention of venues in a community. This can change through legislation and publicans electing to align with different trusts. While some funding partnerships for development personnel and/or programmes have been in place for years, they cannot be guaranteed. The more local, club, or school-centred a programme is, and can demonstrate meaningful community outcomes, the greater the chance funding can be sustained.

Gaming Trusts, like most philanthropic organisations, want to help shape communities with their funding. While grants for equipment are likely to continue, increasingly applications which show how involvement in sport is making a positive difference to their organisation and community, not in terms of victories and titles won, but through more opportunities to play sport, engage volunteers, and change behaviour by being in a team, will have greatest appeal to funders.

Questions

1. Who can apply for Gaming Trust funding? List the items clubs and schools can seek this funding for?
2. Why are Gaming Trusts increasingly looking to ensure their funding for community sport is also benefiting individuals and communities?

While the partnerships with most central governments have been skewed towards elite sport development, they have also made contributions to assist NSOs formulate community sport plans and programmes (Nicholson et al. 2011). In many cases, they come with specific directives as to where (e.g. targeted regions and/or groups) and/or what (e.g. improved health, social inclusion) any investment should be allocated. Such partnerships have also required NSOs to transform their operations and modernise their organisational capability, before central governments will consider them investment fit, and be confident public or national lotteries funding will be used effectively to achieve agreed community sport outcomes (SPARC 2009a).

While most partnerships are positive, some are restrictive in terms of their compliance, servicing, and management requirements, cost–benefit, lack of clarity, and short-term nature (Collins 2010). These have created conflicting pressures for NSOs, their constituent bodies, SDOs, and volunteers in trying to effectively deliver their core business sport, but at the same time satisfy their partners' expectations and differing outcomes (Bloyce et al. 2008; Green, M. 2007; Shilbury et al. 2008).

The 'top-down' 'development of sport' process requires clear objectives and a long-term commitment from NSOs and their partners, especially central governments, to support and invest in their national community sport programmes and regional delivery structures. The implementation process, and its subsequent change management practice, is an incremental one. Any lack of commitment and resourcing by either NSOs and/or their partners can be a major constraint to progress, and place SDOs and volunteer-based community providers under real pressure. This can happen because of: limited organisational capability and capacity, including a lack of vertical integration within a sport; uncoordinated national plans with ambiguous objectives and outcomes; short-term programmes; insufficient or unsecured funding from partners often with their own agendas; inexperienced SDOs with a high turnover; limited consultation and unrealistic expectations of volunteers; and inability of NSOs to monitor and evaluate the effectiveness of their plans programmes and SDOs.

REVIEW QUESTIONS

1. Why have NSOs established regional networks of SDOs?
   - What key skills do SDOs require?
2. Why are partnerships essential for NSOs to develop their sports at a community level?
3. Why and how has the role of volunteers changed since NSOs intervened in the 'development of sport' process?

CONCLUSION

The 'development of sport' process within community sport has traditionally been an uncoordinated 'bottom-up' process reliant upon knowledgeable and enthusiastic volunteers. They have been instrumental in forming teams and clubs, and influencing schools, to offer a range of participatory opportunities for people to be involved in sport; and establishing regional and national associations to govern and administer the organisation of their sport.

In the last three decades, a raft of changes has adversely impacted participation rates in volunteer-led, organised community sport. The response to this has seen NSOs initially themselves, then later with investment and support from central governments, increasingly becoming involved in the 'development of sport' process through planned, 'top-down' interventions into community sport. Their purpose has been to revitalise, integrate, and strengthen their sports at a community level to assure their future sustainability. To achieve this, NSOs have drawn on the knowledge of practitioner managers, and principles derived from the various sport and participant development models, to formulate national sport development plans, pathways, and programmes. These have been designed to grow their sports, by increasing the appeal, diversity, and availability of their sporting opportunities to attract and retain more participants. Regional networks of sport-specific SDOs, funded through various partnership arrangements have been engaged to work with volunteers to facilitate the implementation of these national plans and programmes in clubs and schools.

In many cases, these NSO interventions have revived the community foundation of their sports, increasing participation and contribution and improving the capability and infrastructure of their regions, clubs, and schools (see Chapters 8 and 9). This involvement by NSOs, the creation of partnerships, especially with central governments, the engagement of SDOs, and the often unrealistic expectations placed on volunteers, however, have not always been a smooth process.

REFERENCES

Astle, A. M. (1999). *New Zealand Cricket: National development plan.* Planning document. New Zealand Cricket, Christchurch.

Astle, A. M. (2006). *National coach education plan and programme.* Planning document. New Zealand Cricket, Christchurch.

Astle, A. M. (2009). *New Zealand Cricket: National development plan and programme.* Planning document. New Zealand Cricket, Christchurch.

Astle, A. M. (2011). *Community sport implementation plan: Collaborative delivery and outcomes.* Planning document. Sport and Recreation New Zealand, Wellington.

Astle, A. M. (2014). *Sport development – Plan, programme and practice: A case study of the planned intervention by New Zealand Cricket into cricket in New Zealand.* PhD, Massey University, Palmerston North, New Zealand.

Astle, A. M., Dellaca, K., & Pithey, R. (2013). *Canterbury Cricket Association: District reviews* (Report). Christchurch: Canterbury Cricket Association.

Bailey, R., Collins, D., Ford, P., MacNamara, A., Toms, M., & Pearce, G. (2010). *Participant development in sport: An academic review.* 1–134. Retrieved from www.sportscoachuk.org/sites/default/files/Participant%20Development%20Lit%20Review.pdf website.

Bailey, R., Toms, M., Collins, D., Ford, P., MacNamara, A., & Pearce, G. (2011). Models of young player development in sport. In I. Stafford (Ed.), *Coaching children in sport* (pp. 38–56). Abingdon, Oxon: Routledge.

Baker, D. (2002). *Kids sport: A very real guide for grown ups* (2nd ed.). Sydney: New South Wales Department of Sport and Recreation.

Balyi, I. (2001). Sport system building and long-term athlete development in British Columbia. *Coaches Report, 8*(1), 22–28.

Balyi, I. (2002). Long-term athlete development: The system and solutions. *Faster, Higher, Stronger, 14,* 6–9.

Bloom, B. S. (Ed.). (1956). *Taxonomy of educational objectives, the classification of educational goals – Handbook I: Cognitive domain.* New York: McKay.

Bloyce, D., & Green, K. (2011). Sports development officers on sport development. In B. Houlihan & M. Green (Eds.), *Routledge handbook of sports development* (pp. 477–486). London and New York: Routledge.

Bloyce, D., Smith, A., Mead, R., & Morris, J. (2008). 'Playing the game (plan)': A figurational analysis of organisational change in sports development in England. *European Sport Management Quarterly, 8*(4), 359–378.

Bramham, P., & Hylton, K. (2008). Introduction. In K. Hylton & P. Bramham (Eds.), *Sports development, policy, process and practice* (2nd ed., pp. 1–9). London: Routledge.

Bowers, M. T., & Green, B. C. (2016). Theory of development of and through sport. In E. Sherry, N. Schulenkorf, & P. Phillips (Eds.), *Managing sport development: An international approach* (pp. 12–27). London and New York: Routledge.

Charlton, T. (2010). 'Grow and sustain': The role of community sports provision in promoting a participation legacy for the 2012 Olympic Games. *International Journal of Sport Policy, 2*(3), 347–366.

Collins, M. (2010). Conclusions. In M. Collins (Ed.), *Examining sports development* (pp. 289–318). London and New York: Routledge.

Côté, J. (1999). The influence of the family in the development of talent in sport. *The Sport Psychologist, 13*, 395–417.

De Bosscher, V., & van Bottenburg, M. (2011). Elite for all, all for elite? An assessment of the impact of sports development on elite sport success. In B. Houlihan & M. Green (Eds.), *Routledge handbook of sports development* (pp. 579–599). London and New York Routledge.

Eady, J. (1993). *Practical sports development.* Harlow: Longman.

Geenty, M. (2011, June 21). Expanded Pearce Cup one of the options for Wellington. *The Dominion Post*, p. C10.

Gilson, C., Pratt, M., Roberts, K., & Weymes, E. (2000). *Peak performance: Business lessons from the world's top sports organizations.* London: HarperCollinsBusiness.

Green, B. C. (2005). Building sport programs to optimise athlete recruitment, retention, and transition: Toward a normative theory of sport development. *Journal of Sport Management, 19*, 233–253.

Green, M. (2007). Olympic glory or grassroots development? Sport policy priorities in Australia, Canada and the United Kingdom, 1960–2006. *The International Journal of the History of Sport, 24*(7), 921–953.

Green, M. (2009). Podium or participation? Analysing policy priorities under changing modes of sport governance in the United Kingdom. *International Journal of Sport Policy, 1*(2), 121–144.

Gryphon Governance Consultants. (2011). *Organisational change in seven selected sports: What can be learnt and applied?* Sport and Recreation New Zealand, Wellington.

Harris, S., Mori, K., & Collins, M. (2009). Great expectations: Voluntary sports clubs and their role in delivering national policy for English sport. *Voluntas, 20*, 405–423.

Houlihan, B. (2000). Sporting excellence, schools and sports development: The politics of crowded policy spaces. *European Physical Education Review, 6*(2), 171–193.

Houlihan, B., & White, A. (2002). *The politics of sports development: Development of sport or development through sport?* London: Routledge.

Inkson, K., & Kolb, D. (1998). *Management perspectives for New Zealand* (2nd ed.). New Zealand: Longman Paul.

Lindsey, I. (2011). Partnership working and sports development. In B. Houlihan & M. Green (Eds.), *Routledge handbook of sports development* (pp. 517–529). London and New York: Routledge.

Martin, A. J., Eagleman, A. N., & Pancoska, P. (2014). A case study of regional development organisation: Development in triathlon. *Journal of Applied Sport Management, 6*(1), 72–90.

Meylan, C., Koutstaal, J., Priestman, B., Eaddy, S., Rumpf, M., & Herdman, J. (Eds.). (2011). *National player development framework: Players first.* Auckland: New Zealand Football.

Nicholson, M., Hoye, R., & Houlihan, B. (2011). Conclusion. In M. Nicholson, R. Hoye, & B. Houlihan (Eds.), *Participation in sport: International policy perspectives* (pp. 294–308). London and New York: Routledge.

Ryan, G. (2007). Sport in 19th-century Aotearoa/New Zealand: Opportunities and constraints. In C. Collins & S. J. Jackson (Eds.), *Sport in Aotearoa/New Zealand society* (2nd ed., pp. 96–111). South Melbourne and Auckland: Thomson.

Sam, M. (2011). New Zealand. In M. Nicholson, R. Hoye, & B. Houlihan (Eds.), *Participation in sport: International policy perspectives* (pp. 238–253). London and New York: Routledge.

Shilbury, D., & Kellett, P. (2011). *Sport management in Australia: An organisational overview* (4th ed.). Sydney: Allen and Unwin.

Shilbury, D., Sotiriadou, K., & Green, B. C. (2008). Sport development. Systems, policies and pathways: An introduction to the special issue. *Sport Management Review, 11*(3), 217–223.

Sotiriadou, P., Brouwers, J., & De Bosscher, V. (2016). High performance development pathways. In E. Sherry, N. Schulenkorf, & P. Phillips (Eds.), *Managing sport development: An international approach* (pp. 63–76). London and New York: Routledge.

Sotiriadou, K., & Shilbury, D. (2009). Australian elite athlete development: An organisational perspective. *Sport Management Review, 12*, 137–148.

Sotiriadou, K., Shilbury, D., & Quick, S. (2008). The attraction, retention/transition, and nurturing process of sport development: Some Australian evidence. *Journal of Sport Management, 22,* 247–272.

SPARC. (2006). *Coach development framework.* Wellington: Sport and Recreation New Zealand.

SPARC. (2009a). *Sport and recreation – Everyone. Every day. Sport and Recreation New Zealand's Strategic Plan 2009–2015.* Wellington: Sport and Recreation New Zealand.

SPARC. (2009b). *Sport and Recreation Pathway.* Unpublished document. Sport and Recreation New Zealand, Wellington.

SPARC. (2009c). *NZ Sport and Recreation Pathway.* Unpublished powerpoint. Sport and Recreation New Zealand, Wellington.

SPARC. (2010). *Community Sport Strategy Phase 1: 2010–2015.* Unpublished document. Sport and Recreation New Zealand. Wellington.

Sport England. (2008). *Grow, sustain, excel: Strategy 2008–11.* London: Sport England.

Sports Coach UK. (2008). *The UK coaching system: The UK coaching framework.* Leeds: The National Coaching Foundation/Coachwise Business Solutions.

Sports Coach UK. (2009). *The UK coaching framework: The participant development model user's guide.* Leeds: The National Coaching Foundation/Coachwise Business Solutions.

Stothart, B. (2000). The development of sport administration in New Zealand: From kitchen table to computer. In C. Collins (Ed.), *Sport in New Zealand society* (pp. 85–97). Palmerston North, NZ: Dunmore Press.

Vail, S. E. (2007). Community development and sport participation. *Journal of Sport Management, 21,* 571–596.

PART II

Getting started in sport development

CHAPTER 3

Formulating a sport development plan

Planning is an essential requirement for sport development practitioners, irrespective of their level of operation within a sport organisation. It is inextricably linked to ensuring their own effectiveness and the future success of sport development programmes. For many practitioners, however, planning is perceived as a time-consuming task that takes them away from their core sport development business. Most prefer to do sport development rather than spend time planning how, when, and where to do it.

Most NSOs produce strategic plans for their national body every three to five years, however, few have the holistic vision to design whole-of-sport plans that cover their sport and its organisation. Some NSOs engage external consultants to create their plans, many compiling them to satisfy external agency requirements, such as central governments and commercial sponsors, rather than advancing their sport (Sport NZ 2015). These practices limit the potential analytical and ownership opportunities the planning process affords NSOs to create a blueprint for the future development and delivery of their sport.

This chapter is aimed at practitioners, especially SDMs and their SDO, needing to formulate sport development plans to revitalise and grow their sport at a community level. It explains how successful plans must be underpinned by extensive research and consultation, clearly defined goals, objectives and outcomes, integrated strategies and initiatives, monitoring and evaluation procedures, and a long-term commitment and sustainable investment from their sport organisation. It does this within a context that acknowledges the importance of planning and management of sport in a businesslike manner, but also recognises sport has an "extra quality and element of commitment, desire, enjoyment and voluntary input which can never totally relate to purely business operation" (Watt 2003: 131).

This chapter will:

1. Discuss the purpose of strategic planning for sport organisations, their motives for producing strategic plans, and the scope and priorities of these plans.
2. Describe whole-of-sport plans, their purpose, and the usefulness of creating whole-of-sport overviews for sports organisations.
3. Explain the differences between strategic planning and whole-of-sport planning, highlighting the value of each in formulating a sport development plan.
4. Explore the necessity of undertaking preparatory research and consultation to inform strategic thinking and build an evidence base on which to construct a plan and make decisions.
5. Present a model to illustrate the sequence of steps in the planning process, and an account of each step, including establishing methods to monitor and evaluate a plan.

6. Consider the systems and procedures needed to underpin the application of a plan, prepare a budget, and secure partnerships to fund a regional SDO network to implement its derived programme.
7. Discuss the importance of communicating the plan, especially to engage stakeholders.

STRATEGIC PLANNING

Planning is the first and most important function for a sport organisation. It should underpin their every organisational and operational undertaking and pervade all its levels. The planning process helps structure thinking, provide direction, facilitate decision-making, coordinate the effective use of resources, and direct purposeful actions. It allows all staff and stakeholders to clearly understand the organisation's purpose and focus, their role and responsibilities, and the need for them to work together to achieve an agreed set of objectives and outcomes.

Sport organisations, however, have been slow to engage in the planning process and formulate plans. Historically, most sport organisations at all levels have been led, developed, and administered by volunteers, motivated by love of their sport and desire to contribute to its running, but with little interest in complicating their pastime with management practices, such as planning, which they associated with paid work (Harris, Mori, and Collins 2009).

Over the last three decades, this has changed as NSOs gradually professionalise, often influenced by central government sport policies, and adopt businesslike practices to ensure their capability and fitness for investment to deliver these policies (SPARC 2009a). This has required many NSOs to improve their governance, leadership, and management systems and capabilities, and produce strategic plans that "articulate what they intended to achieve and how success would be determined" (Robson, Simpson, Tucker, and Leach 2013: 3). The formulation of strategic plans reflects the maturing of NSOs, as they transform from their previous amateur volunteer administrations and governing structures, to becoming more corporate bodies, supported by professional boards, and full-time, specialist staff with proven leadership, management, and sporting skills and expertise.

This businesslike approach to the management, organisation, and capability has also permeated their regions, clubs, and schools, with increasing numbers of these entities producing strategic plans to meet funding requirements, or satisfy criteria to qualify for ClubMark or equivalent recognition (England – www.sportenglandclubmatters.com/club-mark; NZ – www.sportcanterbury.org.nz/new-zealand/for-clubs). ClubMark is a quality assurance system of the minimum standards clubs should have in place to operate effectively and safely. To enable this, local authorities and RSTs have provided courses to upskill SDOs and volunteer administrators to become more proficient in planning, as well as offering their services to assist regions, clubs, and schools create their own strategic plans.

Strategic planning provides sport organisations with the opportunity to review their purpose (i.e. why do we exist?), focus, and performance. It allows them to systematically evaluate their current state as an organisation and that of their sport, discuss their contemporary relevance and results, prioritise options for future improvement, and decide on the steps necessary to implement these. Their strategic thinking is often guided in this planning process by sports organisations gathering and considering information to answer the following set of questions: 'where are we now?', 'where do we want to be in the future?', 'how are we going to get there?', and 'how will we know if we have got there?'.

REVIEW QUESTIONS

1. What are the benefits of planning for a sport organisation?
2. Why were sport organisations slow to engage in the planning process?

STRATEGIC PLANS

Strategic planning is a systematic process, typically driven by senior management, through which sport organisations can agree, and elicit commitment from their staff and stakeholders, to priorities which are essential to their purpose (Astle 2002). These priorities are documented within strategic plans which highlight their goals, identify the objectives, strategies, initiatives, and outcomes to guide their pursuit of these goals, and allow progress towards them to be monitored (see Facts and figures 3.1).

FACTS and FIGURES 3.1

Strategic planning and plans

Strategic planning and the specifications for compiling strategic plans are well documented in sport management publications (Emery 2011; Hoye, Smith, Nicholson, Stewart, and Westerbeek 2012; Lussier and Kimball 2014). Sport-specific accounts of strategic planning, often with templates and examples, are obtainable on national sport agency websites (Australian Sport Commission – www.ausport.gov.au/; Sport England – www.sportengland.org/; Sport NZ – www.sportnz.org.nz/) and in their publications (Sport NZ 2015), while Robson, Simpson, and Tucker's (2013) *Strategic Sport Development* provides a comprehensive account from a sport development perspective.

The time frame for strategic plans is usually three to five years, although they must be regularly reviewed and refreshed over this period to ensure they remain relevant. To translate strategic plans into more workable modules, sport organisations create annual operational or business plans. In these, the long-term objectives and outcomes of the strategic plan are broken down into short-term (one year or less) objectives and outcomes, that become the focus of the daily and monthly work schedules of management and staff. Annual operational plans detail "the 'means' to achieve the 'ends' defined by the strategic plan" (Sport NZ 2015: 43).

Some NSOs produce lengthy and elaborate strategic plans, which can create issues of ownership, as often they are too internally focused, and/or prepared more as a requirement to access funding from central government sport agencies or corporate sponsors than as a purposeful plan of action for the organisation and its sport (Sport NZ 2015).

The goals of NSO strategic plans tend to emphasise their effective performance as a national body, winning by their elite players and/or teams, and growth of participation in their sport. These are reflected in objectives which concentrate on the NSO's organisational leadership and management functions (e.g. quality of governance and management, calibre of staff and financial viability); and their operational expectations to achieve elite success and increase grassroots participation (Hoye et al. 2012) (see Figure 3.1).

Strategic plans for NSOs are the 'master plan' for their sport organisations, which sit over a network of plans for each of their key functions (e.g. high-performance plan, community sport plan) (see Figure 3.1). In effective sport organisations, these permeate down, and are replicated at each layer within their sport (see Figure 6.2). For example, while NZC's MA plans were tailored to meet regional needs and challenges, there were also aligned with its 'master plan' (see Chapter 6). The importance of such organisational and strategic togetherness is reflected in Tennis New Zealand's 'One Team' thinking and objectives (see Chapter 8).

To ensure alignment between these plans, and better balance their high performance and participation objectives, it is imperative for NSOs to also prepare whole-of-sport plans (see Figure 3.1). This provides them with an overview of the interdependence of these objectives, and relative importance of each to the sport and its system of development and delivery. Strategic plans focus primarily on the corporate functions of the sport organisation (e.g. NZC), while whole-of-sport plans concentrate on the sport itself and its system of development and delivery (e.g. cricket in NZ).

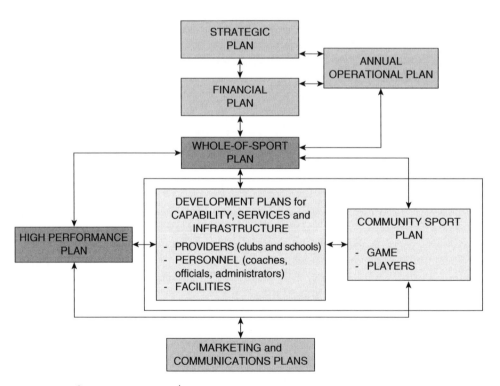

FIGURE 3.1 Sport organisation plans

Source: © Astle.

WHOLE-OF-SPORT PLANNING

Whole-of-sport plans require NSOs to identify the framework of integrated and aligned development pathways that underpin the entirety of their sport operations from community participation to elite performance. They include everyone who is engaged in a sport – players, coaches, officials (referees/umpires), administrators, and volunteers, and all levels within a sport organisation involved in its delivery (Sport NZ 2015). This provides NSOs with an overview of their sports as an interconnected whole, allowing them to order their priorities, and apportion their resources to more effectively support both their participation and high-performance objectives.

The first step in whole-of-sport planning is the design of a whole-of-sport overview (see Figure 2.2). This is not complicated, but research and consultation with key stakeholders are prerequisites to its formulation. In NZ, the 'Sport and Recreation Pathway' (see Figure 2.4) provides NSOs with a theoretical guide to identify the sequence of integrated and aligned pathways that span their operations from community to high-performance sport (SPARC 2009b, 2009c).

Because it is participant-centric, a whole-of-sport overview begins by identifying the bottom-to-top multiple strands of conventional or 'competitive' playing options and recreational or 'social' opportunities that form their player development pathways (see Figures 3.2, 4.1, and 9.1). The modification of sports with different formats, player numbers, scheduling, durations, equipment, and playing surface dimensions, while more reflective of the recreational strand, is increasingly straddling these pathways (e.g. T20 in cricket). This is evident in hockey's pathways (see Figure 3.2).

Once player development pathways have been determined, they can be surrounded by similar integrated pathways with comparable progressions of development opportunities for coaches, officials, and administrators aligned to each other and the player pathway (see Figure 3.2). For example, NZC's entry-level MILO Have-A-Go Cricket initiative for children aged 5–7 years was matched by a similar coach education course that encouraged the involvement of parents and teachers (see Chapter 4). It provided them with the requisite know-how and resources to run the programme, teach their children the basic skills of the game, and provide a fun first experience of cricket (Astle 2000).

A whole-of-sport overview provides NSOs, their staff, and stakeholders with a one-page, 'big picture', end-to-end, and side-to-side model of their sport and its operations. It represents a clear and informative illustration of its interconnected delivery system and support structure of vertical pathways and their horizontal layers that bind their sport together. This visual image has the potential to stimulate meaningful discussion throughout an entire sport organisation about its appropriateness, functioning and priorities, opportunities for improvement and resource allocation, and roles and responsibilities within this of the sport's different entities and stakeholders.

GETTING STARTED: FORMULATING A SPORT DEVELOPMENT PLAN

Some SDMs and SDOs will be appointed to positions where the expectations of their role will already be clearly articulated within an existing sport development plan (see Case study 3.1). Others will need to define their own role and responsibilities, at whatever level they are

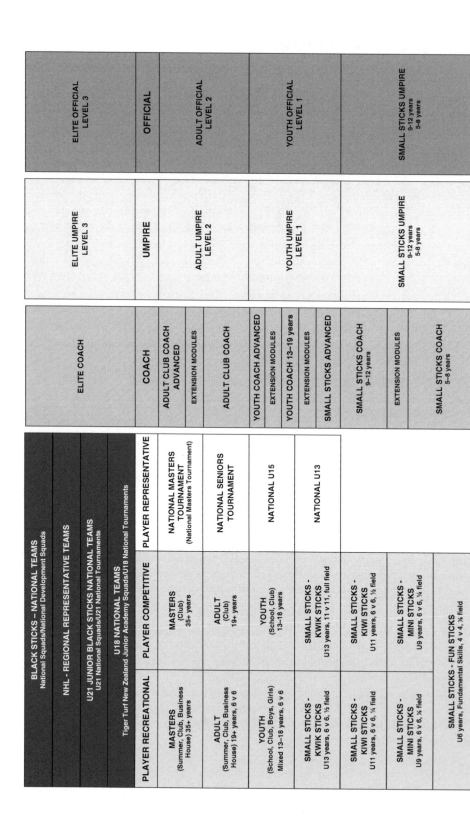

FIGURE 3.2 Hockey New Zealand: whole-of-hockey overview

Source: abridged from Francis 2011: 3

operating, by leading the process of advocating for and formulating a sport development plan for their sport. They will need to consult with, and persuade, staff and stakeholders of the benefits of a plan to revitalise their sport at a community level and explain how they intend to achieve this and measure its impact. At the national level, this is the first step in influencing change in a sport organisation's direction and approach to the development and delivery of community sport, and lays the foundation for the subsequent design and implementation of a sport development programme.

CASE STUDY 3.1

International Cricket Council global development plans

Kieran McMillan, East Asia Pacific Development Manager, International Cricket Council, Melbourne, Australia

The International Cricket Council (ICC) appointed its inaugural global development manager in 1998, and in 1999 launched its first global development plan (1999–2004). Its objectives were to grow and improve the quality of the game within both full members (currently 12 countries) (e.g. Australia, England, India, Afghanistan) and associate members (currently 92 countries) (e.g. Canada, Kenya, Nepal, Scotland). The ICC divided the world into five regions, each with a regional manager, to oversee the plan's implementation.

In my six years as regional manager for the East Asia Pacific region, I have implemented the two most recent global development plans (2011–2015 and 2016–2019). These plans, like the preceding ones, focused on building a bigger and better global game, through strategies to:

1. **Significantly grow participation,** with the goal being 50 million participants globally by 2023, with 40% being female. To achieve this the ICC aims to design a number of community cricket participation initiatives, including a children's curriculum to be delivered in schools, a flexible game format that reflects the changing ways people want to engage with organised sport, and establish a training and education framework for coaches, umpires, curators, and scorers with an accredited workforce to deliver it. All members will be expected to deliver participation initiatives to attract more girls into cricket.
2. **Sustain competitive excellence** by improving high-performance programmes in associate members, and ensuring the pathway of ICC tournaments is open for all members, with a global ranking system in place (men and women). The aim is to have leading associate members excelling in the 2020 World T20 and 2023 Cricket World Cups, and T20 to be an Olympic sport in 2024 or 2028.
3. **Provide greater access to cricket** through research and innovation into equipment, facilities, and formats that provide more cost-effective and simpler access to cricket; bringing all cricket formats (e.g. indoor cricket, disability cricket) under the ICC umbrella; and increasing broadcast reach to 150 countries by 2023.

These strategies are underpinned by a suite of organisational development programmes (e.g. governance, professional development) to improve associate members' capability; investment that incentivises performance against strategic priorities and ensures the basics are in place (e.g. strategic plan, budgeting); and a network of supportive partnerships with full members, broadcasters, sponsors, governments, and NGOs.

The impact of the 2011–2015 global development plan saw an increase in participation of over 1 million in associate members, with an annual growth rate over 20%. This greater participation footprint in associate member countries has seen them attract more support and investment from central governments and sponsors. This, and improvements in governance and administration, have ensured associate members have a stronger, more professional foundation on which to grow and sustain the game.

To achieve these global development outcomes, there has been a change in ICC's approach, with staff moving from delivery-based 'tracksuit' roles in the field to more strategic-based 'suit' roles in the boardroom; a greater prioritisation of engaging girls and women in cricket; and targeting investment and support into fewer, 'high priority' countries, rather than equally across all associate members.

Despite their success, the ICC development programmes still face challenges. Among these are:

1. **The struggle to transition a large number of participants** from the 'sampling' or awareness phase into regular players (i.e. playing a minimum of five or six matches). Modified formats, along with better data collection to gain a deeper understanding of what participants want from their experience, are seen as key to improving transition.
2. **The insufficient number of coaches**, especially in emerging cricket countries, where accessing volunteers is difficult, and cricket is often a new sport, so not well understood. The strategy to create a global coaching pathway with an accredited delivery workforce will assist, but more appropriate resources need to be designed for parents to increase their understanding of cricket, and encourage their involvement in their children's entry-level initiatives.
3. **The requirements of traditional cricket**, such as a large oval and expensive equipment. The ICC needs to lead research and innovation into designing more cost-effective equipment, lightweight portable pitches, and formats requiring less space to allow 'cricket anywhere, anytime'.

Questions

1. When did the ICC launch its first global development plan? What were its original objectives? Are these still the same today?
2. How has the ICC's approach changed in implementing its plans?
3. How similar are the challenges facing the ICC's global development programme to those of a club or school in a sport of your choice? Select one challenge and indicate how your club or school has sought to overcome it.

Planning is a deliberate and proactive process that requires SDMs and SDOs to consider their sport and its development and delivery, project ahead, chart a course of action, and act upon it. Although it impinges on their time and the immediate, daily delivery and servicing of their sport, a lack of planning impacts their effectiveness, with their efforts tending to be sporadic and reactive, rather than attending to priorities essential for the future development of their sport.

Planning allows practitioners to research, consult, analyse, and make systematic decisions about their intended development programme, underpinning framework of pathways and initiatives, and system for their delivery. From a national perspective, the incorporation of these into a sport development plan provides a compelling value proposition to convince a NSO's CEO and board, its RSOs, clubs, and schools, and funding partners to commit long term to turning the plan into practice

Before formulating a sport development plan, practitioners need to clarify their thinking about its objectives, and how much of the whole-of-sport system will be their responsibility to achieve these objectives. Are these objectives to attract new participants (Grow), support and motivate existing participants to keep playing (Sustain), and/or provide enhanced opportunities to nurture talented performers (Talent Development) (Bloyce and Green 2011)? To determine which objectives, practitioners first must define sport development within the context of their sport organisation's agenda, and then use this to delimit the scope of their sport development programme.

For example, NZC's NDP concentrated on growing and sustaining cricket in clubs and schools which equated to the Sport and Recreation Pathway's Learn and Participate stages. Its scope was 'community cricket' in clubs and schools, it did not include developing talented players. Other sports, include responsibility for the Learn and Participate stages, and most of the Perform stage, in their community sport development programmes, leaving only Excel to high performance. This inclusion of the Perform stage of regional representative teams in community sport, unfortunately means the SDOs' development work is regularly compromised by the intrusion of representative demands. Even despite NZC's tighter delineation of its programme's scope, this has still occurred, where high performance has increasingly focused almost solely on Excel or its 'professional game', hampering the effective operation of their community cricket coordinators (Astle 2014) (see Chapter 5).

Once practitioners define the purpose and focus of sport development, they can scope the extent of their operation within a sport organisation, and distinguish their development role from high performance (Astle 2014). While 'development' is about presenting a set of relevant, attractive, and accessible sporting opportunities for individuals in community sport; 'high performance' is differentiated by the talent identification process which elevates a minority of these individuals from community sport into the representative pathway with its advanced menu of regional, national, and international playing and coaching opportunities. This delineation provides a clear boundary of responsibility for practical purposes of planning and programme delivery.

REVIEW QUESTIONS

1. What is the difference between strategic plans and whole-of-sport plans?
2. What do each of these types of planning provide SDMs in formulating sport development plans?

Key steps in formulating a sport development plan

To initiate the planning process, SDMs should, where possible, form a small group of SDOs and/or experienced volunteers to consult with, share ideas, and contribute to the process. If they are able to assemble a planning group, they must lead it, identify the key steps, establish a schedule and agendas for regular workshops, delegate tasks, and set a timeline to keep the process on track.

Because it takes time, NSO leadership needs to commit adequate time and resources to the process, and not compel SDMs to produce sport development plans, which for whatever reason, lack the necessary foundational research, consultation, and analysis. The urge to skip to doing, rather than spending sufficient time preparing properly, is a recipe for poorly thought out plans that lack direction and fail to achieve their objectives.

When drafting a sport development plan, it's important to record where a sport organisation wants to go and how it is going to get there. Irrespective of the plan type, the planning process tends to follow a similar series of steps. While the sequence of these steps can vary between sport organisations, they are all necessary to the planning process. The steps include:

1. Undertaking preparatory research, consultation, and analysis.
2. Deciding a vision statement.
3. Determining goals and objectives.
4. Establishing strategies to meet these objectives.
5. Identifying initiatives, reflective of these strategies, to achieve the objectives.
6. Considering the systematic procedures and structure of a regional and local delivery network to implement these initiatives.
7. Establishing monitoring and evaluation procedures.

This sequence of steps is neither linear nor discrete, as the planning process is circular and continuous (Emery 2011; Lussier and Kimball 2014) (see Figure 3.3). There is often movement back and forth between the steps, which allows timely and informed adjustments to be made, as the plan and its associated programme are reviewed and refreshed to respond to new circumstances and challenges.

Research, consultation, and analysis

The first challenge facing many practitioners is the need to combat the desire and organisational pressure to take action immediately without appropriate preparation and planning (Hoye et al. 2012). The latter is essential for practitioners to locate information sources and seek expert advice as a basis to analyse their sport, reflect, and make decisions about its future direction.

There are several information sources SDMs can access to undertake a situational or environmental analysis of the current state of their sport and its organisation, ascertain its needs and those of its participants, and assess its capability and capacity to respond to these (see Facts and figures 3.2). These include:

- Examining examples of their own and other sport organisations' plans, and available literature from practitioner and academic sources, for insights into planning and plan formats.

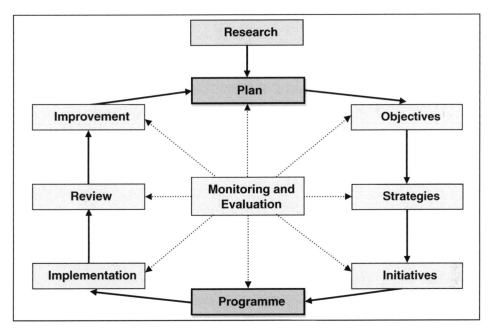

FIGURE 3.3 Steps in the formulation of a 'development of sport' plan and programme
Source: Astle (1999: 3).

- Establishing a contact network of practitioners within their sport, other sports, and national and regional sport agencies, to exchange ideas and gather information about community sport development through discussions, field observations of programmes and collecting resources.
- Undertaking surveys of clubs and schools, and reviews of a cross-section of stakeholders with an interest in their sport and its organisation, to ascertain their views on the current state, issues, and perceived needs of their sport and its participants.

FACTS and FIGURES 3.2

SPARC's community sport strategy: research and consultation

In 2008, NZ's national sport agency SPARC, before formulating its community sport strategy (SPARC 2010), undertook an extensive review of community sport (SPARC 2009d). This included: a search of the academic literature; an examination of international models of community sport interventions (e.g. Australia, Canada, UK) and domestic models of NSOs with established innovative community sport programmes (e.g. cricket, rugby); and extensive consultation with community sport practitioners to capture their first-hand knowledge and lived experiences. The latter included discussions with 17 focus groups, each with a broad cross-section of about 30 people, three meetings with Māori communities, and interviews with targeted national, regional, and local stakeholders from 27 different NSOs, RSTs, local government, disability groups, Gaming and Community Trusts, and secondary school and youth organisations. These findings provided the factual foundation of SPARC's community sport strategy.

Question

What is the situation of community sport in your country? Does central government have a community sport strategy? If so, what is its focus and purpose?

The first two sources raise questions for practitioners and their sport organisation about: 'what is sport development?', 'who and what should be the focus of such development and why?', and 'what strategies need to be adopted and initiatives designed to achieve this?' The third source of primary data provides first-hand information about the characteristics, strengths, issues, and needs of a sport and its participants in clubs and schools, and possible changes and improvements that could be made. The involvement of stakeholders increases their understanding and acceptance of change, and the need for their collaboration if any improvements are to be made in their sport at a community level. It allows stakeholders to view "the process much more positively, feeling ownership of the strategy and acting in ways that make the implementation process more effective" (Robson et al. 2013: 5). For NZC, stakeholder reviews provided a clear mandate for change and endorsed their leadership to create "a common vision and direction for the game thus providing a holistic approach for all levels of administration and participation in the game" (NZC 2000: 4).

There are several methods for collating the information collected. A simple and effective way is to use a SWOT (strengths, weaknesses, opportunities, and threats) analysis. "As a situational audit it examines the most influential factors that affect the sport organisation at a moment in time and becomes the fundamental building block as to where you will be in the future" (Emery 2011: 6). The four SWOT categories identify a sport's internal strengths and weaknesses, with respect to its capability, capacity, and resources, and potential external opportunities and threats to be optimised or countered that arise from social, political, and economic changes. This bank of factual data provides SDMs with forward planning options to capitalise on strengths and maximise opportunities, while reducing weaknesses and minimising threats (Emery 2011). It allows them to assess the current shape and status of their community game ('where are we now?'); guide their short-, medium-, and long-term decisions and measurable direction, apparent in their vision, goals, and objectives ('where do we want to be in the future?'); set strategies and initiatives to action these ('how are we going to get there?'); and determine outcomes and performance measures they expect to achieve ('how will we know if we have got there?') (see Case study 3.2).

CASE STUDY 3.2

New Zealand Rugby: community rugby plans

Brent Anderson, Head of Community Rugby, New Zealand Rugby, Wellington, New Zealand

The New Zealand Rugby Football Union (NZRFU) in 2006 became the NZRU, and since 2013 NZR. The NZRFU began its community rugby involvement post-1996, when 'trickle-down' funding from the game's professionalisation allowed it to intervene to counter declining participation in clubs and schools. A national Club Rugby Manager was employed, along with a network of 27 Rugby Development Officers (RDOs), one in each provincial union; and an entry-level 'McDonald's Small Blacks' modified programme for children was introduced, followed later by non-tackle 'Rippa Rugby'. In 2001, the intervention's scope was widened when a national Community Rugby Manager was appointed.

Following the loss of hosting the 2003 Rugby World Cup, the NZRU appointed a new board and CEO who took a more strategic approach to the sport. They realised investing in community rugby would pay long term, keeping rugby strong, and supplying the talent pipeline. A plan was required to develop community rugby, provide a business case for budget resources, and give direction to the provincial unions.

The Community Rugby Manager, and a small working group, were charged with this task. Extensive consultation with provincial union and school stakeholders, a National Club Forum, and detailed research were undertaken to ascertain the state of the community game. This underpinned the first 'Community Rugby Plan 2004–2006' introduced in 2004. It "outlined many of the strategies and initiatives that have since become cornerstones of New Zealand's community rugby structure" (NZRU 2008: 4).

Two further community rugby plans (2008–2011, 2013–2015) consolidated and extended these strategies and initiatives. A fourth plan for 2017–2019 is currently being completed. The intervening year between the plans has a 'business as usual' focus, and is used to review, consult, and research prior to rewriting the next plan.

The focus of the community rugby plans on 'more players and more communities participating' has become a key strategy. It fits within the sport's post-2008 strategic vision of 'inspiring and unifying New Zealanders', and provides a context for its community rugby practitioners to define their purpose, and design strategies and initiatives to create a lifelong love of rugby.

The community rugby plans are underlain by a programme of integrated community rugby development initiatives covering: Small Blacks, secondary school and teenagers, club, and coaching and refereeing. While these have been constant through the plans, the fourth plan will also highlight new variations and potential participants (e.g. Indian communities in Auckland playing seven-a-side rugby).

The plans' intent has shifted over time. The initial two plans were concentrated on growth and increasing participation, particularly to expand the talent base. The third and new fourth plans are more focused on the environment the game is played in, so are more player-centric and about creating a lifelong love of rugby. In other words, there has been a shift from primarily recruitment to retention through quality experiences, as measured by participant satisfaction.

The buy-in by the provincial unions to delivering the community rugby plan initiatives is encouraged through NZR funding. They are required to report progress regularly to NZR, and the plans' performance is publicised through the NZR's 'Scoreboard' system of targets and results. The success or otherwise of these are regularly reviewed.

The direction, support, and guidance provided to provinces, clubs, and schools by the community rugby plans and their initiatives have significantly impacted community rugby. Since the first plan in 2004, player numbers have increased 25% from 120,000 to 150,000, trained coaches 50% from 8,000 to 12,000, only referee numbers have remained static. The plans have focused provincial unions' actions and maintained traditional support for the game, despite the challenges of constant change.

Questions

1. When did the NZRFU first intervene into community rugby? What made this possible? What was its purpose?
2. What was the first community rugby plan's strategic focus, which has continued through its subsequent plans?
3. How has the intent of these plans shifted over time, and why?
4. Why do you think this change is becoming a recurring theme in organised sport?

Clubs and secondary schools use this information to produce a strategic plan, most of the objectives of which focus on improving the capability of their organisation and developing and delivering their sport. In other words, it is primarily a sport development plan (see Case study 3.3).

CASE STUDY 3.3

Sydenham Cricket Club: strategic plans

Graham Harris, President, Sydenham Cricket Club, Christchurch, New Zealand

The Christchurch earthquakes in 2010 and 2011 destroyed much of the central city, damaging the infrastructure of many community sports' clubs. Sydenham Cricket Club (CC) was one of these clubs. Established in 1895 at Sydenham Park, it's the largest senior cricket club in Christchurch, with its teams playing in the Christchurch Metropolitan Cricket Association (CMCA) men's and women's competitions.

The earthquakes' impact on the club's players and performance of its teams, and its clubrooms, training, and playing facilities, prompted the club to engage Sport Canterbury, the local RST, to facilitate formulating a strategic plan (2011–2014). This provided the club with a focus, direction for its rebuild and future development, and timeline to achieve this over the plan's duration and beyond.

The strategic plan's mission was 'Providing cricket for enjoyment and success' through a vision to be 'Canterbury's club of choice'. It emphasised four key areas: operations (strong leadership, financial strength, systems, and succession plans to ensure ongoing effectiveness); facilities (quality playing and training amenities, welcoming and attractive clubrooms); participation (clearly defined player development pathways, recruitment and retention strategies, success of its premier teams); and communications (improved information flows within the club, stronger links with the junior club).

The plan provided the impetus for the selection of a proactive club committee to drive the changes required in the club to achieve its strategic objectives. The club has achieved financial security through key sponsorships and fundraising; rebuild and upgraded its clubrooms into a modern, fit for purpose, complex; resurfaced its artificial practice nets; appointed an experienced coach to strengthen its coaching and create a club playing vision for success; and improved its communication through a refreshed club website with up-to-date information and statistics, monthly 'Beyond the Boundary' newsletter, and new Facebook page for members' feedback.

In 2016, the club realising the value of planning, went through a similar process building on its 2011–2014 plan, to create its current strategic plan (2017–2020). This expanded its mission to 'Providing quality cricket for our community, fostering a culture of enjoyment, development and success', with a vision of 'Building on Sydenham's rich history to be Canterbury's club of choice'. Its key areas were extended by one, and reprioritised with participation and pathways being the central focus, surrounded by a strong sustainable club; communications, marketing, and partnerships; our people (i.e. volunteers); and facilities. These changes, which reflect the club's understanding of its role as a provider not just of opportunities, but also meaningful experiences that meet players' needs to enjoy, participate, and perform, have underpinned its ongoing popularity and sustainable growth. Furthermore, the Christchurch City Council, as part of its long-term plan to improve city sports facilities, has renovated Sydenham Park and installed new cricket blocks for 2018, further improving the club's infrastructure.

The club's planning and preparation off the field has had tangible rewards on the field. Since the earthquakes, while player numbers in other city clubs have fluctuated, Sydenham CC's has remained stable with 12 men's and women's teams, and a rapidly growing junior club of 37 junior teams (up 11 teams), together with 50 entry-level participants. Together the senior and junior clubs have over 650 players. Additionally, the Sydenham CC's premier team, after struggling for several years, in 2015/16 won the CMCA premier two-day competition, and in 2016/17 the T20 competition. Its lower grades have also won their competitions and individual players have been selected in Canterbury representative men's, women's, and age-group teams. The club's next steps are to work in partnership with its junior club to build a more integrated overall club player development pathway; and through its involvement with local secondary schools and a combined entity (South West Youth), expand its four youth teams back to the nine it fielded prior to the earthquakes.

Questions

1. When and why did Sydenham CC formulate a strategic plan?
2. Was the first plan's intent club-centric or participant-centric? Did this intent change in the second plan, and how?
3. What impact has strategic planning had on the club's participation and performance?

Vision statements

A sport development plan usually has only a vision statement, because as a subsidiary plan, it defers to the mission statement headlining the sport organisation's strategic plan. A vision statement is a short, precise, easy-to-read, overarching description about long-term direction and improvement. It defines a future position a sport organisation would like to reach in the longer term with respect to sport development. "A good vision statement should provide future direction; express an identifiable benefit to key stakeholders; and motivate and inspire people towards a common goal" (Sport NZ 2015: 25). For example, Sport NZ's vision statement is "Enriching lives through sport – everyone, every day" (Sport NZ 2012: 8).

Goals and objectives

Goals state the broad targets that a sport organisation wants to achieve in the three- to five-year duration of its sport development plan. To accomplish these, they set four to six objectives, worded in specific, measurable, achievable, realistic, and time-bound (SMART) terms that represent the steps they need to take to reach each of their goals in this time period. In other words, sport organisations "set goals that they then strive to attain, and they write explicit objectives to help them get there" (Lussier and Kimball 2014: 100).

Development goals and objectives reflect a sport organisation's definition of development and whether its focus is on growth, sustainability, and/or talent development, and the derived scope of its community operations. The objectives also encompass each of the interconnected elements of the 'development of sport' process (see Figure 2.1), which are integral to a sport realising its development goals at a community level. Table 3.1 matches these elements with the objectives from NZC's national development plan, whose general goals were to 'grow' and 'sustain' participation in cricket in clubs and schools (Astle 2009).

REVIEW QUESTIONS

1. What sources of information are useful in undertaking a preparatory situational analysis of the state of a sport?
2. Why is it essential in the preparatory stage of planning for SDMs to define the meaning and scope of sport development?
3. Create a SWOT analysis for a club you are familiar with, identify in each category at least three features, and highlight one for future improvement.
4. Use the internet to identify the vision statement for two NSOs.
5. Identify for a RSO you are familiar with one of its goals, then list the objectives set to achieve this goal.

Strategies

Central to a sport development plan are the strategies adopted by sport organisations to achieve their goals and objectives. Strategies are usually about the competitive positioning of an organisation. While sport organisations do not necessary perceive themselves in

TABLE 3.1 New Zealand Cricket's national development plan objectives

'Development of sport' elements	Objectives
Player	1. To increase the number of people playing cricket.
	2. To provide more opportunities for skill development, enjoyment, and advancement.
Game	3. To offer a range of versions of the game to cater for players' different needs, interests, ages, and abilities.
Coach (volunteer)	4. To increase the number of parents and teachers as volunteers, especially trained as coaches.
Sport provider and facility	5. To improve the capability, infrastructure, and services of clubs and schools, including their linkage.

Source: Astle (2009).

competition with others, increasingly they are competing against other sports and recreation and leisure activities for their share of the participatory market, especially for children at the entry level to their sports (Shilbury and Kellett 2011).

Astle's (1999) model of strategies was adopted by NZC and embedded in its national development plan to develop cricket in NZ (see Figure 3.4 and Table 3.2). Known as the seven 'Rs', these strategies included: research, recognition, recruitment, retention, restructuring, resourcing, and review. They emerged from an earlier ACB suggestion that 'development' incorporated four 'Rs' of research, recruitment, retention, and restructuring (Gilson, Pratt, Roberts, and Weymes 2000).

As Shilbury and Kellett (2011: 269, quoting the Commonwealth of Australia 2009) note, "strategies must be clearly articulated and acted upon in a coordinated way. It is only a combination of all actions together that will lead to success." Without such a framework of strategies it is easy to waste time, effort, and limited resources dealing with community sport development issues in a fragmented way through reactive 'stop-gap' measures.

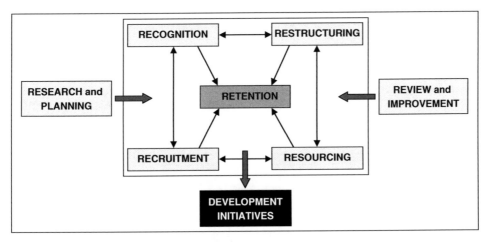

FIGURE 3.4 Integrated development strategies

Source: Astle (1999: 5).

TABLE 3.2 Development strategies adopted by New Zealand Cricket

Strategies

Research	To prepare a cohesive plan as the basis for designing and implementing a comprehensive national development programme.
Recognition	To increase the profile, level of awareness and interest, and promote the benefits of participation in cricket within the community.
Recruitment	To expand participation in the sport by ensuring every individual, irrespective of age, ability, interest, or gender, has access to relevant, attractive, and affordable cricket playing opportunities, experiences, and services.
Retention	To maintain the interest, support the involvement, service the needs, and develop the competencies of individuals so they can participate and progress in the game to the level they desire.
Restructuring	To revitalise clubs and schools by improving their organisation, infrastructure, and services, as well as enhance and modify the game by increasing its flexibility and adaptability to cater for the varied needs and expectations of individuals.
Resourcing	To provide appropriate information, support, and funding (where available) to strengthen the capability of clubs and schools and their paid and volunteer personnel to attract, nurture, and keep individuals in the game.
Review	To evaluate the success of these strategies to continually improve the quality and effectiveness of the national development programme, its initiatives and their delivery.

Source: Astle (1999, 2009).

Initiatives

Initiatives, or specific actions, make the link between strategies and objectives, and should reflect the key 'development of sport' elements (see Figure 2.1). Examples of initiatives and these elements include: modified formats (game), different competition types (player), innovative coach development courses and resources (coach), club capability measures (provider), and new and improved facilities (facility).

Initiatives need to be integrated within a sport organisation's whole-of-sport framework of pathways. They must be affordable to implement and offer a value proposition to achieve the 'buy-in' of volunteers who will deliver them. The design of initiatives, and their inclusion in comprehensive development programmes, are the subject of Chapter 4.

Implementation

Careful consideration needs to given to how the plan, through its associated programme, is going to be introduced. Existing development initiatives are mainly delivered by volunteers in clubs and schools. The implementation of new initiatives is often facilitated by regional networks of SDMs and SDOs, whose role is to inspire, educate, coordinate, and support volunteers to deliver these in their clubs and schools. To appoint SDOs will require a national

SDM to carefully consider and justify their value to a NSO's CEO and board, by answering such questions as: 'what will be their role and responsibilities?', 'how many will be required?', 'how will they be sustainably funded?', 'how will they be managed remotely?', and 'how will their performance be measured?'. Answers to these questions about SDOs are discussed in Chapter 5.

For practitioners to be effective, cost-efficient, and timely in implementing sport organisations' initiatives, the process needs to be planned and systematic, so everyone involved at every level within organisations knows, understands, and is accountable for their delivery. This requires NSO SDMs to coordinate and standardise, at national, regional, and local levels, a hierarchical system of plans, procedures, and accountabilities to facilitate implementation (Astle 2014). This system provides the framework within which SDOs operate. It defines their workflow, determines their targets and accountabilities, specifies their requirements to record data and report regularly, and guides their performance appraisals.

Although this national system of plans and procedures for implementation is best standardised, the actual delivery of the programme needs to remain flexible to accommodate local and regional variations and best practice solutions. The translation of plans into practice through the implementation of sport development programmes is examined in Chapter 6.

Monitoring and evaluation

Monitoring and evaluation (M&E) are ongoing processes that regularly review the relevance of the contents of a sport development plan, and applicability of the design and implementation of the programme that turns the plan into practice (see Figure 3.3). Monitoring involves observing, recording, and reporting information to assess the programme's performance against predetermined criteria, while evaluation is about making a judgement about the performance in terms of comparing actual versus planned results, and determining if change is required (Sport NZ 2014). Together these processes are necessary to ensure the plan remains flexible and responsive to change, and to monitor progress and measure the performance (impact and effectiveness) of the programme and its delivery, and where necessary, make corrective adjustments for its continuous improvement.

A regular review of a sport development plan and its programme needs to be scheduled annually, and then revised as required. In addition, to this constant reviewing of the plan, in particular its objectives and strategies, each initiative, once designed, needs to be initially piloted with select clubs and schools to ensure its effectiveness, and once implemented be regularly assessed to measure its impact.

A programme's impact is usually assessed by measuring outputs (quantitative indicators, e.g. number of participants), and/or outcomes (qualitative indicators, e.g. evidence of capability improvements, such as strategic plans), set for each of a plan's objectives (see Figure 7.1). Some sport organisations merge these and call them all just outcomes (SPARC 2009a, 2010). Once these outcomes have been decided, a suite of measurable values or key performance indicators (KPIs), which demonstrate if a sport organisation is on track to achieving its objectives can be agreed on, and appropriately linked with these outcomes. KPIs, like the plan's objectives, need to be written in SMART terms, and assigned targets (see Table 3.3). As Emery (2011: 47) suggests, "the main benefit of using SMART objectives and KPIs is they act as targets that can engage and motivate individual and team performance towards measurable achievement".

TABLE 3.3 Examples of sport development outcomes and KPIs with targets

Outcomes	KPIs with assigned targets
1. An increase in people participating in the sport	An increase in participation in the sport by 'x'%
2. An increase in the number and capability of coaches servicing the sport	An increase in the number by 'x' of coaches recruited into the sport An increase in the number by 'x' of coach development courses An increase in the number by 'x' of coaches trained by completing coach development courses
3. An improvement in the capability of clubs to deliver the sport	Complete 'x' number of club health checks Complete 'x' number of club strategic plans

Source: © Astle.

SDMs need to establish a standardised system for collecting the necessary data to measure these KPIs, and for reporting and tracking their progress. For each KPI, baseline data is needed, as a benchmark or reference point from which to measure future performance. The KPI targets, and their recording and reporting requirements, can then be incorporated into annual service level agreements (SLAs) and signed off with each RSO. SLAs not only indicate their accountabilities for NSO sport development investment, but also act as a planning guide to assist their SDOs prepare regional plans specifying how, where, and when they will deliver each outcome and its associated KPIs.

The establishment of M&E methods serves many purposes. These include: reviewing the effectiveness of a sport development plan and its objectives; gauging the performance of SDMs and SDOs in implementing these; collecting evidence to assess the impact of its programme and initiatives; reporting on progress and trends; and identifying issues, and where necessary, taking timely and informed corrective action to adjust the plan and/or improve the programme. This makes planning a continuous and active process (Emery 2011).

REVIEW QUESTIONS

1. What are strategies? What strategies were important in NZC's NDP? Why are these strategies applicable in most sport development plans?
2. Why are systems and procedures important in implementing a sport development plan?
3. Select any sport organisation and identify two of its sport development outcomes and associated KPIs. How successful have they been in achieving these outcomes?

Financial plan and funding partnerships

What are the financial implications of a sport development plan (i.e. the cost of its emergent programme and its implementation)? This requires a financial plan, including a budget, to turn the plan into action, by making "clear the match between stated outcome, key initiatives, and the application of financial resource" (Sport NZ 2015: 46). SDMs need to carefully consider the cost of designing, resourcing, and implementing a sport development programme (expenditure), especially SDO salaries and operating costs; and identify possible sources of funding to cover this cost (income) and ensure its viability.

While a NSO may contribute funding to its sport development programme, the level and sustainability of this will depend on its own financial viability, and identifying alternative funding options for sport development. Some NSOs receive financial backing from central government for their programmes (SPARC 2009a; Sport England 2008). Others, who get less from this source, are more reliant on both external funding partnerships with corporate sponsors, Gaming Trusts, and local authorities, and/or internal funding arrangements with their RSOs, clubs, and schools. The main item of expenditure is to establish and maintain the SDO network. Some of their expenditure can also be offset by sponsors providing SDM and SDO vehicles, mobile phones, laptops, clothing, equipment, and products to market the sponsors' brands and grow the sport's profile.

In creating a financial plan, most NSOs will have their own accountant or access to a financial adviser to provide SDMs with advice. If NSOs have preferred suppliers of clothing, equipment, and publishing, indicative prices can be sought from them, which SDMs can use in their budgets to estimate the unit price of items, such as outfitting a SDO, or printing resources.

Irrespective of the quality of the plan and its programme, for it to become reality, a NSO's CEO and board must be convinced of its value proposition for the sport and its affordability. They will require a financial plan that provides realistic partnership options for funding the programme and its implementation, and clearly indicates their level of financial contribution, if they are to commit long term to its ongoing support and investment.

Communication, ongoing education, and acceptance

The success of a plan is dependent on how inclusive the planning process has been in its formulation, how widespread the completed plan is disseminated inside and outside the sport, and how well its key messages are communicated and accepted by staff, stakeholders, and sponsors. If a sport development plan's purpose is to revitalise and grow community sport, it has to be accepted and supported at a community level, with club and school volunteers involved from the start of the planning process. Their views on the state of their sport at this level, its strengths and weaknesses, and potential opportunities and challenges, need to be canvassed in the initial consultation stage (Gryphon Governance Consultants 2011). Ironically, these beneficiaries of sport development plans are not always included in the planning process, yet are expected to be involved in their implementation (Harris et al. 2009).

Once a sport development plan is complete, it needs to be communicated widely throughout a sport organisation to get 'buy-in' from all those with a stake in the organisation. Large sports may create a specific communication strategy to achieve this objective through their internal and external media channels. Small sports will more likely use every internal communication means available (e.g. forums, newsletters, emails, websites, and social media) to reach as wide an audience as possible (see Case study 3.4). Everyone needs to be familiar with the plan, its associated programme and key messages, and understand what needs to be done if the organisation is to achieve its goals, objectives, and outcomes. Keeping the plan front and centre provides the organisation with direction and creates a sense of shared ownership and commitment to work together collaboratively to implement the plan.

CASE STUDY 3.4
Value of websites and social media

Ryan Astle, Digital Marketing Specialist, Jade Logistics Group; and Vice President, Old Boys' Collegians Cricket Club, Christchurch, New Zealand

A digital presence is becoming increasingly important for sports clubs to communicate with members, recruit new players, and retain current ones. Traditional communication and marketing through print and radio advertisements are being replaced with digital strategies, such as social media and a website, which are seen as more effective.

When searching for a new sports club, more people use search engines, such as Google, to find out what is available locally. Obviously, without a website or social media presence clubs are unlikely to appear in these searches. Conversely, the greater a club's digital presence and the more new content produced, the greater the likelihood these will appear in search results.

However, it's not just about quantity, the quality of club posts on social media and websites should appeal to both current and prospective players. For instance, posting photos and videos of current players enjoying their sport provides positive experiential proof which aids recruitment.

Social media providers, like Facebook, allow for both public and private channels. Private groups are useful for communicating to current participants, especially information not relevant to the public (e.g. team selections). Public pages are better for recruitment and informing the wider community about the club, its performance, future direction, and events.

To be effective in the digital space, clubs must understand the relationship between social media and their website. People are more likely to check social media than websites, so it is important to regularly post concise but compelling content there. These posts should use imagery where possible, and encourage people to click to the website, where more detailed and informative content can be hosted.

Questions

1. How have digital strategies made communication and marketing more effective for sports clubs?
2. Why should sports clubs have both a website and social media presence?

Producing a one-page sport development plan summary has the advantage of it being clear, accessible, simple to update, and easy to distribute at meetings, through organisation newsletters, SDO manuals, and online. It's also useful for SDOs in their ongoing task of informing and educating stakeholders about the requirements of the plan and its programme, as at RSO and club levels there is a high turnover of volunteers (Astle, Dellaca, and Pithey 2013).

REVIEW QUESTIONS

1. Locate a sport organisation's annual report and identify a funding partnership it has with a corporate sponsor. What is the partnership's value and how does it benefit the development of community sport?
2. When, why, and how should a sport development plan be communicated to ensure its understanding, acceptance, and ultimately its success?

CONCLUSION

A plan is a blueprint for success. The planning process allows SDMs and SDOs, in sport organisations at all levels, to apply a systematic research and decision-making process, to organise sport development within the framework of a plan comprising a vision, goals and objectives, strategies and initiatives, and measurable outcomes in KPIs, to revitalise and grow community sport. Such a plan keeps everyone on the same page, working towards the same agreed outcomes, and measuring progress along the way.

Strategic plans, which have become increasingly commonplace within NSOs, and their constituent RSOs, and often clubs and schools, have provided SDMs, SDOs, and volunteers with a template to clarify their thinking and structure their operations. The more recent use of whole-of-sport plans, which allow a sport's delivery and support systems to be viewed in their entirety, have encouraged SDMs and SDOs to design whole-of-sport overviews, not only to understand the interconnectedness of their sports and their pathways of opportunities, but also to make decisions about the scope and purpose of their sport development plans.

The importance of thorough preparation in the planning process and need to follow a logical sequence of steps in formulating a sport development plan have been highlighted. It is of considerable benefit for practitioners to invest fully in this research and systematic analysis, not only to clarify their strategic thinking about their sport and its current circumstances, but also to assemble a factual base for strategic decision-making about sport development, and its practical application to their sport in determining its future direction and priorities. This preparatory research and thinking is considered the most beneficial aspect of crafting a sport development plan, as it gives SDMs a rich, in-depth, 'big picture' depository of knowledge about their sport (Sport NZ 2015).

The sequence of steps and their importance in the planning process, and how the completed sport development plan as a working document is not an end in itself but a means to harness a sport organisation's strengths and use these to seize opportunities to revitalise and grow sport at a community level, have been emphasised. Success is not necessarily a function of getting everything right in the first place, but rather having the resilience and capability to adjust one's plans continuously to take advantage of change, innovation, and best practice solutions (Hoye et al. 2012).

Above all, a sport development plan and its derived programme need to provide a value proposition for those with a stake in it, especially volunteers in clubs and schools. NSO leadership also needs to be convinced of the plan's benefits and affordability of its programme.

To implement the latter generally requires partnerships to be formed to underwrite the establishment of a SDO regional network. The effectiveness of this implementation, relevance of the plan, and impact of the programme, require systems to monitor their progress and performance.

REFERENCES

Astle, A. (1999). *New Zealand Cricket: national development plan.* Planning document. New Zealand Cricket, Christchurch.

Astle, A. (2000). *MILO Have-A-Go cricket coaching manual for children 6–8 years.* Christchurch: New Zealand Cricket.

Astle, A. (2002). *Strategic planning: The plan and the process.* Christchurch: New Zealand Cricket.

Astle, A. (2009). *New Zealand Cricket: national development plan and programme.* Planning document. New Zealand Cricket, Christchurch.

Astle, A. (2014). *Sport development – Plan, programme and practice: A case study of the planned intervention by New Zealand Cricket into cricket in New Zealand.* PhD, Massey University, Palmerston North, New Zealand.

Astle, A., Dellaca, K., & Pithey, R. (2013). *Canterbury Cricket Association: District reviews* (Report). Christchurch: Canterbury Cricket Association.

Bloyce, D., & Green, K. (2011). Sports development officers on sport development. In B. Houlihan & M. Green (Eds.), *Routledge handbook of sports development* (pp. 477–486). London and New York: Routledge.

Emery, P. (2011). *The sports management toolkit.* London: Routledge.

Francis, I. (2011). *2011 Hockey New Zealand Community Sport Plan.* Draft Annual Association Community Hockey Plan. Hockey New Zealand, Auckland.

Gilson, C., Pratt, M., Roberts, K., & Weymes, E. (2000). *Peak performance: Business lessons from the world's top sports organizations.* London: HarperCollins Business.

Gryphon Governance Consultants. (2011). *Organisational change in seven selected sports: What can be learnt and applied?* Sport and Recreation New Zealand, Wellington.

Harris, S., Mori, K., & Collins, M. (2009). Great expectations: Voluntary sports clubs and their role in delivering national policy for English sport. *Voluntas, 20,* 405–423.

Hoye, R., Smith, A., Nicholson, M., Stewart, B., & Westerbeek, H. (2012). *Sport management: Principles and applications* (3rd ed.). London and New York: Routledge.

Lussier, R. N., & Kimball, D. C. (2014). *Applied sport management skills* (2nd ed.). Champaign, IL: Human Kinetics.

New Zealand Cricket. (2000). *District review.* Planning document. New Zealand Cricket, Christchurch.

Robson, S., Simpson, K., & Tucker, L. (Eds.). (2013). *Strategic sport development.* London and New York: Routledge.

Robson, S., Simpson, K., Tucker, L., & Leach, R. (2013). Introduction. In S. Robson, K. Simpson, & L. Tucker (Eds.), *Strategic sport development* (pp. 1–24). London and New York: Routledge.

Shilbury, D., & Kellett, P. (2011). *Sport management in Australia: An organisational overview* (4th ed.). Sydney: Allen and Unwin.

SPARC. (2009a). *Sport and recreation – Everyone. Every day. Sport and Recreation New Zealand's Strategic Plan 2009–2015.* Wellington: Sport and Recreation New Zealand.

SPARC. (2009b). *Sport and recreation pathway.* Planning document. Sport and Recreation New Zealand, Wellington.

SPARC. (2009c). *NZ sport and recreation pathway.* Powerpoint presentation. Sport and Recreation New Zealand, Wellington.

SPARC. (2009d). *Community sport review findings*. Sport and Recreation New Zealand, Wellington.

SPARC. (2010). *Community sport strategy: 2010–2015*. Planning document. Sport and Recreation New Zealand, Wellington.

Sport England. (2008). *Grow, sustain, excel: Strategy 2008–11*. London: Sport England.

Sport New Zealand. (2012). *Strategic plan 2012–2015*. Wellington: New Zealand Government.

Sport New Zealand. (2014). *Nine steps to effective governance: Building high performing organisations* (3rd ed.). Wellington: Sport New Zealand.

Sport New Zealand. (2015). *Planning in sport*. Wellington: Sport New Zealand.

Watt, D. C. (2003). *Sports management and administration* (2nd ed.). London: Routledge.

Websites

www.ausport.gov.au/

www.sportcanterbury.org.nz/new-zealand/for-clubs

www.sportengland.org/

www.sportenglandclubmatters.com/club-mark

www.sportnz.org.nz/

CHAPTER 4

Designing a sport development programme

Once a sport development plan is completed, a sport development programme can be designed and implemented. The plan presents a conceptual framework for the programme's construction, providing structure and direction for the design of its specific initiatives.

Central to the design of a programme is the initial research and consultation undertaken as part of the planning process, and subsequent whole-of-sport overview created to provide a holistic view of a sport. The former identifies the current state of a sport and indicates areas for future improvement, while the latter enables strategic decisions to be made about the scope of the programme. These decisions will influence the mix of initiatives needed to meet the plan's objectives and outcomes.

For initiatives to be enduring, they need to be integrated within a sport's overall programme and embedded in the pathways that underpin its development and delivery system. If they are not, evidence suggests they are likely to be piecemeal and often short-lived (Sport England 2007). For example, efforts to increase participation are unlikely to be sustained without concurrent improvements in coaching, club, and school capability, and facilities (Shilbury and Kellett 2011). For this reason, stand-alone initiatives are questioned in terms of their failure to transition participants into community sport pathways (Bowers and Green 2016), their cost–benefit for volunteer and SDO efforts, and their long-term impact on community sport (Partington and Robson 2013).

In designing a sport development programme, a SDM first needs to decide what level in their sport (e.g. children, youth, adult) the programme will initially target, and then in what order the other levels will be addressed. For each level consideration needs to be given to which existing initiatives should be retained, what new initiatives need to be created and piloted, and when and how these will be implemented.

This chapter will:

1. Identify the underpinning pathways of community sport in which to embed a sport development programme's initiatives and indicate why they need to be both integrated and aligned.
2. Discuss the requirement for change and innovation in community sport in the last three decades, and the role of game diversification and modification in making sport more available, accessible, and relevant for wider participation.
3. Explore the theories, policies, and programmes that have influenced the planning of sport development programmes, and content of initiatives designed to meet the needs of community sport participants.

4. Briefly outline NZC's NDP as a context in which to examine MILO Have-A-Go Cricket, its branded, entry-level initiative, including its purpose and objectives, support resources and piloting, and procedures and training needed to ensure the quality of its delivery and experience for participants.

FOUNDATION RESEARCH AND FRAMEWORK

The preparation of a whole-of-sport overview during the planning process gives a SDM the opportunity to create an end-to-end 'big picture' view of their entire sport and its development and delivery systems, and determine the scope of their sport development programme. Is its scope only club and school sport, or does it also include regional high-performance sport, and if so, to what level? In NZ, the scope of NZC's NDP originally focused on the former, while hockey's programme incorporated club, school, and up to and including U18 representative hockey.

Once the programme's scope has been delimited, then the first level to concentrate on must be decided. Many sports initially focus on the entry-level of children aged 5–12 years playing sport in primary schools and junior clubs. This is a logical starting point to capture the initial interest and involvement of children (and their parents and teachers) in sport, the objective being to provide relevant and appealing opportunities for children to participate, and their parents and teachers to become involved in the game as coaches, as a prerequisite to creating a strong foundation on which to build other initiatives directed at youth and adult levels.

The purpose and effectiveness of existing initiatives must be assessed, and either discarded or retained with or without amendment, and new initiatives identified and included to complete the sequence of initiatives necessary to achieve a sport development plan's objectives and strategies for each level within community sport (e.g. children, youth, adults). Together the sequential sets of initiatives for these three levels comprise an integrated, community-focused 'development of sport' programme. It's crucial for SDMs when designing new initiatives to put themselves in the shoes of participants and coaches, to ensure they are both appropriate to their needs and capabilities and those of the sport (see Pause and ponder 4.1).

PAUSE and PONDER 4.1

Standing in the customer's shoes: questions for initiative design

The first step in designing matching player and coach development initiatives is to undertake research, collect player development and coaching resources from different sports and sports agencies, and consult with experienced volunteers and SDOs. Then put yourself in the shoes of the participant, then subsequently those of the coach, which at junior level is usually a parent or teacher, to determine their diverse needs and capabilities, and balance these with those of your sport and its club and school providers. Below is a list of questions to guide the process:

1. What is the initiative's purpose and objectives, and where does it fit into the sport's pathways?
2. Who is the initiative's target audience?
3. What are the varying needs and capabilities of (a) participants, and (b) their coaches?
4. How will the initiative be structured for (a) participants, (b) coaches, and (c) clubs and schools, and what support materials will be required for each (e.g. equipment, coaching resources, organisational handbook, and administrative procedures)?
   a) **For participants**: What will be the duration of the initiative – a season, a module, a day festival? How long will each session be? It is suggested 45–60 minutes for entry-level children, then increasing in subsequent initiatives according to age, and sporting and social skills development (stage). How will each session be structured in terms of sections and their duration (see Figure 4.3)? What skills will be included, and how will each skill be developed through the sessions? What equipment will be required? What will this and registering in the initiative cost?
   b) **For coaches**: Who will they be? What coaching resources need to be produced and what will they cost? How will the coaches be trained, where, by whom, and for how long? Will they be assessed? Will there be a cost? What support and equipment will they require?
   c) **For clubs and schools:** How will the initiative be marketed? What will be required to organise and administer it (i.e. how will participants be recruited, from where, by whom, and when and how will they be registered in the initiatives)? What will be the cost to run the initiative? What extra facilities (i.e. playing and practice surfaces), equipment, and coaches will be required?
5. Who will design the playing initiative, coaching course and resources, organisational handbook and administrative procedures (i.e. the SDM, a group of practitioners, or an external agency)? Make sure they are easy to use, fun for participants, and add value to club and school programmes.
6. How will the initiative be tested (i.e. what sample of clubs and schools will be used to pilot these)? Who will evaluate the pilot and recommend any changes? How and when will it be launched? What resources and training requirements will SDOs need to implement the initiative?

NB: There are undoubtedly many other questions. These are just to get started! Keep reflecting and standing in the customer's shoes to get the perspective of being a recipient of the initiative, and work systematically through the process. Good luck.

Question

Why is it always important to stand in the customer's shoes? How does their perspective differ from considering the needs of a sport?

It is important to realise "the concept of 'development' inherently involves change. For something to develop, or be developed, it must be changed" (Doherty and Rich 2015: 130), which implies growth and/or improvement. In this context, initiatives are seen as innovative activities aimed at increasing and/or improving participation, contribution and/or capability to grow, sustain, and and/or foster talent in community sport. For example, initiatives may take the form of: new modified skill development activities and/or game formats to create a wider selection of playing opportunities for participants; improved coaching frameworks and courses to ensure the supply of more skilled coaches to service participants needs; health checks and planning to enhance the capability and capacity of clubs and schools to deliver these playing opportunities; and establishment of more and better facilities to allow a greater number of participants to experience these opportunities.

THE UNDERPINNING PATHWAYS

A framework of integrated and aligned pathways needs to be designed to underpin a sport development programme. In forming these pathways, existing participatory and high-performance initiatives for players need to be distinguished, then from a community sport perspective, potential new initiatives identified. This acknowledges player recruitment, development, and retention as the central function of community sport, but must be comple-mented by aligned pathways, within an integrated and organised delivery system, provided by clubs and schools with the appropriate capability, infrastructure, and services.

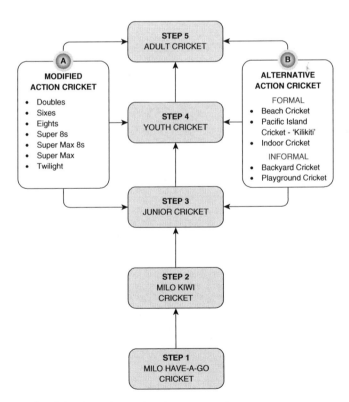

FIGURE 4.1 New Zealand Cricket: player development pathway

Source: Astle (2000a: 8).

In NZC's case, the player development pathway was not linear, but multidirectional, especially as players progressed from junior cricket upwards. It comprised a central, conventional pathway of five stages of participatory opportunities spanning community cricket from entry-level to adult cricket, with clubs and schools offering a planned progression of skill development, modified game formats, and competitive challenges at levels appropriate to the age, ability, and interest of players (Astle 2000a) (see Figure 4.1). Adjoining this conventional pathway, were two parallel pathways of more social, recreational 'modified action cricket' (e.g. twilight cricket, six-a-side), organised by either individual schools, clubs, regional associations, or independent providers; and 'alternative action cricket' (e.g. backyard cricket, indoor cricket), set up and run by groups of friends, ethnic communities, or commercial operators.

The availability of this diversity of options increased cricket's popularity and appeal to a wider audience of participants. In this way, cricket has accommodated both those seeking a more intense competitive challenge, and those interested in a more relaxed social experience. Many players participate concurrently across these different pathways, progressing at variable rates and with different motivations, thereby creating their own individual, often intertwining, development pathways.

After formulating the player development pathway to support the development of players and sustain their participation, NZC needed to align it with a matching coach development pathway to provide the required coaches and quality coaching. This pathway comprised a progression of educative opportunities for coaches that aligned with the stages in its player

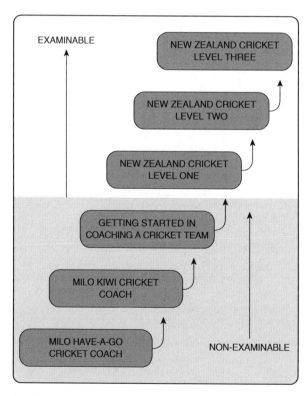

FIGURE 4.2 New Zealand Cricket: coach development pathway

Source: Astle (2000a: 7).

development pathway (see Figure 4.2) (Astle 2000a). Both pathways had to be synchronised because for players to develop, they require coaches, especially parents and teachers, trained to upskill them at a level commensurate with their age and ability. Any growth in player numbers had to be balanced by an increase in coach numbers, if players were to be developed and retained.

The matching player and coach development pathways formed the backbone of NZC's NDP. They allowed for the first time in community cricket coaches to step the same sequence as the players. As Goldsmith (2009: 1) noted, "the whole point to coaching is to create an environment which provides appropriate coaching to athletes at the appropriate time in their development".

REVIEW QUESTIONS

1. Why have NSOs, since the 1990s, introduced sport development programmes to influence their sports at a community level?
2. What preliminary preparation is advisable for practitioners prior to planning and designing a sport development programme? What initial decisions are needed to determine the programme's parameters?
3. What is a sport development initiative? List three types of initiatives evident in sport development programmes, and for each identify their purpose.
4. What pathways underpin a community sport development programme?
5. What is a pathway? Why does it need to be integrated and aligned with other pathways?

GAME AVAILABILITY AND RELEVANCE: DIVERSIFICATION AND MODIFICATION

In the 1990s, a raft of social, economic, and political changes began to impact organised sport causing participation rates to decline (see Chapter 2). A few NZ NSOs (e.g. cricket, rugby, netball) responded to this decline by introducing change and innovation through 'development of sport' programmes to grow and sustain their sports at a community level. Within these programmes, they identified integrated pathways of initiatives that offered more relevant opportunities, broadening their sports' appeal to better meet the contemporary needs and demands of current and prospective participants. In the last decade, other NSOs have been assisted by central government sport agency investment and specialist support, using whole-of-sport planning, to create similar programmes, with frameworks of pathways and initiatives to attract, recruit, and retain participants.

Two processes, diversification and modification, underpin the initiatives within these community sport pathways. Diversification refers to the number and types of opportunities available for participation in a sport. The number of opportunities correlates with the number and geographical spread of different providers of a sport (e.g. clubs, schools, business houses, commercial operators), while the types of opportunities represent the different formats of the sport that these providers offer for participation.

An example of diversification in cricket in NZ was the introduction of midweek competitions. Historically, cricket opportunities for adults were delivered through cricket clubs on Saturdays. In the 1970s, a combination of an increasing community interest in new competitions with shorter version formats, the availability of artificial pitches, and advent of national daylight saving provided the catalyst for midweek, twilight cricket. Subsequently, associations, clubs, and private providers have organised various 11-a-side, eight-a-side, and six-a-side limited over, social, twilight competitions for 'business house' or 'mates' teams. These competitions and formats continue to gain in popularity (e.g. Last Man Stands – see Case study 4.4).

Modification has seen sports altered through changes to rules, duration, scheduling, equipment, and facilities (Phillips and Warner 2016), expanding the variety of opportunities available to meet participant needs and demands (see Chapter 1). Although examples of modification have existed for many years, they became more commonplace in the 1980s when central government sport agencies in countries such as Australia (Australian Sports Commission) and NZ (Hillary Commission for Sport and Recreation) introduced modified sports programmes for primary school-aged children (5–12 years), known as Aussie Sports and KiwiSport respectively, to improve children's 'physical literacy' (Australian Sports Commission 1986; Hillary Commission 1988).

NSOs were encouraged to develop age-appropriate versions of their sport that catered specifically to the needs, development stage, and abilities of children. These provided entry-level, high-quality experiences for children to have fun, understand the basic structure of games, and acquire their fundamental and sport-specific skills in a simplified setting. To achieve this, NSOs changed and customised their sports through simplified rules, shortened games, reduced team numbers, rotation of player positions, smaller playing spaces, and appropriate size and weight equipment (Hillary Commission 1998; Phillips and Warner 2016). However, "where such modifications have been introduced it has been important that the integrity of the game should not be altered and the participants see and experience the game as very similar to the adult model" (Lee and Smith 1993: 260).

Although the KiwiSport programme in NZ successfully increased the number of children participating in sport and number of teachers trained as coaches, it also had its limitations. As a programme it was considered more an end in itself, than part of an integrated pathway for participants that led to youth and adult sport. While it trained teachers as elementary coaches it had limited success in transferring this into the coaching culture of clubs or the coach development pathways of NSOs (National Research Bureau 1996). Despite these shortcomings, KiwiSport introduced several key principles that have influenced the design of sporting initiatives in most sports in NZ over the past three decades. These include the need:

- to ensure sport is participant-centred not sport-centred;
- to ensure sport at a community level is relevant, accessible, and appealing, with stage appropriate opportunities, including progressive skill development and competition, particularly for children, commensurate with their level of physical, intellectual, and emotional development, and with each stage dovetailing into a player development pathway;

- to design and deliver high-quality entry-level initiatives that inspire participants and equip them with the foundational competence and confidence to optimise their future involvement and possible progression to higher levels in sport;
- to embrace the concept of modified sports, for all ages, abilities, and genders and incorporate these in their pathways; and
- to engage with teachers (and parents) and provide them with practical, easy-to-use coaching resources, and opportunities to train as coaches, at a level appropriate to their participants.

The dual processes of diversification and modification have enhanced the adaptability of what and how sports are played, and the flexibility of when and where they are played. These two concepts of adaptability and flexibility are integral to the 'development of sport' at a community level. They allow sports to remain contemporary in their appeal and accessibility, meeting the changing needs and demands of current participants, and targeting specific groups of prospective participants in terms of age, ability, interest, and/or gender.

Flexibility means sports such as cricket, which was once a Saturday dominant game, while still played on weekends is now also played on midweek evenings during the summer. This allows multi-use of facilities and enables more parents to become involved as coaches at times better suited to their routines. Parent availability and influence is key to their children's participation (Toms and Fleming 2003).

Adaptability through game modification has also been enhanced through the premise of 'less is more'. That is, the fewer players in a team (i.e. six or eight), usually means games are shorter, but each player's involvement, action, enjoyment, decision-making, and skill development opportunities is much greater. Unless players have the opportunity to have contact with the ball through batting, bowling, wicketkeeping, or fielding, they are unlikely to develop their cricket skills or have a quality experience, and so are more likely to drop out of the game. Fewer players means there are more gaps, more chances to score runs, more running in the field as there are fewer fielders, more turns at each skill set, and so more involvement and chances for each player to develop.

A study of junior cricket in South Australia found the amount of time a player is actively involved in a game increases significantly in reduced team number, shorter formats of the game (Johnswood 2006) (see Table 4.1). They used this evidence to introduce six-a-side and eight-a-side formats into junior cricket. More recent research has confirmed the benefits of modification and been used by Cricket Australia (2017) to underpin its junior pathway (see Facts and figures 4.1 and Case study 4.1).

TABLE 4.1 'Less is more': player involvement in different game formats

Active involvement	12-a-side	8-a-side	6-a-side
Percentage of players on the field involved in each ball	23.3%	36.7%	43.7%
Percentage of players in the match involved in each ball	13.6%	22.9%	29.1%

Source: Johnswood (2006: 5).

FACTS and FIGURES 4.1

Game modification for junior cricket

Cricket Australia recently conducted a three-year nationwide research project to examine the way junior cricket is delivered. Their findings strongly recommend the importance and benefits of game modification to create a progression of formats for developing junior cricketers. They included reductions in player numbers, time and overs, pitch lengths and boundary sizes, and use of appropriate size and weight equipment. These produced the following positive game outcomes:

- 43% more runs scored off the bat
- 13% more balls hit
- 66% more boundaries
- 35% fewer runs from wides
- 53% more balls bowled on a good length
- 24% fewer 'dot' balls bowled

Feedback from the cricket community endorsed these modifications with:

- 87% participants enjoying the cricket experience more
- 88% coaches considering their coaching was more effective
- 76% parents indicating their children had more fun and developed better skills
- 74% clubs supporting the shorter game time

Source: Cricket Australia (2017).

Questions

1. What key advantages were revealed by Johnswood and CA's research on reduced team numbers for junior cricketers?
2. How did this benefit their development?

CASE STUDY 4.1

MILO T20 Blast: Cricket Australia's Children's Learn the Game initiative

Michael Peacock, Cricket Australia Junior Participation Specialist, New South Wales, Sydney, Australia

In 1983, the Australian Cricket Board introduced its national development programme to increase participation by introducing children to cricket at an early age. They began by devising entry-level initiatives in their player development pathway to enable children to have fun learning the game and its fundamental skills.

Today, Cricket Australia (CA) offers three integrated age and stage appropriate initiatives in its pathway that allow boys and girls from five to 16 years to progress, depending on their ability and experience, at their own pace. These include: 'MILO in2CRICKET' which introduces 5–8-year-old children to cricket, teaching them its fundamental skills; 'MILO T20 Blast' which gives 7–12-year-olds their first experience of playing modified games; and 'play Cricket' which transitions 9–16-year-olds into competitive club cricket.

MILO T20 Blast is a new playing and marketing initiative, which had its origins in the highly publicised and attended Australian professional T20 'Big Bash League' (BBL) for men and 'Women's Big Bash League' (WBBL), launched in 2011 and 2015 respectively. Each league features eight city-based franchise clubs who play in the evenings during December/January in Australia.

MILO T20 Blast is closely linked with the BBL and WBBL and has leverage off its huge national and regional media promotion, including television and Big Bash website, www. bigbash.com.au. Each MILO T20 Blast Centre is aligned with a BBL club in their state, children registering in the initiative receive player packs with their BBL club playing shirt, hat, and drawstring bag.

MILO T20 Blast spans the gap between MILO in2CRICKET and play Cricket. It's a fun, social cricket initiative for 7–12-year-old boys and girls, that for most is their 'first taste' of cricket. Games are eight-a-side, 16 overs per innings, played for 90 minutes, usually on midweek evenings, instead of four to six hours on a weekend. The initiative runs at the same venue for eight weeks during the summer. It's played with simple rules, modified equipment, and a rubber ball on local cricket club outfields and community parks. Everyone gets to bat, bowl, and field in an atmosphere similar to the BBL with live music between overs. A 'Skill Zone' is created for children waiting to bat to keep them engaged through small-sided games.

The equipment and public address system is supplied by CA, and the initiative is delivered by paid accredited coaches and coordinators. These personnel are trained by one of CA's 10 Junior Participant Specialists appointed to implement its junior player pathway, especially MILO T20 Blast.

Designed to remove barriers to participation, like cost, time, equipment, and coaching, the initiative has provided opportunities for children to play, their parents to volunteer, and them as families to become fans of the BBL and WBBL. In three seasons since its inception, over 22,000 children have registered in MILO T20 Blast playing in boys, girls, and mixed teams. The retention rate of participants is 70–80%, compared to as low as 20% prior to this initiative.

Questions

1. What is MILO T20 Blast? Where does it fit in CA's player development pathway?
2. How does it differ from other initiatives in its origins and marketing?
3. What barriers has MILO T20 Blast needed to overcome to ensure it is relevant, accessible, and appealing?
4. What impact has this had on recruitment and retention?

The game modification in cricket in NZ since the late 1990s was also evident in rugby (Small Blacks) and netball (Future Ferns), both initiating modified introductory programmes to attract and retain children (see Facts and figures 4.2). In the last decade, other sports have followed suit (e.g. hockey – 'Small Sticks', see Case study 4.3; tennis – 'Hot Shots', see Case study 8.4; football – First Kicks, see Chapter 9) (Astle 2011). A number of sports have also embraced modified versions at youth and adult levels, especially for social and recreational competitions formats (see Case study 4.2). In some cases, these formats have been adopted and marketed as either a showpiece for the elite (e.g. cricket – T20; rugby – Sevens; netball – Fast5), or refashioned into alternative versions, often delivered by private franchises (e.g. touch rugby, futsal – see Facts and figures 9.2) (Astle 2014).

FACTS and FIGURES 4.2

Modified sports programmes

In NZ, rugby and netball have devised entry-level, modified initiatives (e.g. 'Small Blacks' – rugby, 'Future Ferns' – netball) for children aged 5–12 years that take account of their age, ability, and size. To cater for their needs, they have reduced team numbers, playing areas, equipment size, and game time, and simplified rules for players and referees. Each initiative comprises a sequence of appropriate, age-based modules that allow children to progress and develop, have fun in a safe environment, and learn the fundamental and sport-specific skills and tactics of these sports in small-sided teams. The following websites detail these initiatives:

www.smallblacks.com/how-to-play/
www.mynetball.co.nz/futureferns/home.html

Questions

1. Select one of these websites and identify the modifications rugby or netball have made in their entry-level initiatives to meet children's needs.
2. Does a sport you are familiar with have a modified initiative for children? If so, name it and indicate how it has been modified for children?

CASE STUDY 4.2

Cricket Blitz: an alternative, modified social initiative for schools

Adrian Dale, former Cricket Development Manager, Auckland Cricket Association; and Mark Cameron, former CEO, Auckland Cricket Association, Auckland, New Zealand

In 2014, the Auckland Cricket Association (ACA), one of NZC's six MAs, faced with declining junior club and secondary school cricket numbers, and an over-focus on clubs as the prime providers of the game, undertook a SWOT analysis of the state of community cricket. This identified:

- Cricket competes with other sports for young people.
- Access and exposure to cricket for many young people is difficult.
- An early experience of the game is necessary for lifelong involvement.
- Cricket is mainly club-based, whereas most other sports are school-based.
- Young people like playing for their school with friends.
- Saturday club cricket is seen as too long, competitive, and dominated by better players.
- A number of modified formats of cricket already exist.
- More cricketers enjoy playing modified formats midweek.
- ACA has the opportunity to develop a modified version of cricket to reach a wider audience of young people.

Through the analysis, it became obvious schools were an untapped market for cricket, especially non-traditional cricket schools with high Asian and/or Polynesian populations; and to grow participation the ACA needed to challenge current perceptions of cricket and adopt a more appealing, social, modified format to attract a wider cohort of young people.

To address this, the ACA designed Cricket Blitz, a new, fun, learn by playing, modified format that removed many barriers (e.g. cost, equipment, travel, technical proficiency) to more 9–17-year-olds playing cricket. It allowed students to play with their mates in school-based teams, instead of playing conventional cricket on Saturdays for clubs.

Cricket Blitz is an eight-a-side game with 16 overs per side. Its batting and bowling rules allow maximum involvement and equal opportunity, with everyone getting the chance to bat, bowl, and field. Games are played midweek after school, on artificial pitches, and last about 1 hour 45 minutes. The ACA organises umpires and provides all equipment. It's free for schools to enter and students to play.

Cricket Blitz competitions cater for: Years 5/6 Mixed, Years 7/8 Boys, Years 7/8 Girls, Years 9/10 Boys, Years 9/10 Girls, Years 11–13 Boys, and Years 11–13 Girls. Round-robin games are played in each grade over six weeks in locally based pools, before semi-finals and finals are played at a central cricket venue.

Before introducing Cricket Blitz, careful ACA research and analysis allowed them to develop the game. ACA cricket development staff then visited schools in Auckland to explain and 'sell' the benefits of Cricket Blitz and get 'buy-in'. Identifying key contacts in schools and regularly communicating with them was essential to building credibility. Registrations, draws, and information on Cricket Blitz are on the ACA website.

The goal in establishing Cricket Blitz was to have 160 teams entered in the various grades. In 2015, 128 teams entered, in 2016, 150 teams, and in 2017, 168 teams. The initiative has succeeded in increasing junior and youth participation, and raising cricket's profile, especially in non-traditional cricketing schools in South and West Auckland. It is hoped the 16 cricket clubs in Auckland will eventually take over and manage the initiative, creating links with schools, and providing opportunities for players excited by Cricket Blitz to continue playing post-school.

Source: Auckland Cricket Association (2015, 2017).

Questions

1. What is Cricket Blitz?
   - Why did the ACA design it and who is its target audience?
2. How did the ACA determine the need for this initiative?
3. Where and how did they market the initiative?
4. How important are schools versus clubs in providing community sport in your sport and/or country?
5. Why did the ACA decide to focus on schools and what type of schools?

REVIEW QUESTIONS

1. Define diversification and modification, and indicate how each process has increased the availability of sporting opportunities? In a sport of your choice, identify an example of each process.
2. What advantages has modification created for community sport? Why is modification necessary for sports to thrive? How has it been applied to children's sport and why?

PROGRAMME PLANNING AND INITIATIVE DESIGN

The current cohort of SDMs and SDOs can draw on a significant body of theoretical and practical knowledge, including the various participant-centric, stage-based models outlining the provision of playing opportunities and individual player development (Côté 1999; Balyi 2001, 2002); central government modified sport and more recent fundamental movement skills (FMS) programmes to improve children's 'physical literacy' (SPARC 2010); existing NSO 'development of sport' programmes; and increasing needs to cater for lifelong participation and the emergence of new markets.

These can inform and influence their thinking in determining the sequential pathways of opportunities within their programmes, and their understanding of the requirements of participants at the different stages of their playing cycle when designing new initiatives. They also provide a wide range of modification ideas and small-game activities, which can be easily adopted and adapted in designing these initiatives. Irrespective of the influence, the design of player development initiatives must be participant-centric, identify the target audience of participants, devise appealing initiatives which meet their needs, and ensure their delivery is consistent and effective.

The influence of stage-based participant models

Stage-based development models have ensured recent programmes are participant-centric, with pathways of opportunities structured around stages of development, and featuring progressions of initiatives whose content reflects the characteristics of participants at each stage and caters for their specific needs and motivations (see Case study 4.3). For example, the NZ 'coach development framework' details player characteristics (physical, social, emotional, and cognitive) and needs for a range of coaching communities from early childhood to adults, to guide NSOs and coaches in designing their coach development programmes (SPARC 2006). The practical implications of this have significantly impacted the approach of coaches to their coaching, in terms of not only 'what' they coach, but also 'who' they are coaching, and 'how' they should tailor their coaching to the age/stage and needs of their players (Astle 2006).

Some coaches have adopted a 'teaching games for understanding' (TGfU) or 'game sense' approach to 'how' they have sought to improve the competencies of their players (Bunker and Thorpe 1982). This approach is based on teaching players the skills and tactics of their sport by playing modified games that pose tactical and strategic problems for players to solve. "The coach acts as a facilitator, setting up a game and where appropriate asking open-ended questions of the players to encourage them to consider and evaluate their tactical decisions" (Ferguson and McMillan 2009: 2). TGfU places the focus on players learning game awareness and tactical appreciation in a game situation, allowing them to figure things out for themselves, through their own decision-making and problem-solving.

The influence of increasing physical literacy and fundamental movement skills

In addition to seeking to increase participation in community sport, central governments in countries such as Australia, Canada, NZ, and the UK have also sought to improve children's FMS, because of an ongoing concern about a decline in their 'physical literacy' (Active Healthy Kids Australia 2016; SPARC 2007, 2010; Sport NZ 2012) (see Facts and figures 4.3). While many factors shape young people's engagement in sport, Côté (1999) and Balyi (2001, 2002) both placed a strong emphasis on children developing physical literacy through mastering FMS. Most of these skills are developed through informal play, physical activities in schools, and modified sports programmes in schools and clubs. The potential benefits of the acquisition and mastery of FMS which contribute to physical literacy include: an active lifestyle, lifelong interest and participation in sport, excellence in elite sport, and improved health and well-being.

FACTS and FIGURES 4.3

Physical literacy and fundamental movement skills

For further information on physical literacy and FMS, and the initiatives different countries have introduced to deliver these, refer to their national sport agency websites (e.g. Sport England, www.sportengland.org; Sport NZ, www.sportnz.org.nz). For a literature review of this subject, see Richards (2017) on the Australian Sports Commission's website: www.clearinghouseforsport.gov.au.

To support this trend, central government sport agencies have implemented policies, provided investment, and designed FMS resources to increase physical literacy, especially in primary school children. They have encouraged NSOs to mix FMS with sport-specific skills in their entry-level modified player development initiatives (SPARC 2007). In the UK, the Youth Sports Trust has created a framework to guide those delivering physical education and sport in primary schools to provide appropriate learning opportunities for children to develop their physical literacy (Youth Sports Trust 2013). In NZ, a government funding initiative, administered by SPARC (now Sport NZ), known as KiwiSport (different from the earlier KiwiSport modified sport programme), has invested in NSOs and RSTs to develop organised sport to achieve 'more kids, more opportunities and better skills' among school-aged children in clubs and schools (Astle 2011; SPARC 2010).

Increasingly, these modified, introductory initiatives have created new, appealing opportunities for NSOs to recruit children (and their parents) into their sports (see Case study 4.3). They have also attracted sponsors keen to access this market segment, who gain exposure by branding these initiatives with their name and logo (e.g. ANZ 'futureFERNS' netball, 'New Zealand Post Small Sticks' hockey). In designing such initiatives, the advantage for a sport (and a sponsor) is that they are part of a pathway of opportunities for children (e.g. NZC's MILO initiatives catered for children from 5 to 12 years); they are not a stand-alone proposition (see Case study 4.4). Many of these initiatives now have an online presence through websites and social media specifically designed to foster children's interest, promote their sport's menu of opportunities and experiences, and acknowledge sponsors' support (see Facts and figures 4.2).

CASE STUDY 4.3
Hockey New Zealand's Small Sticks programme

Jack Clayton, Community Hockey Manager – Young People, Hockey New Zealand

In 2010, Hockey New Zealand (HNZ), with SPARC assistance, devised a whole-of-hockey plan (HNZ 2010). This identified six national projects to develop hockey in NZ. The first three formed its subsequent community sport plan (Francis 2011), namely: grow and sustain participation; strengthen its delivery structure, especially volunteer coaches and umpires; and improve regional capability to deliver. The Community Sport Plan based on a whole-of-sport framework featured a central integrated player development pathway, serviced by similar and aligned pathways for coaches, umpires and officials (see Figure 3.2).

The player pathway's first four steps comprised the 'Small Sticks' programme of children's initiatives: Fun Sticks (4–6 years), Mini Sticks (7–8 years), Kiwi Sticks (9–10 years) and Kwik Sticks (11–12 years). These provide a sequence of modified game formats for children, with reduced team numbers, smaller playing surfaces and customised equipment, appropriate to their age and ability. The programme's objective is to grow and sustain participation in community hockey by attracting children and fostering their lifelong love of hockey through a small-sided, games-based approach built on skill development.

In 2011, Small Sticks was piloted in 11 of HNZ 32 Associations, and then launched nationwide in 2012. It's both a school-based marketing and recruitment initiative and a club-based playing and coaching programme. Small Sticks 'taster' sessions are delivered in primary schools by trained regional development managers and part-time hockey development coaches to build relationships with schools, create an interest in hockey, and actively recruit children into the Small Sticks programme run in local junior hockey clubs. The Small Sticks in-school initiative provided playing equipment to schools, in-service training and a teaching resource for teachers, four 30-minute coaching sessions per class for children, and a festival day at the end of the sessions at a local hockey club. The class sessions are repeated in years two and three using new drills and games that match children's age and stage of hockey development.

Although the Small Sticks programme with its nationally branded, standardised, and modified game formats, was initially resisted by some associations keen to maintain existing junior hockey formats, it has been quickly adopted because of its consistent game formats, session plans, equipment and promotional material, and coach and umpire development resources, which make it easy to promote to clubs and schools.

By 2015, three seasons after Small Sticks was introduced, its taster sessions had been delivered to 70,000 children in primary schools. This has seen the number of boys and girls registering as regular participants in junior hockey clubs rise to 25,823, an increase of 21.6% over this period. Small Sticks success has also attracted commercial sponsorship from New Zealand Post, backing from Sport NZ, and support from RSTs with KiwiSport funding.

Questions

1. What was the purpose and structure of HNZ's community sport plan?
2. Where does Small Sticks fit in the plan? What are its main features and objectives?
3. How is Small Sticks both a school-based and club-based programme?
4. Why has Small Sticks been successful?

The move to a participant-centric approach covering the lifespan

NSOs' shift to a more participant-centric emphasis has increasingly embraced diversity and inclusion. This has seen the provision of multiple pathways of initiatives, and the realisation that future growth in their sport lies not just with children, but also catering for specific groups, such as mature-aged adults (see Facts and figures 4.4), disabled people (see Case study 10.1), and new immigrant ethnic groups with a passion for their sport (e.g. Indian cricketers who now comprise 40% of cricketers in Auckland, NZ, and 35% of amateur cricketers in the UK) (Walker 2017) (see Case studies 4.2 and 4.4).

The current ageing population in developed countries, has seen a significant increase globally of older age adults, swelled by the wave of ageing 'baby boomers' (born between 1945 and 1964). It is predicted by 2030 that one billion, or one in every eight of the world's population, will be 65 years and older. To capture this sizeable ageing market NSOs are introducing different social and competitive sport initiatives in their community sport pathways for mature-aged adults of varying ages, abilities, and interests (see Facts and figures 4.4).

FACTS and FIGURES 4.4

Masters sport

In addition to NSOs, there are separate organisations that govern and administer Masters sports events. For example, the World Masters Games, the largest global multi-sport event, is overseen by the International Masters Games Association.

The World Masters Games follows the Olympic model, with summer and winter versions held every four years in a different city of the world. These games are open to masters athletes of all abilities and ages, with the qualifying age being over 35 years in most sports. Rather than competing for their country, participants compete for themselves and their own motivations.

The first World Masters Games, held in Toronto, Canada in 1985, involved 8,305 participants, representing 61 countries, participating in 22 sports. Since then the popularity of the event and participation have increased considerably. The ninth World Masters Games was held in Auckland, NZ in 2017. Over 25,000 participants and 3,500 coaches and managers from 100 countries competed in 45 disciplines, more than double the 11,327 athletes in the 2016 Olympic Games in Rio de Janeiro, Brazil.

Furthermore, the sport-related cost of staging the World Masters Games in Auckland was $US24m or $US960 per participant, compared to $US16.2b or $US1.43m per athlete to host the Olympic Games in Rio de Janeiro.

At a national level, countries such as NZ and Australia also have their own Masters Games, for both multi-sports and single sports. The New Zealand Masters Games, which is an annual multi-sport event, began in 1989. It had 1,500 entrants involved in 29 sports, today over 8,000 participants compete in 67 sports.

Questions

1. List four differences between the World Masters Games and the Olympic Games.
2. Does a sport you are familiar with cater for masters players? If so, what game modifications are made to accommodate their participation?

These 'sport for life' initiatives allow older adults, known variously as 'seniors', 'veterans', or 'masters', to continue to play or re-enter sport for a range of competitive, fitness, personal achievement, health, well-being, friendship, and enjoyment reasons (Medic 2010). Such initiatives are usually flexible, with each sport determining its own age criteria for entry (i.e. over 30, 35, or 40 years depending on the sport and competition), and incorporating appropriate modifications, like smaller field sizes, reduced match or competition durations or distances, limited physical contact, and different size and weight equipment (Richards 2016).

REVIEW QUESTIONS

1. What influences are evident in the thinking of practitioners designing sport development programmes?
2. What evidence is there of these influences in the design of current entry-level initiatives for children?
3. Take one influence (e.g. a model, theory or policy), and indicate how it has impacted an initiative in a sport of your choice.
4. What is physical literacy?
    -   What are FMS? What role do they play in physical literacy?
    -   Why is it important to develop physical literacy early in children?
5. Why are so many people engaging in masters sport? What implications does this have for sport delivery?

NEW ZEALAND CRICKET'S NATIONAL DEVELOPMENT PROGRAMME

NZC's NDP was launched in 2000. It heralded NZC's first intervention into community cricket and aimed at changing the development and delivery of cricket in clubs and schools, to counter declining participation in the game, and ensure the sport's future growth and sustainability (Astle 2014). Cricket in other countries is at different stages in their planning and implementation of national programmes to achieve these objectives (see Case study 4.4). NZC's programme was underpinned by two aligned pathways (see Figures 4.1 and 4.2), and overlain by two sets of integrating initiatives, each with its own development strategies, that straddle the three levels (children/junior, youth/secondary, adult/club) of the community game. These initiatives were implemented to revitalise and grow community cricket.

CASE STUDY 4.4

Cricket Scotland's participation programme

Ian Sandbrook, Head of Participation, Cricket Scotland, Edinburgh, Scotland

Cricket Scotland's (CS) participation strategy has only been formalised in our recent Strategic Plans (2012–2015 and 2016–2019). This is reflected in CS's vision of 'Inspiring Scotland to Choose Cricket', strapline of 'More Opportunities, Great Experiences', and strategic outcome of a 20% increase in committed participants (those playing in regular competitions, irrespective of format) by the end of 2019.

CS's participation programme is strongly influenced by three key partners. The International Cricket Council and Sport Scotland who are our largest funders, and England and Wales Cricket Board (ECB) who have influenced our programme design, as we use several of their programmes (e.g. coach education pathway, All Stars Cricket) and their research to shape what we do.

Currently, there is no clearly defined national player development pathway underpinning cricket in Scotland. There is an historic pathway – kwik cricket, club age-group leagues, and national junior and senior cup competitions – that cater for existing participants. These are 'business as usual' initiatives, that in many cases are static in numbers. reflecting a contraction in the 'traditional' game in the UK. To counter this, CS has in the last decade embedded national initiatives into this pathway. These include, as part of our school engagement strategy, six national primary and secondary schools, boys and girls, modified competitions, which have stimulated the creation of school teams and entries in these competitions, increased recognition of cricket as a sporting option, and contributed to growing participation. Our task now is to transition these school players into local clubs.

In 2017, the introduction of the ECB's entry-level initiative, All Stars Cricket (5–8 years), provided our first formal step in redesigning the player development pathway from the bottom up, as we seek to have nationally led initiatives at each pathway stage. These will primarily focus on modified versions of the game and skill development and be delivered by clubs providing dual traditional and modified pathway opportunities catering for how people want to play and engage with cricket. In year one, All Stars Cricket registered 1,000 children in 40 centres throughout Scotland. This has transformed many clubs, as none previously offered cricket for 5–8-year-olds, so these are all new children to the game.

CS has a development network of 14, including three regional participation managers, and eight local authority, partner CDOs, who work with regional associations and clubs to deliver our initiatives, and support local opportunities for growth. However, they face a range of challenges:

- **Perception and awareness of cricket in Scotland**, where it is a minority sport and seen as English, exclusive and time-consuming by many, despite having a strong tradition and comparatively large playing numbers (70,000). Cricket has a low profile and receives little media coverage. To address this, CS has been proactive in embedding cricket in primary schools and introducing All Stars Cricket.
- **A very traditional mindset within our clubs.** However, for them to continue to exist they must change to remain relevant. CS has introduced Thriving Clubs, a club development initiative focused on clubs becoming 'more than cricket' with respect to community engagement, income generation, and membership growth; partnered with the commercial provider of a popular new format of cricket (i.e. Last Man Stands); and invested more into identified growth areas (e.g. female cricket, black and minority ethnic cricket focusing on the Asian community in Greater Glasgow).
- **Disjointed organisational structure,** with limited integration between CS and its volunteer-led, regional associations, and clubs. This has hindered our 'top-down'

intervention to improve the community game. Recent improvements in CS's governance and leadership has provided a catalyst to professionalise our regional structures, with memorandums of understanding drafted, to foster greater collaboration and development of the sport.

- **Lack of funding** to achieve this has necessitated prioritising commercial strategies to grow our revenue.
- **Lack of facilities,** especially suitable indoor complexes and artificial pitches in a country with inclement weather and short summers. A facilities audit is being undertaken to ascertain what exists, where and its standard, and a strategy launched to increase artificial facilities in clubs and schools, and develop indoor complexes at regional hubs.

Our programme has positively impacted cricket in Scotland, contributing to a greater awareness of cricket, and a 150% growth in participation in the last five years to over 70,000 in 2016. Although traditional club numbers have dropped slightly, growth has come from modified formats, which is indicative of the game's future. More importantly, we have broadened the approach and mindset of our clubs to developing and delivering the game to ensure it remains relevant.

Questions

1. What is CS's participation strategy? How is participation defined? How does this differ from participation statistics used in tennis (see Pause and ponder 8.1)?
2. When did CS introduce a national player development pathway? What was its first initiative, target audience and impact?
3. Apart from weather, what do you think is CS's main challenge? How have they tried to counter this?
   - Is this challenge apparent in a sport you are familiar with? If so, how has it been addressed?

The two sets of initiatives were the MILO initiatives and Community Cricket initiatives (Astle 2009). The MILO initiatives were aimed at primary school and junior club cricket to rekindle interest in the game and increase player and coach numbers. They were designed to create a range of appealing opportunities and experiences that attracted children (5–12 years) into cricket to have fun and learn its fundamental skills, and encourage their parents' and teachers' involvement as coaches (see Case study 6.1). Nestlé NZ, through its MILO brand, underwrote the MILO initiatives (see Case study 2.4).

The Community Cricket initiatives were introduced to strengthen and integrate the game in secondary schools and clubs. Their purpose was to improve the health and well-being of secondary schools (School Support) and clubs (Club Assist) by systematically addressing issues that impact their capability, organisation, infrastructure, and services, and consequently their ability to provide a supportive environment to meet the needs of players and volunteers.

The focus here is on the MILO initiatives whose key objectives were:

1. To encourage more children to participate in cricket for their school or local club.
2. To ensure they have a positive experience within a stimulating environment, where the emphasis is on fun, skill development, and enhancement of their competence and confidence so they can enjoy the game.
3. To involve more parents and teachers in the game and encourage them to train as coaches appropriate to the level of their children, and support them with sufficient quality coaching resources (Astle 2009).

The main development strategies at this level concentrated on recognition, recruitment, and retention. Retention underlying the other two strategies to ensure their long-term participation and involvement in cricket, by improving the skills of children to play and enjoy the game (Toms and Fleming 2003), and training parents and teachers as coaches to organise and run their programmes (Hopkinson 2014).

THE DESIGN OF A SPECIFIC INITIATIVE: MILO HAVE-A-GO CRICKET

Entry-level MILO Have-A-Go Cricket was launched in 2000 as the cornerstone of NZC's development programme. It provided the foundation on which other initiatives were built and helped ignite a resurgence in the sport (McConnell 2003). MILO Have-A-Go Cricket was a player and coach development initiative, with a standardised system of delivery, each step prescribed by procedures and supported with resources. It provided a high-quality introductory experience for children that set the context for a lifetime of involvement in the game. Similar objectives are increasingly evident in other sports' entry-level initiatives, especially the understanding of playing sport for life (see Case studies 4.1, 4.3, and 8.4).

Support resources

The MILO Have-A-Go Cricket coaching manual provided both organisational guidelines for this first step on NZC's player development pathway, and instructional content for beginner coaches taking their first step on its coach development pathway. It outlined only those fundamental cricket skills appropriate to the initiative and provided a set of structured session coaching plans, each with a sequence of activities and drills for coaches to use to progressively develop these skills in their players. There were 12 session coaching plans, each scheduled for 90 minutes, although this was flexible, subdivided into seven different sections. Each session detailed the skills to be taught, drills and small-sided games to be played to develop these skills, equipment required and appropriate time to be spent on each activity (see Figure 4.3) (Astle 2000a). As Nolen (2001: 6) noted:

> the coaching manuals contain all the skills parents need to know and all the drills and games that would be coached each session. The benefits of these manuals were that the parents need not have a knowledge of cricket, as everything is explained in simple terms.

An operational handbook was produced for the MILO Summer Squad (MSS), the network of part-time seasonal CDOs employed to implement the MILO initiatives (Astle 2000b). It outlined the different initiatives and provided step-by-step instructions on their implementation. This included procedures for: school visits; delivery of MILO Cricket Skills Awareness Lessons to Years 1–6 boys and girls in primary schools and their associated active recruitment measures; setting up and running MILO Have-A-Go Cricket Centres; and training parents and teachers as coaches. The handbook also highlighted the MSS's role in profiling the game; NZC's expectations of their personal and professional appearance and performance; their need to be fully conversant with each initiative, its objectives and benefits, and how they were most effectively delivered; and the processes of evaluation and regular reporting.

Any sport looking to develop and grow its community base must have a presence in the captive market of primary schools. Visits to primary schools must be carefully planned and sessions structured with a specific purpose to have a positive cost–benefit for the sport. While one-off visits by high-profile players to primary schools create excitement and may generate publicity, evidence shows they have negligible value for recruitment as they are quickly forgotten.

From cricket's perspective, the prime purpose of primary school visits was to raise awareness, market the game, and actively recruit participants and teachers as coaches. To ensure their effectiveness these were well organised. Introductory letters and booking forms were created for MSS to arrange their visits and run the MILO Cricket Skills Awareness Lessons. For the latter, the MSS were provided with structured lesson plans that offered a fun 'taste of cricket' to ensure consistency in their delivery and intended recruitment message; recruitment packs for students with registration information about MILO Have-A-Go Cricket Centres in their community; coaching manuals for teachers (Astle 2000a); and an evaluation form to elicit feedback from schools on the value of the visits. Similar systematic procedures with support resources were also devised for the MSS to establish the MILO Have-A-Go Cricket Centres (see Figure 4.4), including information booklets, administration handbooks, and registration receipt books (Astle 2000c, 2000d).

Sets of promotional giveaways were designed for MILO Have-A-Go Cricket participants. For each session specific giveaways were distributed to each child (e.g. cap, ball, player cards, and posters). These were created to heighten children's interest and ongoing involvement, profile the game and NZC's national Black Cap and White Fern players, and promote the MILO brand.

NZC in combination with MILO designed distinctive, branded sportswear for the MSS to wear when delivering the MILO initiatives. The clothing colours and logos reflected the partnership between NZC and MILO, and clearly identified the MSS as part of NZC's delivery network. NZC also purchased MILO-branded plastic cricket equipment, and donated starter kits of this to each MILO Have-A-Go Cricket Centre to kick-start its programme. The kit size depended upon the number of children registered.

Piloting

Before investing time and resources in implementing a development initiative nationwide, it is strongly recommended a pilot study is first undertaken with a sample of clubs and/or schools. A key to MILO Have-A-Go Cricket's success was its preliminary pilot to assess its ease of use, accuracy of content, and effectiveness. This process allowed amendments to be made and revealed how to best market and implement it to a wider audience.

○ Session I

1. Introduction and Warm up — 10 minutes

EQUIPMENT: 4 cones to mark out given area, bucket full of balls
ACTIVITY: KEEP THE BUCKET FULL

- Players surround the coach who stands with a bucket full of balls in the centre of a given area marked out by the four cones
- As quickly as possible the coach tries to empty the bucket one ball at a time by rolling or throwing the balls in all directions
- The players retrieve the balls, one at a time, and return them to the bucket with the aim of never letting the bucket become empty

2. Ball handling — 10 minutes

EQUIPMENT: 1 ball per player
SKILLS:

- **Hand to hand throw:** Player to hold the ball in one hand at about head height and throw it to the other hand at waist height. Change hand positions and repeat gradually getting faster
- **Drop, bounce and catch:** Player to drop and bounce the ball and catch it with two hands underneath by 'making the hands into a cup'
- **Belly button catch:** Player to drop the ball at chin level and allow it to roll down the chest before catching it near the belly button (navel)

3. Batting — 10 minutes

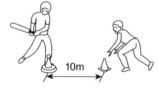

10m

EQUIPMENT: 1 bat, 1 batting tee, 1 cone, 1 ball per pair
SKILL:

- Briefly explain to all the players how to stand [STANCE], to hold [GRIP] and swing [BACKSWING] the bat, and drive the ball [FRONT FOOT DRIVE] [see section on 'The Basics - Batting']
- Divide the players into pairs - one player [batter] takes up his/her stance with the bat behind the batting tee facing his/her partner who stands beside the cone about 10 metres away
- The batter steps forward and drives/hits the ball off the batting tee to his/her partner who stops it and returns it to the batter to place on the batting tee
- Each player has 6 drives/hits then changes over

4. Fielding — 10 minutes

EQUIPMENT: 1 ball per pair

SKILL:

- Briefly explain to all players how to throw [UNDERARM THROWING] and to catch [CATCHING] a ball [see section on 'The Basics - Fielding']
- Divide the players into pairs
- In pairs players to roll a ball to each other. Encourage each player to step towards their partner with the opposite foot to the preferred hand when they roll the ball
- Extend the skill to each player throwing/lobbing a ball underarm to their partner - one bounce, one catch

5. Bowling — 10 minutes

EQUIPMENT: 2 cones, 1 ball per pair
SKILL:

- Briefly explain to all players how to hold [GRIP] and bowl [ACTION] a ball overarm [see section on 'The Basics - Bowling']
- Divide the players into pairs and get them to stand in two lines beside the cones which are set 10 metres apart
- Each player in line A turns side-on facing his/her partner with feet comfortably apart, looking over the front shoulder, front arm up high, bowling hand gripping the ball correctly down beside the back leg
- Each player then bowls to his/her partner in line B by pulling the front arm down into the front hip, and swinging the bowling arm over straight, letting the ball go above the ear, before bringing it down across the body
- The players in line B stop the ball, then adopt the above side-on position and bowl the ball back to the players in line A

6. Cricket game — 30 minutes

EQUIPMENT: 1 bat, 1 set of stumps, 3 cones, 1 batting tee, 1 ball
GAME: TEE BALL DRIVE CRICKET

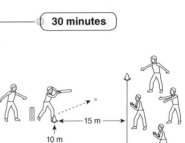

- Briefly explain to all the players how to stand [STANCE], to hold [GRIP] and swing [BACKSWING] the bat, and to drive [FRONT FOOT DRIVE] a stationary ball off a batting tee
- Divide the players into two even groups and decide which group is batting and which is fielding
- Set up the batting tee with the stumps 1.5 metres behind and a cone at right angles 10 metres away. Place the other two cones 10 metres apart 15 metres in front of the stumps
- One player from the fielding group acts as the wicketkeeper [Ⓦ], the rest spread out behind the two cones in front of the stumps
- Each batter [Ⓑ] drives/hits the stationary ball off the batting tee and scores as follows:

  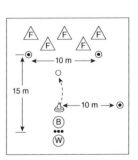

  - 1 run for hitting the ball between the cones
  - 1 run for running with the bat around the cone at right angles to the stumps and back passed the batting tee (crease)

- The batter is out if the fielders [⚐] catch the hit ball, or stop the ball and return it to the wicketkeeper before the batter passes the batting tee
- The wicketkeeper places the ball on the batting tee for each batter
- Each batter has 3 drives/hits. Once all the first group have batted, the groups change over
- The group with the most runs in the allotted time wins

7. Warm down and conclusion — 10 minutes

ACTIVITIES:

- Upon the word 'Go' players jog together and touch three targets identified by the coach [e.g. cone stumps, tree], then return back to a given area
- Rotate each arm in circles - 5 forward and 5 back; then rotate both arms together in circles - 5 forward and 5 back
- Loosely shake arms/hands and legs
- Breathe deeply and relax

FIGURE 4.3 MILO Have-A-Go Cricket session 1

Source: Astle (2000a: 24–25).

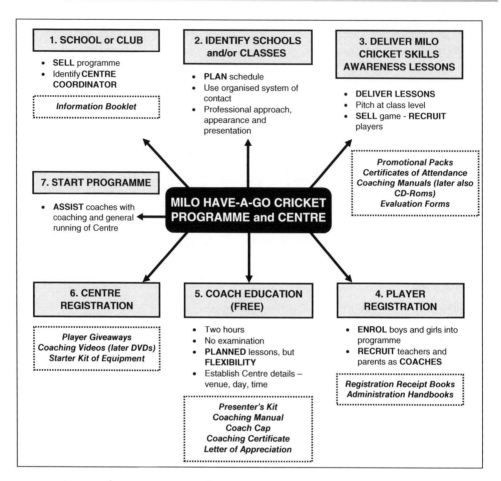

FIGURE 4.4 Steps and support resources for establishing a MILO Have-A-Go Cricket Centre
Source: Astle (2003: 10).

MILO Have-A-Go Cricket was piloted in 2000 in eight centres, a mix of junior clubs and primary schools. Their success, in terms of the effectiveness of MILO Have-A-Go Cricket to attract new recruits to cricket and involve parents as coaches, highlighted the initiative's potential. The pilot also attracted Sky Television's attention, who produced a short documentary of the initiative and showed it nationwide. This was an added bonus for promoting the value and benefits of MILO Have-A-Go Cricket and NZC's fledgling NDP.

Subsequently, a MILO Have-A-Go Cricket coach education course was trialled. This demonstrated that even pitching the course at an introductory level to parents was still a challenging experience for many. While some had 'coached' teams previously, many had essentially been 'minders' rather than coaches required to give specific cricket instruction. The course provided them with the basic guidelines and rudimentary cricket skills needed to run MILO Have-A-Go Cricket and assist coach their children.

Along with the pilot, training sessions were run pre-season (August/September) in 2000 and 2001, in each MA for its MSS, to explain the NDP's objectives and strategies, and the key features of MILO Have-A-Go Cricket and how to most effectively market and deliver it. The training included primary schools visits, where a MILO Cricket skills awareness lesson was demonstrated with classes to the MSS, before they conducted and evaluated the same lesson with different classes.

Delivery

After the MSS school visits, when children registered in MILO Have-A-Go Cricket within their primary school or local cricket clubs, their parents and teachers were encouraged to become involved as 'coaches'. This was crucial to support the growth in player numbers and enhance their skills, so they could compete and enjoy the game and increase the likelihood of their ongoing involvement (Toms and Fleming 2003).

Active recruitment measures were required to increase the number of coaches. Historically, community cricket did not have a 'culture of trained coaches'. Like many sports, there were some parents and teachers with a cricket background who were 'coaches', a few were trained, the rest were enthusiastic 'minders'. This meant many young cricketers did not have qualified coaches, so few received skill development opportunities. Players tended to learn by trial and error and/or copying role models, such as older siblings, peers, or players seen on television (Toms and Fleming 2003).

This constraint of insufficient coaches and lack of coaching, prompted NZC to:

1. Encourage more parents and teachers to become involved, and train them as beginner coaches so they could assist with coaching their children. This required removing the barriers to undertaking a coaching course, such as; cost, time and assessment.
2. Simplify the coaching of the game by reducing its technical aspects to a minimum, so only skills fundamental to the level they were going to coach, were included.
3. Adopt 'group coaching' in which several coaches were involved in coaching a group of children, rather than the previous one 'coach' per team.

These became key objectives of the MILO Have-A-Go Cricket coaching course. The two-hour courses were free and non-examinable. They provided parents and teachers with the necessary knowledge and resources to coach their children and organise and run the programme. The quality of their first experiences as coaches, and those of their children as participants in the programme, were crucial to the long-term involvement of both in the game (Hopkinson 2014). Each 'trained' coach received a coaching manual, cap, and accreditation certificate. Their MILO Cricket Centres were provided with copies of a MILO Have-A-Go Cricket video (later DVD), which illustrated the skills to be developed and how the programme operated (Astle 2000e), an administration manual (Astle 2000d), and a starter kit of cricket equipment.

To increase parent and teacher involvement as coaches, 'group coaching' was introduced. This was where a group of three to four trained coaches work collaboratively as a unit with 15–20 children, making for a more effectively organised and better run session, than one conducted by an inexperienced coach on their own. It ensured a ratio of one coach to every five or six children to provide simple instructions, demonstrations, and guidance, and maximise children's opportunities to have fun and learn fundamental cricket skills in small groups. Small groups mean children have more opportunities, involvement, decision-making, and a greater likelihood to acquire the skills to stay in the game (Hopkinson 2014). Group coaching is now evident in all elite professional teams, however, it's not common in sports at a junior level. In winter sports (e.g. rugby, football), many junior teams have a coach (not always trained) and a manager to assist with supervision, but not always with coaching.

Once an initiative's purpose and objectives are decided, a SDM can then determine its content. This could be a SDM's responsibility, if they possess the expertise and skills, or it may be contracted to an internal or external individual or working group to research and complete under the SDM's instruction and supervision. Once an initiative is created, it should be piloted to assess its content and effectiveness in achieving its objectives. Failure to do this can be costly. An untested, ill-conceived initiative can not only waste limited community sport funding, but also damage SDOs' credibility and their relationship with volunteers who they have convinced to deliver it in their clubs or schools. Feedback from the pilot can be used to create training guides for SDOs and procedures for their effective implementation. For an initiative to be successful it needs to be part of an integrated programme, easy to access and introduce, and add value to community sport.

REVIEW QUESTIONS

1. What were the objectives, strategies, outcomes, and target audience of NZC's MILO Have-A-Go Cricket initiative?
2. How can a practitioner ensure the effectiveness of a sport development initiative prior to delivery?
3. In your experience, why are some sport development initiatives effective, and others are not?

CONCLUSION

Planning a sport development programme and designing new initiatives to integrate into its underlying pathways takes a sport development plan's blueprint and translates it into a practical format ready for application in community sport. This chapter highlighted the importance of preparation, with practitioners refreshing and informing their strategic thinking from the databank of research and consultation used to formulate their plan. This allowed the purpose of the programme to be defined, its framework of pathways to be identified, the scope of its community sport operation to be delineated, and its initial focus to be determined, prior to the design of new initiatives to achieve its desired outcomes.

Over time, diversification has expanded the number of providers and types of participatory opportunities in traditional organised sports. Facing change in recent years, NSOs often with central government assistance, have also increasingly embraced modification to customise these opportunities, by designing more adaptable and flexible formats of their sport, to increase their relevance and appeal to a broader spectrum of participants of varying ages, abilities, and interests. Modification is particularly evident in entry-level, age- and stage-appropriate development initiatives created for children to suit their size, ability, skill level, and experience, and improve their competence, confidence, and enjoyment of sport.

Current practitioners have access to a wider collection of literature, models, and resources than their predecessors, which provides them with a broad set of principles and practical examples to draw on in creating programmes, pathways, and initiatives within their sports. These influences are evident in current player development initiatives, which have become more participant-centric, appropriate to the specific needs of participants in different phases of their playing cycle, and cater for both lifelong involvement and talent development. To be successful, these initiatives must be integrated within the pathways of sport development programmes if sports are to expand their horizons and offer more diverse and modified options to satisfy current participants and target new markets, such as mature-aged adults, disabled athletes, and particular ethnic groups.

A specific initiative, NZC's entry-level MILO Have-A-Go Cricket initiative, is explored in terms of its content, support resources, procedural systems, piloting, and structured delivery through trained group coaches. Practitioners need to systematically consider these requirements in designing and implementing their own programme initiatives, if they are to be accepted by volunteers in clubs and schools, and effective in achieving their expected outcomes (see Pause and ponder 4.2).

PAUSE and PONDER 4.2

Do's and don'ts of designing and implementing a community sport development programme

Do's

1. **Do** establish a framework of integrated and aligned pathways across all levels of community sport within which to embed initiatives.
2. **Do** be prepared to modify your sport and create a sequence of initiatives that maximise the involvement and enjoyment of participants.
3. **Do** pilot initiatives as it is better to identify flaws and make amendments sooner rather than later.
4. **Do** involve parents wherever possible and provide opportunities for them to become volunteers, especially coaches.
5. **Do** aim for long-term incremental growth as most successful programmes take at least 10 years to realise their potential and accumulate data to showcase their impact.

Don'ts

1. **Don't** prioritise one-off visits to schools as these will soon be forgotten and the benefit for recruitment is minimal.
2. **Don't** just focus on appealing to one particular age-group, as the point of a sport development programme is to allow people to participate at whatever age or stage they want.
3. **Don't** introduce short-term or stand-alone initiatives, or chop and change initiatives without careful thought and notice.

4. **Don't** alienate commercial, government, and education partners as their support is essential to a sport development programme's success.
5. **Don't** allow funding allocated to community sport to be diverted into high-performance programmes which benefit only a few.

REFERENCES

Active Healthy Kids Australia. (2016). *Physical literacy: Do our kids have all the tools? The 2016 report card on physical activity for children and young people.* Adelaide, South Australia: Active Healthy Kids Australia.

Astle, A. M. (2000a). *MILO Have-A-Go Cricket coaching manual for children 6–8 years.* Christchurch: New Zealand Cricket.

Astle, A. M. (2000b). *MILO initiatives: Guidelines for MILO Summer Squad cricket development officers.* Instruction manual. New Zealand Cricket, Christchurch.

Astle, A. M. (2000c). *MILO Have-A-Go Cricket information booklet.* New Zealand Cricket, Christchurch.

Astle, A. M. (2000d). *MILO Have-A-Go Cricket administration handbook.* New Zealand Cricket, Christchurch.

Astle, A. M. (2000e). *MILO Have-A-Go Cricket coaching video for children 6–8 years* [Video]. Auckland: ibrow productions.

Astle, A. M. (2003). *MILO Summer Squad cricket development personnel.* Powerpoint presentation. New Zealand Cricket, Christchurch.

Astle, A. M. (2006). *National coach education plan and programme.* Planning document. New Zealand Cricket, Christchurch.

Astle, A. M. (2009). *New Zealand Cricket: national development plan and programme.* Planning document. New Zealand Cricket, Christchurch.

Astle, A. (2011). *Community sport implementation plan: Collaborative delivery and outcomes.* Planning document. Sport and Recreation New Zealand, Wellington.

Astle, A. M. (2014). *Sport development – Plan, programme and practice: A case study of the planned intervention by New Zealand Cricket into cricket in New Zealand.* PhD, Massey University, Palmerston North, New Zealand.

Auckland Cricket Association. (2015). *Cricket Blitz.* Planning document. Auckland: Auckland Cricket Association.

Auckland Cricket Association. (2017). *Innovation excellence award: Cricket Blitz.* Entry for New Zealand Sport and Recreation Awards. Auckland Cricket Association, Auckland.

Australian Sports Commission. (1986). *An introduction to Aussie sports.* Canberra: Australian Sports Commission.

Balyi, I. (2001). Sport system building and long-term athlete development in British Columbia. *Coaches Report, 8*(1), 22–28.

Balyi, I. (2002). Long-term athlete development: The system and solutions. *Faster, Higher, Stronger, 14,* 6–9.

Bowers, M. T., & Green, B. C. (2016). Theory of development of and through sport. In E. Sherry, N. Schulenkorf, & P. Phillips (Eds.), *Managing sport development: An international approach* (pp. 12–27). London and New York: Routledge.

Bunker, D., & Thorpe, R. (1982). A model for the teaching of games in secondary schools. *Bulletin of PE, 18*(1), 5–8.

Côté, J. (1999). The influence of the family in the development of talent in sport. *The Sport Psychologist, 13,* 395–417.

Cricket Australia. (2017). *Australian cricket junior formats.* Unpublished Powerpoint presentation to New Zealand Cricket. Cricket Australia, Melbourne.

Doherty, A., & Rich, K. (2015). Sport for community development. In M. T. Bowers & M. A. Dixon (Eds.), *Sport management: An exploration of the field and its value* (pp. 124–145). Urbana, IL: Sagamore Publishing.

Ferguson, C., & McMillan, K. (2009). *Teaching games for understanding.* Christchurch: New Zealand Cricket.

Francis, I. (2011). *2011 community sport plan.* Planning document. Hockey New Zealand, Auckland.

Goldsmith, W. (2009). *Coach education – Ten dumb things we do and call it coach education.* Retrieved from www.sportscoachingbrain.com website.

Hillary Commission. (1988). *KiwiSport: Play it cool. Activities manual.* Wellington: Hillary Commission for Recreation and Sport.

Hillary Commission. (1998). *KiwiSport: Sport the way kids want it.* Wellington: Hillary Commission for Sport, Fitness and Leisure.

Hockey New Zealand. (2010). *Whole of Hockey's business plan: To fuel the growth and sustainability of hockey throughout New Zealand.* Planning document. Hockey New Zealand, Auckland.

Hopkinson, M. (2014). *The impact of coaching on participants.* Leeds: Sports Coach UK.

Johnswood, B. (2006). Less is more for young cricketers: South Australia endeavours to break the mould. *Overview, 1*(4), 5.

Lee, M., & Smith, R. (1993). Making sport fit for children. In M. Lee (Ed.), *Coaching children in sport: Principles and practice* (pp. 259–272). London: E & FN Spon.

McConnell, L. (2003). *Quiet revolution underway in New Zealand cricket*, pp. 1–2. Retrieved from www.cricinfo.com/newzealand/content/story/124760.html website.

Medic, N. (2010). Understanding masters athletes' motivation for sport. In J. Baker, S. Horton, & P. Weir (Eds.), *The masters athlete: Understanding the role of sport and exercise in optimizing aging* (pp. 105–121). London and New York: Routledge.

National Research Bureau Ltd. (1996). *Survey of the KiwiSport programme.* Wellington: Hillary Commission.

Nolen, J. (2001). *Business report for Sport Waikato.* Law and Management. Partial fulfilment of course work for 1087.301 Practicum in the Leisure Industry, University of Waikato, Hamilton.

Partington, J., & Robson, S. (2013). A different ball game? In pursuit of greater strategic collaboration between sport-specific and community sport development. In S. Robson, K. Simpson, & L. Tucker (Eds.), *Strategic sport development* (pp. 217–240). London and New York: Routledge.

Phillips, P., & Warner, S. (2016). Community sport. In E. Sherry, N. Schulenkorf, & P. Phillips (Eds.), *Managing sport development: An international approach* (pp. 77–89). London and New York.

Richards, R. (2016). *Mature-aged sport and physical activity.* Retrieved from www.clearinghouseforsport.gov.au/knowledge_base/sport_participation/community_participation/mature-aged_sport_and_physical_activity website.

Richards, R. (2017). *Physical literacy and sport.* Retrieved from www.clearinghouseforsport.gov.au/knowledge_base/sport_participation/community_participation/physical_literacy_and_sport website.

Shilbury, D., & Kellett, P. (2011). *Sport management in Australia: An organisational overview* (4th ed.). Sydney: Allen and Unwin.

SPARC. (2006). *Coach development framework.* Wellington: Astra Print.

SPARC. (2007). *Developing fundamental movement skills.* Wellington: Sport and Recreation New Zealand.

SPARC. (2010). *Community sport strategy: 2010–2015.* Planning document. Sport and Recreation New Zealand, Wellington.

Sport England. (2007). *Impact in 3D: a learning guide for practitioners in community sport.* Retrieved from www.sportengland.org/research/evaluating_impact.aspx website.

Sport New Zealand. (2012). *Fundamental movement skills among children in New Zealand.* Wellington: Sport New Zealand.

Toms, M., & Fleming, S. (2003). *Why play cricket. . .? A preliminary analysis of participation by young males.* Retrieved from www.canadacricket.com/archives/2003/whyplay.htm website.

Walker, P. (2017). Cricket's battle for the working classes: Breaking the grass ceiling. In L. Booth (Ed.), *Wisden cricketers' almanack* (154th ed., pp. 55–61). London: John Wisden & Co.

Youth Sports Trust. (2013). *Primary school physical literacy framework: Supporting primary schools to develop the physical literacy of all their pupils.* Retrieved from www.youthsporttrust.org/sites/yst/files/resources/documents/physical_literacy_framework.pdf website.

Websites

www.bigbash.com.au

www.mynetball.co.nz/futureferns/home.html

www.nzmg.com/

www.smallblacks.com/how-to-play/

www.sportengland.org

www.sportnz.org.nz/

www.worldmastersgames2017.co.nz/

CHAPTER 5

Establishing a sport development delivery network

In recent years, NSOs have formulated sport development plans (see Chapter 3), and created programmes (see Chapter 4), with specifically designed initiatives to revitalise and grow their sports in clubs and schools. To implement these, NSOs must decide whether to rely on volunteers, engage SDOs, or use a combination. Such decisions are influenced by a NSOs capability, financial resources, participant numbers, and degree of integration with its constituent RSOs. NSOs of many small- and medium-sized sports, often of necessity, use their volunteers, while NSOs of larger sports have opted to establish regional SDO networks to implement their national programmes, with volunteers still delivering specific initiatives in clubs and schools. This chapter focuses on sport-specific SDOs engaged by NSOs.

Academic literature on SDOs is limited – especially for those engaged in sport-specific roles, because paid SDOs are only a recent phenomenon. The few studies that exist are mostly confined to examining the views and experiences of SDOs working for local authorities in the UK (Bloyce and Green 2011; Bloyce, Smith, Mead, and Morris 2008), or considering their demographics and access to education, training, and career advancement opportunities (Girginov 2008; Nesti 2001; Pitchford and Collins 2010). Watt (2003) briefly discusses the roles and skill requirements of SDOs, although a more in-depth coverage of these competencies is provided by Eady (1993). Apart from these studies, the subject of SDOs has been "largely neglected and under-explored" (Bloyce et al. 2008: 359).

This lack of research offers an opportunity to examine the role and responsibilities of sport-specific SDOs. NZC's community cricket coordinators (CCCs), instrumental in implementing their NDP, are used to explore "the reality of 'doing' sports development from the perspective of the SDOs themselves in order to enhance our understanding of sports development in practice" (Bloyce and Green 2011: 477).

This chapter will:

1. Identify two main types of SDOs, the sports organisations they work for, and their roles.
2. Indicate which sports initially engaged SDOs, and why; and the role of central governments in their employment, and reasons for this.
3. Explain the emergence and structure of NZC's delivery network to implement its development programme as a context for analysing its regional CCCs as an example of sport-specific SDOs.

4. Consider the planning and job analysis to scope the role of a CCC.
5. Explore the characteristics of the CCCs, the challenges they face, and how they and NSOs have tried to mitigate these.

SPORT DEVELOPMENT OFFICERS

Increasingly sports organisations are engaging SDOs with a specific remit to implement programmes designed to increase participation in their sports. The intent of their role, however, varies according to whether their prime responsibility is to grow participation to ensure their sport's future sustainability ('development of sport'), or to address a range of social welfare issues ('development through sport') (Astle 2014; Houlihan and White 2002). The answer reflects how the organisation engaging the SDOs interprets sport development (see Chapter 1).

Since 2000, two types of SDOs have emerged in NZ: generic SDOs and sport-specific SDOs. This is consistent with the UK experience, where SDO roles vary according to the needs, ideals, and aspirations of the sports organisation for whom they work (Eady 1993; Houlihan and White 2002). Generic SDOs are mainly employed by local authorities, and/or RSTs in NZ, and are involved in 'development of sport' activities across a range of sports in a geographic region and/or with a targeted population group (e.g. children, youth, women, disabled). Sport-specific SDOs are engaged by a NSO and/or its RSOs to promote and develop one particular sport (e.g. cricket). This chapter focuses on the latter.

REVIEW QUESTIONS

1. Why is there a lack of research on SDOs?
2. Why are sport organisations increasingly keen to engage SDOs?
3. What are the two main types of SDOs? Differentiate between them in terms of their focus and purpose.

NEW ZEALAND CRICKET: THE EMERGENCE OF A PROFESSIONAL DELIVERY STRUCTURE

In 1998, NZC appointed its inaugural national development manager (NDM) to formulate a national development plan and programme (see Case studies 5.1 and 5.2). The latter comprised initiatives which offered a range of opportunities to participate in the game, and made improvements to the capability of clubs and schools to provide and service these; and established a national to local delivery network of cricket development personnel and volunteers to implement these initiatives at a community level within clubs and schools (Astle 2009, 2014) (see Chapter 4). The object of NZC's intervention was to repackage the game in order to revitalise grassroots cricket, to counter a steady decline in participation during the mid-1990s, and ensure the sport's future sustainability.

CASE STUDY 5.1

International cricket development manager

Kieran McMillan, East Asia Pacific Development Manager, International Cricket Council, Melbourne, Australia

For six years, I have worked for the International Cricket Council (ICC) as their East Asia Pacific (EAP) Manager. There are five regional managers in Europe, the Americas, Africa, Asia, and East Asia Pacific responsible for implementing its global development programme. I am based in Melbourne, Australia, at Cricket Australia (CA).

Prior to my ICC appointment, I had acquired considerable development experience in NZ as a CCC for Auckland Cricket, then their game development manager for five years. NZC's NDP is well respected and gave me an in-depth understanding of the principles of sport development and challenges facing community cricket; and provided opportunities for me to work with NZC and present strategies we had adopted in Auckland to counter such challenges at their development conferences. A key aspect of my ICC role is working with different cultures where cricket has limited tradition or history; my experiences working in South Auckland to grow participation among Polynesian communities, and short term in Japan to assist develop a junior participation strategy, have significantly benefitted my ICC role.

As EAP manager, I report to ICC's development services manager based in Dubai. We catch up weekly by Skype, meet as regional managers with ICC senior management in Dubai every six months, and every 12 months have a global meeting of managers and their development staff.

I have two staff, both based in Melbourne, one responsible for organising and delivering the ICC's regional qualifying events for EAP men, women, and U19 players in ICC's global tournaments, ensuring member federations (MFs) comply with ICC membership criteria, and overseeing their financial reporting. The other works directly with MFs on their cricket development plans to help them grow the game.

The focus of my role is to grow cricket beyond its traditional boundaries, provide leadership and support to our MFs to build strong and sustainable cricket systems within their countries; and ultimately, push towards ICC's long-term vision of being the world's favourite sport. My main contributions include:

- Developing strong relationships within CA to leverage their support and expertise to accelerate the growth of cricket in emerging nations.
- Working with Japan Cricket to implement a new governance structure and develop a new long-term strategic plan.
- Providing assistance to Cricket Papua New Guinea to become a more professional organisation that has over the last five years risen to 15th in the world rankings, recorded the second highest participation rate of all sports in their country, introduced full-time professional contracts for its elite athletes, and negotiated a television deal to broadcast its home international matches free-to-air nationwide.

All development roles have their challenges. My most significant have been the need to:

- **Overcome cultural and language barriers** by learning to listen and seek to deeply understand first. For example, it takes many visits to Japan to appreciate the cultural etiquette and different way of conducting business. I have learned the language and demonstrated a commitment and respect to understanding their unique perspectives and approach. Only now am I in any position to influence change, with the solutions I propose being very different and more appropriate from those I may have thought were best beforehand.
- **Change perceptions of my ICC role from that of 'policeman' to 'trusted adviser'**. As a major funder of MFs and its global governing body, there is a perception you are the 'big boss' who determines what can and can't be done. This undermines trust and honesty and hinders our ability to genuinely provide support. We have worked hard to change this, and position ourselves as mentors, to develop collaborative relationships with MF boards and management.

Questions

1. What previous development experiences were important to being appointed as the ICC EAP manager?
2. What subsequent learning assisted the greater acceptance and ability of the manager to influence change?
3. What is an important lesson for SDOs to understand when working with different ethnic groups within a sport?

CASE STUDY 5.2

National cricket development manager

Ian Sandbrook, Head of Participation, Cricket Scotland, Edinburgh, Scotland

I became Head of Participation for Cricket Scotland (CS), based in Edinburgh, in 2014. Critical to attaining this position was my proven track record of seven years of practical knowledge and experience of community sport development, acquired as the CCC, then operations manager, facilitating and managing the implementation of NZC's NDP in the Manawatu, NZ.

I have six national staff, each with specific roles to implement our participation initiatives: a national female participation manager and part-time disability cricket development officer, based in Edinburgh; three regional participation managers, based in Nairn, Stirling, and Glasgow; and a community engagement coordinator, based in Glasgow, responsible for developing cricket among its disadvantaged and black and minority ethnic communities. There are also eight development officers the regional managers manage or co-manage with funding partners (e.g. local authorities) (see Case study 4.4).

I formally report quarterly to CS's CEO and twice a year to its board. Because CS is dependent upon key funding partnerships with the International Cricket Council (ICC) and its regional body, ICC Europe, and Sport Scotland, Scotland's national sport agency, I also prepare a range of reports quarterly, half-yearly and annually for them against various performance criteria and outcomes.

The main focus of my role is achieving 20% growth in committed participants (those playing in regular cricket competitions, irrespective of format) by 2019. Creating greater engagement and integration with our regional associations and clubs, has been an important first step to enable us to introduce three key initiatives:

- Curriculum for Excellence Resource, a cricket-based, educational initiative, aligned with the Scottish primary schools' curriculum, has allowed us to start embedding cricket into primary schools.
- All Stars Cricket, a new, entry-level England and Wales Cricket Board (ECB) initiative we negotiated to use, provides a more professional approach to recruiting children into clubs.
- Thriving Clubs, a bespoke club development programme, has changed our way of working with clubs, for the provision of cricket initiatives and community development.

Introducing these initiatives, however, has not been without challenges, which we have needed to circumvent.

- **Poor governance and leadership as a national body** with a consequent disconnect from our cricket community base. Subsequent governance and personnel change at CS has totally changed our approach, enabling relationships to be re-built, and us to intervene to develop the community game.
- **A very traditional approach to cricket delivery by most clubs**. This is slowly changing as we educate stakeholders and volunteers about the need to modernise the game and its delivery to keep it relevant and appealing, and they witness the impact of the national initiatives we have introduced.
- **A lack of people on the ground to implement and manage initiatives.** Although the number of development staff has grown to 14, including the eight local development officers, which has increased our delivery effectiveness.

Questions

1. What tasks frequently take SDMs away from their core development business?
2. Why are these tasks deemed necessary?
3. List three challenges that can limit change. In a sport of your choice, how have they overcome traditional attitudes of clubs?

Between 1998 and 2004, NZC assembled a small team to design its NDP and lead and manage its implementation by an emergent regional and local delivery network (see Figure 5.1). It was funded by NZC in partnership with its cricket associations, supported by sponsorship from Nestlé New Zealand through its MILO brand, Gaming Trust funding from the New Zealand Community Trust (NZCT), and sport development investment from the national sport agency SPARC.

The establishment of the delivery network began in 1999, when full-time cricket development managers (CDMs) were appointed to manage and monitor the introduction of the NDP in each of NZC's six major associations (MAs). From 2001 onwards, mainly full-time CCCs were engaged in each MA and their constituent district associations (DAs) and metropolitan clubs, to implement the programme's community cricket initiatives, aimed at restructuring and resourcing the game and its organisation to support and retain players in secondary schools and clubs; and supervise the seasonal MILO Summer Squad (MSS) to implement the MILO initiatives, focused on recruiting and retaining children to play cricket in primary

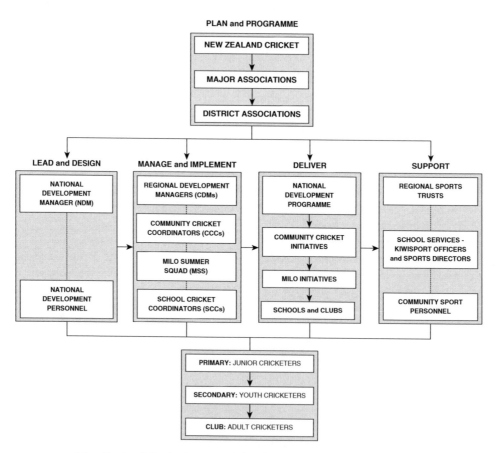

FIGURE 5.1 New Zealand Cricket's national development programme delivery structure

Source: Astle (2009: 27).

schools and junior clubs, and engaging and training their parents and teachers as coaches. From 2008, part-time school cricket coordinators (SCCs) were employed to assist the CCCs improve the organisation and delivery of cricket and retention of youth players in targeted secondary schools. The latter two groups were mainly young, part-time employees charged with delivering specific tasks during the summer.

COMMUNITY CRICKET COORDINATORS

The CCCs were mainly full-time personnel, with the requisite skills and experience, keen to develop careers as permanent SDOs. They transformed the NDP into practice, marketing its benefits, convincing volunteers of its value, and motivating and training them to deliver it in clubs and schools. They were instrumental in facilitating NZC's 'top-down', 'development of sport' process and its resultant impact on the sustainable growth of community cricket (Astle 2014).

Their requirements and role

The initial task in establishing NZC's SDO network was to scope the CCC role. This involved: first, undertaking a job analysis to determine the general requirements and person specifications for a CCC (see Appendix 5.1), and incorporating these into a generic job description for cricket associations to use in advertising for their CCCs (see Appendix 5.2); second, considering how these positions might be funded, managed, and held accountable; and third, convincing NZC's CEO and board these positions were necessary and needed to be full-time, not part-time seasonal, to neutralise concerns about their role in winter.

In formulating a sport development plan, a SDM must consider how its associated programme will be delivered. If SDOs are to be engaged for this purpose, SDMs need to ascertain their workforce requirements, and undertake the necessary planning and job analysis to ensure they recruit the right people as SDOs (Emery 2011). This involves determining their roles, skills and qualities required, numbers needed, and level of funding to underwrite a delivery network. While some NSOs have human resources (HR) strategies and personnel to assist SDMs address these questions, because HR practices vary considerably across sport organisations, many SDMs will have to seek their own answers (Lussier and Kimball 2014).

Their skills

Eady (1993), and later Watt (2003), listed the core professional skills they believed SDOs in the UK needed to have, or acquire, to successfully execute their role. These included: leadership, self management, planning, dealing with people, marketing, influencing, understanding, communicating, organising, sourcing, monitoring, persevering, and being patient. A similar list was identified by NZC's NDM for the CCC positions (see Appendix 5.1). This required self-motivated individuals, with passion, commitment and drive, and the interpersonal skills and practical ability to enthuse people, especially volunteers, to 'buy-in' to NZC's programme, and initiate change in clubs and schools.

A job analysis, identifying position specifications, and composing a job description (see Facts and figures 5.1), can be compiled using information from several sources. First, search the internet for job descriptions and position specifications of SDOs employed by similar sport organisations (see Facts and figures 5.2). Second, identify from your plan's objectives and strategies the potential tasks a SDO will need to fulfil (see Figure 5.2). Third, determine the position's scope in terms of the outcomes you expect them to achieve (e.g. clubs and schools to be serviced, initiatives delivered, players recruited, and coaches trained).

FACTS and FIGURES 5.1

Job descriptions

A job description outlines the role and responsibilities associated with a particular position. These are specified within a job description template that usually includes:

- job or position title
- employing sport organisation – its purpose and vision
- description of position
  - responsibilities
  - reporting line and relationships
- essential and desirable requirements
  - knowledge, skills, and abilities
  - education and experience
- location of position
- hours of work
- remuneration – salary and benefits
- sport organisation's website
- timelines for candidates' application, closing date, interviews, and appointment
- application procedures and contact details for forwarding applications

Question

Which of the above elements are important to you in a job description, and why?

FACTS and FIGURES 5.2

SDO job descriptions and position specifications

Very good generic job descriptions and position specifications for SDOs can be viewed online on UK websites, such as www.prospects.ac.uk/job-profiles/sports-development-officer. For more specific details, refer to the SDO positions advertised under 'Vacancies' on NSO websites, and those of central government sport agencies (e.g. Australian Sports Commission, www.clearinghouseforsport.gov.au/). Use these sport-specific websites to advertise SDO positions, and compile accurate SDO job descriptions and person specifications to secure the right people. This ensures qualified candidates see these positions and apply.

Question

Check, and amend where necessary, your own CV so it provides sufficient information to ensure you are the right person for a SDO role.

REVIEW QUESTIONS

1. Describe the delivery structure set up to implement NZC's programme, how was it funded, and what was its role in relation to volunteers in clubs and schools?
2. What is a job analysis? What does it entail and why is it necessary?
3. Explain the difference between a job description and a position specification.

Their funding partnerships

Because most of NZC's funds were assigned to high performance, additional funding had to be sourced to implement its NDP. To achieve this, NZC created partnerships with its MAs, DAs and metropolitan clubs, and externally with various funders and sponsors, to secure sufficient funding to appoint the CCCs. While most partnerships funded CCC salaries, other arrangements were negotiated to cover their operating costs (e.g. vehicles), provide office space (e.g. RSTs), supply promotional product (e.g. MILO), and access specialist support and resources (e.g. SPARC, Sport NZ).

At the national level, the initial catalyst came from an injection of sponsorship funding from Nestlé New Zealand, through its MILO brand. This prompted NZC to finance, with partnership funding from SPARC and NZCT, 75% of each CCC's remuneration package, with 25% being contributed by associations or metropolitan clubs allocated a CCC. This shared funding underwrote the phased employment of 30 CCCs. The internal partnership contribution of 25% ensured there was local ownership and acceptance of the CCCs, something not always apparent in other sports, where SDOs had been imposed by NSOs on their RSOs. It was also instrumental in the delivery network growing and spreading quicker than anticipated, with the number of CCC positions nearly doubling in 10 years. Of the 59, 51 were full-time positions in MAs and DAs, comprising 39 CCCs fully focused on development, and 12 club managers (Astle 2014). The latter were engaged in Auckland, by each of its principal clubs, as part of their 'Club is the Hub' scheme, to undertake a mix of administrative, coaching, and development duties.

At regional and local levels, an array of alliances was also built with Gaming and Community Trusts, business sponsors, local councils, and RSTs. The RSTs, in particular, were vital partners in supporting the NDP in many DAs, providing professional office space for their CCCs. Instead of operating from a 'home base', they had access to RST facilities and resources, staff knowledge and experience, community contact networks and databases, especially with schools, and professional development opportunities. In return, the credibility of the CCCs and profile of the NDP with its quality initiatives and resources, saw the relationship with the RSTs become one of mutual interest rather than just a client. Cricket was able to provide the RSTs with a prototype of a successful development programme for other sports in their communities. Those CCCs in major metropolitan clubs (mainly in Auckland), and largest DAs, had offices in their cricket complexes.

Their selection and tenure

The CCC positions were advertised locally and appointments made, usually in conjunction with the MA CDM, with the proviso the appointee was to be an integral part of, and managed by, the MA, DA, or metropolitan club. The formation of the CCC network comprised three phases (Astle 2014).

The first, when the programme commenced in 2000, was notable for the tendency of associations and metropolitan clubs to employ someone as a CCC who was already in their service, without taking heed of whether they had the capability to do the job. This arose from the initial lack of awareness of the type of person to appoint, despite the availability of NZC's CCC job description and position specifications (see Appendices 5.1 and 5.2), and there being no repository of trained SDOs in NZ. A similar tendency occurred in football (see Case study 9.1). In cricket's case, the first appointed CCCs had mainly worked part-time, in locally funded, seasonal coaching and talented player development programmes. While most were equipped to deliver the MILO initiatives in primary schools and junior clubs, few had the attributes to deliver the more complex Community Cricket initiatives to improve the capability of secondary schools and clubs.

The second phase saw CCCs with the requisite competencies appointed from the positions advertised or being shoulder-tapped by CDMs. Most were in their mid-thirties to mid-forties, and more experienced in work and life than cricket development. They brought with them a strong work ethic, passion for cricket, commonsense understandings, a pragmatic approach and impressive people skills acquired from previous occupations, such as stock agent, milk vendor, teacher, bank officer, and real estate agent (Astle 2014). Invariably, all had a voluntary involvement in sport, and some also had part-time employment coaching cricket and/or other codes.

The third and current phase has seen a better understanding of the requisite CCC skills. Increasingly, younger individuals in their twenties have been appointed with tertiary or sport-related qualifications, such as business management, law, coaching, physical education, and sport and recreation (Astle 2014). While they lacked the life experience of the phase two CCCs, they bring many academic qualities to the role, and the capabilities associated with their various disciplines. Despite their academic credentials, they still need to be immersed in practical cricket development to understand the objectives of its initiatives, learn to deal with a diverse range of mainly volunteer stakeholders, be able to effectively sell and deliver the programme to them, and build credibility in their cricket communities. This is because, as Pitchford and Collins (2010: 272) found for similar SDOs within the UK, there was "a poor match between underpinning knowledge and job functions".

This recent establishment of national and regional SDO delivery networks in cricket and other sports (Astle 2011) has created a potential career pathway for SDOs in NZ. For CCCs who have moved into other employment, their acquired skills have provided a strong foundation for their advancement. Many CCCs have gained senior leadership, management, and coaching roles in MAs, NZC, the ICC (see Case study 5.1), and in sport development in other NSOs in NZ and overseas (see Case studies 5.2 and 5.3).

The stability of tenure of the CCCs has been significant in cricket's development. Having a stable SDOs base is critical to building strong relationships with stakeholders, especially volunteers in clubs and schools. Where SDO turnover is high, clubs and schools become reluctant to engage with them, as changing personnel frequently means a lack of continuity in programme delivery and support.

The continuity of CCC involvement has been crucial to their effective operation (Astle 2014). A survey of 14 CCCs in 2015 identified nine had contributed to the programme for over four years, four of these for over 10 years (Astle 2015). Evidence shows for a CCC to be at their most effective took around three years. In the first year, they are engrossed in learning their role, intricacies of the programme initiatives, and familiarising the stakeholders in their community with these. In the second year, aware of the annual schedule of tasks, they become more confident and competent in their delivery. By the third year, they knew their role, how to deliver the initiatives, who the stakeholders are and among them the change agents driving the programme. Because of their accumulated knowledge and experience, and the respect and credibility they built up in their communities they could tap into local resources, network with other CCCs, and innovate by modifying national initiatives to better fit the local scene and achieve improved outcomes (see Figure 7.4 and Case Study 7.4).

Their training

The 2015 survey revealed a mix of CCCs appointed in phases two and three (Astle 2015). All had previous or current experience as cricket players, coaches, and/or managers. Nine CCCs had tertiary qualifications, with bachelor degrees in the arts, science, teaching, business, sport management, and sport and leisure. Several also brought existing knowledge, skills, and experience acquired from other previous, 'people-related' occupations to their role, such as bank officer, public service administrator, teacher, and capability manager. Because of the newness of the concept, most had no specific sport development training, prior exposure to it in the field, or a sport development qualification from a tertiary institution. Access to such training and qualifications in NZ was still non-existent at the time of the 2015 survey. In contrast, England by 2016 had 86 tertiary providers offering 'sport development' courses (www.ucas.co.uk), which had doubled in 10 years (Pitchford and Collins 2010).

Although opportunities to work in sport development in NZ have expanded, there is "no formal consideration of the person specification and. . . training needs" of those employed as SDOs (Nesti 2001: 196). Pitchford and Collins (2010) signalled this same concern in the UK and led them to advocate for a national, accredited framework for the education and training of SDOs. While a set of national occupational standards for sports development has been established in the UK (www.skillsactive.com/standards-quals/sports-development), only four of its 22 standards apply to the core function of working with volunteers and facilitating the development and delivery of community sport. Most of the remaining standards are management focused. Such a framework has to be specific to sport development and community sport, underpinned with a knowledge and practical experience of the dynamics of working in the field, and an understanding of the skills required to engage with community stakeholders, especially volunteers, to initiate change to improve and/or increase sporting opportunities in clubs and schools. This lack of specificity with respect to sport development, in favour of a more generic, theoretical sport management focus in these standards, is possibly the reason why they are not acknowledged by practitioners in the UK (Robson, Simpson, Tucker, and Leach 2013). Perhaps as Eady (1993: 73) suggests, this practical specificity may be best provided "from within the profession with SDOs themselves moving into academic or private sector roles servicing and supporting their former colleagues".

Few sports have the expertise, capability, or resources to conduct intensive induction training for new SDOs, football in NZ being the exception (see Chapter 9). Most SDOs are appointed individually within a sport, at different times and by different RSOs, depending upon available vacancies, funding, and suitable candidates. Their training is provided on the job and offsite, through attending NSO conferences and workshops offered by the likes of a local authority or national sport agency. While on-the-job training is usually conducted by their SDM, or an experienced SDO, who act as a mentor to help develop their knowledge, expertise, and confidence. For most SDOs, this comprises an initial orientation to the role, its requirements, responsibilities, and expectations (see Appendix 5.3), followed by ongoing, practical job training. The former is critical for a SDO's understanding of role clarity and annual tasks, networking and information sharing, and accountability and reporting (Astle, Dellaca, and Pithey 2013). The latter involves the SDO 'shadowing' or working closely with their mentor, who provides in-field demonstrations and explanations of specific tasks, then supervises the SDO undertake these supported by the mentor's guidance and constructive feedback. This form of training was valued the most by the CCCs surveyed in 2015 (Astle 2015). While 'learn by doing' may seem an old adage, it both signals the existing gap between 'knowing' (theory) and 'doing' (practice) and identifies it as still the most effective way for SDOs to become familiar with their roles (Lussier and Kimball 2014). It should be emphasised that ongoing SDO training is essential to the consistency and quality of their practice.

The orientation and training of NZC's CCCs was undertaken by their MA CDM (see Appendix 5.3). This including an explanation of the programme and its objectives, in-field demonstrations of the delivery of the NDP initiatives, and opportunities to network with other CCCs in their MA, especially through season preview and review meetings, and attendance at NZC's national development conference. These networking opportunities also allowed the NDM to meet with each CDM and their CCCs to update them on the NDP, explain new initiatives and resources, discuss any issues, and exchange ideas. At the same time, it allowed the CCCs to meet with their colleagues, and share information and best practice.

Each CCC was supplied with two operational manuals which detailed the procedures for delivering the MILO and Community Cricket initiatives (Astle 2000, 2001a). These were to ensure that their efforts were planned and standardised. A generic annual schedule of tasks so they could see the job unfolding in its entirety month by month, and a selection of coaching and development resources to assist them market and deliver the various initiatives.

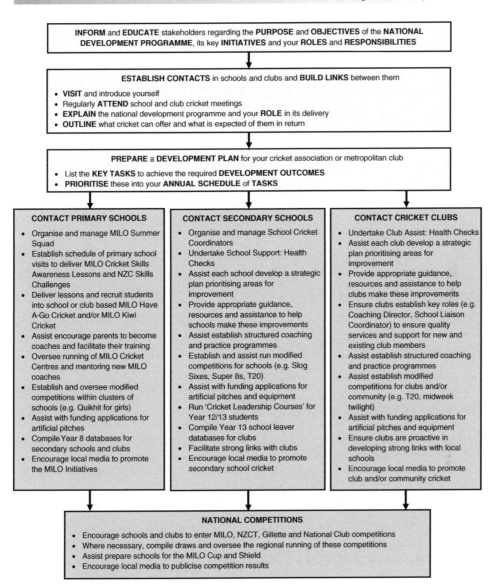

INFORM and EDUCATE stakeholders regarding the **PURPOSE** and **OBJECTIVES** of the **NATIONAL DEVELOPMENT PROGRAMME**, its key **INITIATIVES** and your **ROLES** and **RESPONSIBILITIES**

ESTABLISH CONTACTS in schools and clubs and **BUILD LINKS** between them
- **VISIT** and introduce yourself
- Regularly **ATTEND** school and club cricket meetings
- **EXPLAIN** the national development programme and your **ROLE** in its delivery
- **OUTLINE** what cricket can offer and what is expected of them in return

PREPARE a **DEVELOPMENT PLAN** for your cricket association or metropolitan club
- List the **KEY TASKS** to achieve the required **DEVELOPMENT OUTCOMES**
- **PRIORITISE** these into your **ANNUAL SCHEDULE** of **TASKS**

CONTACT PRIMARY SCHOOLS
- Organise and manage MILO Summer Squad
- Establish schedule of primary school visits to deliver MILO Cricket Skills Awareness Lessons and NZC Skills Challenges
- Deliver lessons and recruit students into school or club based MILO Have A-Go Cricket and/or MILO Kiwi Cricket
- Assist encourage parents to become coaches and facilitate their training
- Oversee running of MILO Cricket Centres and mentoring new MILO coaches
- Establish and oversee modified competitions within clusters of schools (e.g. Quikhit for girls)
- Assist with funding applications for artificial pitches
- Compile Year 8 databases for secondary schools and clubs
- Encourage local media to promote the MILO Initiatives

CONTACT SECONDARY SCHOOLS
- Organise and manage School Cricket Coordinators
- Undertake School Support: Health Checks
- Assist each school develop a strategic plan prioritising areas for improvement
- Provide appropriate guidance, resources and assistance to help schools make these improvements
- Assist establish structured coaching and practice programmes
- Establish and assist run modified competitions for schools (e.g. Slog Sixes, Super 8s, T20)
- Assist with funding applications for artificial pitches and equipment
- Run 'Cricket Leadership Courses' for Year 12/13 students
- Compile Year 13 school leaver databases for clubs
- Facilitate strong links with clubs
- Encourage local media to promote secondary school cricket

CONTACT CRICKET CLUBS
- Undertake Club Assist: Health Checks
- Assist each club develop a strategic plan prioritising areas for improvement
- Provide appropriate guidance, resources and assistance to help clubs make these improvements
- Ensure clubs establish key roles (e.g. Coaching Director, School Liaison Coordinator) to ensure quality services and support for new and existing club members
- Assist establish structured coaching and practice programmes
- Assist establish modified competitions for clubs and/or community (e.g. T20, midweek twilight)
- Assist with funding applications for artificial pitches and equipment
- Ensure clubs are proactive in developing strong links with local schools
- Encourage local media to promote club and/or community cricket

NATIONAL COMPETITIONS
- Encourage schools and clubs to enter MILO, NZCT, Gillette and National Club competitions
- Where necessary, compile draws and oversee the regional running of these competitions
- Assist prepare schools for the MILO Cup and Shield
- Encourage local media to publicise competition results

FIGURE 5.2 Community cricket coordinator's key tasks

Source: Astle (2009: 33).

Because many SDOs work in relative isolation, it is important they receive regular performance appraisals by their SDM and/or RSO committee/administrator to help them continuously improve. Unfortunately, this is not done well by sport organisations, with many lacking the procedures and/or having SDMs with the competencies and confidence to evaluate their SDOs. An effective appraisal provides SDOs with valuable evaluative and developmental feedback on their performance, indicating what they are doing well, identifying areas for possible improvement, establishing goals for the next six or 12 months, and deciding on future professional development opportunities.

REVIEW QUESTIONS

1. Why are partnerships critical to the formation and sustainability of SDO networks? Then in a sport of your choice, identify the key partners that support its SDOs.
2. How have the characteristics of current CCCs changed from their earlier counterparts? Do you think this change is reflected in current SDOs in other sports, and if so, why?
3. Why is stability of tenure for SDOs important to their effectiveness?
4. Identify the two main types of training offered to SDOs, which is the most effective? Describe the type of training you have received in a job? What type of training is most effective for you and why?

Their work programme

The CCCs were employed primarily to implement the Community Cricket initiatives, aimed at revitalising and strengthening the game in clubs and secondary schools, to oversee the delivery of the MILO initiatives in primary schools and junior clubs, and ensure both sets of initiatives were integrated into one coordinated community cricket delivery system (Astle 2014) (see Figure 5.2). They used the Community Cricket initiatives' Club Assist and School Support health checks to audit the performance of clubs and secondary schools respectively, and provide detailed feedback on their strengths and areas needing improvement (Astle 2001b, 2001c) (see Facts and figures 6.1). The latter were prioritised, then incorporated as goals into a development plan and assigned actions, time frames and responsibilities to achieve these. Such plans provided the focus for developing clubs and secondary schools, their resource allocation, and the CCC's work programme.

The CCCs in the DAs generally operate differently from those in the larger metropolitan centres. In the DAs they worked in a vertical delivery structure of clubs, secondary schools, and primary schools, with the object of creating links to integrate them together. In the metropolitan centres, different delivery mechanisms were negotiated with NZC to suit their regional structures. Auckland introduced the initiatives through its existing principal clubs, as part of their 'Club is the Hub' scheme, with club managers (instead of CCCs) responsible for delivering the initiatives (Astle 2003). Wellington opted for a centralised, horizontal structure with their CCCs accountable for a specific level of the game to implement the initiatives (e.g. primary/junior, secondary/youth or club/adult). While Christchurch and Dunedin started with a vertical structure, with each CCC allocated a cluster of clubs and schools, they later adopted a similar horizontal system to Wellington. Although this provided each CCC with a broad overview of their level of responsibility, it hindered the integration of the community game, constraining its coordinated development.

In the last decade, both Wellington and Christchurch, have reduced their CCC numbers, instead adopting an 'arm's length' approach to development. They have used the CCC funding to provide annual grants to their premier clubs, and in return set criteria for them to undertake a limited number of development tasks. Unfortunately, the accountability for this funding and where it is applied is subject to question in terms of its efficacy (Astle et al. 2013).

To alleviate this, Wellington has introduced SLAs with their clubs to increase their answerability and more effectively monitor agreed outcomes (Snedden 2017).

As regional change agents the CCCs not only introduced the national initiatives, but infused the community game with key development principles, especially game modification (see Case study 5.3). This required the CCCs to possess the interpersonal and organisational skills to establish a network of individuals and agencies in their communities, particularly in clubs and schools, to influence change to existing practices and introduce the new initiatives. Being the focal point of this network, the CCCs were influential in fostering close relationships within and between clubs and schools.

CASE STUDY 5.3
Regional cricket development officer

Michael Peacock, Cricket Australia Junior Participation Specialist in New South Wales

I was appointed as a sport-specific junior participation specialist (JPS) in 2014 by Cricket Australia (CA), one of 10 JPS positions throughout Australia. These are national roles, but based in State Cricket Associations, where they are responsible for delivering national initiatives within each state, with the prime focus being to promote and grow the new MILO T20 Blast initiative for 7–12-year-old children (see Case study 4.1).

I qualified for the position because of my knowledge and understanding of the game as a player, sport management degree from NZ, and cricket development experience in Christchurch, NZ.

Based in Cricket New South Wales' (NSW) office at Sydney Cricket Ground, I am part of a Participation Team of four, including a participation manager and schools coordinator employed by Cricket NSW, and two JPSs (myself and another) engaged by CA. As JPSs we each operate in the different catchment areas of NSW and Australian Capital Territory (ACT) designated to the two Sydney-based Big Bash League (BBL) club franchises – the Sydney Sixers and Sydney Thunder.

I am responsible for 11 of NSW/ACT's 21 regions aligned to the Sydney Thunder club franchise. Each region has a development manager (DM) who oversees their school and club cricket development initiatives. I help these DMs introduce and deliver the MILO T20 Blast in their regions.

My main responsibilities are to:

1. Introduce CA's nationally recommended junior pathway to Junior Cricket Associations within the NSW/ACT regions, with a strong focus on MILO T20 Blast.
2. Align CA's, Cricket NSW's and Cricket ACT's MILO T20 Blast promotional strategies.
3. Increase the conversion of children sampling school-based cricket activities, such a MILO in2CRICKET sessions and MILO T20 Blast 'Gala Days' run by the regional DMs, into sustainable club-based participation.
4. Train and educate a workforce of private providers, casual employees, and volunteers as coaches to effectively deliver the MILO T20 Blast initiative.

I have two managers: my reporting manager is CA's national field manager in Melbourne, and my direct manager is Cricket NSW's participation manager. I report to them fortnightly, and am appraised twice annually by my reporting manager, who also arranges two conferences per year for the JPSs to get together and share ideas.

My main contribution has been to ensure sustained growth, over the past three seasons, in participation in MILO T20 Blast in my NSW/ACT territory. In this time, participant numbers have increased from 860 to 6,575, with the number of girls increasing from 32 to over 1,000, and 70–80% of these participants now transitioning into junior club cricket.

Despite the success of the MILO T20 Blast initiative, my biggest challenge is trying to influence junior cricket associations in NSW/ACT to adopt CA's national junior player pathway and embed it in their junior cricket programmes. The national pathway is not mandated by CA, therefore some volunteer-led associations, refuse to run national initiatives, such as MILO T20 Blast, preferring to retain their existing junior formats.

As the MILO T20 Blast has grown, we have more success stories and statistics to convince associations to adopt the initiative. We are also better prepared to counter objections through the increased benefits (e.g. marketing and promotion, free equipment, participant packs, trained coaches, links to the BBL and WBBL) both CA and Cricket NSW are able to offer, if they incorporate MILO T20 Blast into their junior player pathways.

Questions

1. What is the role of a JPS? How does this differ from most SDO roles?
2. How has CA tied their promotion and development of their junior player pathway to their professional BBL? What advantages does this offer junior cricket?
3. What impact has MILO T20 Blast had on participation in the Sydney Thunder franchise?
4. What is the biggest challenge to extending this impact? How universal is this challenge to efforts to develop community sport?

The CCCs immersed themselves in the game and its organisation. They created community networks, linked the main providers, and connected participants with programmes whether they be players, coaches, or administrators. They inspired a genuine interest in cricket in schools for youngsters to have fun, make friends, and enjoy participating in various forms of the game. They offered encouragement and assistance to enthuse, train, and provide resources to parents and teachers as coaches and administrators. As a consequence, they gained the trust and respect of the cricket communities they serviced, who valued them and the role they played in ensuring the long-term health of the game. Their enthusiasm was infectious and their credibility crucial to the spread and impact of the NDP.

In the last decade, without constant guidance, support, and being held to account by NZC, the CCCs' role has been diluted by associations and metropolitan clubs. The 2015 survey showed CCCs allocated less than half (45%) of their time to fulfilling their core development responsibilities fundamental to growing and sustaining the game. The time they have to achieve these objectives is increasingly under pressure from other management, administration, and coaching tasks they also need to complete. CCCs now assign almost an equal amount of their time (43%) to these responsibilities, with the remaining 12% spent on travel, meetings, and overseeing facilities.

While there is always a need to undertake management and administration tasks, these consume 28% of their time. This overburdening was a consequence of both NDP's success, and as the 'paid person' being overloaded with tasks previously done by volunteers (Astle 2014). This latter factor saw the CCCs spend 15% of their time servicing summer and winter coaching programmes, especially for age-group representative players.

Their challenges

Along with the increasing amalgam of tasks facing CCCs, a 'gatekeeper' mentality by some administrators and volunteers, who failed to grasp the benefits of the CCC's role or the NDP's objectives, created conflicting pressures for the CCCs (Astle 2014). These were similar to the challenges experienced by local authority SDOs, arising from changing central government policies in the UK, which affected their hands-on delivery of sport-specific outcomes (Bloyce and Green 2011; Bloyce et al. 2008).

The effective operation of the CCCs was dependent upon the support of MA and DA administrators, and club and school volunteers. Some of these personnel, however, struggled to grasp the specificity of the CCC's role, so acted as gatekeepers to the effective spread of the programme. Their attitudes arose from a mix of: reluctance to change; lack of understanding of the programme's objectives and benefits; strong preference for short-term high-performance goals; and belief the CCCs were at the association's disposal to use as they saw fit, whereas in fact they were funded by NZC to achieve national development outcomes (Astle 2014).

To alleviate this constraint required an ongoing educative process because of the constant turnover of administrators and volunteers. It was essential that NZC and its NDM, the MA CDMs, and the CCCs themselves continuously communicated the development message to all levels of the community game (Astle et al. 2013).

Initially, many CCCs were the only full-time employees in their associations. As paid cricket operatives, the expectation of many administrators and volunteers, was they were available to do 'all things cricket' in their communities. For this reason, CCCs were often 'hijacked' by the encroachment of administrative and coaching responsibilities on their core development role, including those previously done by volunteers (Astle et al. 2013). As one CCC noted: "the nature of being a CCC means we are often asked to do things which aren't in our job description. As we are passionate people we very rarely say no which means we are often stretched" (Astle 2015: 25).

A significant imposition on the CCCs was coaching. This was indicative of many associations being over-consumed by their representative programmes, and NZC's high-performance expectations, despite there being no nationally coordinated plan for young talented player development (11–17 years). This has seen considerable talent development fall on the CCCs' shoulders through coaching age-group representative teams. While most CCCs enjoyed this involvement, they frequently became overloaded during the summer, which negatively impacted their development work, especially with secondary schools and clubs.

REVIEW QUESTIONS

1. How have the CCCs' roles and responsibilities changed over time? What has caused this, and why? What tensions has it created for the CCCs?
2. What main challenges face the CCCs? If you were a CCC, how would you overcome these challenges? How can NSOs counter these challenges?

In the 2015 survey, the CCCs also expressed frustrations over the uncertainty of development funding from various partners (e.g. NZC, MAs, DAs, Gaming Trusts); limited progress within specific areas of the game (e.g. female and secondary school cricket); and lack of strategic direction and support for community cricket from NZC. In its 2017 'One Cricket' review of community cricket, NZC has recognised this and is seeking solutions (Snedden 2017) (see Case study 7.1).

CONCLUSION

This chapter used NZC's CCCs to examine the formation and features of a regional delivery network of sport-specific SDOs. The efforts and effectiveness of the CCCs (see Pause and ponder 5.1), have been instrumental in significantly increasing player numbers, and making improvements in the infrastructure and services within clubs and schools to support and sustain this increase (see Chapter 6).

PAUSE and PONDER 5.1

Ten principles for being an effective sport development officer

1. **Research, plan and prepare.** Be well organised, enthusiastic, know your business, and deliver (i.e. 'know what you want to do' and 'do what you say you are going to do'). This is essential for credibility.
2. **Seize the initiative and look for opportunities to introduce appropriate change**. Remember it should be systematic, sustainable, and add value, not ad hoc.
3. **Be adaptable and flexible.** For example, this applies equally to endorsing game modification and the concept of 'less is more', to adjusting your own schedule to deliver initiatives at a time to suit customers.
4. **Monitor – be census-driven – as a measure of performance.** Collect evidence, set up accurate databases, take photographs, engage with and monitor the media. SLA targets set by NSOs are yours, not those of the NSO, as the outcomes affect the quality of the programme and the derived opportunities and experiences in your community.

5. **Understand, adhere to, and focus on your core business**. Don't be side-tracked and try to do all things.
6. **Focus on areas of strength.** Work with those who want it, before attempting to convert the reluctant and inactive.
7. **Don't assume anything!** Promote and sell your programme not just to external stakeholders, but also to those inside your sport organisation. Spread the word also about your role and expectations.
8. **Engage and recognise volunteers.** Make their life easier by clarifying their roles and acknowledging their vital contributions.
9. **Develop and understand key community networks and partnerships.** Take opportunities to expand the impact of your sport and positive brand exposure for sponsors and funders. Provide quality service; value and be accountable for their support and investment; achieve agreed outcomes; be the best you can be.
10. **Look to be proactive.** Be innovative and look to continuously improve.

Questions

1. Which two of these principles do you think are the most important if SDOs are to be effective, and why?
2. If you are a SDO, the application of which principles have been most beneficial in your involvement in sport development?
3. If you are not an SDO, what contact, if any, have you had with SDOs? What things did they do well? How might things have been done better?

The role and challenges of the CCCs were explored within the context of NZC's planned intervention into grassroots cricket. This highlighted the need for the ongoing commitment, clear direction, and active involvement by NSOs to preserve the integrity of the development role, and the gains these practitioners have made.

Therefore, in establishing a regional delivery network of SDOs to facilitate the implementation of a national development programme, NSOs need to:

- have clear expectations of the skills, roles, and responsibilities they require of their SDOs;
- educate RSO administrators and management committees of these expectations, and their responsibilities to oversee, support, and be accountable for the performance of their SDOs;
- ensure their SDOs are trained appropriately to understand the objectives that underpin their planned programme, and are able to explain these confidently to stakeholders;
- provide clear direction for their work programmes, and a system of accountability for their performance; and
- commit to their programme long term, 10 years plus, to enable their SDOs to effectively use it to revitalise and sustainably grow their sports at a community level.

In the past decade, some NSOs in their search for role clarity and greater accountability have changed the focus of their SDO position titles from 'development' to 'participation' (e.g. sport participation officer). This has reiterated the core purpose of these positions, and reinforced with administrators and volunteers, that they are not a 'jack-of-all-trades' at their disposal, but a specialist appointed to increase participation in order to grow and sustain their sport in clubs and schools.

REFERENCES

Astle, A. M. (1998). *Position requirements for a cricket development officer.* Planning document. New Zealand, Christchurch.

Astle, A. M. (2000). *MILO initiatives: Guidelines for MILO summer squad cricket development officers.* Instruction manual. New Zealand Cricket, Christchurch.

Astle, A. M. (2001a). *Community cricket initiatives: Community cricket coordinators' manual.* Instruction manual. New Zealand Cricket, Christchurch.

Astle, A. M. (2001b). *Club assist: Health check.* Checklist. New Zealand Cricket, Christchurch.

Astle, A. M. (2001c). *Secondary school: Health check.* Checklist. New Zealand Cricket, Christchurch.

Astle, A. M. (2003). *Community cricket initiatives: Report and recommendations 2002–03.* Board report. New Zealand Cricket, Christchurch.

Astle, A. M. (2007). *Community cricket coordinators: Orientation/induction checklist.* Training guideline. New Zealand Cricket, Christchurch.

Astle, A. M. (2009). *New Zealand Cricket: National development plan and programme.* Planning document. New Zealand Cricket, Christchurch.

Astle, A. M. (2011). *Community sport implementation plan: Collaborative delivery and outcomes.* Planning document. Sport and Recreation New Zealand, Wellington.

Astle, A. M. (2014). *Sport development – Plan, programme and practice: A case study of the planned intervention by New Zealand Cricket into cricket in New Zealand.* Unpublished PhD thesis, Massey University, Palmerston North, New Zealand.

Astle, A. M. (2015). *Development of sport in practice: Sport development officers – New Zealand Cricket's community cricket coordinators.* Unpublished survey.

Astle, A. M., Dellaca, K., & Pithey, R. (2013). *Canterbury Cricket Association: District reviews* (Report). Christchurch: Canterbury Cricket Association.

Bloyce, D., & Green, K. (2011). Sports development officers on sport development. In B. Houlihan & M. Green (Eds.), *Routledge handbook of sports development* (pp. 477–486). London and New York: Routledge.

Bloyce, D., Smith, A., Mead, R., & Morris, J. (2008). 'Playing the game (plan)': A figurational analysis of organisational change in sports development in England. *European Sport Management Quarterly, 8*(4), 359–378.

Eady, J. (1993). *Practical sports development.* Harlow: Longman.

Emery, P. (2011). *The sports management toolkit.* London: Routledge.

Girginov, V. (2008). Management of sports development as an emerging field and profession. In V. Girginov (Ed.), *Management of sports development* (pp. 3–37). Oxford: Elsevier/Butterworth-Heinemann.

Houlihan, B., & White, A. (2002). *The politics of sports development: Development of sport or development through sport?* London: Routledge.

Lussier, R. N., & Kimball, D. C. (2014). *Applied sport management skills* (2nd ed.). Champaign, IL: Human Kinetics.

Nesti, M. (2001). Working in sports development. In K. Hylton, P. Bramham, D. Jackson, & M. Nesti (Eds.), *Sports development: Policy, process and practice* (pp. 195–213). London: Routledge.

Pitchford, A., & Collins, M. (2010). Sports development as a job, a career and training. In M. Collins (Ed.), *Examining sports development* (pp. 259–288). London and New York: Routledge.

Robson, S., Simpson, K., Tucker, L., & Leach, R. (2013). Introduction. In S. Robson, K. Simpson, & L. Tucker (Eds.), *Strategic sport development* (pp. 1–24). London and New York: Routledge.

Snedden, M. (2017). *Positioning cricket for the future.* Unpublished One Cricket Project Report. New Zealand Cricket, Auckland.

Watt, D. C. (2003). *Sports management and administration* (2nd ed.). London: Routledge.

Websites

www.clearinghouseforsport.gov.au/
www.prospects.ac.uk/job-profiles/sports-development-officer
www.skillsactive.com/standards-quals/sports-development
www.ucas.co.uk

The role of a community cricket coordinator (CCC) is extremely important. A CCC as a representative of NZC, their association or metropolitan club, and national development programme sponsors, provides 'a window on the sport' and is its 'eyes, ears and voice of cricket' in the community. As often the first contact with children, young people, principals, teachers, parents, club players and administrators, and the game's official representative, a CCC has to be well presented, thoroughly prepared, professional, and enthusiastic.

Roles	Experience
At various times a CCC will need to be a: <ul><li>Leader</li><li>Planner</li><li>Sales person</li><li>Teacher</li><li>Coach</li><li>Role model</li><li>Organiser</li><li>Influencer</li><li>Negotiator</li><li>Facilitator</li><li>Diplomat</li><li>Change agent</li></ul>	Preferably: <ul><li>A university graduate with a teaching or sports management background and familiarity with secondary school and club sport development, delivery, and interaction</li><li>Not a current first class or international player, but needs to have playing/coaching experience and a passion for cricket</li></ul>

Technical skills

- A knowledge and understanding of:

  o The principles of cricket
  o Current coaching principles (Level I or II cricket coaching qualification)
  o The structure and organisation of secondary school and club cricket

- Ability to enthuse children and young people to play cricket, encourage volunteers to become involved, and facilitate appropriate coaching and training for both
- Ability to:

  o Meet and effectively communicate with school principals and teachers, club and district cricket officials, parents and volunteers as well as young people and children
  o Utilise, support, and enhance existing structures and organisation within secondary schools and clubs to create delivery systems and an environment conducive to retaining young people and adults as players, coaches, and administrators
  o Identify and form links between the game's three levels (primary, secondary, and club) to address attrition at the interfaces, and to integrate the cricket community and meet its needs

Position skills	Personal qualities
<ul><li>Effective self-management</li><li>Presentation skills – written and oral</li><li>Organisational skills</li><li>Marketing and negotiating skills</li><li>Ability to facilitate meetings, courses and workshops</li><li>Problem solving</li><li>Delegation</li><li>Time management</li><li>Financial accountability</li></ul>	<ul><li>Enthusiastic, energetic, confident, committed</li><li>Professional personal presentation</li><li>Strong interpersonal skills</li><li>Reliable and punctual</li><li>Ability to work with a diverse range of ages, abilities, and interests</li><li>Self-motivated – able to work independently and with initiative</li><li>Organised and hard-working</li><li>Open to new ideas</li><li>Patience, perseverance, and resilience</li></ul>

Source: Abridged from Astle (1998).

Roles	Responsibilities
Reports and relationships	• To report regularly to an appointed management committee of an association or metropolitan club. • To report regularly to the MA CDM providing feedback on the implementation and impact of NZC's NDP within an association or metropolitan club. • To initiate and maintain contact with the local regional sports trust (KiwiSport coordinator and regional sports director) regarding their needs for junior, youth, and adult cricket within the community.
Focus and implementation	• To actively promote, integrate, revitalise, strengthen, and grow the game at all levels (primary, secondary, club) and to elevate the profile of cricket within the cricket community of the association or metropolitan club. • To facilitate the implementation, management, and expansion of NZC's NDP, including the MILO and Community Cricket initiatives, in within an association or metropolitan club. • To formulate a strategic development plan for the association or metropolitan club to ensure all initiatives are delivered to clubs and schools and agreed outputs and outcomes are achieved. • Where necessary, organise and manage the effective operation of part-time MSS personnel in primary schools and junior clubs, and SCCs in select secondary schools.

Establish links and facilitate flows	• To initiate and maintain contact with contributing primary, intermediate, and secondary schools and metropolitan club or clubs of an association, and facilitate the development of appropriate links between them by:
	
	  o identifying and establishing contact between the teacher-in-charge of cricket and/or school cricket coordinator in the contributing schools and appropriate liaison person in the metropolitan club or clubs of an association and developing a rapport between them;
	  o establishing a strong, supportive relationship with coaches in contributing schools;
	  o taking an active interest in the efforts, achievements and future aspirations of players in contributing schools and facilitate their effective and seamless transition to the next level of the game;
	  o creating databases of Year 8 cricket players (and their parents as coaches) moving to secondary school and Year 13 cricket players leaving school, including an indication of future intentions and possible movements; and
	  o taking stock of the facilities in the cluster of schools and clubs and how they might best be utilised, developed, and shared.

Deliver programme	• To increase participation levels in terms of playing numbers and volunteer supporters (e.g. coaches, scorers, administrators). • To prepare and conduct sessions in primary schools and junior clubs for the various MILO initiatives (MILO Cricket Skills Awareness Lessons, MILO holiday clinics, MILO Have-A-Go Cricket, MILO Kiwi Cricket, New Zealand Cricket Skills Challenge, Quikhit). • To assist establish, promote and run appropriate competitions and game formats in primary schools and junior clubs to make the game more accessible, meet player needs, and cater for their varying ages, interests, abilities, and genders. • To promote and encourage entry into national school, club and district competitions (e.g. MILO Cup, MILO Shield, Gillette Cup, NZCT Cup (Girls), NZCT Cup (Junior Boys), National Club competitions)

(continued)

Roles	Responsibilities

	• To foster and promote in secondary schools intra-school and inter-school matches and tournaments and modified formats (e.g. Slog Sixes).
	• To organise and run cricket leadership courses (coaching and umpiring) in secondary schools to develop young people as leaders in cricket.
	• To assist organise and conduct coach education courses and distribute coaching resources to parents, teachers, and volunteers in conjunction with the CDM.
	• To implement the Community Cricket initiatives by undertaking School Support and Club Assist health checks (standard or abridged) and provide guidance, assistance and information to secondary schools and clubs on:
	
	  o developing strategic plans;
	  o establishing efficient organisational, management, and financial systems;
	  o providing appropriate playing opportunities and experiences for all players;
	  o putting in place a coach coordinator, coaches and a high-quality coaching programme;
	  o attracting and recognising volunteers;
	  o upgrading and/or installing facilities; and
	  o purchasing and maintaining equipment.
	
	• To arrange with RSTs and facilitate the training and upskilling of volunteers within secondary schools and clubs so they are better equipped to take on leadership, management, and administrative roles.
	• To promote and acknowledge the positive contribution to cricket of parents, teachers, and volunteer supporters who assist in the delivery and organisation of the game.

Measurement of effectiveness	• To report regularly on progress against the service level agreement outcomes and KPIs for the national development programme, and assist in evaluating its impact and effectiveness by:
	
	  o Assisting collect player and coach statistics to establish an accurate database for the association or metropolitan club to be used for comparative and future development purposes.
	  o Assisting in compiling an accurate asset register of facilities, including grounds, turf and artificial playing surfaces, and practice complexes within the cricket community.
	  o Contributing regularly at the MA seasonal preview and review meetings, and when required at NZC's annual national development conference, to share information and best practice.

Source: Abridged from Astle (2009: 81–83).

| ✓ | *Orientation/induction checklist* |

Introduction

- Welcome
- Introduce to key stakeholders
- Introduce to RST personnel where appropriate
- Issue with MSS manual
- Issue with CCC manual
- Outline association's regional development plan and general objectives
- Outline NDP's general objectives and initiatives
- Emphasise the importance of professional appearance, planning, preparation, teamwork, and timeliness
- Emphasise the importance of being self-motivated, proactive and innovative, but at the same time purposeful and patient
- Emphasise the importance of achieving development outcomes
- Indicate risk management need for 'reasonable care' in working within cricket community

Routines and requirements

- Hours of work
- Place of work – office/work space
- Vehicle availability and use
- Telephone/mobile phone availability and use
- Issue MSS and NZCT CCC clothing

Resources

- MILO resources, including promotional and programme giveaways
- School Support/Club Assist resources
- Coach education resources and presenter's kit
- Cricket leadership course

Responsibilities

- Discuss position, outline role and expectations
- Outline MILO initiatives, including school visits – purpose and organisation
- Explain and demonstrate with class MILO Cricket Skills Awareness lessons
- Explain and demonstrate with class New Zealand Cricket Skills Challenge
- Explain and assist run the MILO Have-A-Go Cricket coach education course
- Explain and assist run the MILO Kiwi Cricket coach education course
- Explain and assist run the Getting Started coach education course
- Outline Community Cricket initiatives
- Assist facilitate a health check
- Assist run a cricket leadership course

(continued)

- Assist organise and run a modified format competition, e.g. Quikhit (girls only), Slog Sixes
- Promote national development competition entries and assist with local preliminary matches
- Assist establish primary school, secondary school, and club partnerships or delivery agreements
- Assist compile a local development plan and annual schedule of tasks for the DA or metropolitan club

Recording

- Administration of MILO Cricket Centres, including giveaways and starter kits
- Database of MILO Cricket Centre coordinators
- Database of trained coach contact details
- Database of Year 8 and Year 13 cricket players' contact details
- Monthly reports of MILO and Community Cricket initiative outcomes

Source: Astle (2007).

CHAPTER 6

Implementing a sport development programme

Putting the plan into practice

Change is a fact of life. To be effective, NSO SDMs need to know how to strategically respond to change emanating from internal and external challenges to their sports' well-being. These challenges often require NSOs to make major changes to the organisation, development, and delivery of their sport. They require SDMs to recognise the need for change, design strategies to address these challenges, and provide leadership to implement these and guide their organisation through the change process (Parent, O'Brien, and Slack 2012). As Snedden (2017: 6) highlighted with respect to NZC's 'One Cricket' review:

> For the game of cricket to stay relevant and important to New Zealanders, what and how we deliver the game must keep adapting to the ever-changing needs of our actual and potential customers. We must not only strive to keep up with change, we must strive to lead change.

The intentional 'development of sport' at community level by NSOs inevitably involves major organisational change. NZC's planned, 'top-down' intervention to influence the development and delivery of cricket within clubs and schools induced a sequence of such change. This witnessed the formulation of a national development plan with clearly defined objectives and strategies; design of an innovative NDP embracing a series of initiatives to address these; and establishment of a regional delivery structure of CCCs to implement the initiatives, and in conjunction with volunteers in clubs and schools, translate the programme into practice. This chapter examines the change process that permeates a sport's organisation, its sport and its volunteers to enable this to occur.

This chapter will:

1. Discuss how NSO size and complexity affects their ability to initiate successful organisational change, and the factors influencing them to undertake such change.
2. Consider the possible variables of the organisational change process within a sport organisation, and its importance for NSOs to remain current and their sport to stay relevant and thrive.
3. Examine change models in business corporations and compare these with a sport practitioner's model of the approach required to introduce change into volunteer-run community sport.
4. Explore the role and characteristics of regional SDO and local volunteer change agents, and their significance in translating 'development of sport' change into practice.

5. Consider the use of health checks by SDOs to assess and improve club and school capability to sustain change.
6. Explain the national to regional system of plans, SLAs and reporting procedures necessary to underpin the change associated with implementing a NDP and monitor its progress.

TIME FOR CHANGE

Before introducing change, such as intervening into community sport to increase participation and ensure its success, NSOs first need to know why and how it aligns with their purpose, and why and how they intend to introduce it. This requires NSOs to understand their core purpose, that is 'why they do what they do', not just 'what they do' (Gryphon Governance Consultants 2011).

The ability of sport organisations to understand their purpose and respond to change is critical to their future success. Differences in this respect saw disparities between sports widen during the 1990s and early 2000s. Some NSOs remained volunteer-controlled organisations with simple structures, whereas others were rapidly becoming more complex corporate bodies, supported by entrepreneurial boards and professional staff with proven management, business, and sporting skills (Hindson 2006). The impetus for such organisational reorientation was either driven by a desire to improve what they did, often forced by financial or leadership crises; or for some NSOs, externally directed by central government sport agencies, who made formalised planning, professionalisation, and improved capability, prerequisites for the receipt of funding, often to prepare elite athletes for Olympic Games (Gryphon Governance Consultants 2011; Slack and Hinings 1992).

This variability among NSOs was often further exacerbated by similar capability constraints at regional and club levels; general complacency at these levels about their sport's appeal; and inflexible programmes catering more to preparing a few representative players than the enjoyment of most participants. This situation reflected the perceived high-performance demands of the sport, rather than the changing expectations of its club and school participants.

In NZC's case, their ability to respond to community sport challenges and change their approach, emanated from urgent internal and external governance, management and high-performance upheavals that rocked the NSO in the mid-1990s (Grey and Gilbertson 1998). This provided the catalyst and a mandate for change, and following a major review of its operations (NZC Review Committee 1995), it resurged in the latter half of the decade, equipped with a new board, new CEO, specialist managerial staff, and clearly defined vision and goals (Astle 2014).

During this period, NZC's resolve was tested as it restructured from a traditional amateur, volunteer-led sports organisation with few paid staff into a professional organisation capable of overseeing the newly emerging professional status of the sport and managing "the complex social, legal and economic issues and commercial interests of players and the sport business" (Hindson 2006: 32). Greater organisational capability, a more holistic view of the sport, improving alignment between NZC and its associations, and increasing revenue from sponsorship and media rights provided NZC with not only an understanding of the need, but also the resources, for the first time, to intervene into cricket at a community level, to expand the game's participation base and enhance its profile as a sport (Astle 2014).

THE CHANGE PROCESS

Sports organisations are in a constant state of change. Although change is a complex and continuous process, the magnitude, speed, and impact of specific changes varies considerably. According to Parent et al. (2012: 116), "throughout the lifecycle of a sport organisation, it will move through long periods of convergent, gradual change that will be punctuated by short periods of frame breaking, radical organisational change". While most change in sport is subtle and continual, the sequence of changes arising from the systematic intervention by NSOs to revitalise and integrate the organisation, development, and delivery of their sport at a community level, is more frame-breaking change. It introduces a planned, 'top-down', innovative programme and delivery structure which challenges the status quo replacing existing 'ad hoc' regional approaches with coordinated pathways of national initiatives.

To be effective, the scale of such change has to be accepted by most, and pervade the culture (i.e. patterns of behaviour, mindsets, and values) of the entire sporting organisation from top to bottom. This requires a clearly articulated and agreed vision of the change; capable leadership; sufficient resources; a coordinated plan and implementation schedule; and an understanding of the value proposition (i.e. the aggregate or bundle of benefits offered by the change) (Gryphon Governance Consultants 2011; Sport NZ 2015). These must be regularly and openly communicated with stakeholders. Because of the whole-of-sport magnitude of such organisational change, the commitment and funding timeframe for its progressive implementation needs to be long-term (i.e. 5–10 years) to embed it within a sport (see Chapter 11).

According to Slack (1997), organisational change is an alteration or modification in a sport organisation's technology; strategies, structures, and systems; people, including their mindsets and behaviours; and/or products and services. Change in these variables are "what organisations must adapt to, adjust, shift, or re-create to stay current, to keep or grow their market share, or to remain viable as an organisation" (Lussier and Kimball 2014: 164). The scale and complexity of the change introduced by NSOs through comprehensive sport development programmes sees all these variables impacted by their intervention.

REVIEW QUESTIONS

1. Why do NSOs vary in their ability to change? How is this influenced by the community levels of their sports?
2. What provided the catalyst for NZC to make change in the mid-1990s, what changed, and how did this influence future change to revitalise the development of community cricket?
3. If change is to be effective, what needs to occur in a sport organisation, and how long does this take?
4. What is organisational change and what variables are affected by it?

THE THEORY

The increasing interest in understanding organisational change within sports organisations has seen a growth in academic literature on the topic and within it new theoretical perspectives on change (Lyras 2008; Slack 1997). Most of these address the transformation of volunteer-led NSOs into professional institutions, often initiated by central government policies and funding requirements (O'Brien and Slack 2003; Slack and Hinings 1992). They look to account for the complex nature of organisational change and suggest this is best accomplished using a combination of theoretical approaches (Lyras 2008; Lyras and Welty Peachey 2011; Slack 1997); or identify the directions of change within organisations and recommend maintaining a balance between 'top-down' structural change and incremental 'bottom-up' improvements in organisational culture and capabilities (Beer and Nohria 2000). Slack (1997) highlighted the role of change agents in organisational change, that is, individuals who champion, lead, and implement the change, and their need to commit to the vision and have the energy and enthusiasm to develop a new culture within the organisation. The transformational leadership provided by change agents within NSOs and their RSOs is critical to the success of their 'development of sport' interventions. This is not a case of coming in, making sweeping changes, then leaving. It is about introducing, leading, and managing ongoing innovation and change to ensure over an extended period (5–10 years) it is internalised in the game and its organisation.

While these theoretical perspectives on organisational change provide new ways of looking at change, they offer limited practical solutions to the process, that is, to present an understanding of the sequence of practical steps NSOs must take to successfully implement major change through its organisation to impact community sport. Several researchers have considered the latter and designed models that conceptualise change as a process comprising a series of stages (Kotter 1996; Lewin 1951). These models have drawn criticism from researchers because of their simplicity, current relevance in the case of Lewin's model, and inability "to capture the temporal dynamic of change, or to address the fact that change is rarely a smooth or sequential process" (Slack 1997: 224). However, the intuitive appeal of these change models to sport practitioners is their simplicity, as they provide an uncomplicated means of framing the change process that is easy to explain and for stakeholders to understand.

A MODEL OF CHANGE

Tradition is a powerful force in maintaining the status quo. Change in a traditional, conservative sport such as cricket is not easily achieved, even if the change is perceived as advantageous. The introduction of NZC's NDP challenged the status quo (see Chapter 5). Such change required: better alignment, communication, and collaboration through cricket as a sporting organisation; improvement in the capability of its associations, clubs, and schools to implement the programme's initiatives; and alteration of the mindsets and behaviours of community stakeholders, especially volunteers, to accept and deliver these to participants.

The process of change, and how NZC planned and led the revitalisation of community cricket in NZ, involved a sequence of phases that began in the NSO, and then diffused through the sporting organisation. These were incorporated into a model by Astle to illustrate the change process from the perspective of a practitioner-manager (Astle 2011, 2014) (see Figure 6.1).

A subsequent survey of organisational literature revealed similar sequences of change proposed by Lewin (1951) and Kotter (1996). There is uncertainty, however, about the extent to which their corporate models of organisational change are applicable to sport organisations. According to Gryphon Governance Consultants (2011: 16) in a corporate setting it is possible to drive change through, however:

> for a change process within a sport. . . to be successful, the organisation must negotiate with volunteers. The negotiation happens at every stage of discussion, agreement, implementation and reviewing of the change process.

The change process undertaken by NZC, while similar to the Lewin and Kotter models, resembled more closely Astle's model, the main difference being the former corporate models assume change is imposed, and must be right to avoid stakeholder resistance and get 'buy-in', while Astle's sport organisation model recognises if change is to be pervasive and long-term, it must first be negotiated with and broadly accepted by key stakeholders (see Pause and ponder 6.1). All three models strongly advocate the importance of the need to continuously 'sell' (i.e. communicate and educate), and demonstrate the purpose and benefits of change. In cricket's case, this was because of uncertainty about the change and an ongoing desire to maintain the status quo, particularly among volunteers and regional administrators unwilling to take a wider view, where the perception was all is well locally.

PAUSE and PONDER 6.1

The do's of organisational change in sport

1. Understand your core purpose as a sport organisation, before introducing change.
2. Determine the objective of any proposed change, and ensure it aligns with and strengthens your core purpose. Remember ill-directed change is counterproductive, diverting limited resources, and dissatisfying staff and stakeholders.
3. Ensure the change process is driven by positive and committed leadership and involves all levels of the organisation.
4. Engage regularly with stakeholders throughout the process and communicate constantly the objective and benefits of change to get their acceptance and 'buy-in'.
5. Underpin change with detailed planning based on research and consultation with stakeholders, including a step-by-step implementation guide, and outline of funding requirements, sources, and long-term viability, especially if a SDO network is to be established.
6. Design and test initiatives to assess their effectiveness, and ensure they represent a value proposition for clubs and schools, before launching them nationwide.
7. Agree on the desired outcomes of change, establish a pre-change baseline or benchmark, and systems to measure and report these outcomes against this to show change has occurred.

8. Educate stakeholders by providing training and development opportunities to empower them to support and maintain change.
9. Improve the capability, capacity, infrastructure, and services of clubs and schools to adopt change.
10. Recognise regional and local variances, accommodate innovative solutions to deliver change as 'one size doesn't fit all', and encourage the sharing of best practice ideas.

Above all, remember that for 'development of sport' change to succeed requires a corresponding change in the mindsets and behaviours of stakeholders, and this takes time and commitment from a sport organisation to the process (5–10 years), for it to pervade and influence all its levels.

Questions

1. Why does change in community sport take at least five years?
2. Which three of the above measures do you think SDOs must put in place if change is to be successful in a sport organisation?

The Astle model identifies seven phases of change, together with a series of responses that represent specific actions to adapt to and introduce change (see Figure 6.1). The phases comprise:

1. Understanding the need for, and having a willingness, to change.
2. Readiness for change.
3. Planning and preparation for change.
4. Stakeholder acceptance of change.
5. Selling change.
6. Implementing change.
7. Evaluating change.

The phases were not perceived as linear, but more circular in providing ongoing feedback and positive reinforcement of the change becoming accepted as new practice. As Gryphon Governance Consultants (2011: 24) argued, "organisational change undertaken to achieve sport development, growth and sustainability, is not a linear process. It is a circular journey that is never completed." All the stages had to be addressed by NZC in planning and introducing its community cricket development programme. Astle's later experiences as a SPARC/Sport NZ consultant/facilitator suggested the speed NSOs moved through the phases and sequence of these can vary according to: a NSO's commitment and time frame; available investment; degree of vertical alignment within their sport; current level of capability; timeliness and quality of planning; programme design completion; relevancy and appeal of initiatives; receptivity by their volunteer base; coverage and skills of the delivery network; and effectiveness of national and regional partnerships. Such major change in multi-level sports organisations is inevitably slow and incremental, especially as it diffuses down through loosely linked, volunteer-based community levels.

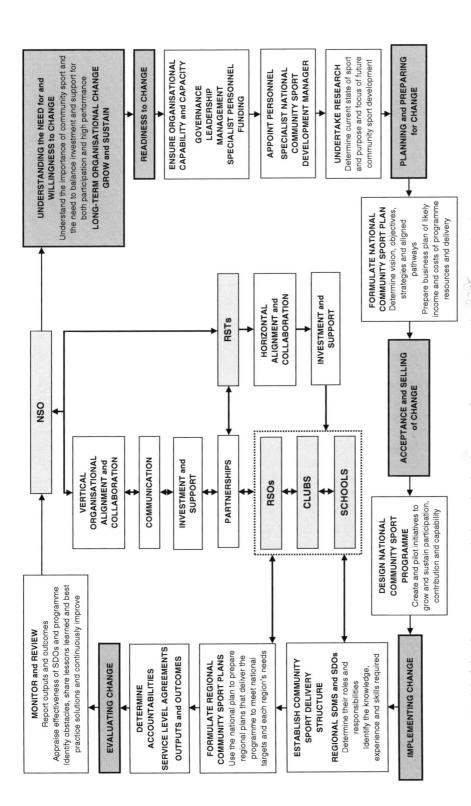

FIGURE 6.1 Model of the change process underlying the development of community cricket in New Zealand

Source: Astle (2014: 201).

TABLE 6.1 The phases and responses in the change process underlying New Zealand Cricket's intervention into community cricket

Phases	Responses
1. **Understanding the need for, and having a willingness, to change**	**Strategic plans**
	These were NZC's plans for itself as the NSO. While they reflected its vision for cricket in NZ, they were not necessarily subscribed to by its MAs and DAs in their regional plans. They did, however, indicate:
	a. An understanding of the need for change
	NZC's first strategic plans in the 1990s (NZC 1992, 1996) recognised 'why' it needed to influence cricket in NZ. Initially, this was to increase participation, primarily to expand its pool of talented players. There was no clear indication of 'what' this required and 'how' it would be accomplished.
	b. A willingness to change
	After the Hood Report in 1995 (NZC Review Committee 1995), a new NZC board, CEO, and specialist staff adopted a holistic view of the sport. This recognised the interdependence of community cricket and high-performance cricket, and the need to balance the development of both for the long-term organisational health of the game, rather than previously just high-performance cricket. They acknowledged this would require a comprehensive community cricket development plan and programme (the 'what') and appointment of national and regional personnel to formulate and deliver these (the 'how').
	NSO capability and capacity
	This was NZC's first meaningful response to the 'how' and involved appointing a national development manager (NDM) in 1998 to lead, design, and manage the process, and subsequently assemble a small development department, with responsibility for the development and delivery of cricket in clubs and schools.
2. **Readiness for change**	**Research, whole-of-sport overview, pathways**
	NZC moved beyond rhetoric, as they overcame the obstacles to change (e.g. lack of capability, availability of funding), to turn their 'development of sport' vision into action. According to Weiner (2009: 1), such readiness for change within an organisation refers to "shared resolve to implement change (change commitment) and shared belief in their collective capability to do so (change efficacy)". This aptly described NZC's situation, where like the first stage in the Lewin (1951) and Kotter (1996) models, readiness was created by 'unfreezing' existing mindsets and prompting a 'sense of urgency' through provoking dissatisfaction with the status quo in which participation in community cricket was declining, and proposing an appealing vision for the future development of the game.
	This readiness included NZC board's commitment to support change to the community game by appointing a NDM to create a 'big picture' overview of the sport through consultation, observation, and research. This provided a context in which to define 'development', identify its scope (i.e. community cricket in clubs and schools), determine its objectives, devise integrated, and aligned player and coach development pathways (Astle 1999), and ascertain the sequence of change and resources (e.g. financial, human, and informational) required to implement it. These presented NZC with a framework for change.

3. **Planning and preparation for change**	**National development plan**
	The above research was incorporated into a comprehensive national development plan. It was underpinned by an integrated series of development strategies (i.e. the seven 'Rs'; see Chapter 3), with linked sets of initiatives designed to grow and sustain community cricket (see Chapter 4). A 'top-to-bottom' organisational delivery structure was proposed to implement these initiatives. Each initiative was supported by standardised implementation procedures and resources.
4. **Stakeholder acceptance of change**	**National development programme**
	The plan was presented to the MA CEOs, who despite initial reservations about the extra work involved, and tagged funding by NZC to engage CDMs to facilitate the development of community cricket, accepted the plan and its emergent programme. This began in 2000 with the MILO initiatives, followed later by the Community Cricket initiatives, which together spanned the community levels of the game.
5. **Selling change**	**Collaboration with national and regional partners**
	Once the plan and its proposed programme was accepted by the MA CEOs, their benefits for the sustainable growth of community cricket needed to be sold to the DAs and metropolitan clubs. They had to be convinced of their value as NZC required them to commit 25% of their funding to employ a CCC or equivalent to implement the programme in their clubs and schools (see Chapter 5). As the programme evolved and its impact became apparent, initially through pilots, it became easier to market its mutual benefits to possible partners. In addition to the cricket partnerships with the MAs, DAs and metropolitan clubs, support for the programme was forthcoming regionally from RSTs, and nationally from SPARC, New Zealand Community Trust, New Zealand Cricket Foundation and corporate sponsors MILO, Gillette, and Pasgaards.
6. **Implementing change**	**Regional delivery structure**
	Most of the funding from NZC and its partners was used to establish a regional delivery network of CDMs, CCCs and a part-time, seasonal MSS and SCCs to implement the programme. Their number was dependent upon available funding and identification of suitable candidates. The process to get nationwide coverage was incremental, but by 2008 the network had almost doubled that anticipated by NZC (see Chapter 5).
	Regional development plans
	Once the programme commenced in 2000, each MA CDM was required to formulate a regional development plan and annual operational plan that addressed the delivery of its initiatives, inclusive of how their mutually agreed targets (outputs and outcomes) were to be achieved. Attached to these regional plans were the contributory plans of the CCCs in each of their constituent DAs and/or metropolitan clubs (see Figure 6.3).
	Service level agreements
	Each year the annual operational plans were signed off by the NDM and SLAs negotiated with each MA. These outlined the role and responsibilities of both NZC and the MAs in delivering the programme, level of development funding to be invested by NZC and each MA's contribution, and expected targets to be attained. In turn each MA apportioned its responsibilities, funding, and targets among its DAs and/or metropolitan clubs through subsidiary SLAs (see Figure 6.3).

(continued)

TABLE 6.1 *(continued)*

Phases	Responses
	Delivering national development programme
	The CDMs and CCCs were the primary agents of change at a community level. They were responsible for marketing the NDP and facilitating its implementation in clubs and schools. Overall, they successfully achieved the desired change of growing community cricket, increasing its flexibility, relevance, and appeal, although not always without obstacles.
7. **Evaluating change**	**Monitoring and reviewing for improvement**
	As the programme evolved, the annual collection of participation data through the NZC Census, and feedback from the regular reporting of the regional delivery network, was used to gauge trends and identify areas requiring improvement. Increasingly as the CDMs and CCCs, gained experience and confidence in their roles, they shared their lessons learned and practical solutions to local issues at the annual national development conferences, and contributed to designing new NZC initiatives and resources (see Figure 7.4 and Case Study 7.4). These opportunities to measure and evaluate the programme and its effectiveness provided constant impetus for further innovation and continuous improvement in both the programme and scope of its impact.

Source: Astle (2014: 202–204).

THE PRACTICE

NZC's response to each change phase in Figure 6.1 is elaborated in Table 6.1. It began in 1995, when leadership and management issues forced organisational change within the national body (Grey and Gilbertson 1998). The subsequent appointment of a new board, CEO and cricket operations manager mobilised commitment to further change. NZC adopted and articulated a more holistic vision for the sport, and through transformational leadership, provided a sense of direction and understanding of the need for change, and impetus for the design and implementation of a national development plan and programme to achieve this. This change process was initiated by NZC; led, designed, and guided by its NDM through its plan's vision, objectives, strategies, and initiatives; and translated into practice by its delivery network of CDMs and CCCs, who promoted and facilitated the actual change. They informed and persuaded volunteers in clubs and schools to accept and institute the proposed initiatives, overcame obstacles to their introduction, and where necessary, devised practical solutions to achieve the desired change.

NZC's programme challenged the status quo of existing practices and promoted change in the community game and its clubs and schools. The programme required a more 'hands-on', direct approach to: recruit and retain players and coaches, and restructure and resource clubs and schools to improve their organisation, services, infrastructure, and linkage. No longer was the previous laissez-faire approach of volunteers appropriate. Many sports were competing for players, especially primary school and junior club players, for cricket to flourish it had to be proactive, adapt, and be more organised in its pursuit of expanding its base. Complacency was not an option.

The programme offered an innovative, national approach to providing more contemporary sporting opportunities and experiences, and every occasion was used to inform and motivate regional administrators and local volunteers to convince them of their benefits. This required a persuasive value proposition of the programme's advantages and a guarantee that NZC would underwrite it. Any change had to be integrated, progressive, and add value as it required local 'buy-in' and contribution of funding to support the proposed delivery structure.

REVIEW QUESTIONS

1. What type of organisation does the Astle model apply to, and how does it differ from the Lewin and Kotter models?
   - What is 'readiness' and why is it important for sport organisations in the change process?

A CASCADING SYSTEM OF CHANGE AGENTS

Once the need for change has been accepted, with 'buy-in' from key stakeholders, its theoretical and conceptual dimensions must be embodied in a meaningful plan and programme. This formative phase of change is mainly the responsibility of national change leaders, especially a NSO's SDM (and national development staff) who plan and lead change, and create partnerships to underwrite it and enable continuous improvement within their sport organisation. The subsequent transformative phase of turning change into practice at a community level, involves regional and local change agents. This is where the real work of change begins. It is regional change agents (i.e. SDOs) who implement the programme and its new initiatives, promoting their benefits, and convincing local change agents (i.e. influential volunteers) to persuade their clubs and schools to adopt and deliver them.

In the change diffusion process there is a significant gap between the national design and local delivery of change. For sport organisations to diffuse change across this gap is not easy because of intervening obstacles at each level. To alleviate this requires NSOs to improve the vertical integration, engagement, and communication within their sport organisations. Localised resistance can be lessened by NSOs better understanding the role and importance of volunteers, and not assuming they will accept change unquestioningly and deliver new initiatives. They need to be consulted, convinced of the initiatives' value, and assisted to improve their capability to deliver these (Harris, Mori, and Collins 2009). This necessitates SDOs, as regional change agents, to be well trained, have credibility, and equipped with interpersonal skills to enthuse and support volunteers adopt the change (see Chapter 5). Among these volunteers, SDOs need to identify local change agents capable of spreading the change within clubs and schools. These are respected individuals, who convinced of the value of the change, are able to influence others in their own clubs and schools to adopt and deliver the change.

These regional and local change agents represent a cascading system responsible for diffusing change conceptualised in sport development plans, via programmes and initiatives, into practice within a sport organisation from national to local levels. They ensure national change becomes a local reality. It is imperative change agents receive constant guidance, support, and ongoing commitment from NSOs to ensure consistency of the change process and sustainability of its funding, as change takes time to embed in a sport organisation.

SPORT DEVELOPMENT OFFICERS AS REGIONAL CHANGE AGENTS

In the position specification for NZC's CCCs (see Appendix 5.1) is that of being a regional change agent, responsible for leading change before, during, and after the 'development of sport' change process (Schulenkorf 2010). Before: to encourage and persuade volunteers in clubs and schools to be involved in the process; during: to facilitate the introduction of the change, and guide and support volunteers to execute it; and after: to ensure through the ongoing education and training of volunteers, especially administrators and coaches, they have acquired sufficient knowledge, skills, and capability, to become local change agents empowered to introduce, manage and maintain the process within their clubs and schools (see Case study 6.1) (Phillips and Schulenkorf 2016).

CASE STUDY 6.1

Teachers as local change agents

Nigel Brooke, Manager – Community Cricket, Central Districts' Cricket Association, New Zealand

In many organised sports in NZ, a more balanced approach is needed to develop their sport in clubs and schools, as both are critical to their long-term future. In some sports, however, there still remains a strong belief, all participants should play for clubs and not schools. This was contested by Patrizia Torelli, who as Cricket Australia's participation services manager in the mid-2000s, tasked to reintroduce cricket into schools, cautioned:

> Once the 'schools' market is excluded from any form of development then it is virtually impossible to infiltrate again. . . [Because children]. . . all must go to school. . . it is one point you can guarantee access. Clubs are not able to access new participants in the same way.
>
> (Personal correspondence, quoted in Astle 2006: 13)

The initial thrust of NZC's NDP was aimed at boys and girls aged 5–12 years. It provided more opportunities for children to participate, have fun and learn the fundamental skills of cricket, and involve their parents and teachers in the game and train them as coaches. NZC's CCCs and MSS visited primary schools to conduct MILO Cricket Skills Awareness Lessons with classes, and enthuse boys and girls to register in the programme's initiatives (e.g. MILO Have-A-Go Cricket, MILO Kiwi Cricket) run by schools or local junior cricket clubs. Teachers were required to be present at these lessons to upskill them and assist deliver the cricket skills and games. After each visit, schools received for staff use, coaching manuals, and CD-ROMs of ready-to-use lessons, based on 'cricket', covering the curriculum.

For cricket in NZ, primary school teachers are an important resource, often being local change agents promoting cricket initiatives to youngsters and their parents in their school and community. In some associations, the CCCs ran in-service training courses to inform teachers about the MILO cricket initiatives and upskill them as MILO coaches and users of the cricket resources in their teaching programmes. This enabled the CCCs to engage with teachers, many of whom were female, few with any knowledge of cricket, and enlighten them on the opportunities and experiences cricket offered their students, and the free cricket coaching and teaching resources available to them for use in their classrooms, physical education programmes, or with their school teams.

In the Horowhenua-Kapiti District Association, the local CCC facilitated in-service training courses for over 160 teachers in 14 primary schools. Many of these teachers became influential change agents who advocated for cricket; promoted its benefits; and became involved in running MILO initiatives in their schools at lunchtime or after school; teaching cricket skills in their physical education programmes; entering boys' and/or girls' school teams in local or national competitions; and encouraging children and their parents to join local cricket clubs.

Questions

1. Why is it important for sports to ensure schools are an integral part of the equation in developing community sport?
2. What advantages do teachers have as local change agents for a sport?
3. How and why did cricket upskill teachers to ensure they were more effective change agents?
4. How did teachers and schools benefit from this?

What makes an effective regional change agent in terms of their personal attributes and professional capabilities? From Appendix 5.1, five characteristics, which reflect 'people' or 'interpersonal skills', are identified as prerequisites:

1. An outgoing and engaging personality, with a proactive approach, who leads by example (i.e. walking the talk), plans and prepares, has a strong and effective work ethic, and is well organised, professionally attired, and punctual.
2. A knowledge of their sport and the people involved in it, with an in-depth understanding of the vision and benefits of change, and ability to clearly articulate these.
3. An aptitude to champion change, challenge the status quo, ask questions and be questioned, negotiate and persuade stakeholders to 'buy-in' to change, but remain patient yet persistent, and build trust, mutual respect and credibility.

4. An ability to engage and work closely with volunteers, appreciate their importance and contribution, be approachable and receptive, and build a network of relationships within the community.
5. The skills to train and empower volunteers to take ownership of change, and support them accommodate regional differences, needs, and solutions (see Case study 6.2).

CASE STUDY 6.2
Cricket development officer: a regional change agent

Emma Campbell, Cricket Development Officer, Otago Country Cricket Association, Club Manager, Queenstown Cricket Club, and Programme Coordinator, Sports Coaching Solutions Ltd, Queenstown, New Zealand

I have worked in cricket development roles for 15 years in NZ, the Netherlands, and England. For the past three seasons, I have been based in Queenstown, NZ, where I balance being a part-time CDO for Otago Country District Association, club manager for Queenstown Cricket Club (CC), and run my own coaching and development company, Sports Coaching Solutions.

My CDO role focuses on promoting and growing cricket, mainly at junior level, within the Queenstown Lakes region, primarily in the tourist towns of Queenstown and Wanaka. I work with seven primary schools in Queenstown and five in Wanaka. I have built strong relationships with each school through constant communication with their Sports' Coordinators, and an organised schedule of regular visits. During these visits, I run structured skill-based activities and fun, modified cricket games with Years 1–8 classes, to enthuse children to register in Queenstown CC or Albion CC in Wanaka.

When I became the CDO, Queenstown CC had one senior (adult) team and 90 junior players. Since then through the school visits and community promotional efforts, player numbers have tripled to 230 junior players who play on Saturday mornings; and 80 seniors who play Friday twilight cricket, with 30 also playing Saturday afternoon club cricket. The junior players comprise: Years 1–3 who are involved in skill and small-sided game sessions; Years 4–6 play eight-a-side; and Years 7–8 play 11-a-side; the latter two groups are in school-based teams with their mates and begin each Saturday with a 30-minute skill session. We also host a midweek, twilight, social six-a-side competition that caters for 36 adult teams, and annually I run two midweek, social cricket festival days for schools – one each for Years 5–8 boys and girls. In 2016/17, this involved over 450 children. This rapid growth in player numbers is attributed to: Queenstown being one of NZ's fastest growing regions; the rapport I have created with schools and the structured programme I use to attract junior players to the club; the integrated player pathway I have established in the club which caters for entry-level to adult players; and the availability of coaches I have trained to service these players within a supportive club environment.

As a CDO, I constantly facilitate change, adopt new ways to grow the game (e.g. festival days), and ensure my school and club programmes are well organised and enticing for players. I regularly canvass feedback which allows me to modify and add value to my programmes.

My major challenges are: the lack of facilities, especially playing fields, as Queenstown continues to grow and land prices rise, and with cold winters no indoor training options; the considerable distances players and parents have to travel; the absence of coordinated regional pathways for young talented players; and the breakdown of NZC's coach development programme. To overcome these challenges, I continue lobbying the council for more sports venues; provide quality programmes making the travel to attend worthwhile; arrange winter trainings for talented players in local halls; and use my own expertise to train our coaches appropriately.

The key for me as a regional change agent is building trust and rapport with people. I do this by being open, engaging and using humour to break down barriers and illustrate the value of my programmes. If players are not having fun, they won't come back! I also constantly seek improvement so players can see the benefit of being involved in well organised programmes, that provide them with quality opportunities and experiences.

Questions

1. What is the role of the CDO? List four strategies she used to ensure her effectiveness in this role, and four measures of this effectiveness.
2. What personal attributes and professional capabilities have made the CDO an effective regional change agent?
3. How do these compare with the characteristics of regional change agents listed in the text?

VOLUNTEERS AS LOCAL CHANGE AGENTS

SDOs as regional change agents are tasked with facilitating national change at the local level with volunteers in clubs and schools of varying size and complexity. To establish a foothold among these, NZC's CCCs, although well prepared to market change especially its MILO initiatives (Astle 2009), encountered three different types of parent and teacher volunteers. The first type was receptive and easily convinced of the benefits of change, and readily introduced the new initiatives into their club and school programmes. Indeed, the receptivity of primary school teachers encouraged some CCCs to upskill them as local change agents to promote cricket and the initiatives in their schools (see Case study 6.1). The second type were initially cautious, but over time, having observed the impact of the change in neighbouring clubs and schools, adopted the initiatives into their programmes. The third type were more resistant to change. Interestingly, when this type did change, some became strong proponents for the initiatives. It was the first type of volunteers, who were open and responsive to change, that initially became the CCCs network of local community change agents (see Case studies 6.3 and 6.4).

CASE STUDY 6.3

Local change agent – junior rugby club volunteer

Craig MacFarlane, Investment Coordinator, Planning, Investment and
Performance, Sport New Zealand, and Junior Convenor/Chairperson,
Upper Hutt Rams Junior Rugby Football Club, Upper Hutt, New Zealand

Since 1999, I have volunteered at Upper Hutt Rugby Football Club (RFC) as a coach, manager, and senior club committee member, and also been a player. From 2011, when my children began playing, I became involved with the junior club, coaching across all the grades from nursery (3–4-year-olds) to an U12 years team in 2017; serving as its secretary; then in 2016 was appointed its junior convenor/chairperson. I brought to this role my passion for rugby, and considerable community sport development experience working previously as a rugby development officer for the Wellington Rugby Football Union (WRFU), and currently the national sport agency, Sport NZ.

The Upper Hutt RFC in 2014 amalgamated with the Rimutaka RFC to become the Upper Hutt Rams RFC, with responsibility also for the Upper Hutt Rams Junior RFC and Rimutaka Junior RFC, each of whom has their own delegated autonomy. The club is located at Maidstone Park in central Upper Hutt city, which has a population of 42,000 and is part of the greater Wellington region.

The Upper Hutt Rams Junior RFC currently has 390 players with a nursery grade and 20 teams spread across the U6 to U13 years grades. The U6 to U11 years teams play within Hutt Valley, the U12 and U13 years teams play across the greater Wellington region. Since 2013, despite the excitement generated by the 2011 Rugby World Cup held in NZ, there has been a steady decline in junior club players from 371 down to 309 in 2016, the most significant decline of the six of 19 junior clubs in the Wellington region to experience a decline.

The election of a new junior committee in 2016, including my appointment as junior convenor/chairperson, allowed me to use my sport development experience, and understanding participation needed to be supported by quality club infrastructure and services, to tackle our decline in junior players by:

1. Distributing a simple survey to players' parents for feedback on their child's experience of playing rugby for the club; the quality of the environment, opportunities, coaching, and facilities the club provided, and its organisation, communication, and areas needing improvement.
2. Improving and expanding communication with families through weekly emails; monthly newsletters; our website, especially for registrations; and most significantly Facebook. Regular coaches and managers meetings, and a more streamlined Grade Convenors structure have also ensured better decision-making.

These measures had an immediate impact. The feedback has seen the club focus on three key areas of improvement – player, coach, and club development. Together with enhanced communications, this has seen player numbers rise in 2017 by 25% to 390.

As a local change agent, it has been important to understand the key participation drivers for young people and provide relevant and appealing opportunities and experiences to meet their needs and expectations of their parents. My background in sport enabled me to recognise the value of planning to provide direction, understand the importance of volunteers so we have the right people driving the club in that direction, and seek partnership support for the club. For example, creating greater links between the junior and senior clubs, and connecting with the Upper Hutt primary schools' sports coordinator network, Upper Hutt City Council, WRFU, and our neighbouring Rimutaka Junior RFC. Rugby as a sport, however, also needs to deal with injury-adverse parents concerned about risks, such as concussion, and develop age and stage (i.e. ability) appropriate grades and formats, if the game is to continue to flourish.

Questions

1. What was the local change agent's role and what measures did he take to address declining junior rugby numbers?
2. Who did he involve in this process and how effective were the measures?
3. What personal attributes and professional qualities made him an effective local change agent in his club?

CASE STUDY 6.4
Local change agent – cricket club volunteer

Lauren Shaw, Secretary/Treasurer, Maniototo Cricket Club, Ranfurly, Otago Country Cricket Association, New Zealand

Maniototo Cricket Club (CC) is located in Ranfurly, a small rural town of 1,000 people in the Maniototo district of Otago. The Maniototo CC has a senior section of two teams and junior section of over 50 children. Since 2004, I have been the senior section's voluntary secretary/treasurer. In 2014, this role was expanded to include the junior section, and I also became a junior Years 5/6 team coach.

In the widespread Otago Country Cricket Association (OCCA) region, club players can travel up to two hours for a game. This places tremendous financial and time strains on both players travelling and parents transporting children to away matches.

Our biggest challenge in a rural community is attracting and retaining cricketers. While the Maniototo CC has a good base of junior players, it loses many at secondary school age who leave the district to attend boarding schools in Dunedin and Oamaru. This leaves insufficient numbers at Maniototo High School to field a full team, so their youth cricketers play in the club's two senior teams, alongside experienced players in their thirties and early forties.

Because country cricket has traditionally been an all-day sport, especially away matches, its sustainability has been increasingly threatened by people working weekends, and the availability of alternative, less time-consuming sport and recreation activities. The introduction of shorter version T20 cricket, and provision of age- and stage-appropriate formats and quality coaching by club coaches for our junior cricketers have eased these threats.

My role as a local change agent is to ensure our club is well organised, caters for the needs and demands of cricketers in a rural community, and is receptive to change in the game's development, but flexible in its delivery to best suit our circumstances of being a rural club. I also keep our players, coaches, and parents informed about new initiatives and upcoming club activities; and regularly communicate with the OCCA to arrange for their CDO to come and run coaching sessions for our players and training for our coaches.

Questions

1. What was the local change agent's role and how has she influenced the club and its players?
2. What challenges does this rural cricket club face, and how have they tried to overcome these?

Many of these local change agents were trained by the CCCs as coaches to deliver NZC's MILO initiatives, so they saw first-hand their value in attracting, developing, and retaining players and coaches. It was this group of volunteers who became influential in persuading others within their own clubs and schools of the merits of change. Through their stories of success, and the visible impact of the MILO initiatives on increasing player and coach numbers and skill levels, they convinced other clubs and schools to register in the programme. CCCs used these change agents in local and regional forums to advocate the success of the initiatives. As Astle (2014: 158) stated:

> having successful working exemplars of. . . the programme and its initiatives; and a growing number of local advocates for the programme, its resources, delivery structure and ultimately its impact; provided very persuasive advertisements of their benefit. They demonstrated what was achievable, how it could be accomplished, and what was required in terms of commitment, effort and funding.

These local change agents were not deterred by the demands of change or obstacles that sometimes confronted the delivery of the MILO initiatives in their club or school. To overcome these, they often resorted to their own local knowledge and experience to find innovative solutions. Two examples include:

- In a rural area (Wairarapa), with small, widely spread, country primary schools that catered for 5–12-year-olds, and where many students were transported to school by bus, teachers decided to run MILO Kiwi Cricket for all their students, irrespective of age. In conjunction with the regional CCC, they ran lunchtime coaching sessions once a week in each school during November/December, to teach their children cricket skills and how to play the game. This saved parents from transporting teams, because of the distances involved, to other schools which they had done all winter for sport. In the second half of the cricket season, during February/March, they formed clusters of neighbouring schools, and organised interschool, midweek afternoon matches.

- In a major metropolitan area (Auckland), a large city cricket club (Waitakere CC), after promoting MILO Have-A-Go Cricket in six neighbourhood primary schools, received 180 registrations from 5–7-year-old boys and girls. Because of transport difficulties and the club's limited facilities, the club convenor approached the schools and organised to run the programme for the registered children from each school on their own grounds. The CCC trained parents from each school as MILO coaches, and the club organised a coordinator for each school. The initiative was run on midweek evenings at each school, on a day that suited most parents, as it was they who transported their children and assisted deliver the programme.

This ability of local change agents to adopt and share such solutions is integral to the emergence of a 'learning culture' within a sport organisation. It allows volunteers and SDOs to learn and gives them licence to be creative and use local resources and circumstances to adapt solutions that 'best fit' variances between clubs and schools, and within communities (Gryphon Governance Consultants 2011) (see Chapter 7). This is essential for successfully implementing change in community sport.

REVIEW QUESTIONS

1. What are change agents? Who are regional and local change agents most likely to be, and what roles do they perform?
   - List two key qualities for a regional change agent to effectively influence change?
   - What is meant by a 'value proposition', and the need for 'buy-in' by volunteers for change to succeed?
   - In your club or school, identify a local change agent, and list three skills they exhibit that enables them to persuade others to adopt change.
   - Identify a situation where you have resisted change. Why did you resist it? By what means could a change agent have overcome your resistance?

CHANGE AND THE NEED FOR IMPROVED CLUB AND SCHOOL CAPABILITY AND CAPACITY

In addition to identifying and using local change agents in clubs and schools, it is equally important for SDOs to work with volunteer administrators to improve the capability of clubs and schools so they can plan, implement, and manage the delivery of new initiatives. This is critical for them to offer a well organised and supportive environment for current and future players, satisfy their varying needs, and cope with their increasing numbers and demands.

Many development initiatives introduced by NSOs, despite their best intentions and marketing efforts, struggle because they either have had limited engagement or 'buy-in' from volunteers who they expect to deliver these initiatives (Harris et al. 2009); and/or their clubs and schools are not equipped to adopt change or receive and retain an increase in players. Evidence of this is provided by the failure of legacy projects associated with major sporting events to increase grassroots participation, because their clubs and schools lack the capability, infrastructure (e.g. facilities), or services (e.g. coaching) to accommodate and sustain any increase (Macrae 2017) (see Facts and figures 1.2).

To ensure change generated by NSOs to increase participation is not thwarted, NSOs need to assist improve the capability, capacity, infrastructure, and services of their clubs and schools to support any positive impact of their development programmes on participation. To accomplish this, NZC issued its CCCs with 'health checks' to systematically assess the organisation and performance of clubs and secondary schools (see Facts and figures 6.1 and Figure 6.2); and a range of instructive resource booklets to assist them improve their capability and capacity to plan, develop, and deliver the game. The booklets offer guidance and information on how to improve club management and organisation, game modification and delivery, and services and facilities, present templates and exemplars of easy to adopt best practice, and identify potential funding sources.

FACTS and FIGURES 6.1

Health checks

What is a health check? It is a structured sequence of cricket-specific questions that CCCs use to examine the effective functioning of cricket within a cricket club or secondary school. The questions cover:

- **Organisation** – strategic planning, leadership, management, communication, financial management, employees
- **On the field** – players, men's cricket, women's cricket, junior cricket
- **Off the field** – coaches and coaching, volunteers
- **Facilities** – clubrooms/pavilion, playing and practising facilities, health and safety, equipment

Instead of a SWOT analysis, a CCC uses a health check with a cross-section of club or secondary school members to systematically consider each question and determine their level of compliance on a 0–5 scale. There is no '3' in the scale, so decisions need to be made on their compliance being below average and allocated 0, 1, or 2, or above average and assigned 4 or 5.

On completing the health check, it is easy to identify areas of strength (4 or 5) and those needing improvement (0, 1, or 2). The latter can be listed and ranked to identify their priorities.

Four to six of these priorities can then be selected by the club or secondary school and incorporated into a strategic plan to provide them with clear objectives and direction. For each objective an action plan can be compiled with details of what, how, who, and when it will be implemented.

NZC designed separate health checks for cricket clubs (Club Assist: Health Check) and secondary schools (School Support: Health Check), reflecting the differences in their operation and provision of the game (Astle 2001a, 2001b). In 2007, each health check was modified to include standard and abridged versions (Astle 2007a, 2007b, 2007c, 2007d). The abridged versions are best suited to small clubs or schools, these include only the essential questions, and take an hour to administer; the more detailed standard versions are for larger clubs or schools, and take three hours.

Questions

1. What is a health check and why is it used?
2. How is it useful in assisting a club prioritise, improve its capability, and plan for the future?

Subsequently, in NZ other sports organisations have created club audits, such as Sport NZ, but none have devised appraisals of secondary school sport provision. In 2016, Sport NZ replaced its previous organisation development tool for NSOs and RSOs, and online Club Warrant of Fitness for clubs to self-assess their capability, with a new online tool, Sport Compass (www.sportcompass.nz), to enable sport organisations improve their operations. To undertake the latter, Sport NZ provides links on its website for organisations to best practices and resources (www.sportnz.org.nz/en-nz/our-partners/Developing-Capabilities/Development-and-support/SportNZ-Repository/ODT-Resource-Links/). This is an online equivalent of NZC's resource booklets, but without the hands-on assistance of its CCCs to facilitate the health checks, but more importantly, assist clubs and secondary schools tackle their identified areas needing improvement, to effectively deliver new initiatives and sustainably grow participation.

CHANGE IMPLEMENTATION SYSTEMS AND PROCEDURES

Planning was essential at all levels of the game, to implement the change initiated by NZC through its NDP and achieve its objectives and outcomes. A coherent system of development planning and SLAs, with regular recording and reporting procedures, was introduced to provide direction and drive accountability through the sport organisation (see Figure 6.3). This was driven 'top-down' by NZC through its plan and associated systematic procedures, to ensure there were clear responsibilities and accountabilities in the regional development plans and annual operational plans of its six MAs and their constituent DAs and metropolitan clubs, with respect to the effective use of NZC's funding and delivery of expected outcomes. This reflected the claim by Bradbury and Inkson (2006: 140) that "broad plans at the top of the organisation are translated downwards to more specific plans for subsidiary units until, if the process is carried to its logical conclusion, each person has a plan for his or her work".

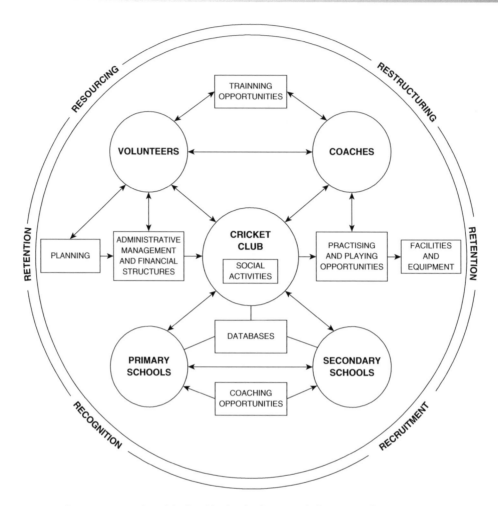

FIGURE 6.2 Community cricket club: health check elements, linkages, and strategies
Source: Astle (2009: 32).

A prudent and prescriptive approach was adopted to ensure the accountability through SLAs for the funding allocated by NZC to implement its NDP. 'Accountability' referred to the need to attain agreed national KPI targets commensurate with the funding invested by NZC into its MAs, DAs, and metropolitan clubs. This confirmed Eady's (1993: 18) contention that "in many organisations it is the advent of sports development which has provided the impetus for the production of clearly stated objectives and targets". This was certainly the case at NZC, where across other areas of the business there was only a professional expectation that national funding would be used to best effect, there was no specificity as to what, where, and how it should be done, as required through the NDP (Astle 2014).

The planning process provided a structure through which the objectives of change, in the form of the NDP, were clearly identified, development funding was appropriately allocated and directed, and accountabilities defined with respect to expected KPIs and targets. This was a two-way, interactive process between NZC and its MAs, and the MAs, and their DAs

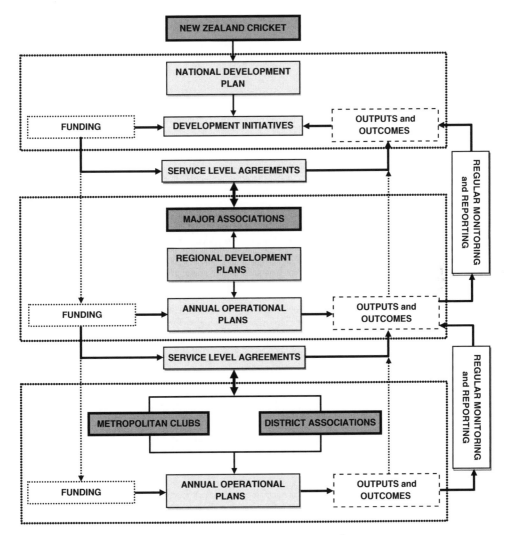

FIGURE 6.3 New Zealand Cricket's planning, implementation, and reporting system

Source: Astle (2001c: 20).

and clubs. It delineated and integrated the work programmes of the CDMs and CCCs and prescribed a constant flow of feedback on performance, progress, and best practice between them and NZC's NDM.

REVIEW QUESTIONS

1. Why do SDOs need tools, such as health checks, to assess clubs and schools? What are they looking to achieve? How important is this in the change process?
2. List the systems and procedures sport organisations need to ensure national to local change is structured, effective, and sustainable.

CONCLUSION

In the last three decades, many NSOs for varying reasons, particularly concern over declining participation rates, have realised the need for change. This chapter discusses the organisational change process and a practitioner's model of change in sport organisations (Astle 2011, 2014), conceptualised similar to the corporate models of Lewin (1951) and Kotter (1996), as a series of stages. Based on the design and implementation of NZC's development plan and programme, the model comprised a sequence of seven phases that NZC, and subsequently other NSOs, followed in planning and introducing programmes to improve their development and delivery of community sport. Unlike the Lewin and Kotter models, where business organisations could impose change in a corporate environment, this is not the case in sport organisations where the delivery of change is dependent upon volunteers. The Astle model, highlights the need for NSOs early in the process, to consult with volunteers about the plan for change and their role in it, and then ensure the programme devised to initiate change presents a value proposition, so volunteers 'buy-in' and willingly deliver it.

The chapter also considers in a 'top-down' 'development of sport' change process, the importance of transformational change leaders, change agents, health checks to identify and improve the capacity of clubs and schools to adopt and sustain change, and integrated organisational systems to anchor and underpin its delivery. At a NSO level, change leaders (SDMs) must engage with all levels of their organisation, and use the feedback, especially from community volunteers, to undertake detailed planning and programme design, and guide and enable regional change agents (SDOs) to implement the change in their communities. In turn, SDOs need to possess the 'people skills' to persuade and empower a network of local change agents (influential volunteers) to promote and deliver change within clubs and schools. SDOs also need the tools and resources, such as health checks, to assess and improve the capability of clubs and schools to absorb change and sustain the delivery of development initiatives. Furthermore, to underpin a national to local 'development of sport' change process, and support the effective operation of SDOs and volunteers, NSOs must implement an organisation-wide framework of planning, accountabilities, recording and reporting to ensure its effective functioning, regular monitoring, ongoing improvement, and sustainable impact.

REFERENCES

Astle, A. M. (1999). *New Zealand Cricket: National development plan.* Planning document. New Zealand Cricket, Christchurch.

Astle, A. M. (2001a). *Club assist: Health check.* Checklist. New Zealand Cricket, Christchurch.

Astle, A. M. (2001b). *Secondary school: Health check.* Checklist. New Zealand Cricket, Christchurch.

Astle, A. M. (2001c). *Community cricket initiatives: Community cricket coordinators' manual.* Instruction manual. New Zealand Cricket, Christchurch.

Astle, A. M. (2006). *Community cricket initiatives report 2005–06.* Board report. New Zealand. Christchurch.

Astle, A. M. (2007a). *Club assist: Health check (standard version).* Checklist. New Zealand Cricket, Christchurch.

Astle, A. M. (2007b). *Club assist: Health check (abridged version).* Checklist. New Zealand Cricket, Christchurch.

Astle, A. M. (2007c). *School support: Health check (standard version).* Checklist. New Zealand Cricket, Christchurch.

Astle, A. M. (2007d). *School support: Health check (abridged version)*. Checklist. New Zealand Cricket, Christchurch.

Astle, A. M. (2009). *New Zealand Cricket: National development plan and programme*. Planning document. New Zealand Cricket, Christchurch.

Astle, A. M. (2011). *Community sport implementation plan: Collaborative delivery and outcomes*. Planning document. Sport and Recreation New Zealand, Wellington.

Astle, A. M. (2014). *Sport development – Plan, programme and practice: A case study of the planned intervention by New Zealand Cricket into cricket in New Zealand*. PhD, Massey University, Palmerston North, New Zealand.

Beer, M., & Nohria, N. (2000). Cracking the code of change. *Harvard Business Review, 78*(3), 32–144.

Bradbury, T., & Inkson, K. (2006). Strategy and planning. In S. I. Leberman, C. Collins, & L. D. Trenberth (Eds.), *Sport business management in Aotearoa/New Zealand* (2nd ed., pp. 130–146). South Melbourne, Victoria: Thomson Dunmore Press.

Eady, J. (1993). *Practical sports development*. Harlow: Longman.

Grey, H., & Gilbertson, D. (1998). *New Zealand Cricket*. Unpublished case study by the Hillary Commission and D. Gilbertson. Hillary Commission, Wellington.

Gryphon Governance Consultants. (2011). *Organisational change in seven selected sports: What can be learnt and applied?* Sport and Recreation New Zealand, Wellington.

Harris, S., Mori, K., & Collins, M. (2009). Great expectations: Voluntary sports clubs and their role in delivering national policy for English sport. *Voluntas, 20*, 405–423.

Hindson, A. (2006). The evolution of sport management in New Zealand. In S. I. Leberman, C. Collins, & L. D. Trenberth (Eds.), *Sport business management in Aotearoa/New Zealand* (2nd ed., pp. 24–41). South Melbourne, Victoria: Thomson Dunmore Press.

Kotter, J. P. (1996). *Leading change*. Boston, MA: Harvard Business School Press.

Lewin, K. (1951). *Field theory in social science: Selected theoretical papers*, Ed. D. Cartwright. New York: Harper and Row.

Lussier, R. N., & Kimball, D. C. (2014). *Applied sport management skills* (2nd ed.). Champaign, IL: Human Kinetics.

Lyras, A. (2008). Organisational change theory: Sport for peace and development. *Chronicle of Kinesiology and Physical Education in Higher Education, 19*(2), 14–16.

Lyras, A., & Welty Peachey, J. (2011). Integrating sport-for-development theory and praxis. *Sport Management Review, 14*, 311–326.

Macrae, E. (2017). Delivering sports participation legacies at the grassroots level: The voluntary sports clubs of Glasgow 2014. *Journal of Sport Management, 31*(1), 15–26.

New Zealand Cricket. (1992). *The game plan: A plan for New Zealand's cricketing future*. Christchurch: New Zealand Cricket.

New Zealand Cricket. (1996). *Four year strategic plan*. New Zealand Cricket, Christchurch.

New Zealand Cricket Review Committee. (1995). *A path to superior performance: Report of the New Zealand Cricket Committee, August 1995*. Christchurch: The 'Hood Report', an independent report submitted to New Zealand Cricket.

O'Brien, D., & Slack, T. (2003). An analysis of change in an organisational field: The professionalisation of English rugby union. *Journal of Sport Management, 17*, 417–448.

Parent, M., O'Brien, D., & Slack, T. (2012). Organisational theory and sport management. In L. Trenberth & D. Hassan (Eds.), *Managing sport business: An introduction* (pp. 99–120). London and New York: Routledge.

Phillips, P., & Schulenkorf, N. (2016). Coaches, officials and change agents in sport development. In E. Sherry, N. Schulenkorf, P. Phillips, & L. a. N. York (Eds.), *Managing sport development: An international approach* (pp. 107–118). London and New York: Routledge.

Schulenkorf, N. (2010). The roles and responsibilities of a change agent in sport event development projects. *Sport Management Review, 13*(2), 118–128.

Slack, T. (1997). *Understanding sport organisations: The application of organisation theory.* Champaign, IL: Human Kinetics.

Slack, T., & Hinings, B. (1992). Understanding change in national sport organisations: An integration of theoretical perspectives. *Journal of Sport Management, 6,* 114–132.

Snedden, M. (2017). *Positioning cricket for the future.* Unpublished One Cricket Project Report. New Zealand Cricket, Auckland.

Sport New Zealand. (2015). *Planning in sport.* Wellington: Sport New Zealand.

Weiner, B., J. (2009). A theory of organisational readiness for change. *Implementation Science, 4*(67), 1–6. Retrieved from www.implementationscience.com/content/4/1/67 website.

Websites

www.sportcompass.nz

www.sportnz.org.nz/en-nz/our-partners/Developing-Capabilities/Development-and-support/SportNZ-Repository/ODT-Resource-Links/

CHAPTER 7

Monitoring and evaluating the programme

The increasing involvement and intervention by NSOs to develop their sports at a community level, coupled with greater expectations by partners, especially central governments sports agencies, has seen NSOs become more conscious of the need to monitor and evaluate the effectiveness of their programmes and how they are being delivered. This has required NSOs to measure performance against agreed outcomes and KPIs (Astle 2011). Their efforts, however, have often been hampered by a limited awareness of how, where, and what information should be gathered; outcomes that are frequently too broad, ambitious, and unclear; and a lack of baseline data resulting from ineffective data collection and interpretation methodologies.

Such limitations arise from NSOs' lack of understanding of the necessity and commitment to collect quality data, and difficulties posed in its collection by the lack of clarity over the definitions of key terms such as 'participation'. Few NSOs have invested in qualified personnel or systems to ensure the effective collection and analysis of robust data across the multi-levels of their sports organisations (Nicholson, Hoye, and Houlihan 2011). As a consequence, few NSOs have the capability to rigorously measure and assess the effectiveness of their community sport plans and programmes, have baselines from which to measure their performance, or appreciate the value of good data for planning, resource allocation, and programme design. Instead many NSOs in Australia, England, and NZ, rely on national sport agency activity surveys of once a year involvement by adults in sport and recreation. These provide views of sport sampling rather than participation, and give NSOs an overly optimistic impression of their participant numbers, but little evidence of the effectiveness and impact of their 'development of sport' programmes.

National sport agencies also often set vague and unrealistic community sport targets, and without the provision of adequate funding and resources, expect NSOs to deliver on these (Houlihan 2011a). In NZ, SPARC set arbitrary targets of 500,000 more adults participating and over one million volunteering in sport and recreation by 2015 (SPARC 2009). Australia and England have similar overly ambitious, difficult to measure targets. Furthermore, at a national level, frequent direction changes in community sport policies and programmes; and programmes being short-term with vague outcomes; and at a regional level, high SDO turnover and conflicting pressures for SDOs whether to deliver quantity (i.e. grow participant numbers) or quality (i.e. establish the infrastructure and support services necessary to sustain such growth) (Bloyce and Green 2011) have hindered the collection of longitudinal sport participation data making it difficult to analyse trends over time. Where participation statistics have been collected in a systematic way over time, such as by NZC between 2002 and 2012, they provide a reliable indicator of the long-term impact and success of a community sport development programme (Astle 2014).

While monitoring and evaluation (M&E) are critical at each stage of the planning cycle, this chapter will:

1. Examine why the M&E process is increasingly important for NSOs to measure and assess the performance of their 'development of sport' programmes, what factors constrain the process, and the reasons for this.
2. Discuss M&E in the planning process, the difference between monitoring and evaluation, and how each is used to measure and assess sport development programmes.
3. Consider the terminology associated with monitoring, and difference between outputs and outcomes as used by NZC to measure the performance of its NDP.
4. Discuss the system of collecting and analysing participation statistics introduced by NZC to provide reliable and comparable evidence of the long-term impact of its programme, and why its statistics differ considerably from national sport agency participation surveys, and the usefulness of the latter for NSOs.
5. Consider the monitoring system used by NZ's national sport agency to measure the performance of NSOs allocated community sport investment.
6. Use evidence from a longitudinal case study of NZC's programme, to explain its impact on the sustainable growth of participation in community cricket.
7. Explore the emergence of a 'learning culture' within NZC's regional delivery network, and its importance in fostering the creation and horizontal transfer of innovative local solutions.

REVIEW QUESTIONS

1. Why are NSOs now more aware of the need to monitor and evaluate the performance of their development programmes?
   - List three factors that constrain the process and reasons for this.
2. What is an arbitrary target with respect to participation? Give an example.
   - Why are such targets likely to change and what impact does this have on NSO programmes?

MONITORING AND EVALUATION

Sport development as a concept implies change. But "if this change cannot be measured how do we know that it has occurred?" (Simpson 2013: 125). Practitioners frequently perceive M&E as too complex, time-consuming, and demanding, and for these reasons they are not well understood, or undertaken for the wrong reasons. Too often they are seen as compliance to satisfy the demands, or justify the investment, from NSOs, national or regional sport agencies, and/or investors, rather than an opportunity to critically reflect on their own effectiveness, and the impact of the programme they are implementing.

M&E are threaded through the planning and design process (see Figure 3.3), where they represent the ongoing scrutiny of each step in planning a sport development intervention, such as: objective setting, programme design (strategies and initiatives); outcome and KPI identification, implementation, review, and ultimately, continuous improvement. The evidence collected is used to ascertain: 'what works?', 'what doesn't work?', and 'what needs to change, and how?'

Too often M&E is collapsed into one term, when in fact they are "two complementary, though distinct processes" (Simpson 2013: 125). Monitoring involves observing, recording, and reporting information as evidence of a sport organisation's performance. Evaluation reflects on this evidence to determine whether a sport organisation's performance is on track, or if change is required, or constraints alleviated, to make improvement (Sport NZ 2014). Monitoring of a sport development programme is mainly the responsibility of SDOs and volunteers. The collation of the evidence they collect, together with feedback from in-field SDO appraisals, independent reviews (see Case studies 7.1 and 9.1) and online surveys, and its use for evaluation purposes to improve (formative) and/or prove (summative) a programme's effectiveness (Houlihan 2011b), is usually a SDM's domain. Formative evaluation uses the quantitative and qualitative data collected to review a programme during its planning, design, and implementation to continuously improve the efficacy of its strategies, initiatives, systems, and procedures. While summative evaluation assembles the collected evidence, often as facts and figures, to prove at the end of each season, the success, or otherwise, of the programme to a sport's CEO, board, corporate sponsors, and national sport agencies.

CASE STUDY 7.1
New Zealand Cricket's One Cricket Review

Martin Snedden, Board Member and Project Lead, One Cricket Review, New Zealand Cricket, Auckland, New Zealand

NZC's NDP affected a marked change in attitudes towards the 'development of sport' process in NZ. Cricket was considered by Sport NZ "as one of the best sports in terms of programme delivery at grassroots level for children and adults" (Alderson, Cleaver, and Leggat 2012: B24).

The success of NZC's programme during its first decade (1998–2008) and its impact on the sustainable growth of cricket in clubs and schools was characterised by planning, innovation, community buy-in, and accountability. This contrasts since 2009, when NZC took its 'eye off the ball', of no planning, ad hoc innovation, loss of community confidence, little accountability, and limited influence on clubs and schools.

The latter reflects a shift in understanding and commitment by NZC's leadership, away from a holistic vision of the sport, back to prioritising high performance, especially the professional game, without due concern for its impact on community cricket which has been gradually marginalised. Seniority of its NDM role was reduced negating their advocacy and influence on the leadership of NZC and its MAs. Previous tagged development funding was untagged and no longer accountable, allowing MAs and DAs to use it for non-development purposes; and no planning saw its NDP languish and became fragmented. Long-term funding partners (e.g. MILO, Gillette) terminated their sponsorships; and CCCs and volunteers received little guidance and support to develop community cricket.

The success of the 2015 Cricket World Cup in NZ encouraged NZC to rewiden its approach to the game, to ensure it remained relevant and thrives. This was encapsulated in its strategic plan 2016–2020 vision 'A game for all New Zealanders; a game for life', and strategy of 'Growing the Game' (nzc.nz/media/9531/nzc-strategic-plan.pdf). To realise this vision and strategy, NZC instigated its 'One Cricket' Review of the game. This comprised two phases. The first was a stocktake of the health of the game, including research by PricewaterhouseCoopers (PwC 2016), an investigation of women and cricket (NZC 2016), reports on the state of cricket in each DA (Hill 2017), and insights from Sport NZ on actual and potential customers (Snedden 2017a). This revealed the extent to which "NZC has dropped the ball in terms of its guardianship, leadership and support of community cricket" (Snedden 2017b: 25).

The second phase consists of seven workstreams (Snedden 2017a). One is focused on community cricket and its effective development and delivery within clubs and schools. While participation in community cricket has grown, less so since 2008/09, there have been declines in the last decade in secondary school cricket, and traditional adult men's and women's cricket, although these have been compensated by increases in various social, modified cricket formats (Astle 2014; Astle and Hill 2017; Snedden 2017a, 2017b). CCC numbers to service the community game have also declined, with their roles being discontinued by MAs and DAs, or filled with administrative and coaching tasks (Astle 2015) (see Chapter 5). Furthermore, NZC's funding to its MAs and DAs is now untagged, so less has been available for community cricket development, and with no accountabilities this has been further diluted by some DAs allocating it to representative cricket (Snedden 2017b).

To address these community cricket issues, several One Cricket initiatives have been implemented:

- In Otago, its DAs were reviewed to assess the state of the community game, and recommendations made to NZC to increase its support and funding to the Otago Cricket Association (OCA) to rebuild its regional delivery network, urgently address club and school issues, and improve cohesion between the OCA and its DAs (Astle and Hill 2017).
- In Canterbury, a shared services partnership has been established between the Canterbury Cricket Association (CCA) and its DAs, to more effectively utilise their development staff and administrators to improve the capability, development, and delivery of the community game (Snedden and Hill 2017). A system of accountabilities has been introduced, including planning, partnership agreements, SLAs, agreed outcomes and reporting against these, and regular opportunities created for staff to share ideas and coordinate their skill sets to improve community cricket across Canterbury.
- In Canterbury, a progressive junior cricket player development pathway, comprising a sequence of modified, age and stage appropriate, modified formats, was introduced for 2017/18 (CCA 2017). Based on research into junior cricket by Cricket Australia (2017), NZC intends to adopt this nationally in 2018/19 (see Facts and figures 4.1).

Without a 'big picture' vision, however, these initiatives only patch NZC's floundering NDP. It had been nine years since NZC updated its national development plan (Astle

2009a). "Currently, there is no plan" (Snedden 2017b: 24), although NZC is committed to formulating a participation plan (Snedden 2017b). Because this was not completed first, there is currently no blueprint to provide a coordinated overview of intended change and future direction.

The dramatic juxtaposition in NZC's programme demonstrates there is no room for NSO complacency, as a lack of leadership, loss of focus, or diminishing commitment, can quickly undermine its foundations, lessen its effect, alienate its practitioners, and dissipate volunteer trust.

Questions

1. What is 'One Cricket' and what prompted its instigation?
2. What did its first phase conclude?
3. Although the second phase has involved several pilots, what is needed to direct the programme's restoration, and ultimately what will its effectiveness depend upon?

While the academic literature mentions the importance of monitoring inputs (application of resources to create a programme) (Coalter 2013; Sherry, Schulenkorf, and Phillips 2016) and the formative evaluation of sport development programmes (Coalter 2013; Houlihan 2011b), in reality this is frequently beyond the scope of many practitioners, because of their available time, limited resources, lack of awareness of its usefulness, and their own paucity of knowledge and expertise to undertake such tasks. For these reasons, the collection and analysis of data by practitioners needs to have a clearly articulated purpose, be planned, so it is straightforward, and not excessive so it reduces their "responsiveness, flexibility and innovation" (Eady 1993: 38) (see Facts and figures 7.1).

FACTS and FIGURES 7.1

Recording: basic data to collect

Number of players

This can be collected using information from player databases, or counting team numbers in a club, school or competition and using a multiplier (e.g. cricket uses a multiplier of 15 players for each 11-a-side team; this takes account of different players who play during a season).

- Number of primary school aged players (5–12 years):
  o Playing for primary schools v. junior clubs
  o Male v. female
- Number of secondary school aged players (13–17 years):
  o Playing for secondary schools v. senior clubs
  o Male v. female

- Number of adult players (18 years and over):
  - o Playing for senior clubs
  - o Male v. female
- Total number of players:
  - o Total number
  - o Male v. female

Number of volunteers

- Number of coaches
  - o Total number of coaches (a 'coach' is one who calls him/herself one)
  - o Number of these coaches trained and their qualification level
  - o Details for each coach – gender, address, telephone/mobile, email
- Number of officials (umpires/referees)
  - o Total number of officials
  - o Number of these officials trained and their qualification level
  - o Details for each official – gender, address, telephone/mobile, email

Capability

For each club and secondary school:

- Heath check:
  - o Being implemented
  - o Completed
- Strategic plan:
  - o Being implemented
  - o Completed
- Website:
  - o Being implemented
  - o Completed
- Coaching and practice plan:
  - o Being implemented
  - o Completed
- Facility audit:
  - o Being implemented
  - o Completed

This data is easy to collect and record. More difficult data is related to factors such as: ethnicity and length of time players have been involved.

Nevertheless, in designing a programme, there is a need for constant checking (formative evaluation – whether they see it as this or not) by practitioners, especially SDMs, to ensure it is closely aligned with their development plan's objectives; and sufficient funding is available to create the necessary support resources for the programme (see Chapter 4) and establish and maintain a delivery system to implement it at a community level (see Chapter 5). For these reasons, individual initiatives within a programme need to be devised so they are integrated within its pathways, have a clearly defined purpose, target audience and intended outcomes, and be aligned with specific strategies that contribute to achieving the programme's objectives. As mentioned in Chapter 4, initiatives must be piloted to ensure they are fit for purpose, easy to apply, and effective in accomplishing their strategic objectives. SDOs and volunteers also must be trained and conversant with the purpose of initiatives, how they need to be delivered, and what the expectations are in terms of outputs and outcomes (see Chapters 5 and 6). It is these outputs and outcomes SDOs record and report and SDMs collate to review the programme, in order to improve and prove its ongoing efficacy and impact.

Increasingly, enlightened SDMs and SDOs are monitoring and evaluating their development strategies and initiatives. Using simple email questionnaires, or readily available online tools such as Survey Monkey, they are able to elicit feedback from participants on the value and appropriateness of these, and any changes required to better meet participants' needs (see Case study 7.2).

CASE STUDY 7.2

Surveys to evaluate community cricket initiatives

Email questionnaire

James Carr, Cricket Development Officer, Southland Cricket Association, Invercargill, New Zealand

In 2016/17, a new initiative for girls only, 'Girls' Smash', was introduced as a regional initiative in Southland. It was a fun, modified six-a-side format for girls aged 5–10 years. It was marketed in the community, and 206 girls registered and were divided into 30 teams. Cricket equipment was supplied by the Southland Cricket Association, parents and teachers were trained as coaches, and short skill sessions were run prior to matches. These, and the match, took 75 minutes.

After the season, a simple email questionnaire was sent to a sample of 22 girls seeking their feedback on the initiative and its relevance. Their responses indicated:

- 79% had learned about the initiative through the CDO's promotional visits to their primary schools, the rest by a mix of word of mouth, an advertising poster, and Facebook.
- 91% indicated the initiative had increased their interest in cricket and excited them to play again next season.

Such feedback highlighted the importance of face-to-face school visits, and the fun the girls had learning cricket skills and playing a modified, girls only game in a short time frame.

Survey Monkey

Mike Harvey, General Manager, Christchurch Metropolitan Cricket Association, Christchurch, New Zealand

In 2016, the Christchurch Metropolitan Cricket Association (CMCA) used Survey Monkey to gather information from club and secondary school stakeholders as part of its consultation process to assist identify the organisation's priorities in formulating its strategic plan 2017–2019. Information was sought on: the reasons stakeholders played cricket and joined a club; the challenges clubs, secondary schools, women's cricket, and facility developments face; how they rated the CMCA's performance and what its future priorities should be. This provided valuable feedback to the CMCA on the direction and focus of its plan, and the strategies it needed to consider in leading, developing, and supporting community cricket over the next three years.

Questions

1. What did the CDO's email questionnaire confirm about the effectiveness of the recruitment strategy and girls' initiative? What were the reasons for the effectiveness of each?
2. Using the internet, find out what Survey Monkey is and how to use it?
3. What did the CMCA use the survey for?
4. Have you used a simple survey? What type of survey and what was its purpose? What was the feedback used for?

How sport organisations evaluate depends on their own needs, budget, and demands of external investors. They should, however, evaluate enough to provide a level of confidence in the effectiveness and impact of their programme, and to communicate a convincing case to stakeholders (Sport NZ 2015a).

REVIEW QUESTIONS

1. How is M&E often perceived by practitioners and why?
2. Why is M&E central to the planning process?
3. What is monitoring and who is most likely to undertake this?
4. What is evaluation and whose responsibility is it?
5. What is the difference between formative and summative evaluation? Give an example of each.

MONITORING PERFORMANCE: OUTPUTS AND OUTCOMES

In M&E, the language used by both practitioners and academics is not consistent, making it difficult to interpret what NSOs want to achieve with their sport development programmes

(Simpson 2013). Although terms such as outputs and outcomes have variations in meaning, they are often used interchangeably (Coalter 2013; Simpson 2013), frequently confusing practitioners. Sport NZ (2015a: 38) maintains whether something is an output or an outcome depends on perspective, so practitioners should not get too hung up on terminology, as "the terms are less important than achieving a shared understanding of what must be done, when, and towards what end".

NZC's NDP was measured by attaining agreed KPI targets with its six MAs. These targets comprised objective, quantitative outputs, or short-term results of the programme (e.g. numbers of players and coaches), and more subjective, qualitative outcomes or intended long-term changes in mindsets, behaviour, and structure anticipated through the programme (i.e. evidence of tasks completed leading to improvements, such as in provider capability, e.g. school and club health checks) (see Figure 7.1) (Astle 2014). The quantitative measures were statistical indicators of performance and counted annually in NZC's participation census.

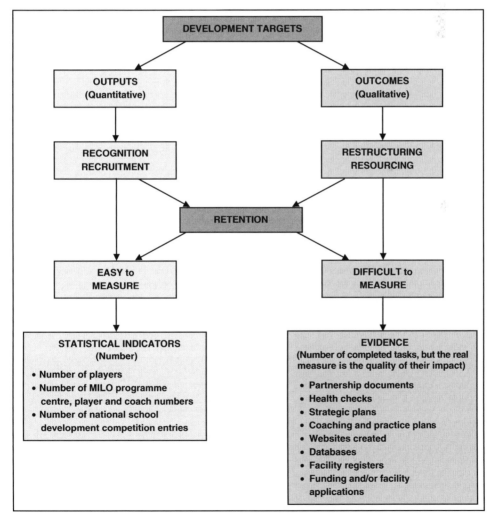

FIGURE 7.1 Recording and measuring New Zealand Cricket's development progress

Source: Astle (2009a: 62).

The qualitative measures were usually indicative of improvements, despite a lack of specific proof (Sport NZ 2015a). For example, while NZC did not collect player retention data, long-term evidence showed a sustained increase in player numbers. It was observed that more and better coaches were influential in such retention, therefore information collected by NZC showing increases in both coach numbers and qualifications was by implication considered significant in player retention.

For this reason, Eady (1993: 38) noted "outputs are relatively easy to define and measure, outcomes are more difficult to pin down". This has seen practitioners place a greater reliance on quantitative variables but using these as absolute measures of progress in community sport has its limitations. These arise from variable definitions of participation and inconsistent methods of collection (Houlihan 2011a; Mander 2013). Both these issues have been apparent in NZC Census figures, although between 2001/02 and 2011/12 a consistent system of collection improved the reliability and accuracy of the data (Astle 2014). A subsequent change in NZC's method of collection has reduced the validity of this information and its usefulness in evaluation and future planning (Snedden 2017a).

REVIEW QUESTIONS

1. What are outputs and outcomes? Give an example of each.
   - Is it important for practitioners to differentiate between outputs and outcomes? If not, why?
2. Why do practitioners concentrate more on collecting quantitative outputs? Do these have limitations?

OUTPUTS AS PARTICIPATION STATISTICS: FACT OR HYPERBOLE?

The key measure of success of NZC's NDP was the growth of the game as measured by annual incremental changes in player numbers. For over 35 years, NZC has conducted an annual census of participation. Prior to 2001/02, this was based upon returns collected from clubs and schools in the first half of the cricket season (November/December) by administrators from each of its MAs and their constituent DAs. There was no formal collection procedure in place, and because some administrators had limited involvement with clubs and schools, the census was a low priority at a time of the year when their focus was on representative cricket. This often led to inaccuracies that NZC needed to follow-up and attempt to have corrected. The 2000/01 NZC Census noted it was "very disappointing to conclude that associations appear to have very little interest in accurately determining a key measure of the state of the game within their boundaries" (NZC 2001: 5).

In 2002, a more systematic method of collecting reliable participation metrics was introduced that used a clearly defined set of procedures, definitions, and multipliers. This saw the census date moved to the latter half of the season (February/March); the collection of information become the responsibility of each MA CDMs and CCCs because of their detailed knowledge of community cricket; and the use of NZC generated standardised enumeration forms for each MA and its DAs. Instead of counting individual cricketers from each club and school, many of whom had limited or inaccurate databases, data was obtained by counting their number of teams, and corroborated for each association through competition entries. Multipliers were applied to these team statistics to calculate player numbers (NZC 2002). For example, a player multiplier of 15 was used for each 11-a-side team. While this multiplier may overestimate player numbers in 'competitive' teams in larger clubs and schools, it tended to underestimate those in 'social' teams and smaller rural clubs and school teams whose player base could range from 20 to 30 players over a season. Lesser multipliers were used for six-a-side (8) and eight-a-side modified cricket (10), while entry-level MILO Have-A-Go and Kiwi Cricket numbers were based on annual registrations received by NZC. To determine which players were eligible participants, 'participation' required a player to play at least six games during a season.

The use of the same multipliers from 2001/02 until 2011/12 provided a consistent measure of player numbers, which grew over this period from 75,479 to 111,829, and as such, was an accurate indicator of progress (Astle 2014; NZC 2012). For this reason, the census became a valuable document used at all levels of the organisation to analyse trends, gauge the effectiveness of existing development initiatives, offer evidence for the design of new initiatives, underpin strategic planning and resource allocation, and apply for external funding. It is possible to contest NZC's Census figures, based on teams and multipliers, as they do not preclude double-counting players involved in both Saturday and midweek competitions. The ongoing application of the same multipliers, however, while not negating this, did provide NZC with a consistent method of measuring participation.

NZC, like the NSOs of several other large organised sports in NZ, has tried without success to improve its collection of statistics using a national web-based player database (see Case study 7.3). Recently, NZC engaged CricHQ (www.crichq.com/) to create such a system for player registrations; however, as yet it is neither reliable nor useful (Snedden 2017a). Only New Zealand Rugby has a comprehensive national registration system for rugby players, coaches, officials, and administrators (www.nzrugby.co.nz/rugby_regis tration). For many smaller sports (500–10,000) collecting statistics is often easier and more accurate. Many have databases of their participants. although this depends upon the capability of volunteer administrators. Statistics from 34 smaller sports submitted to Sport NZ show a 35% increase in participants between 2011/12 and 2015/16 from 82,188 to 116,320 (MacFarlane 2016).

CASE STUDY 7.3
A cloud solution to recording and reporting participation data

Ryan Astle, Digital Marketing Specialist, Jade Logistics Group; and Vice President, Old Boys' Collegians Cricket Club, Christchurch, New Zealand

Recording and reporting accurate participation data is important for sports clubs and schools for planning, resource allocation, and securing funding. Many sports, however, still have poor data collection and collation systems using paper or computer (i.e. Microsoft Excel) methods. It is now easy for SDOs and volunteers to record and share data using a cloud software solution. A 'cloud' solution is simply software hosted on the internet, accessible on any device anywhere in the world, as opposed to software installed on a computer's hard drive. There are several free applications, such as Google Forms (www. docs.google.com/forms), which offer many benefits over paper-based forms or computer-based databases.

Once a club or school has created an online survey using a provider like Google Forms – which is similar to creating a form in Word – they will be provided with a link. This can be shared with participants by any appropriate communication means (e.g. via email or social media).

Participants can then receive a link to the online survey which they can complete in their own time. This can be done on any device with a web browser (e.g. Chrome, Internet Explorer) and internet access. Supplementary information can be provided to participants, such as terms and conditions, via a hyperlink from the survey.

Paper-based forms typically completed by participants can lead to administration errors because of illegible handwriting and manual data-entry. A cloud solution solves this problem, providing accurate data with participants able to choose predefined options or type and edit text.

They offer instant results with no need to manually calculate percentages or create graphs. For example, Google Forms collates all responses and automatically produces tables and graphs. Access is available to view raw individual responses, and data can be exported and saved in different formats ready to be printed or sent as an email attachment.

Permissions can be set to control access to results. For instance, committee members could be added as administrators of a survey, with permission to edit questions and see the responses submitted.

As with all technology, there are potential challenges in utilising a cloud software approach. Users may forget to fill out the survey or lack access to technology. These issues can be minimised through follow-up communications and providing a secondary method of collecting information (i.e. letting users complete the survey on a SDO's device).

Questions

1. What is a 'cloud' solution and where can it be accessed?
2. What advantages does it have over more traditional methods of recording and reporting participation data?
3. In a sport you are familiar with, what method is used to record participation data? What data do they record, how accurate is it, and how is it reported?

An alternative measure of cricket 'participation' is used by Sport NZ in their *Active New Zealand Survey* of adults (16 years and over) who participated in various sports at least once in the previous 12 months. Its 2007/08 survey indicated cricket participation had increased to 237,965, only exceeded by golf and tennis (SPARC 2008). While this broad definition of 'participation' highlighted cricket's popularity as a sport, it did not meet NZC's tighter definition, which required individuals to play at least six games during a season. For this reason, there is no comparison between the level of participation recorded by the NZC Census of 100,348 players in 2007/08 (NZC 2008), and SPARC's figure for the same period of 237,965 players. Furthermore, when 52,406 junior cricketers aged 5–12 years in the NZC Census are subtracted, leaving just 47,942 youth and adult players (NZC 2008), the comparison with SPARC's figure is even further exaggerated. The only conclusion is SPARC's figure is a reflection of those over 16 years of age who may have an active interest in cricket, but only 'sampled' rather than 'participated' in the sport over the survey period.

Since 2010/11, NZC instead of processing its own participation data, contracted an external company to collate its census. While this did not alter the collection methodology, from 2012/13 it changed how the information was processed, and how total participation numbers were determined. The latter now include individuals who had experienced "one-off type cricket awareness lessons even though they did not then go on to participate in. . . [NZC's]. . . playing framework" (Snedden 2017a: 21) (see Pause and ponder 7.1). For this reason, by 2016/17 NZC's player numbers had jumped to 175,000. This figure correlates with Sport NZ's broad definition of sport participation used in its 2013/14 *Active New Zealand Survey*, which revealed 187,000 cricket players aged 16 years and over in NZ (a significant drop from SPARC's 2007/08 survey) (SPARC 2008; Sport NZ 2015b). These Sport NZ survey figures are extrapolations, based on once-a-year experiences of cricket from a sample of more than 6,000 individuals aged 16 years and over (Sport NZ 2015b). The use of such figures raises a critical question: "Does a 'participant' include those that enjoyed a single 'experience'?" (Mander 2013). The answer from cricket's pre-2012/13 perspective was categorically 'no'!

PAUSE and PONDER 7.1

Pliable participation statistics

In 2016/17, NZC recorded its participation as 175,000 which included junior players having a single exposure or experience of cricket. During the first decade of the twenty-first century, however, as NZC's NDP gathered momentum, participation numbers increased, as did the number of junior players who sampled cricket awareness or holiday programme opportunities provided by the CCCs to increase interest and potential recruitment into the game. During this period these sampling numbers were never used by NZC as a measure of participation, but as an indicator of the exposure of children to cricket and the programme's sponsor MILO. The following table shows how easy it is for a NSO to misinterpret participation.

New Zealand Cricket: participation v. sampling

Season	Participation number	Sampling number	Total number
2001/02	85,812	82,540	168,352
2003/04	91,413	95,119	186,532

Season	Participation number	Sampling number	Total number
2005/06	97,262	93,188	190,450
2007/08	100,348	107,941	208,289
2009/10	106,916	96,317	203,233

Questions

1. If NZC had added its sampling and participation figures together, by what percentage would this overestimate its actual participation?
2. Why do NSOs use the larger figure? Do such figures have any value in the formative evaluations of their development programmes?
3. For a sport you are familiar with, what are their current participation numbers, and how have they been measured? Are they an accurate measure of their development of community sport efforts?

Sport England uses its *Active People Survey* to produce a similar broad measure of sport participation (www.sportengland.org/research/about-our-research/active-people-survey/) (see Facts and figures 2.1), which Simpson (2013: 123) describes as "helpful to a degree", although questioning the validity of its collection methods. The Australian Sports Commission, until 2010, used its annual *Exercise, Recreation and Sport Survey* to determine participation by people aged 15 years and over (www.ausport.gov.au), but since 2010 has accessed similar information collected by the Australian Bureau of Statistics in its biennial adult *Participation in Sport and Physical Recreation* survey (www.abs.gov.au).

Mander (2013), in discussing tennis participation in Australia, argues the selective use of participation numbers from national surveys by NSOs frequently distorts reporting and leads to exaggerated comments about the state of individual sports, often to satisfy stakeholders, especially central government agencies, to justify their ongoing sport development investment (see Pause and ponder 8.1). For this reason, Mander (2013: 1) asserted Tennis Australia's claims about participation "cannot be supported by any substantial and verifiable evidence due to current data collection deficiencies and resultant inadequate information reporting". A similar conclusion is drawn in Chapter 8 regarding Tennis New Zealand's recent use of participation statistics.

The collection and analysis of good quality sport participation data is a perennial issue for most sports. While there are limitations to the longitudinal participation data collected by NZC through its annual census, the systematic and coordinated collection procedure, clear definition of 'participation' and use of consistent multipliers ensured data collected could be utilised with some degree of confidence in its NDP programme to demonstrate trends over time.

REVIEW QUESTIONS

1. What indicator did NZC use to measure the success of its NDP?
   - How did NZC define participation?
   - What is a multiplier? Give an example. Why did NZC use multipliers?
2. How did NZC improve its method of collecting and analysing participation statistics?
3. How do national sport agencies define participation in their sport and recreation surveys?
   - Why do NSOs use these participation statistics? Do they provide a genuine measure of the impact of their programmes?

OUTCOMES AND KEY PERFORMANCE INDICATORS

NZC used both outputs and outcomes to measure and assess performance. In doing so, it considered outcomes to be qualitative indicators of longer-term changes in mindsets and systems in the organisation and delivery of community sport. In NZ, SPARC made no distinction between outputs and outcomes, classifying all measures of NSO performance as outcomes. These outcomes reflected the key goals and objectives of SPARC's strategic plan 2009–2015 (SPARC 2009) and community sport strategy (SPARC 2010).

For over two decades, NZ's national sport agencies provided NSOs with sport development investment that had variable outcomes and little accountability. Since 2009, a 'development of sport' refocus by SPARC heralded a change in their expectations of NSOs. This required NSOs receiving 'community sport investment' to be accountable for this funding, and identify and/or devise strategies and initiatives to effectively deliver SPARC's six agreed community sport outcomes (SPARC 2010) (see Table 7.1).

For each of SPARC's outcomes, one or more SMART (specific, measurable, achievable, relevant, and time-bound) KPIs were established (see Table 7.2), against which all NSOs' performance was assessed. Because of variance in NSO characteristics and differences in their delivery methods, SPARC negotiated a schedule with each NSO, including only those outcomes and KPIs pertinent to that sport. For example, motor racing did not deliver a FMS programme, so this outcome and KPI were not applicable to them. Once a schedule of relevant outcomes and KPIs was established, NSOs were then required to identify their strategies and initiatives to successfully deliver these (see Table 7.2).

In the first year of investment, many NSOs first had to establish monitoring systems and baseline data. For these NSOs, their investment schedules specified KPI targets would only be negotiated when baseline data had been gathered. For those NSOs with available baseline data, KPI targets were negotiated for 2010/11 and beyond (see Table 7.2) (NZC 2010).

TABLE 7.1 NSO community sport outcomes

SPARC strategic focus	Community sport outcomes
Participation	An increase in the level of fundamental movement and basic sport skills in primary school-aged children.
	More young people participating in sport through clubs and organised events.
	More young people participating in organised sport in primary and secondary schools.
	An increase in the number of adults participating in clubs and organised events.
Contribution	An increase in the number and quality of volunteers, especially coaches.
Capability	Improved ability of national and regional sporting organisations to deliver sport in communities.

Source: Astle (2011a: 4).

TABLE 7.2 New Zealand Cricket: sample of community sport investment plan outcomes and KPIs

SPARC		New Zealand Cricket	
Outcomes	Key performance indicators	NSO strategies and initiatives	Measures
An increase in the level of fundamental movement and basic sport skills in primary school-aged children	X increase in the number of children participating in FMS programmes	MILO Cricket Skills Awareness Lessons in primary schools or through holiday programmes MILO Have-A-Go Cricket MILO Kiwi Cricket New Zealand Cricket Skills Challenge	9% increase in number of children participating in FMS programmes 2009/10 baseline: 10,900 registered participants 2010/11 + 2.5% = 11,173 2011/12 + 3.0% = 11,500 2012/13 + 3.5% = 11,881
More young people participating in organised sport through primary and secondary schools	X increase in the number of young people participating in formal organised sport through primary schools	MILO Have-A-Go Cricket MILO Kiwi Cricket New Zealand Cricket Skills Challenge Integrated Junior Cricket pathway programme – competitive and social, modified and traditional, midweek and weekends, girls and boys MILO Cup (boys) and Shield (girls) primary schools' national competitions	6% increase in number of 11,500 young people participating in organised sport through primary schools and junior clubs 2009/10 baseline: 61,050 2010/11 + 1.5% = 61,966 2011/12 + 2.0% = 63,187 2012/13 + 2.5% = 64,713

| X increase in the number of young people participating in formal organised sport through secondary schools | Integrated Youth Cricket pathway programme – competitive and social, modified and traditional, midweek and weekend, girls and boys

Interschool fixtures

Gillette Cup (senior boys), New Zealand Trust Cups (girls and junior boys) national secondary school cricket competitions

Secondary School Coordinators operating in select secondary schools to strengthen and grow the game | 6% increase in number of young people participating in organised sport through secondary schools

2009/10 baseline: 19,950
2010/11 + 1.5% = 20,249
2011/12 + 2.0% = 20,648
2012/13 + 2.5% = 21,147 |

Source: NZC (2010) and Sport NZ (2015a).

REVIEW QUESTIONS

1. How did SPARC measure NSOs' performance?
    *   What is a KPI? Provide an example of an aligned outcome, KPI, and KPI target.
    *   What is a baseline, and how is it used to measure progress?

THE IMPACT

"One of the challenges for sport development resides in the paucity of longitudinal data on the long-term outcome or impact of interventions" (Simpson 2013: 122). The absence of such evidence has frequently been equated with the absence of impact (Houlihan 2011b). In 2014, Astle used his experience and insights as a practitioner-manager to construct an in-depth, longitudinal case study of NZC's planned intervention during its first decade (1998–2008) to revitalise and grow community cricket (Astle 2014). Player numbers which had declined from the mid-1990s until 2000/01 when NZC's NDP was phased in, subsequently witnessed a significant increase. From 2000/01 to 2008/09 player numbers increased from 75,479 to 104,880, or by 29,401 (see Figure 7.2) (Astle 2014: 221). This represented a 39% increase over this period at an annual average growth rate of 4.9%. This trend continued until 2011/12, when player numbers reached 111,829, an increase of 36,350 players or 48.2% since 2000/01, although the overall annual average growth rate had slowed slightly to 4.4% (NZC 2012). Unfortunately, as mentioned previously, since 2011/12 NZC's method of data processing has changed, making subsequent comparison difficult.

When cricket's growth rate for the period 2000–2008 was compared by Astle (2014) to other sports in NZ with over 25,000 participants, its rate was more than double the nearest sports, which were hockey at 15.2% and netball at 14.6%. (Astle 2011). This comparatively

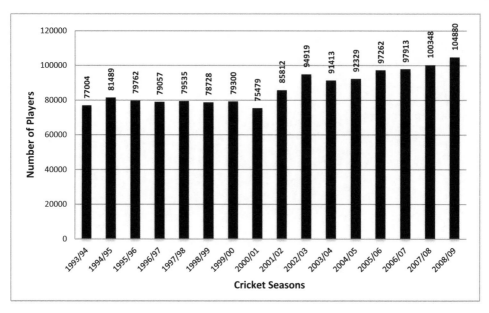

FIGURE 7.2 Total cricket player numbers in New Zealand, 1993/94 to 2008/09

Source: Astle (2014: 221).

high rate of growth in participation for cricket reflected the presence and impact of its emergent regional SDO delivery network in facilitating NZC's NDP. While other factors may have contributed, the constant influence of a cohesive regional delivery network was instrumental in using the programme to increase the game's appeal, secure volunteers, and enhance the organisation of clubs and schools to support this growth in player numbers.

The increase in player numbers was not the only significant indicator of growth in the game between 2000 and 2008. Coach numbers also grew considerably. Following the formulation of NZC's coach development pathway in 2000 (Astle 2000a), and inclusion of introductory, non-examinable MILO Have-A-Go Cricket, MILO Kiwi Cricket, and Getting Started in Coaching a Cricket Team coaching courses, a major increase was recorded in teacher and parent involvement as coaches (Astle 2000b, 2000c, 2004). During this period, 14,814 coaches, 40% female, completed one or more of these three courses. These coaches frequently became so engrossed in the game, initially through their children, they subsequently also volunteered for other vital organisational roles – scorers, umpires, and administrators. Their contribution has been considerable to growing the game and sustaining its growth. While increasing player and coach numbers as outputs are measures of growth, their obvious connectivity was a strong factor in sustaining this growth in the game (see Figure 7.3).

The impact of NZC's NDP on community cricket was widespread. Table 7.3 outlines the various measures used to monitor and evaluate the programme's performance. It summarises its key objectives for each community cricket level and identifies for each objective the expected outputs and/or outcomes. While performance against each of these outputs and/or outcomes was a reflection of the success of the programme, taken together they were indicative of its impact which was showcased by the overall growth in participation (Astle 2014).

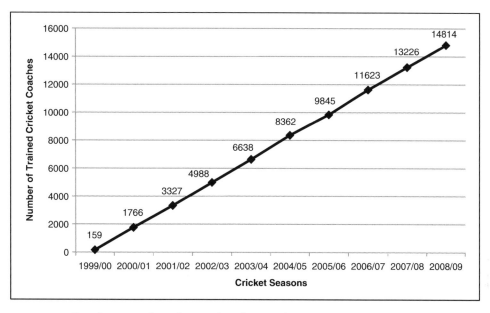

FIGURE 7.3 Cumulative number of trained cricket coaches

Source: © Astle.

REVIEW QUESTIONS

1. What evidence, and over what period, did NZC provide to indicate the impact of its programme?
   - How did this compare with other similar-sized sports during this period?
2. What did NZC suggest was crucial to facilitating its level of impact?
3. What measures, other than participation statistics, were used by NZC to measure impact?

FOSTERING REGIONAL VARIANCES AND SOLUTIONS THROUGH A LEARNING CULTURE

As NZC's NDP matured, while its core development principles remained non-negotiable, its method of delivery was sufficiently flexible to accommodate regional variances as 'one size does not fit all'. The acceptance of such variances by NZC's NDM arose out of a commitment to challenge the status quo, and encouragement and support for the CDM and CCC network to learn and try new ways of doing things to continuously improve their effectiveness and value of the programme in their communities. Coming from an educational background, the NDM understood the importance of perpetual learning, including the creation of an environment conducive to this, and the need for cricket as an organisation and a sport to "be

TABLE 7.3 Development programme objectives, outputs, and outcomes, 2000–2008

Primary/junior level		Secondary/youth level		Club/adult level	
Objectives	**Outputs/outcomes**	**Objectives**	**Outputs/outcomes**	**Objectives**	**Outputs/outcomes**
• More children playing cricket	• Number of children playing	• Maintain broad base of young people playing cricket	• Number of young people playing	• Maintain broad base of adults people playing cricket	• Number of adults playing
• Positive experience - fun and skill development	• Number of students attending MILO Cricket Skills Awareness Lessons and Holiday Clinics • Number of MILO Cricket Centres • Number of MILO participants • Proportion of MILO participants to overall NZC participants • Number of schools entering MILO competitions • Number of students in MILO competitions	• Offer a range of versions of the game to cater for different needs, interests and abilities	• Promotion and support for shorter versions of the game	• Offer a range of versions of the game to cater for different needs, interests and abilities	• Promotion and support for shorter versions of the game
		• More parents and teachers as volunteers, especially trained as coaches	• Number of coaches trained • Volunteers acknowledged	• More volunteers, especially trained as coaches, and the acknowledgement of their contribution	• Number of coaches trained • Volunteers acknowledged
		• More opportunities for skill development, leadership, and advancement	• Establishment and maintenance of national secondary school competitions • Number of schools entered in competitions • Number of students in competitions • Evidence of school coaching and practice plans • Availability of cricket leadership course	• More opportunities for skill development, leadership and advancement	• Maintenance of national club competition • Evidence of club coaching and practice plans
• More parents and teachers trained as coaches and supported with resources	• Number of coaches trained • List of coaching resources • List of specific initiatives and resources for teachers • Equipment donations • Number of facilities supported with funding	• Improved capability – organisation, infrastructure, and services	• Number of School Support health checks • Number of strategic plans formulated • List of resources • Number of facilities supported with funding	• Improved capability – organisation, infrastructure and services	• Number of Club Assist health checks • Number of strategic plans formulated • List of resources • Number of facilities supported with funding
				• Establishment of club–school links	• Evidence of club–school links

Source: © Astle.

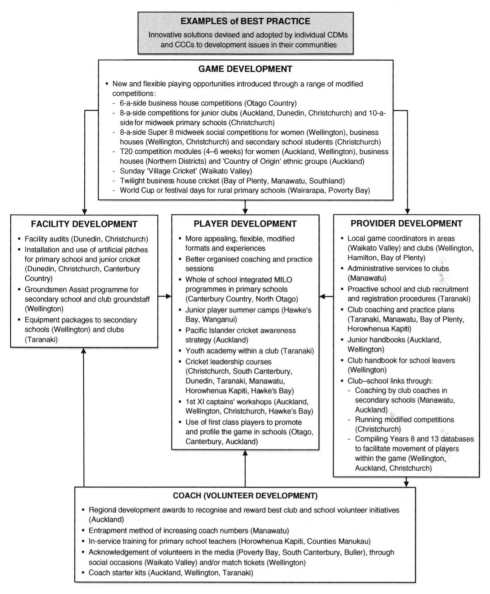

FIGURE 7.4 Innovative solutions designed and adopted by individual CDMs and CCCs

Source: Astle (2014: 238).

prepared to change or modify the way it does things to continue to be successful" (Schein 2010, quoted in Johnson 2014: 229). As Kerr (2013: 72) noted, "accomplished leaders create an environment in which their people can develop their skills, their knowledge and their character. This leads to a learning environment and a culture of curiosity, innovation and continuous improvement." Over time the NDM not only sought knowledge and insights from other sports organisations and practitioners, but also increasingly exchanged ideas with the CDMs and CCCs, many of whom were constantly seeking to improve and contribute to the learning process.

This saw the emergence of a 'learning culture' (Schein 2010) within NZC's NDP, which valued reflection and experimentation, and maximised the collective knowledge and experience of the CDMs and CCCs, whose in-field problem-solving created innovative solutions to local development issues (see Figure 7.4 and Case study 7.4), and saw them increasingly contribute to designing and piloting new national initiatives and resources (Astle 2003, 2006a, 2006b, 2009b; Astle and Clinton 2008). This 'learning culture' recognised "the fact that nobody. . . [has]. . . the capacity to know everything. . . [so encouraged a]. . . commitment to continuous learning and the development of individual problem-solving" (Johnson 2014: 240) within the NDP, enhancing its impact. It also fostered trust, respect, and the horizontal transfer and sharing of individual ideas and solutions by CDMs and CCCs, regionally at MA review meetings, and nationally at annual National Development Conferences and District Forums (see Case study 7.4).

CASE STUDY 7.4
Innovative regional solutions

Integration of MILO initiatives in primary schools

Blair Franklin, former Community Cricket Coordinator, Canterbury Country Cricket Association, New Zealand

The MILO programme, aimed at youngsters 5–12 years of age, comprised an integrated series of initiatives, spanning the primary school curriculum for Years 1–8. Instead of implementing the initiatives individually in schools, the CCC in Canterbury Country persuaded several schools to incorporate the initiatives into a whole-of-school, physical education programme. This saw MILO Have-A-Go Cricket offered to Years 1/2, MILO Kiwi Cricket to Years 3/4, modified cricket matches (MILO Trophy and League) to Years 5/6, and the New Zealand Cricket Skills Challenge and MILO Cup and Shield to Years 7/8. The programme was generic in its skill development opportunities, but specific in its cricket experience. Teachers received in-service training from the CCC, were supplied with appropriate resources to deliver the initiatives to their classes, and provided with ongoing assistance, encouragement and guidance. NZC donated sufficient equipment to each school to kick-start its in-school programme.

Country of origin competition

Peter Clinton, former Cricket Development Manager, and Kieran McMillan, former Community Cricket Coordinator, Auckland Cricket Association, New Zealand

To expand cricket's appeal and grow the game, the Auckland Cricket Association (ACA) set up a 'country of origin' T20 competition to cater for Auckland's culturally diverse communities that share a common interest in cricket. The competition included eight local teams representative of: India, Sri Lanka, Pakistan, Samoa, Niue, Cook Islands, Tonga, and South Africa–Zimbabwe. They played on Sunday afternoons on artificial pitches in South Auckland. The competition's objectives were to bring together these communities, share their experiences of life in NZ, and encourage their ongoing participation in cricket. It also provided an opportunity for them to try T20 cricket, and the ACA to assess the suitability of this format for social cricket.

Questions

1. How did the first solution create a widespread cricket experience in primary schools?
2. What did the second solution provide?

SYSTEM FOR MONITORING AND EVALUATION

Successful 'development of sport' practice requires careful planning, programme design, implementation of initiatives, monitoring of performance, and an overall evaluation of the programme which should be feed into research and programme improvement (Eady 1993). To achieve this, NZC aligned its planning and implementation system from top to bottom (see Figure 6.3). This required each of NZC's six MAs to produce regional development plans and annual operational plans, and sign SLAs to account for NZC annual disbursement of development funding, through a regular monitoring and reporting schedule. Every month, each MA CDM collated and forwarded a report to NZC's NDM on their progress in delivering the agreed KPI targets. The MA reports were based on monthly metrics and feedback from each of their regional CCCs about the delivery of the programme in their schools and clubs. At the end of the season, each CDM aggregated their monthly reports to produce an annual MA summative development report for NZC's NDM (Astle 2009a).

After initially requiring the CDMs and CCCs to fill out a detailed report for each month, the NDM following feedback from these practitioners about the time it took to complete these, condensed their reporting obligations into an easy-to-use, one-page report (Astle 2009a). This enabled them to record numbers against their mandatory participation, coach development, and provider capability tasks, with space provided for bullet-point comments about the programme, school, and club visits, attendance at local and/or regional meetings, and relevant media releases about their activities.

At the end of each cricket season, the NDM undertook a thorough evaluation process, which served both summative and formative purposes. First, a summative evaluation report was prepared for NZC's board, the national sport agency, and key sponsors, with "detailed facts and figures in an objective analysis of the current impact and future direction of the programme" (Eady 1993: 39–40). This was also circulated to the MA CEOs, CDMs, and their CCCs. The report was only completed once the NDM had received all the MA summative reports; attended post-season regional forums with the CDMs and CCCs in each MA; and organised and run NZC's annual National Development Conference, attended by the CDMs and a selection of their CCCs. Second, a formative evaluation was undertaken by the NDM to assess the impact of the NDP and its specific initiatives in each MA; gauge the effectiveness of individual CDMs and CCCs; identify areas needing improvement and/or additional resources; and set KPI targets for the following season (Astle 2014).

REVIEW QUESTIONS

1. What is a learning culture? How is it created? What benefits does it have for SDOs and the programme they deliver?
2. Does your sport organisation or place of employment foster a learning environment? If so, how has it influenced individuals?
3. Identify one innovative solution from Figure 7.4, and then indicate what objective and output/outcome it achieved in Table 7.3, and at what level?
4. What innovative solutions are evident in your sport?
5. What was NZC's evaluation process based on? What did it allow?

CONCLUSION

M&E are continuous processes, although they are often perceived as only summative, rather than also formative. The associated tasks of collecting and collating evidence to undertake these processes are frequently ad hoc or inefficient. This is because NSOs often lack the specialist knowledge, expertise, and resources to identify appropriate programme outcomes or set up adequate monitoring systems, so rely on overstated participation statistics from national sport agency statistics, with their SDOs focused more on implementing programmes, rather than measuring outcomes and reporting their progress. However, to identify the effectiveness and impact of an intervention into community sport, it is essential right from the start of planning a programme that attention is paid to M&E.

M&E is about NSOs scrutinising each phase in the planning, design, implementation, and performance of their programmes to give them confidence they are on the right track, achieving their desired outcomes, and meeting their objectives. From the identification of a programme's objectives, there is a constant need to question, test, and assess the relevance and utility of the programme, its delivery approach and intended outcomes, and establish monitoring systems and baselines to measure and evaluate the extent of its impact.

Many NSOs have begun to increase their awareness of the value and importance of M&E, often driven by the need to regularly analyse data from their programmes to evidence change and justify their progress, and account for the investment provided by national sport agencies and corporate sponsors. While these are mainly summative evaluations, NSOs are also realising, because of their considerable investment of resources in community sport development programmes, the need to better understand why their programme is successful or not, because in doing so "lessons can be learned about the context, the approach, the tools and the intent of the programme" (Sherry et al. 2016: 161).

In this chapter, an example of the M&E process established by NZC for its NDP is used to illustrate from a practical perspective, its benefit and significance in planning, designing and implementing a programme, and regularly assessing its progress and long-term impact. It outlined the systematic data collection methodology and clearly defined definitions and multipliers adopted by NZC, enabling reliable and comparable data to be gathered, to verify its intended outputs/outcomes; and how it used this data to create both annual, formal summative evaluations of the progress and long-term impact of the programme on community cricket, and less conspicuous, but more pervasive, formative evaluations of the programme itself and its delivery to assess its effectiveness and make amendments for continuous improvement. It also showed that constantly seeking such improvement created a 'learning culture' among NZC's practitioners, who used their hands-on knowledge and expertise to devise and share innovative solutions and lessons learned to enhance the programme and its delivery.

REFERENCES

Alderson, A., Cleaver, D., & Leggat, D. (2012, December 5). The shame game: Plenty of opportunities at game's grassroots level. *The New Zealand Herald*, p. B24.

Astle, A. M. (2000a). *Coach pathway: From the backyard to the test arena*. Christchurch: New Zealand Cricket.

Astle, A. M. (2000b). *MILO Have-A-Go Cricket coaching manual for children 6–8 years*. Christchurch: New Zealand Cricket.

Astle, A. M. (2000c). *MILO Kiwi cricket coaching manual for children 7–10 years*. Christchurch: New Zealand Cricket.

Astle, A. M. (2003). *Coaching and practice plans: Implementing an effective coaching plan in secondary schools and clubs*. Christchurch: New Zealand Cricket.

Astle, A. M. (2004). *Coaching a cricket team: Cricket coaching manual for junior and youth cricket*. Christchurch: New Zealand Cricket.

Astle, A. M. (2006a). *The New Zealand Cricket skills challenge*. Christchurch: New Zealand Cricket.

Astle, A. M. (2006b). *Cricket: Game understanding*. Christchurch: New Zealand Cricket.

Astle, A. M. (2009a). *New Zealand Cricket: National development plan and programme*. Planning document. New Zealand Cricket, Christchurch.

Astle, A. M. (2009b). *MILO cricket skills test series*. Draft book. New Zealand Cricket, Christchurch.

Astle, A. M. (2011). *Community sport implementation plan: Collaborative delivery and outcomes*. Planning document. Sport and Recreation New Zealand, Wellington.

Astle, A. M. (2014). *Sport development – Plan, programme and practice: A case study of the planned intervention by New Zealand Cricket into cricket in New Zealand*. PhD, Massey University, Palmerston North, New Zealand.

Astle, A. M. (2015). *Development of sport in practice: Sport development officers – New Zealand Cricket's community cricket coordinators*. Unpublished survey.

Astle, A. M., & Clinton, P. (2008). *Game on! New Zealand Cricket's playing guidelines and policies*. New Zealand Cricket, Christchurch.

Astle, A. M., & Hill, S. (2017). *Otago Cricket Association: District reviews*. Auckland: New Zealand Cricket.

Bloyce, D., & Green, K. (2011). Sports development officers on sport development. In B. Houlihan & M. Green (Eds.), *Routledge handbook of sports development* (pp. 477–486). London and New York: Routledge.

Coalter, F. (2013). *Sport for development: What game are we playing?* London: Routledge.

Eady, J. (1993). *Practical sports development*. Harlow: Longman.

Hill, S. (2017). *Positioning cricket for the future: Data/observations report from phase 1 (2016) visitations to district associations and clubs*. Unpublished One Cricket Project Report. New Zealand Cricket, Auckland.

Houlihan, B. (2011a). Sports development and adult mass participation. Introduction: The neglect of adult participation. In B. Houlihan & M. Green (Eds.), *Routledge handbook of sports development* (pp. 213–215). London and New York: Routledge.

Houlihan, B. (2011b). Assessing the impact of sports development. Introduction: The problems of policy evaluation. In B. Houlihan & M. Green (Eds.), *Routledge handbook of sport development* (pp. 557–560). London and New York Routledge.

Johnson, T. (2014). Winning ways. In T. Johnson with A. Martin, G. Watson, & M. Butcher (Eds.), *Legends in black: New Zealand rugby greats on why we win* (pp. 228–240). Auckland: Penguin Group (NZ).

Kerr, J. (2013). *Legacy: What the All Blacks can teach us about the business of life.* London: Constable.

Mander, C. (2013). Tennis participation reporting in Australia. Retrieved from https://atpca.com.au/tennis-participation-reporting-in-australia-by-colin-mander-2/ website.

MacFarlane, C. (2016). *Sport New Zealand smaller NSOs.* Powerpoint presentation to Tier 4 and 5 NSOs' Forum. Sport New Zealand, Wellington.

New Zealand Cricket. (2001). *New Zealand Cricket census 2000/2001.* Christchurch: New Zealand Cricket.

New Zealand Cricket. (2002). *New Zealand Cricket census 2001/2002.* Christchurch: New Zealand Cricket.

New Zealand Cricket. (2008). *New Zealand Cricket census 2007/08.* Christchurch: New Zealand Cricket.

New Zealand Cricket. (2010). *New Zealand Cricket investment plan guidelines (community sport outcomes).* Planning document. New Zealand Cricket, Christchurch.

New Zealand Cricket. (2012). *New Zealand Cricket census 2011/12.* Christchurch: New Zealand Cricket.

New Zealand Cricket. (2016). *Women and cricket: Cricket and women.* Unpublished Report. New Zealand Cricket, Auckland.

Nicholson, M., Hoye, R., & Houlihan, B. (2011). Conclusion. In M. Nicholson, R. Hoye, & B. Houlihan (Eds.), *Participation in sport: International policy perspectives* (pp. 294–308). London and New York: Routledge.

PricewaterhouseCoopers. (2016). *One cricket stocktake.* Unpublished report. New Zealand Cricket, Auckland.

Schein, E. H. (2010). *Organisational culture and leadership* (4th ed.). San Francisco, CA: Jossey-Bass.

Sherry, E., Schulenkorf, N., & Phillips, P. (2016). Evaluating sport development. In E. Sherry, N. Schulenkorf, & P. Phillips (Eds.), *Managing sport development: An international approach* (pp. 161–176). London and New York: Routledge.

Simpson, K. (2013). Strategic performance management 2: Evaluating strategic sport development. In S. Robson, K. Simpson, & L. Tucker (Eds.), *Strategic sport development* (pp. 119–147). London and New York: Routledge.

Snedden, M. (2017a). *Positioning cricket for the future.* Unpublished One Cricket Project Report. New Zealand Cricket, Auckland.

Snedden, M. (2017b). *Positioning cricket for the future: Interim report on 'support for the delivery of community cricket'.* Unpublished One Cricket Project Report. New Zealand Cricket, Auckland.

Snedden, M., & Hill, S. (2017). *CCA 'One Cricket' pilot: Community cricket delivery support structure.* Unpublished Proposal for Consideration by CCA Member Associations. Canterbury Cricket Association, Christchurch.

SPARC. (2008). *Sport, recreation and physical activity participation among New Zealand adults: Key results of the 2007/08 Active NZ survey.* Wellington: Sport and Recreation New Zealand.

SPARC. (2009). *Sport and recreation – Everyone. Everyday. Sport and recreation New Zealand's strategic plan 2009–2015.* Wellington: Sport and Recreation New Zealand.

SPARC. (2010). *Community sport strategy: 2010–2015.* Planning document. Wellington: Sport and Recreation New Zealand.

Sport New Zealand. (2014). *Nine steps to effective governance: Building high performing organisations* (3rd ed.). Wellington.

Sport New Zealand. (2015a). *Planning in sport.* Wellington: Sport New Zealand.

Sport New Zealand. (2015b). *Sport and active recreation in the lives of New Zealand adults. 2013/14 Active New Zealand survey results.* Wellington: Sport New Zealand.

Websites

www.abs.gov.au

www.ausport.gov.au

www.crichq.com/

www.docs.google.com/forms

www.nzc.nz/media/9531/nzc-strategic-plan.pdf

www.nzrugby.co.nz/rugby_registration

www.sportengland.org/research/about-our-research/active-people-survey/

PART III

Sport development in practice

CHAPTER 8

Changing focus in the development and delivery of community tennis

Alec Astle and Jamie Tong

Tennis is a traditional, organised, individual sport that has a history of conservative and exclusive attitudes, characterised by an over-focus on high performance and preference for the conventional version of the game played by adults in clubs. For this reason, it's been labelled an 'elitist sport', seen as played mainly by 'middle-to-upper classes' in Anglo-Saxon countries, such as Australia, the UK, NZ, and the USA. By the 1990s, challenged by change, the prevalence of these attitudes and perceptions, and presence of fewer high-profile international players, tennis in these countries began to suffer a significant decline in popularity and participation (Wilson 2015). However, this was not the case everywhere. Since the 1990s, tennis participation has grown steadily in Europe (Tennis Europe 2015), and substantial increases have been recorded in Russia and China, stimulated by tennis returning to the Olympic Games and the prospect of winning medals (Marshall 2011).

In this chapter, changes in community tennis in NZ are explored. Until the twenty-first century, tennis was volunteer-driven, dominated by clubs as the main source of competitive community tennis, with limited consideration for the involvement of schools, recreational, or casual players, and content to seek high-performance success, despite a lack of consistent evidence. Over time, tennis grew in popularity and numbers by sticking to what worked well, with few changes required to its delivery or organisation. Such stability is not always possible, however, as tennis found in the 1980s and 1990s, when challenged by social, economic, and demographic changes, its participation numbers tumbled. Although aware of this predicament and potential need for change, inertia restricted the ability of tennis to adapt. Tennis New Zealand (TNZ) lacked the leadership, capability, and resources to adjust its strategies and structures to counter these challenges. For tennis, "the social and technical consistencies that were the very sources of past success and tradition. . . [were also]. . . the seeds of failure once conditions" changed (Parent, O'Brien, and Slack 2012: 109).

After 2000, tennis NSOs in countries such as Australia (Tennis Australia, TA), the UK (Lawn Tennis Association, LTA), NZ (TNZ), and the USA (United States Tennis Association, USTA) began to take stock of community tennis and respond to customer demand to arrest the decline in participation. This necessitated they move outside their previous high-performance and club focus and embrace the wider community of potential tennis players. New development initiatives, based on a game-based approach and modified formats, were introduced to grow the base of their game. These initiatives, which originated from the International Tennis Federation (ITF) global development programme, established in the 1990s (Bowers 2013), provided fun, age and stage appropriate tennis experiences for children, and opportunities for adults to play tennis for social and fitness reasons.

The catalyst for intervention in the UK and NZ, were the external funding inducements and specialist assistance from central government sport agencies, through their 'development of sport' policies to grow community sport participation (SPARC 2009; Sport England 2008). Since 2000 in NZ, SPARC and now Sport NZ, have provided capability and investment support to TNZ, enabling it to intervene 'top-down' to modernise and grow tennis at a community level.

This shift in direction by tennis NSOs is evident in the LTA Chief Executive's (CE) comment:

> We think the growth is going to be in the parks. . . [i.e. casual, individual participation rather than in clubs]. . . We need to strike long-term agreements with local authorities. . . I looked at the old blueprint. It was all about high performance. This is about meat and potatoes.
>
> (www.theguardian.com/sport/blog/2015/mar/17/
> tennis-decline-lta-wimbledon-andy-murray)

This 'meat and potatoes' realisation to take the game beyond tennis clubs was reinforced by TNZ's CE, who stated TNZ's goal moving forward was:

> to provide and promote enticing products and services that encourage more participation by more people in more places. . . This can be achieved by (i) growing the number of clubs and coaches offering existing participation programmes; (ii) developing new participation initiatives that meet the demands of the wider tennis community; and (iii) modernising and opening up tennis to the casual/ pay for play market.
>
> (TNZ 2016: 4)

This chapter will:

1. Describe the origins and factors influencing the growth of tennis in NZ.
2. Consider how conservative attitudes, which preserved the status quo of tennis as an exclusive club-based, predominantly adult sport, and the sport's fixation on elite tennis and constant search for talent, impacted community tennis, contributing to its decline in popularity and participation.
3. Discuss the role of central government sport agencies in improving the organisational capability and integration of tennis in NZ, and TNZ's subsequent adoption of a holistic approach, which balanced its performance and participation aspirations, and fostered the emergence of its national development programme.
4. Explore TNZ's initial foray into development with a stand-alone, school-based initiative, the challenges this presented, and the lessons learned about incorporating initiatives into an integrated development pathway to grow and sustain tennis in schools and clubs.
5. Consider the influences of the ITF and TA on the type and intended audience of the initiatives TNZ introduced into its player development pathway.
6. Examine why and how TNZ changed the regional delivery of its national initiatives from SDOs to local tennis club professionals.
7. Assess the impact of TNZ's intervention on participation in community tennis.

ORIGINS AND GROWTH OF COMMUNITY TENNIS

Modern tennis, known as lawn tennis because it was played outdoors usually on grass courts, began in England in 1850s. It evolved from earlier versions of the game played on hard indoor courts in Europe, mainly by royalty and aristocracy (Bowers 2013). Modern tennis, like other traditional, organised sports, which had their origins in Britain, was introduced into NZ during the 1870s by early British settlers. Initially, tennis was a social pastime (Wilson 2015), mainly for wealthy settlers, who played occasional games on grass courts laid in the gardens of urban mansions and large rural estates (Elenio 1986).

During the 1870s and 1880s, tennis grew in popularity as new waves of immigration bolstered NZ's population, transport and communications improved, and opportunities for engagement in sport increased. Tennis played an important social role in bringing people together in country districts with courts being established in local domains. This was often despite the lack of suitable playing equipment, rough court surfaces, and restrictive dress code and social disapproval of young women participating in such an energetic sport (Elenio 1986). Local clubs began to appear in different parts of NZ, formed by the independent efforts of influential volunteers, keen to establish tennis on a more permanent and continuing basis, for their own and others' enjoyment.

Historically, tennis was one of the very few sports in which men and women played alongside each other. Indeed, the mixed doubles in NZ's tennis championships goes back to at least 1886 (Elenio 1986). Tennis was probably the first sport in which women represented NZ, being selected for inter-colonial competitions against Australian states from as early as 1896 and a NZ women's team played against New South Wales in 1907. There was also a strong Māori involvement in tennis going back to the nineteenth century, with Māori playing tennis on the courts of large farms and sheep stations where they worked, especially in Hawke's Bay, or courts established on some *marae* (Māori meeting grounds). Leaders like Apirana Ngata encouraged Māori participation in tennis, both to promote Māori achievement and foster community identity (Aotearoa Māori Tennis Association 2006).

As club numbers increased in different regions, from the late 1870s they established Provincial Associations (PAs) to administer local inter-club competitions on their behalf and organise inter-provincial matches. In 1886, a national body, the New Zealand Lawn Tennis Association (NZLTA), was formed to run national tournaments and arrange international exchanges, particularly with Australia. The NZLTA and its PAs were voluntary organisations with honorary office bearers and committees (Elenio 1986).

In 1913, Australasia (Australia and NZ) was a founding member of the International Lawn Tennis Federation (ILTF) established to oversee the global growth and uniform development of tennis (Bowers 2013). The NZLTA gained separate membership of the ILTF in 1923, which in 1977 dropped the 'lawn' and became just the ITF.

By 1910, tennis had 9,376 participants, and despite the challenges presented by the First World War (1914–1918) and Great Depression (1929–1935), participation grew rapidly to 32,701 by 1940 (see Figure 8.1). This growth was stimulated by: the national achievements of NZ's first great tennis player and pioneering high-performance female athlete, Kathleen Nunneley, who won the national singles title 13 consecutive times between 1895 and 1907; the international success of New Zealander Anthony Wilding, who pre-First World War was the world's number one ranked player, winning eight Wimbledon titles between 1907 and 1914; the establishment throughout the country of more tennis clubs; the increased presence of tennis in organised sport programmes in schools; and construction by clubs,

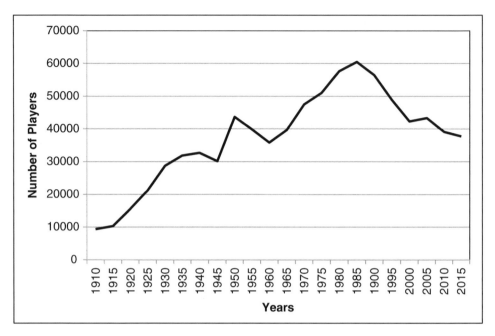

FIGURE 8.1 Registered tennis players in New Zealand, 1910–2015

Source: Te Ara – the Encyclopaedia of New Zealand, www.TeAra.govt.nz/en/tennis; Tennis New Zealand Annual Reports.

schools, and local councils of more lawn and hard court facilities, especially in Auckland, Wellington, and Christchurch. This growth, however, was curtailed by the Second World War (1939–1945), as many tennis club members served overseas with the armed services. By 1945, player numbers had dropped to 30,153.

In 1924, the Census and Statistics Office surveyed NZ's main sports (Census and Statistics 1925). Tennis was the third largest sport, behind rugby and horse racing. At that time tennis had 12 PAs and 19,967 participants. This comprised 11,673 males and 8,294 females, of which 18,045 were adult members of 302 tennis clubs, and 1,922 were school-aged players, 56% of them being girls.

After the Second World War the return of service personnel coincided with a period of economic prosperity in NZ. Higher prices for agricultural exports, industrial growth, rising affluence, increasing mobility, and urban growth and development, fuelled by rapid population growth in the post-war 'baby boom' years (1946–1964) saw the provision of further sports grounds and facilities by local councils. This increased access for many to sport, and combined with regulated working and opening hours, freed Saturdays for people to play club and school sport. Tennis club memberships grew, stimulated by promotional drives by the NZLTA and local clubs, tournaments were resumed, and schools were proactive in encouraging young people to play tennis, with many teachers facilitating this as volunteer coaches. By 1970, NZLTA had 21 PAs and participation had increased to 47,505, before peaking at 60,453 in 1985.

This increased popularity of community tennis also benefited from the rising profile of elite tennis in NZ during this period. This was attributable to three factors. First,

Auckland introduced an annual invitation tournament in 1956, which subsequently has grown in importance, attracting major international tennis players as it has evolved into the current ASB Classic Open tournaments for men and women – one of NZ's major summer sporting events (Romanos 2013). Second was the international success of a group of New Zealand players, the likes of Ruia Morrison, Brian Fairlie, Onny Parun, Marilyn Pryde, Chris Lewis, Russell Simpson, Kelly Evernden, and Brett Steven, on the world tennis circuit and Davis Cup competition. Third was the advent of television in NZ in 1960, and its increasing coverage of professional tennis, including the world Grand Slam tournaments, especially by pay television network Sky.

During the 1990s, however, tennis, like many traditional organised sports in NZ, was impacted by societal change and diversification of sport, recreation, and leisure activities (see Chapter 2), which saw its participant numbers slip to 43,365 by 2005 (see Figure 8.1). At this time, a similar trend was affecting leading tennis nations, such as Australia, UK, and USA, where a combination of: an over-focus on identifying and developing talent, international success, and winning, the prevalence of conservative attitudes and perception of tennis as an exclusive, elite sport, coupled with tennis being both an individualistic and relatively complicated game requiring expensive equipment and venues, saw its popularity fall as tennis participation declined (Wilson 2015).

In NZ, the NZLTA, which was volunteer-led and elite sport-focused, lacked the leadership, vision, capability, and financial resources to coordinate a national response to address this decline in community tennis. The sport itself was fragmented with 25 PAs and 489 clubs characterised by self-interest, duplication of effort, shrinking memberships, ageing facilities, and debt (TNZ 2004). Only 36% of clubs were considered well organised with modern facilities and coaching programmes, 53% had fewer than 50 members, and 64% had falling or static memberships (TNZ 2004). TNZ did not have a shared vision or coherent plan for community tennis, and any of its initiatives "were subject to veto at association level" (TNZ 2004: 13).

At a global level, the ITF in an effort to counter the decline in participation, implemented a global development programme to expand its influence beyond its traditional base, including the introduction of a game-based approach and modified formats to improve the relevance and appeal of tennis to a wider audience of potential participants (see Facts and figures 8.1 and 8.2).

FACTS AND FIGURES 8.1

Tennis: growing the global game

Although tennis participation has declined in traditional tennis-playing nations since the mid-1980s, the ITF has actively sought to spread tennis into new areas of the world. In 1976, it began a global development programme, which became operational in 1991 when regional development officers (RDOs) were appointed. Their role was to assist and advise national associations, conduct coach education courses, introduce children to tennis, run player training workshops, organise regional competitions, and identify talented players. Currently, there are 10 RDOs spread across Africa, Asia, Central and South America, Oceania, and Europe.

The RDOs use the ITF's 'Tennis Play and Stay' campaign, with its slogans of 'serve, rally, score' and 'easy, fun, healthy' to attract children into tennis. They initially used 'Mini Tennis', a modified format, to ensure their enjoyment and continued participation. This represented a change of approach away from traditional repetitive coaching of technique, to getting youngsters on court just having fun playing modified tennis games, with little or no coaching (Bowers 2013).

In 1996, 'Tennis 10s' replaced Mini Tennis, to introduce children under 10 years to tennis. It used 'slower balls', giving them more time to play the game than regular tennis balls (see Facts and figures 8.2). In 2012, another initiative, 'Tennis Xpress', was launched using slower balls to allow adults to learn tennis.

The RDOs' activities have generated a significant increase in ITF membership, particularly among developing countries, with over 100 countries committed to the 'Tennis Play and Stay' campaign.

Questions

1. When, why, and how did the ITF intervene in global tennis?
2. What campaign and modifications has the ITF introduced into tennis?
   - How has this changed the approach to learning to play tennis?
   - In a sport of your choice, what modifications have made it more relevant and appealing to (a) children and (b) adults?

FACTS and FIGURES 8.2

Slower tennis balls: a 'development in sport' innovation

The development of slower-bounce balls has made it easier and more enjoyable for players of all ages to learn to play tennis, compared to the previous use of faster, regular tennis balls. A sequence of slower balls, known as 'red, orange, green' after traffic lights, was adopted by the ITF in 2007 for youngsters involved in Tennis 10s: red being the slowest (75% slower than a regular ball), orange (50% slower), and green (25% slower) (Bowers 2013).

Since the adoption of slower balls, research has shown that children have more fun, hit more balls, and can use more tactics. The inclusion of slower balls in modified formats has been accompanied by the use of lighter, smaller racquets and reduced court sizes.

Since 2012, the ITF has made it obligatory for all under-10-year tennis competitions worldwide to use slower balls.

Question

Can you think of an equipment innovation that has improved the appeal of another sport, and what effect it has had?

COACHING AND DEVELOPMENT

During the 1920s and 1930s, there was limited effort by clubs to actively recruit and develop young players. Tennis was perceived as an adult game, and if young players played, it was alongside adults in tennis clubs, or in school-based competitions. After the Second World War, however, there was a growing awareness by the NZLTA and their PAs of the need to develop junior players, especially those with the talent to potentially become world-class players (Elenio 1986).

To facilitate this, NZLTA established a junior advisory committee in 1963, to organise visits by overseas professionals to conduct coaching clinics for young players, select regional training squads, provide national training and tournament opportunities, send junior teams to Australia and encourage some players to accept tennis scholarships at USA universities (Elenio 1986; Romanos 2013). From 1979, these responsibilities were assumed by a full-time coaching and development officer appointed by the NZLTA, although the junior advisory committee continued to provide recommendations on junior tennis.

A nationwide review of coaching in the 1970s prompted the development of a coaching programme. This involved local professional coaches in clubs and schools and established the foundations for a national coach education programme (Elenio 1986). While this provided a framework for coaching and training coaches, little consideration was given to matching this with the development of the community game to meet participants' needs and what they wanted to play.

Each PA administered its own tennis competitions, and although there was a pathway for talented players, and the game was gradually diversifying to allow midweek ladies tennis and mixed, business house, twilight competitions for adults, there was no nationally coordinated development pathway for community players. Tennis was still seen as an adult game that children could play. In 1988, 'Kiwi Tennis', a modified game for children (5–12 years), was introduced to primary schools, as part the KiwiSport programme instigated by the central government sport agency, the Hillary Commission for Sport and Recreation (Hillary Commission 1988). However, within clubs there were no nationally promoted modified tennis formats for junior players. Clubs and secondary schools were left to deliver their own playing opportunities, with committed coaches, mainly club professionals and teachers, being responsible for coaching and developing players. In secondary schools, annual inter-school fixtures were contested, especially between traditional single-sex schools, and by the late 1970s some of these schools had began arranging their own overseas tours for promising players.

National primary–intermediate schools' tennis competitions for individual boys and girls began in 1983, although since 1999 these have continued as separate North Island and South Island competitions. In 1993, national secondary schools' teams tennis competitions were instigated for boys' and girls' school teams, and then from 1994 mixed teams. These various school competitions are run on a knockout basis, initially in each PA, then in each region, with finals tournaments being organised by the national body.

REVIEW QUESTIONS

1. How was tennis perceived as a sport in the nineteenth century, and why?
2. What was the dominant tennis focus in NZ during the twentieth century of (a) community tennis, and (b) the national body?
3. What factors contributed to the decline in tennis participation at the end of the twentieth century?
4. How did the ITF respond to this decline?

A PLAN FOR RESTRUCTURING AND REVITALISING TENNIS

Until the start of the twenty-first century, tennis in NZ was governed and administered by TNZ, the national body which had replaced the NZLTA in 1989, and its now 25 autonomous PAs, each with its own agenda, constituent clubs and schools. TNZ remained primarily pre-occupied with breeding the next generation of talent and success of its elite players, while the PAs, through their clubs and schools, each fostered the development and delivery of tennis in their own communities.

In 2003, TNZ undertook a comprehensive 'health check' of the state of tennis in NZ, after several attempts in the 1990s to confront the issues facing the game (TNZ 2005). This was triggered by concern about the low profile of tennis in NZ, lack of success of its elite players on the international stage, continuing decline in participation in clubs, and fragmented structure of the sport. Subsequently, TNZ commissioned a group, known as the 'T21 working party', to examine the organisational structure of tennis within NZ, and report on options for the most effective structure for the future. Their report, 'For the Good of the Game' (TNZ 2004), indicated the existing structure of "25 Provincial Associations was so uneven in terms of population, turnover, capability, and responsiveness, that it did not offer a national infrastructure necessary to drive the promotion and development of tennis in New Zealand" (TNZ 2005: 2). It also recommended the need for more professional and strategic leadership and management by TNZ and its board, and the adoption of a more holistic approach to tennis as a sport.

The findings of the report were circulated throughout the tennis community, and after consultation with the PAs, it was agreed the organisation of tennis be restructured and a regional model adopted. Feedback on regional alternatives were sought and collated in the 'Maiden Report', after Sir Colin Maiden who coordinated it (TNZ 2006a). This report called for strong leadership by TNZ, consolidation of the PAs, and common strategic goals to be set across tennis as a sport organisation.

The report and need for restructuring were accepted. It required the 25 PAs to merge into six Regions, or remain autonomous, but linked to a region (TNZ 2006b). "It was believed that this would assist in creating an environment of collaboration, leadership, sustainability and growth in the sport" (Gryphon Governance Consultants 2011: 25). Although this has occurred, the work required to facilitate the change, level of engagement needed to get agreement, and having associations opt out and remain autonomous, added to its complexity and cost (Gryphon Governance Consultants 2011).

This process of restructuring and improvement in organisational capability was supported by the central government sport agency SPARC. They categorised tennis as a 'revitalisation' sport, and provided TNZ with substantial investment and professional advice over a three-year period (2006–2008), contingent upon TNZ's willingness to change, improve its leadership, management, and capability, and complete the regional restructure (TNZ 2006b).

TNZ subsequently adopted a more corporate governance model, and with its six Regions worked to create a more vertically integrated structure for tennis in an effort to function as 'one team' (TNZ 2009). This collaboration provided TNZ with the opportunity to introduce a nationally driven, regionally delivered development programme, to address the ongoing decline in community tennis participation.

AN INCREASING FOCUS ON COMMUNITY TENNIS

Although 'increasing participation' was one of seven priorities in TNZ's 2004–2007 Strategic Plan, community tennis continued to decline. This was attributable to both external factors, such as societal change and sport diversification and commercialisation; and internal causes, including: the conservative and exclusive attitudes of clubs, their members and professional club coaches, the latter keen to preserve the status quo and their livelihoods; the ageing base of club players, expense of upgrading depreciating club facilities and its impact on increasing club memberships, and the disproportionate focus on coaching elite junior players; the lack of age-appropriate, appealing formats for young people; and limited interest in, and accessibility for, recreational and casual players to club courts.

Although TNZ had insufficient capability and resources to address this decline, they realised the environment in which community tennis operated was changing rapidly, and that they "must find ways – actively – to meet the needs of the 21st century" (TNZ 2005: 6). Instead of continuing to just offer traditional tennis, clubs needed to be more attractive, inclusive, and ready to adopt change, take note of customer needs, and provide more appealing, alternative options of the game to enable "the thousands of people who first try tennis on public courts. . . to continue playing the game" (Vail 2007: 579) (see Case studies 8.1 and 8.2).

CASE STUDY 8.1
Community tennis opportunities in the UK

Rob Dearing, Head of Tennis Delivery and Innovation, Lawn Tennis Association, London, UK

Although tennis had its origins in England, where the sport subsequently grew in popularity and profile, by the 1990s its participation began to decline. Some suggested this coincided with UK's dwindling presence in the sport at the elite level, others claimed it was related to the lack of public access to club courts for social, recreational players, the cost of playing, and/or the game being perceived as a middle- to upper-class sport.

In the last decade, the Lawn Tennis Association (LTA) has shifted its strategic focus from prioritised elite tennis to balancing this with improving community tennis, as indicated by its vision to have 'more people playing tennis more often'. The emphasis now is on both creating winners and using the publicity to promote participation, and investing in the grassroots to develop pathways for more players to participate, with the prospect of more talent emerging from a larger pool.

This changing emphasis was evident in the LTA's whole sport plan for Sport England, and the latter's considerable funding support for the LTA to drive tennis participation not only in clubs, but beyond this traditional focus into schools, universities, and wider community through play for free, or pay and play in parks, indoor tennis venues and community facilities.

The LTA's strategic focus shift, reflected in its customer focused structures, initiatives, and campaigns, has seen tennis participation begin to grow following two decades of decline. It has devised a player pathway of different types of tennis opportunities and experiences to meet the needs and interests of a diversity of participants, beginning with entry-level Mini Tennis, which comprises the ITF's red, orange, and green progression of modified formats for 3–10-year-olds. In addition to regular singles and double tennis tournaments, the pathway also includes new, more exciting and time-friendly modified competition formats, such as FAST4 in which first to four games wins; Touchtennis, a fast, five-a-side format played with shorter racquets, foam ball, and portable net on 12-metre courts on any flat surface; and similar to TNZ, Cardio Tennis, and Tennis Xpress. The LTA also partners with the Tennis Foundation to make tennis more inclusive and accessible through Schools Tennis and Disability Tennis. Supporting its player initiatives, the LTA has a large-scale coach and volunteer development programme, which is essential to the continued growth of the sport.

To further expand its participation base, the LTA has designed specific campaigns to attract social, recreational players (e.g. Great British Tennis Weekend, Tennis for Kids). These have sought to remove barriers to participation, such as: perceptions around cost, access, awareness, and having someone to play with, by providing free options to trial tennis, then ongoing opportunities to play. These campaigns annually introduce over 60,000 adults and 20,000 children to tennis.

The LTA invests in clubs to improve or install facilities realising players' experience of the game is critical to their retention. They have also introduced an innovative online court booking and tap in gate entry system, using the ClubSpark (www.club spark.co.uk) technology platform. This allows individuals to reserve a court online, gain access on arrival without the need for staffing at the facility, and have floodlights automatically turned on for evening bookings. In its first 18 months of operation, over 19,000 recreational players used this system to book a court (average six bookings per person). The LTA sees considerable upside for this system in tennis.

Questions

1. Why did tennis decline in UK?
2. What has the LTA done to reverse this decline?

3. What effect have its (a) player pathway and (b) modified formats had on this reversal?
4. What is ClubSpark and how has it benefited tennis participation?
5. Are you aware of another sport with a similar facility access system for casual participants? If so, how effective has this been in increasing participation?

CASE STUDY 8.2
Junior and youth tennis in the USA

Craig Morris, General Manager, Community Tennis and Youth Tennis,
United States Tennis Association, Orlando, Florida, USA

The United States Tennis Association (USTA) is the national body for tennis in the USA,
with responsibility to promote and develop grassroots to professional tennis. In 2017, it
had 653,054 members, down 5.6% from 2015, with 178,471 junior and youth and
474,583 adult members. From a community tennis perspective, a USTA review to address
this decline revealed all its tennis initiatives were performance-oriented, and to engage
more players would require the introduction of easier entry, recreational options that
catered to their needs.

Community tennis is delivered in the USA by multiple providers. The USTA offers
competition tennis with rankings for individuals and teams of all ages. High schools
offer school leagues. Free and pay for play recreational tennis options, both competitive
and social, are available at facilities in parks, schools, hotels and resorts, gated or non-
gated homeowners' association communities and through commercial tennis providers.
Together they cater for the 18.08m people who played tennis in the USA at least once
in 2016. Of these 9.86m were regular players (i.e. playing 10 or more times in the
year), comprising 2.68m junior and youth and 7.18m adult players.

In 2007, the USTA were early adopting and promoting the ITF's 'Tennis Play and Stay'
philosophy to attract more children to play tennis.

In 2017, the USTA launched 'Net Generation', a new, unified children and youth
friendly programme, to attract the next generation of 5–18-year-olds to play tennis and
inspire them to play it more often. The programme provides a pathway of junior and youth
initiatives. It begins by introducing tennis to children in schools through physical education
classes, followed by an easy entry into the sport using shorter courts, lower-bouncing balls
and lighter racquets to have fun and learn the basics of tennis, before progressing through
age and stage appropriate initiatives that cater for the recreational or competitive needs
of young players.

The USTA has created a comprehensive marketing strategy to advertise 'Net
Generation', which began with its launch at the US Tennis Open, and includes its own
website (www.netgeneration.com) and app, through which parents can contact clubs
and coaches approved to deliver Net Generation and enrol their youngsters. It has
also enlisted 32 social media brand influencers, known as 'Netset Ambassadors', aged
5–18 years with a strong social media presence, to showcase Net Generation, by

promoting the brand to their social media followers. Initially, the strategy has targeted and educated providers to sign up under Net Generation. This requires all providers, including coaches, teachers, and volunteers to be accredited by first going through a Safe Play orientation, which includes a background check.

Questions

1. How has the USTA sought to increase participation?
2. What novel approach has the USTA adopted to promote Net Generation directly to participants?
3. Are you aware of any other sports using social media? How effective has it been in promoting participation?

While the restructure of tennis gradually improved the organisational capability and integration within the sport, it was apparent that this would not deliver lasting change. This required TNZ to change its blueprint and adopt a more balanced, holistic approach to their sport, instead of its over-prioritisation of elite tennis. The emergence of this approach is evident in TNZ's later strategic mission "to lead the sustainable growth of tennis in New Zealand and ensure success on the international stage" (TNZ 2012: inside cover). To achieve the former, and imprint lasting, positive change within community tennis, TNZ needed to formulate a national development programme with an integrated player pathway framework (TNZ 2004, 2007).

Fortuitously, the first step in creating this programme occurred in 2006, when two tennis CoachForce Officers, appointed by RSTs in Waikato-Bay and Canterbury, confronted by a lack of existing resources to attract youngsters into tennis and involve teachers as elementary coaches, collaborated to compile *Grasshoppers: New Tennis for Kids* (Wilkinson and Chalmers 2006). This resource, to support an entry-level, mini-tennis programme for primary school children (5–10 years), was subsequently adopted by TNZ as its first national development initiative (see Case study 8.3).

CASE STUDY 8.3

Grasshoppers: Tennis New Zealand's first development initiative

Ian Francis, former National Game Development Manager, Tennis New Zealand, Auckland, New Zealand

Grasshoppers was an entry-level, modified mini-tennis initiative designed to create enjoyment playing tennis among primary school children (5–10 years) that would capture their interest and see them register as junior players in local tennis clubs. Researched and compiled by two CoachForce Officers during 2006, the influences of international tennis development and coaching best practice, KiwiSport modification, and FMS to improve children's physical literacy are evident in Grasshoppers. It was TNZ's first development initiative to increase participation. It presented a new games-based approach to tennis, moving away from traditional repetitive technique coaching, to a more 'learn whilst playing' experience of modified games; and used modified equipment (smaller racquets and courts, and slow-bounce tennis balls), which was not widely used at the time (see Facts and figures 8.1 and 8.2). This allowed it to be played on any flat surface, either outdoors or indoors.

The Grasshopper manual provided a progression of 20 modified tennis games for 5–7 and 8–10-year-olds. Each game, with appealing titles, such as 'Funky Tunes' and 'Space Invaders', comprised an explanation of how to organise and play it, the equipment required, learning outcomes and game understanding questions. These games acted as user-friendly sessions for coaches to conduct primary school visits.

The implementation of Grasshoppers saw TNZ's RDMs and RDOs sign up primary schools to three-year agreements. These ensured each year trained local coaches delivered four 30-minute sessions of the programme to children, and teachers received in-service training to be able to continue delivering tennis and/or its basic sport and movement skills in their physical education lessons. After the in-school sessions, Grasshoppers tournaments were organised so children could play on local club courts to establish a link with them for their future involvement.

Questions

1. What is Grasshoppers? List three advantages it had over traditional tennis.
2. Who were Grasshoppers intended audience and where did it access them?
3. Do you know another sport who targets the school market? If so, how successful have they been in providing children with a 'taste' of their sport?

To drive its national programme, including the implementation of Grasshoppers, in 2007 TNZ, with SPARC sport development funding, appointed its inaugural national game development manager (NGDM). The decision to establish this position reflected TNZ's shifting focus to foster the development and future growth of community tennis, as opposed to their earlier preoccupation with talented player development.

The first task of the NGDM was to launch Grasshoppers. To achieve this, six regional development managers (RDMs) were appointed, one in each Region, later complemented by six regional development officers (RDOs) stationed in key PAs within these regions. This regional team provided the platform for the growth of community tennis in clubs and primary schools. They worked in clubs, using a Club Toolkit, to improve their capability and delivery of services, and implement Grasshoppers in primary schools to excite youngsters to the possibilities of tennis and encourage them to register as junior players in these clubs. TNZ to promote the benefits of tennis has since 2009 also run annual 'Come Play' national open day campaigns to encourage people to visit their local club and try tennis.

During this first phase of TNZ's national development programme, although club tennis player numbers continued to drop from 43,418 (2006/07) down to 39,102 (2010/11), the number of children who sampled tennis through Grasshoppers in primary schools rose significantly from 4,000 (2007/08) to 62,713 (2010/11). Although Grasshoppers only provided a 'taste' of tennis, rather than regular participation, the interest it created raised the profile of tennis at community level. TNZ also began to register casual and recreational participants who played outside regular club-based competitions, and include them in their annual participation census. These players were mainly involved in regional 'business house' twilight competitions.

REVIEW QUESTIONS

1. When and why did TNZ respond to the decline in participation? Who influenced them to intervene 'top-down' into community tennis? What was the nature of this intervention?
2. What was the objective of Grasshoppers? How successful was it in achieving this objective?

A CHANGE IN DIRECTION

Although driven by the sport pyramid analogy of growing the base of club players to increase the possibility of discovering a future champion (TNZ 2011), there was emerging a 'bigger picture' understanding by TNZ to take the game outside clubs, and engage with the wider tennis community to capture the involvement of casual and recreational players. This was evident in the comment by TNZ's CE:

> The challenge that lies ahead is how we continue to engage with all the participants who play tennis, in either organised or unorganised forms of the game, to ensure that we remain relevant and a first choice for those currently playing and for those youngsters who have perhaps tasted tennis through Grasshoppers.
>
> (TNZ 2012: 4)

This thinking coincided with the start of a change in direction in TNZ's development programme, and was apparent in its strategic objective of 'more people playing tennis' (TNZ 2012: 5). A similar change occurred in UK, where the LTA's mission shifted from its previous 'winning' to its current 'more people playing tennis more often' (LTA 2016: 33) (see Case study 8.1). In NZ, this witnessed the appearance of a more inclusive approach to community tennis development, one focused not just on clubs, but on participants and their needs. This approach surfaced from an amalgam of factors:

- The appointment of a replacement NGDM in 2011.
- The ongoing disquiet about declining club numbers.
- The momentum created by Grasshoppers highlighted the need to introduce further participation initiatives and open up tennis to casual and recreational participants.
- The influence of ITF's 'Tennis Play and Stay' campaign, and its rule changes, which from 2012 required the worldwide use of slower bounce balls and smaller court sizes in all

under-10-year tennis competitions (see Facts and figures 8.1 and 8.2 and Case studies 8.1 and 8.2).

• The increasing focus by SPARC on community sport, and the potential of tennis to grow participation in clubs and schools (SPARC 2009).

In 2009, SPARC shifted its focus to concentrate on community sport (SPARC 2009). It partnered with NSOs and RSTs to counter declining participation in clubs and schools. A community sport growth strategy was introduced in 2010 (SPARC 2010), with account-abilities attached to sport development funding to achieve specific community sport participation, contribution (volunteering) and capability outcomes (see Table 7.1). Select sports, with the potential to impact these outcomes, were targeted for specialist support and investment. Seven sports were targeted in 2010, and after collaborative partnerships were established with them, which required the formulation of whole-of-sport plans and community sport development programmes; a further seven sports, including tennis, were added at the end of 2011 (TNZ 2012).

As a targeted sport, community sport development specialists from now Sport NZ, worked with TNZ's new NGDM to: design a whole-of-sport overview identifying the development pathways underpinning the delivery of tennis; determine within these pathways the scope of community tennis; and then use this to draft a community tennis plan to grow participation. Further community sport investment from Sport NZ, allowed the NGDM to appoint two national game development officers (NGDOs), and sustain TNZ's funding support for its regional delivery network of RDMs and RDOs. However, not all clubs welcomed Sport NZ's investment to grow community tennis participation, especially of casual and recreational players, as it would not contribute to club membership and literally "turn them into little more than court-hire agencies" (Roughan 2012: A25).

In the meantime, despite Grasshoppers' success, community club numbers continued to decline. A review of Grasshoppers and its impact on junior club membership in 2012 (Tong 2012) revealed its effectiveness in introducing over 80,000 primary school children to tennis by 2010/11, but provided no evidence of a corresponding transfer of these children into club tennis. Indeed, the overall number of club players had dropped to 39,102 in 2010/11, which including a 10% decline in children under 12 years playing tennis (see Figure 8.2). It was found, while Grasshoppers provided an exposure to tennis and generated interest in tennis in schools, it existed in isolation. It was a stand-alone, in-school initiative, not part of, or leading into, an integrated national pathway of age and stage appropriate, modified tennis initiatives for children in either schools or clubs. There were also ongoing issues with club professional coaches concerned about the impact of school tennis and teacher coaches on their clubs and income, and Grasshoppers' dependency on local coaches and short-term KiwiSport funding. The review concluded that "a more holistic approach needs to be taken and an integrated participation pathway be created with flexible programmes to aid the continued development of young participants" (Tong 2012: 2).

The review advocated a new approach to address the lack of transition of participants from school to clubs, limited menu of appealing opportunities in clubs to attract and retain youngsters, and need for more trained grassroots coaches (Tong 2012). This new approach was underpinned by the design of a player development pathway, with an integrated series of age and stage appropriate mini-tennis initiatives catering for children's needs, which could be delivered in schools and clubs.

Grasshoppers would continue to be used in schools to provide a tennis experience for children, and the opportunity to actively recruit them into the proposed player pathway initiatives.

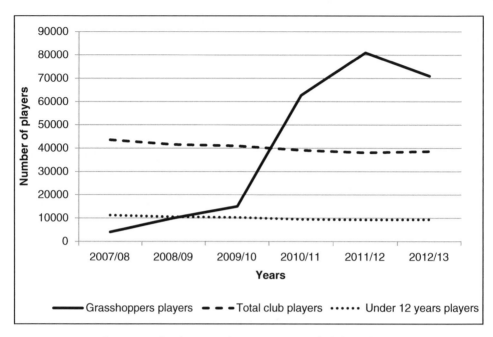

FIGURE 8.2 Grasshoppers school tennis players versus total club and U12 years club players in New Zealand, 2007/08 to 2012/13

NB: Before 2010/11 the statistics collected on children were for under 11 years.

Source: TNZ Annual Reports.

It was also envisaged a coach development pathway be configured to match the player pathway. This was to ensure there were sufficient 'grassroots' coaches trained to run Grasshoppers in schools, and assist professional coaches run future mini-tennis initiatives in clubs.

The emergence of TNZ's new approach was strongly influenced by two close affiliations: first, with the ITF through its global 'Tennis Play and Stay' campaign which introduced its Tennis 10s rule changes in 2012, stipulating all children under 10 years of age worldwide must play tennis with slower-bounce red, orange, and green balls on the appropriately sized courts, and more recently its Tennis Xpress initiative for beginner adults to play tennis using slower-bounce balls, rather than regulation yellow tennis balls (see Facts and figures 8.1 and 8.2); second, with TA and their endorsement of TNZ using and customising their tennis development initiatives – 'Tennis Hot Shots' for children, 'Cardio Tennis' for adults and coach education courses (TNZ 2014a).

REVIEW QUESTIONS

1. Why did TNZ change the direction of its national development programme? What factors influenced this change?
2. What impact has the 'learning by playing' approach and slow-bounce tennis balls had on the development of the community tennis? How have they improved playing tennis, and for whom?

PLANS, PATHWAYS, AND PROGRAMME

Following the groundwork with Sport NZ to create a whole-of-sport framework of pathways to underpin tennis, the NGDM in 2013 used this as a blueprint to compile a community sport 'Participation Strategy' for TNZ (TNZ 2013). This focused on its central player development pathways of integrated opportunities for current and prospective club and school players, to engage both the untapped potential market of people who play tennis, and those who want to play tennis outside the formal membership structure. For example, Sport NZ's *2013/14 Active New Zealand Survey*, identified 209,000 adults over 16 years as having played tennis at least once in the previous 12 months (Sport NZ 2015) (see Pause and ponder 8.1). TA identified a similar latent demand to play tennis in Australia, especially for social and fitness reasons, with a preference for 'pay-to-play' to access tennis facilities, rather than becoming seasonal club members (Richards 2017). While the LTA introduced ClubSpark, an innovative online booking and entry system, to engage more casual and recreational players, who can now use an app to access courts in the UK (see Case study 8.1). For similar reasons, TNZ is keen to establish a comparable system "where people can download an app to their phone and book to play on a court at any participating club in the country" (Long 2017: B6).

Launched in 2014, the Participation Strategy was endorsed by TNZ's Regions. It aligns with TNZ's Strategic Plan (2014–2017), and provides a blueprint for the future growth and development of community tennis in NZ (TNZ 2013). The strategy established an ambitious goal to increase tennis participation in NZ by 20% to 150,000 in 2017. This figure was calculated by combining all registered competitive and 'pay-to-play' casual tennis players. Improving the appeal and accessibility of tennis clubs, increasing participatory opportunities, expanding and reviving competitions, and enhancing the profile of tennis were all identified as key to achieving this goal (TNZ 2013).

To increase participatory opportunities, new initiatives identified in TNZ's player development pathways were piloted and launched. The first was 'Tennis Hot Shots' (see Case study 8.4), aimed at children (5–10 years), which allowed clubs to better cater for children's needs. It comprises a sequence of child-appropriate, mini-tennis opportunities, using the 'traffic light' progression of red, orange, and green slow-bounce tennis balls, modified equipment, and smaller court sizes (TNZ 2015b) (see Facts and figures 8.2), and offers a solution to bridging the gap between school-based Grasshoppers and clubs (TNZ 2015c) (see Figure 8.2). Tennis Hot Shots presents an option for children enthused by Grasshoppers in schools to now register in a pathway of similar child-centred tennis initiatives within clubs.

CASE STUDY 8.4

Tennis Hot Shots: Tennis New Zealand's entry-level initiative

Jamie Tong, National Game Development Manager, Tennis New Zealand, Auckland, New Zealand

Tennis Hot Shots was piloted by TNZ in 2013, then launched in 2014. It is a game-base, starter programme aimed at children under 10 years, played on smaller courts with shorter racquets and slow-bounce balls, and uses the ITF's 'serve, rally, score' slogan to promote a practical 'learning through play' approach. This allows children to learn the skills of tennis, by having fun serving, rallying, and scoring right from the start, without coaching.

Tennis Hot Shots uses slower-bounce balls (see Facts and figures 8.2), so children can develop their skills as they are ready to progress through four sequential pathway stages, each designated by a ball colour and approximate age group. These include: Blue (3–5 years), Red (5–8 years), Orange (8–10 years), and Green (9+ years).

The Tennis Hot Shots programme includes: visiting primary schools to run introductory tennis awareness sessions to excite children to the possibilities of tennis and recruit them into clubs; training coaches to deliver Tennis Hot Shots; implementing Tennis Hot Shots in clubs as their entry level to tennis and the club; and running tournaments for children to test their Tennis Hot Shots skills. Tennis Hot Shots is supported by a coaching manual, equipment, and fence banners for coaches (TNZ 2015b). The manual contains detailed sessions for coaches, tailored to different ages and skill levels of children, with the duration, size of court and racquets used, and bounce of balls increasing progressively through the sessions (TNZ 2015c).

Tennis Hot Shots has its own website (www.tennishotshots.kiwi) and Facebook page (www.facebook.com/TennisHotShotsNZ) which offer information and allow players to share experiences and register online.

In 2014/15, Tennis Hot Shots involved 71,511 children participating at schools, through clubs, receiving coaching, or competing in tournaments. While the majority of children (61,241) just had fun sampling tennis in schools, 10,270 had a more intense experience being coached and playing in clubs and competitions. Although in its early stages, 180 or 58% of TNZ's professional coaches have been trained to deliver Tennis Hot Shots and it is being offered in 87 or 20% of NZ's tennis clubs.

Questions

1. What are the main features of Tennis Hot Shots as (a) a recruitment initiative, and (b) a playing programme?
2. Calculate the percentage of players that Tennis Hot Shots has transferred into clubs? How does this compare with an entry-level initiative in a sport you are familiar with?

Since 2014, TNZ has also added a number of alternative tennis initiatives for adults within its pathways who want to play for social and fitness reasons. Although not mainstream like Tennis Hot Shots, these initiatives, such as Beach Tennis, Cardio Tennis, and Tennis Xpress, are about engaging more casual, pay-to-play adults keen to play recreational tennis. Cardio Tennis is a group fitness-based initiative, combining tennis with cardiovascular exercise in an hour-long aerobic workout, set to fast-pace music. Tennis Xpress caters mainly for beginner adults, where a learn by playing approach, using slower-bounce balls and simple scoring, makes it easy to play.

To complement its 'Participation Strategy' centred on its player pathway, TNZ introduced its 'Coaching Strategy' in 2014, to create an aligned coach development pathway aimed at increasing the number and quality of coaches to meet its players' needs (TNZ 2014b). For each pathway stage, coaches receive appropriate educative opportunities to attain the knowledge and skills commensurate with the age and stage of the players they are coaching (TNZ 2014b).

Since TNZ introduced these club-based development initiatives, club professional coaches have been more receptive to implementing these in their clubs. Instead of their previous resistance to Grasshoppers, they realised the potential of these new initiatives to increase club player numbers, fill their coaching ranks and supplement their income. By 2016, 526 coaches had attended the new 'Coaching Strategy' courses, with 180 professional coaches qualifying to deliver Tennis Hot Shots in their clubs (TNZ 2016). This mindset change by the professional club coaches, and their increasing delivery of the new initiatives, has seen a decline in regional development staff. While a number of Regions still fund their own RDMs and RDOs, TNZ has significantly reduced its funding support for these positions.

This shift in regional delivery to using existing local club professional coaches in sports such as tennis and golf provides a viable, alternative option for programme implementation. If club professional coaches can be convinced of the value of the change and innovation associated with a national development programme, it provides these sports with an in-house source of full-time personnel committed to growing the sport and with it potentially their incomes.

The changing direction of TNZ, and its concern for greater market share of sport participants, saw it change its annual reporting of participation numbers. In 2015/16, instead of reporting just its regular club players, which had declined further to 37,740, and its casual participants which had increased to 21,555, it added a new category of 72,021 national programme participants, most of whom only sampled the sport through Tennis Hot Shots school visits. TNZ began to portray in its reporting it had over doubled its participation numbers to 131,316 (TNZ 2015a). TNZ even altered its strategic objective in line with this debatable statistic to lift tennis participation to 175,000 by 2020 (TNZ 2016). This highlights a key issue in sport development of there being no agreed official definition of 'participation' (Nicholson, Hoye, and Houlihan 2011), to distinguish between regular participants and those just sampling a sport. It also reflects NSOs attempts to satisfy over-ambitious participation outcomes of national sport agencies and their investment accountabilities, and/or present over-optimistic images of the health of their sport to appease stakeholders and sponsors (see Pause and ponder 8.1).

PAUSE and PONDER 8.1

Scepticism about sport participation numbers

Reading media reports on the state of tennis participation in leading tennis countries such as Australia, the UK, and the USA, there is a conflict of statistics about whether the sport is growing or declining. The conflict arises from the source and method of collection of the statistics in these reports and reflect the adage that 'facts are stubborn things, but statistics are pliable'.

Mander (2013), with reference to tennis participation reporting in Australia, argues the selective use of statistics by NSOs is both misleading and counterproductive to assessing how their sport is performing in relation to the effectiveness of their development strategies. The problem is there is no one universal definition of 'participation'. In other words, how is a 'participant' defined, and then how is a 'regular participant' differentiated in terms of time and frequency of participation. A lack of clarity around these definitions has produced confusion and the arbitrary use of undefined participation statistics.

This has seen media select participation statistics that suit their storyline, and sports use broader and broader definitions of participation in their annual reports to satisfy central government community sport participation targets and investment accountabilities and inspire confidence in stakeholders. As Mander (2013: 2) suggests, because tennis participation in Australia remains undefined, "it seems to be morphing over time into a definition that is a long way from the number of people playing tennis".

Defining participation and gathering reliable, comparable data over time to measure and report on participation targets and trends is imperative if NSO development strategies and initiatives are to be effective.

Questions

1. Why is there scepticism over participation statistics?
2. Why do sports selectively use participation statistics? What advantages and disadvantages does this have?
3. How is a participant defined in a sport of your choice? Is this an accurate measure of regular participation?

REVIEW QUESTIONS

1. Why did TNZ replace Grasshoppers with Tennis Hot Shots?
2. How was TNZ's development programme initially delivered? Why is this changing, and how?
3. Why is it difficult to measure participation in sport? How can this make participation statistics used by NSOs subject to different interpretations. How could the validity of these statistics be improved?

CONCLUSION

TNZ has turned a 'development of sport' corner in the last decade, intervening 'top-down' with Sport NZ's support to revitalise and grow community tennis. Historically, tennis in NZ was developed 'bottom-up' by influential volunteers; however, limited efforts were made to extend the game beyond clubs. Participation numbers peaked in the 1980s, and since then the popularity of the game has diminished, and with it a steady decline in those playing community tennis. This was a consequence of a lack of awareness of the deteriorating state of the game, and a resistance to change by conservative club members and their professional tennis coaches steadfast on maintaining the exclusivity of the club domain, adult format of tennis, and ongoing search for talent. The latter was reinforced by TNZ's over-focus on high performance, and belief that international winning and success would inspire prospective participants to want to play tennis and reverse the downward trend in participation.

The selection of tennis by NZ's national sport agencies, initially as a sport for revitalisation, and later targeted to grow its community game, enabled TNZ to improve its capability and that of its new regional centres, adopt a more balanced whole-of-sport approach, and have sufficient sport development funding to intervene to influence the development and delivery of community tennis. This saw a shift in mindset by TNZ, similar to the LTA in UK, away from primarily searching for talent to also fostering a 'play for life' enjoyment of the game, from focusing only on the club player to recognising casual and recreational participants, and from promoting just the traditional version of the game where TNZ's CEO suggests "we provide one size that fits all and expect everyone to fit into that" (Long 2017: B6) to introducing various modified tennis formats.

After being kick-started by Grasshoppers, which raised the profile of tennis in primary schools, but being stand-alone did not transfer youngsters into regular club-based competitions, TNZ has created integrated participation and coaching strategies and implemented aligned player and coach development pathways to grow and sustain community tennis. They have adopted and customised initiatives designed by TA and the ITF, especially Tennis Hot Shots, and incorporated these into its player pathway, and through its coach pathway trained club professional coaches to supplement their regional delivery network. These changes and innovations have revitalised community tennis, providing opportunities for competitive, recreational and casual players, and integrating tennis programmes within and between clubs and schools.

Early signs of TNZ's 'development of sport' intervention are promising. It has cemented entry-level initiatives into its pathway, however, it has yet to venture into secondary school tennis, and to date only introduced alternative social and fitness formats at the adult level. There is also work to be done to capture the casual, recreational tennis market, and qualify the participation figures used to measure its impact (Mander 2013).

REFERENCES

Aotearoa Māori Tennis Association. (2006). *A history of Māori tennis.* Manukau: Aotearoa Māori Tennis Association.

Bowers, C. (2013). *The International Tennis Federation: A century of contribution to tennis.* New York: Rizzoli.

Census and Statistics Office of the Dominion of New Zealand. (1925). *The New Zealand official year-book, 1925.* Wellington: W. A. G. Skinner, Government Printer.

Elenio, P. (1986). *Centrecourt: A century of New Zealand tennis 1886–1986.* Wellington: New Zealand Lawn Tennis Association.

Gryphon Governance Consultants. (2011). *Organisational change in seven selected sports: What can be learnt and applied?* Sport and Recreation New Zealand, Wellington.

Hillary Commission. (1988). *KiwiSport: Play it cool. Activities manual.* Wellington: Hillary Commission for Recreation and Sport.

Lawn Tennis Association. (2016). *Annual review 2016.* London: Lawn Tennis Association.

Long, D. (2017, Sunday, October 15). Tennis NZ reveals future plans. *Sunday Star Times*, p. B6.

Mander, C. (2013). *Tennis participation reporting in Australia.* Retrieved from https://atpca.com.au/ten nis-participation-reporting-in-australia-by-colin-mander-2/ website.

Marshall, A. (2011). *Tennis' global evolution is bringing the sport to new markets: An analysis.* Retrieved from http://bleacherreport.com/articles/594875-the-global-evolution-of-tennis-is-bringing-the-sport-to-new-markets-an-analysis website.

Nicholson, M., Hoye, R., & Houlihan, B. (2011). Conclusion. In M. Nicholson, R. Hoye, & B. Houlihan (Eds.), *Participation in sport: International policy perspectives* (pp. 294–308). London and New York: Routledge.

Parent, M., O'Brien, D., & Slack, T. (2012). Organisational theory and sport management. In L. Trenberth & D. Hassan (Eds.), *Managing sport business: An introduction* (pp. 99–120). London and New York: Routledge.

Richards, R. (2017). *Sport participation in Australia.* Retrieved from www.clearinghouseforsport.gov.au/knowl edge_base/sport_participation/community_participation/sport_participation_in_australia website.

Romanos, J. (2013). Tennis. *Te Ara – the Encyclopaedia of New Zealand.* Retrieved from www.TeAra.govt.nz/en/tennis website.

Roughan, J. (2012, September 15). Price we pay for public funds. *New Zealand Herald,* p. A25.

SPARC. (2009). *Sport and recreation – Everyone. Everyday. Sport and Recreation New Zealand's strategic plan 2009–2015.* Wellington: Sport and Recreation New Zealand.

SPARC. (2010). *Community sport strategy: 2010–2015.* Planning document. Sport and Recreation New Zealand, Wellington.

Sport England. (2008). *Grow, sustain, excel: Strategy 2008–11.* London: Sport England.

Sport New Zealand. (2015). *Sport and active recreation in the lives of New Zealand adults. 2013/14 Active New Zealand survey results.* Wellington: Sport New Zealand.

Tennis Europe. (2015). *2015 European tennis report.* Retrieved from http://tenniseurope.org/news_item.aspx ?id=98374 website.

Tennis New Zealand. (2004). *For the good of the game.* Report of the T21 Working Party. Auckland: Tennis New Zealand.

Tennis New Zealand. (2005). *119th annual report and financial statements.* Auckland: Tennis New Zealand.

Tennis New Zealand. (2006a). *120th annual report and financial statements.* Auckland: Tennis New Zealand.

Tennis New Zealand. (2006b). *Final report of the Maiden Committee to the Board of NZ Tennis Inc. ('Maiden Report')* (Unpublished report). Auckland: Tennis New Zealand.

Tennis New Zealand. (2007). *121st annual report and financial statements.* Auckland: Tennis New Zealand.

Tennis New Zealand. (2009). *123rd annual report and financial statements.* Auckland: Tennis New Zealand.

Tennis New Zealand. (2011). *125th annual report and financial statements.* Auckland: Tennis New Zealand.

Tennis New Zealand. (2012). *126th annual report and financial statements.* Auckland: Tennis New Zealand.

Tennis New Zealand. (2013). *New Zealand's tennis participation strategy 2014–2017.* Planning document. Tennis New Zealand, Auckland.

Tennis New Zealand. (2014a). *128th annual report and financial statements 2013–2014.* Auckland: Tennis New Zealand.

Tennis New Zealand. (2014b). *New Zealand's tennis coaching strategy 2014–2017.* Planning document. Tennis New Zealand, Auckland.

Tennis New Zealand. (2015a). *129th annual report and financial statements 2014–2015.* Auckland: Tennis New Zealand.

Tennis New Zealand. (2015b). *New Zealand Post Tennis Hot Shots: Coach manual 2015–2016.* Auckland: Tennis New Zealand

Tennis New Zealand. (2015c). *New Zealand Post Tennis Hot Shots: Community play deliverer course handbook.* Auckland: New Zealand Tennis.

Tennis New Zealand. (2016). *130th annual report and financial statements 2015–2016.* Auckland: Tennis New Zealand.

Tong, J. (2012). *A review of the Grasshoppers program and its impact on junior club membership in New Zealand.* Unpublished report. Tennis New Zealand, Auckland.

Vail, S. E. (2007). Community development and sport participation. *Journal of Sport Management, 21,* 571–596.

Wilkinson, L., & Chalmers, S. (2006). *Grasshoppers: New tennis for kids – Activities manual for coaches and teachers.* Auckland: Tennis New Zealand.

Wilson, E. (2015). *Love game: A history of tennis, from Victorian pastime to global phenomenon.* Chicago, IL: The University of Chicago Press.

Websites

www.facebook.com/TennisHotShotsNZ

www.sportnz.org.nz/en-nz/communities-and-clubs/Coaching/CoachForce/

www.TeAra.govt.nz/en/tennis

www.tennishotshots.kiwi

www.theguardian.com/sport/blog/2015/mar/17/tennis-decline-lta-wimbledon-andy-murray

CHAPTER 9

A whole of football plan

Alec Astle and John Herdman

Football, or soccer as it is known in North America, "is played, watched and talked about more than any other sport" (Murray 1994: ix). Dubbed variously the 'people's game' or the 'beautiful game', football has achieved its global popularity and strength from its simplicity. It can be played on virtually any surface, in any climate, and with the exception of the offside rule, has rules which are easy to understand and interpret (Murray 1994).

Modern football originated in Britain and was brought to NZ in the nineteenth century by early settlers. While football was the dominant code in Britain, in many of its former colonies football was a minority winter sport to rugby (e.g. NZ, parts of Australia) or a local adaptation (e.g. Australia – Australian Rules Football; USA and Canada – American Football) (Murray 1994). In NZ, football began to be played on an organised basis in the 1880s. In 1891, a national body, the New Zealand Football Association (NZFA), was established; NZ played its first international match in 1904; a national club competition, the Chatham Cup, began in the 1920s; NZFA affiliated with FIFA in 1948; and in 1970 a national inter-provincial soccer league was introduced. The latter provided the foundation for the NZ men's team, known as the 'All Whites', to qualify and play in the 1982 World Cup in Spain. This captured the public imagination in NZ like nothing before and provided an enormous boost for the profile of football in the media (Hilton 1991). However, it did not have a coordinated national development programme, and clubs lacked the capability, infrastructure, and services to capitalise on the excitement and interest created by the All Whites performance (see Pause and ponder 9.1).

PAUSE and PONDER 9.1

Iceland's rise in international football: a tribute to its investment in community football development

Iceland, with a population of 335,000, is the smallest nation to ever reach a major football tournament. It did this when it qualified for the UEFA (Union of European Football Associations) European Championship, or simply 'Euro 2016', held in France. The championship was contested by 24 teams, initially divided into six groups of four teams. Iceland qualified in its group for the round of 16, in which it defeated England, to make the quarter-finals, before losing to France.

Iceland's international success is attributed to not only its obsession with football (Ronay 2016), but the 'top-down' flow of investment from its central government and the Icelandic Football Association (IFA) to build a strong foundation of community infrastructure, capability, and services to support the rise and success of football in Iceland. According to Ronay (2016), this included: constructing purpose-built, heated, community indoor football pitches, open to all and staffed by qualified coaches; purchasing land adjacent to schools and funding the creation of enclosed artificial turf pitches; and establishing a IFA coach development programme to recruit and train coaches. Currently, Iceland has 600 highly educated coaches, all with UEFA qualifications, whose expertise is available right down to entry-level children. As Rafnsson suggested in Ronay (2016), "nowhere in the world do as many kids get to practice as much per week for as long with a qualified coach in such good conditions". Iceland's success has continued with it qualifying for the FIFA World Cup in Russia in 2018.

Questions

1. What role does the IFA play in community football development and how has this contributed to Iceland's international success?
2. What emphasis is placed on coach development and coaching children? How does this vary from sports you are familiar with?

In this chapter, football is explored as an example of a traditional, organised team sport in NZ, which historically has struggled for recognition in a rugby-dominated country. Only in the last decade has football's national body, with assistance from successive central government sport agencies, established a holistic development plan to unify the sport, align its stakeholders, and intervene 'top-down' to fulfil its strategic goals to revitalise and grow community football and develop talented players.

This chapter will:

1. Examine the origins and struggles of football in NZ to become established, gain acceptance in schools, and improve its viability and capability as a sport organisation to involve itself in community football.
2. Explore the purpose and direction of NZF's National Football Development Plan, the coincidence of factors that favoured its formulation, and business proposal to assist fund the implementation of its Whole of Football Plan (WOFP) to grow and sustain community football.
3. Discuss NZF's WOFP, the research and best practice on which it was based, its participant-centric, integrated pathways approach to the 'development of sport', and the different national and regional roles and responsibilities in its implementation.
4. Explain the multi-pathway structure of the WOFP's national player development framework, the importance and stages within this of the community participation pathway, and reasons for initially concentrating on its junior pathways.

5. Consider the national and regional delivery networks created to implement the WOFP, their training, planning and reporting procedures, and challenges to its implementation.
6. Review the WOFP's impact on increasing opportunities and experiences for players, and ultimately on growing and sustaining community football.

THE EMERGENCE AND GROWING PAINS OF COMMUNITY FOOTBALL IN NEW ZEALAND

Historically in NZ, 'football' was used in the titles of its main national and regional organisations; the game, however, was known as 'soccer'. It was predominantly club-based, and although it had a limited following in primary schools, it was actively discouraged in most secondary schools, where rugby was recognised as the national sport (Small 2003). It took until the 1960s before secondary schools allowed their students to play soccer. Since then the game has grown steadily in both clubs and schools. By 2000 there were 104,985 registered soccer players in NZ, with two-thirds of these being junior players (5–12 years of age).

From the late 1980s, junior soccer benefitted from the game's inclusion by the national sport agency, the Hillary Commission for Sport and Recreation (Hillary Commission), in its modified KiwiSport programme (Hillary Commission 1988). Although this was mainly a primary school-based programme, it introduced a number of important modified sport principles for sports in NZ to adopt, including: a participant-centric approach, age and stage appropriate formats, fundamental skill development, and small-sided games with more action and involvement for all players (see Chapter 4). In the early 2000s, the NZFA launched a McDonald's branded, entry-level 'Small Whites' initiative embracing these principles to introduce soccer skills to 5–7-year-old boys and girls (Small 2003), while for soccer grades for 10 years and under team sizes were reduced to six or seven players, and competition points gradually dropped.

Although coaching and coach training programmes had been instigated during the 1970s, there was no nationally coordinated approach to coaching soccer. Many volunteer coaches involved in junior soccer came from non-soccer backgrounds, with little or no formal coach training (Walters 2011). This meant soccer struggled "to develop its players and a quality coaching base, with most activity being heavily dependent on unpaid parent helpers" (Worth 2010: 31). Some coaches, with overseas football experiences, had their own distinct views on coaching and playing the game. Many were outcome-driven and often negative about game modifications for junior players (Small 2003; Walters 2011). The pressure on junior players to win by parents and such ambitious coaches, and their uneven treatment, in terms of lack of game time through substitution practices, contributed to the high attrition rate of players in their early teenage years (13–16 years) (Worth 2010). Other factors included: no integrated national pathway of consistent playing opportunities and experiences; young people playing 11-a-side games too early and not touching the ball; a lack of quality coaching from untrained and unsupported volunteer coaches; overstretched and poorly organised clubs; and a focus on talented player development at the expense of providing quality grassroots opportunities and experiences for all players (Kilgallon 2010; Worth 2010). As such, football was likened to "a bucket with a hole in it", which had a pressing need to stop the leak (Herdman, in Kilgallon 2010: B9).

REVIEW QUESTIONS

1. Why did football struggle for early recognition in NZ?
2. Why did football fail to capitalise on the All Whites' success in the 1982 World Cup?
   - Was this unique to football in NZ? (see Facts and figures 1.2).
   - Compare this with Iceland – what are the reasons for their recent international success in football?
3. How did football, like many sports in NZ, benefit from being involved in the KiwiSport programme?
   - How did this change football's approach to junior football?
   - Why were some coaches resistant to it? How did their attitude contribute to football being described as "a bucket with a hole in it"?

A LACK OF NATIONAL LEADERSHIP, DIRECTION, AND INTEGRATION

By the mid-1990s, soccer like many organised team sports, was under pressure from societal change and the diversification of sports (see Chapter 2), and the NZFA was struggling to not only manage its own business but also accommodate the needs of community football overseen by its 22 provincial associations (PAs) (Small 2003). The administration of football needed to become more professional. The catalyst for change was driven by a financial crisis. By 1998, the NZFA was in debt, it lacked the leadership and management capabilities to implement change and had structures that were financially unsustainable. The NZFA required a financial bailout. This was provided mainly by the Hillary Commission on the proviso it improved its governance, leadership, and organisational structure (Gryphon Governance Consultants 2011).

The Hillary Commission assisted the NZFA to improve its governance and management. NZFA became New Zealand Soccer (NZS), adopted a new board structure, and instigated major structural change which merged its 22 PAs into seven Federations, which was seen as the most efficient and cost-effective way for NZS to manage the sport. To reduce its funding shortfall, NZS doubled the levies of all registered players, and formed a partnership with three Federations to support it financially (Gryphon Governance Consultants 2011). This structural change, however, had limited impact on the delivery of community soccer.

By 2007, NZS again faced funding issues. Another financial rescue package was underwritten by three Federations, together with a Kiwibank loan, and the renamed national sport agency, SPARC (Worth 2010). NZS became 'New Zealand Football' (NZF); restructured its staff, reducing them by two-thirds, so it was financially sustainable; and following further SPARC capability support appointed a new board and CEO. By 2009, NZF had recovered financially through increased sponsorship (e.g. McDonald's, Volkswagen), SPARC funding, and revenue from football events (e.g. All Whites winning Oceania qualification to the

2010 World Cup) (Worth 2010). A Strategic Plan (2009–2011) was produced, with two of NZF's four goals being to 'grow the game' and 'develop world class players' (NZF 2008). The achievement of these two strategic goals provided the context for the formulation of a national football development plan in 2009 (Herdman 2009), and subsequent design of a whole of football plan (WOFP) in 2010 (Herdman 2010).

FORMULATING A NATIONAL FOOTBALL DEVELOPMENT PLAN

After the staff restructuring in 2007, the incumbent coach development officer was elevated to director of football, with a wider range of responsibilities, including formulating a national football development plan (2009–2011) to complement NZF's strategic plan (Herdman 2009). The plan's purpose was to unite the game, address its two strategic goals, and drive football forward. It provided a blueprint for the development of the game with a focus on improving the standard of community football. Its intent was to grow the game by increasing the number of football opportunities available to participants and enriching the quality of their football experience (Herdman 2010).

NZF's decision to devise its national football development plan coincided with a combination of factors favourable to change (Herdman 2010). In 2009, SPARC altered its investment strategy to focus on the development of community sport (SPARC 2009a) (see Chapter 2); NZF's plan provided an indication of football's potential to contribute to SPARC's new community sport outcomes; and because of growing player numbers and increased confidence in NZF's capability, football was targeted by SPARC as one of seven sports to receive additional investment and specialist assistance to achieve these outcomes (Astle 2011a; SPARC 2010a). At a similar time, the All Whites success in qualifying for the 2010 World Cup raised football's profile in NZ and provided a windfall of $NZ4m for NZF to invest in growing the game (Worth 2010).

The director of football, like personnel in similar NSO sport development roles in NZ in the 1990s and early 2000s, did not have a tertiary sport development qualification, but relied on his unique knowledge, understanding, and insights accumulated from past practical experience playing, coaching, and working in football. This significantly shaped the design and direction of NZF's national football development plan, similar to how the combination of previous roles and personal experiences of NZC's NDM had earlier influenced the content and structure of its national development plan (Astle 2014) (see Introduction). These influences of the director of football evident in the plan included his: previous involvement as a regional development officer in community football in NZ; understanding of the urgency to improve the organisation and provision of age and stage appropriate opportunities and quality football experiences for junior participants in NZ, especially compared to the high standard of his experiences of playing club football and coaching junior sides in north-east England; and access to a network of NZF board, Federation CEO, and SPARC personnel, who had specialist knowledge and expertise in sport management, community sport development, coach development, and organisational change. The first two sets of influences were instrumental in the director of football determining the pathways of opportunities and experiences to meet the needs of the football community, and ensuring the game was more organised and meaningful. The latter set of influences was important for the ongoing support, encouragement, and guidance provided to the director of football on the dynamics of sport development, and creation of underpinning systems to fund, market and achieve acceptance from football stakeholders of the mechanics of implementing, managing and monitoring the plan.

Although the plan proposed a major revitalisation of football in NZ from 2011 to 2017, it lacked the necessary financial justification and guidelines for implementation. To remedy these a business plan was prepared which outlined the substantial funding required to launch a project of this magnitude in terms of likely costs, potential revenue sources, and possible risks; and provided an overview of its holistic WOFP, "to grow the sport of football in New Zealand through providing consistent nationwide development initiatives to deliver a consistent high quality experience at all levels of the game" (Herdman 2010: 10). It indicated how the plan would be delivered, with its ultimate goal being NZF having "the capability to deliver football in a seamless manner to all players regardless of age, gender, ethnicity or ability and provide them with a high quality experience tailored to their individual needs" (Herdman 2010: 10). In 2010, the business plan was presented to SPARC, as the potential principal investor, and they agreed to increase their sport development investment in football to assist turn NZF's WOFP into practice (SPARC 2010b). This endorsement by SPARC prompted a range community Gaming Trusts and commercial sponsors (e.g. ASB – Auckland Savings Bank, Volkswagen, McDonald's, Persil, and Nike) to also underwrite the design of the WOFP and its implementation in 2011.

REVIEW QUESTIONS

1. What was the catalyst for the NZFA to change and become more professionalised?
2. What organisational changes occurred? Did this benefit community football? If not, when and how did NZF ensure it did, and what was its focus?
3. What was the purpose and direction of the national football development plan?
4. What three sets of influences underpinned the plan? How did these impact its content?

THE WHOLE OF FOOTBALL PLAN

The WOFP introduced major 'frame breaking' organisational change and innovation within community football (Parent, O'Brien, and Slack 2012) (see Chapter 6). Its intent was to galvanise the efforts and investment of the extended football family to make a lasting change to the quality and consistency of football delivery. The WOFP was described by Herdman (2010: 19) as:

> the road map for the future development of football in New Zealand. It places all stakeholders on the same page with the aim of aligning their thinking and providing the necessary direction to ensure that they can all work together to develop the game in a coherent, effective and efficient manner.

The WOFP was based on three years of preparatory research. During this time, the director of football visited the national bodies of football in the Netherlands, Germany, Switzerland, England, Australia, and Japan to examine their football practices and programmes, interview their coaching and development staff, and gather information about their strategies and initiatives to ascertain what actually works in developing the game. These findings emphasised the importance of "more football, more fun, persuading kids to become 'footballers for life', aiming for quality instead of numbers and crucially, investing just as much into the grassroots as the elite" (Kilgallon 2010: B9).

Back in NZ, the director of football engaged two Auckland University doctorate students to evaluate the information gathered from the visited countries, review the programmes of over 30 other football associations and NSOs both domestically and internationally, and undertake a detailed survey of the academic literature on sport development, especially Balyi's stage-based LTAD model (Balyi 2001, 2002) (see Chapter 2), and SPARC's Sport and Recreation Pathway (SPARC 2009b, 2009c) and Coach Development Framework (SPARC 2006). The best practice evidence and ideas from these were adapted and interwoven into the WOFP's framework of integrated football pathways and initiatives to create a unique NZ approach to football development.

The increased SPARC funding during the WOFP's formulation process allowed the director of football to assemble a small, highly qualified national football development unit (NFDU) of coaching and development personnel. It was the exceptionality of the NFDU and its leadership by the director of football that was fundamental to the design and implementation of the WOFP.

The central feature of the WOFP was its 'development of sport' model, which reflected a balanced, holistic perspective of football in NZ, and provided the sport with a logical and coherent overarching structure. The model presented a 'bottom-to-top', 'side-to-side', whole-of-sport framework in which integrated development pathways for players, coaches, referees, and administrators were aligned into one unified system for football, with players placed at the centre of the process (see Figures 2.2, 9.1, and 9.2). Addressing players' needs through the provision of pathways of age and stage appropriate playing initiatives, and then surrounding these with support mechanisms, such as competition structures, coaching, facilities, and capable clubs, was seen as imperative to ensuring the consistency and quality of players' football opportunities and experiences (Herdman 2010).

The WOFP framework identified four interconnected sets of pathways, pertaining to player, coach, referee, and administrator development (see Figure 9.1). Superimposed on the player pathways were a sequence of initiatives offering age and stage appropriate, modified, conventional, and performance opportunities for recreational, participation, and talented players. These were surrounded by the development pathways for coaches, referees, and administrators to equip them with the capability, requisite knowledge and skills to service and support the needs of players commensurate with their age, ability, and interests. These pathways and initiatives provided a whole of football framework for the development of football in NZ (see Figure 9.2).

Due to the scale of the project and available resources, it was decided the WOFP's initiatives would be implemented from the bottom-up in three stages over six years, commencing in 2011. This would allow resources and attention to be concentrated on one level of the game at a time, and give Federations, clubs, and schools sufficient time to progressively improve their capability and services to accommodate each stage. The focus of stage 1 was predominantly the junior (4–12 years) level of the game, existing youth and senior initiatives, and several projects related to women's, referees and futsal development. The junior level was the logical place to begin as this is "where eager kids (and their parents) get their first taste of the sport" (Herdman 2011: 8). After establishing a strong foundation for the game in stage 1, stages 2 and 3 would subsequently be introduced as NZF's development emphasis moved up to the youth (13–17 years), then senior (18+ years) levels of the game. The same key development principles and strategies adopted at the junior level would also permeate these other levels, always with the goal of creating consistently, high-quality football experiences for all players.

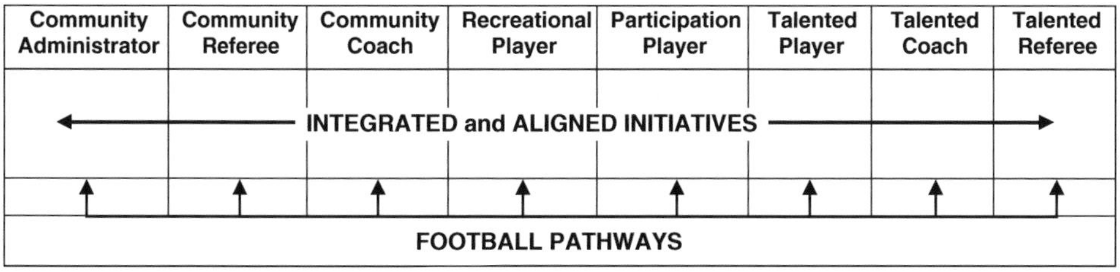

Community Administrator	Community Referee	Community Coach	Recreational Player	Participation Player	Talented Player	Talented Coach	Talented Referee
← ————————— INTEGRATED and ALIGNED INITIATIVES ————————— →								
↑	↑	↑	↑	↑	↑	↑	↑
FOOTBALL PATHWAYS								

FIGURE 9.1 New Zealand Football's whole of sport framework development pathways

Source: Abridged from Herdman (2010: 18).

The WOFP's design and implementation was a 'top-down' intervention. NZF's NFDU had responsibility for leading and managing the plan; devising its initiatives and support resources; sourcing funding for these; and marketing and monitoring the plan and its initiatives, to ensure stakeholders, especially the Federations, were well informed, engaged, and on track. The Federations had to formulate regional football development plans; source community Gaming Trust funding; engage with local councils to secure facilities; establish regional football development units (RFDUs) by appointing football development managers (FDMs) and football development officers (FDOs) with expertise to implement the WOFP in local clubs and schools, and collect performance data for NZF on key outcomes. Clubs and schools, however, were the WOFP's focus. Their role, with NZF and Federation support, was to deliver the WOFP's initiatives, restructure how the game was played and administered, and provide more meaningful football opportunities and better quality experiences for their players (Herdman 2010).

The WOFP provided a clear vision for the cohesive development of the sport and presented an opportunity to achieve much needed alignment across the football community, maximise investment, create greater efficiency and consistency in the organisation and delivery of community football, and ultimately grow and sustain the game.

REVIEW QUESTIONS

1. What was the purpose of NZF's WOFP?
2. List two sources of evidence-based research that underpinned the WOFP?
3. What was the central feature of the WOFP? Describe its structure and objective.
4. Who were critical to the actual delivery of the WOFP and why?

THE NATIONAL PLAYER DEVELOPMENT FRAMEWORK

While the WOFP provided the overarching vision and structure for football in NZ, its nucleus was the participant-centric, national player development framework (see Figure 9.2). The framework's pathways charted a progression of appropriate and appealing football opportunities for all players from entry-level juniors through to senior adult footballers, irrespective of whether their motivation is recreation, personal improvement, or excellence,

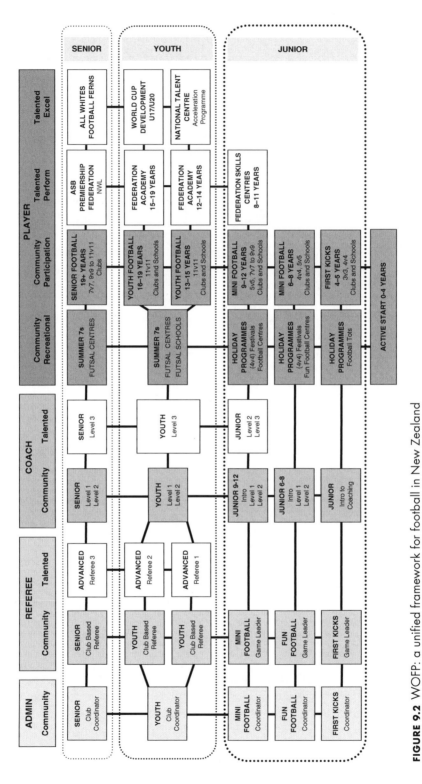

FIGURE 9.2 WOFP: a unified framework for football in New Zealand

Source: Abridged from Herdman et al. (2011a: 6–7).

and takes account of the mix of different support and services that contribute to the quality of their football experience (Meylan, Koutstaal, Priestman, Eaddy, Rumpf, and Herdman 2011).

Although the framework was influenced by Balyi's LTAD model (Balyi 2001, 2002), as it relates to players' physical, mental, and emotional growth and maturation, its development philosophy, game formats, competition structures, and training schedules were designed specifically to meet NZ player needs, and address gaps in their development. Underlying the framework and content of its national initiatives is a series of key principles to guide the long-term development of the game and its players (see Facts and figures 9.1).

FACTS and FIGURES 9.1

Football's guiding development principles

1. **Accumulation of hours and number of touches.** Research indicates it takes 10,000 hours of football-specific practice (i.e. structured coach-led practice) and play (i.e. unstructured backyard football) to reach a high level of technical proficiency. Guidelines are provided on the number of hours players at different stages of development should train and play per week to accumulate these hours, and the progression of small-sided games to ensure junior players get more touches of the football.
2. **Early engagement.** This is advocated for players (i.e. 4–12 years) where the emphasis is on discovery, skill development, and quality of experience, so they acquire an intrinsic motivation and love of football.
3. **Recognising development age.** Differences in the development age of players within the same chronological age group are recognised, and recommendations provided to coaches about being flexible in designing training programmes to cater for the individual needs of young players.
4. **Training emphasis periods.** During maturation, there are optimal periods in the development of young players, when they physically are ready to respond to specific types of training and skill development. Guidelines are provided for coaches on correct training emphasis to maximise these periods.
5. **Football fitness.** Cognisant of players' training emphasis periods, guidance is provided to ensure the physical intensity and football-specific methods of training match players' developmental age.
6. **Four corners approach.** This places players at the centre of the development process to ensure enjoyment, competency, and retention in the game, through football experiences that meet four key player development needs: physical, mental, social/emotional, and technical/tactical. The emphasis on each of these needs varies by age and stage as players progress through the framework.
7. **Age appropriate games.** A progression of age appropriate, modified, small-sided games is promoted for junior players transitioning to conventional 11-a-side football for youth and adult players. At the junior level, small-sided games ensure young players have fun, learn skills, have more touches on the ball and one-on-one situations.

8. **Talent identification and development.** Because player development is dynamic and non-linear, there are multiple pathways offering flexibility, individual optimisation and return routes for players. These pathways begin to distinguish from eight years of age between community and talented opportunities for players.
9. **National framework integration and alignment.** To optimise player development, all stakeholders and providers, need to be aligned and aware of their roles in contributing to player development.
10. **Based on evidence and dynamic.** The framework is underpinned by recent academic research and best practice. Football needs to stay at the forefront of this to ensure a dynamic approach to players' development in the future.

Source: Based on Meylan et al. (2011).

Questions

1. What key concept underpins the first seven principles and how relevant is it to other sports?
2. What is the difference between age and stage?
3. What game modifications are evident in the principles and why?

The framework comprises four pathways for players, within which four of the five stages in SPARC's Sport and Recreation Pathway (SPARC 2009b, 2009c) are used to differentiate between community and talented football (see Figure 2.4). It does this by subdividing community football into 'recreational' and 'participation' players, corresponding to SPARC's pathway 'Learn' and 'Participate' stages; and talented football into 'talented-perform' and 'talented-excel' players, equivalent to SPARC's 'Perform' and 'Excel' stages (Meylan et al. 2011; SPARC 2009b, 2009c).

Community football includes the majority of junior to senior players who play for schools and clubs. It begins with junior players being introduced to fundamental football skills and modified games, through to youth and adult players playing conventional football. The community recreational and participation pathways provide flexibility and "are about ensuring all players regardless of their ability levels and motivations are presented with high quality opportunities. . . to play and enjoy football" (Meylan et al. 2011: 16).

From eight years of age, gifted players are identified and selected to attend talented-perform football. This is the foundation of NZF's talented player pathways and provides opportunities for these young players to receive football specific training with highly qualified coaches, in preparation for higher level regional representative football opportunities. At 13/14 years of age, the very best of these talented players are placed into a talent acceleration programme, with the best coaches and facilities. The long-term intent is for them to achieve national representative honours and a professional status (Meylan et al. 2011).

FRAMEWORK COMMUNITY PARTICIPATION STAGES

The central focus of NZF's national player development framework was community football. Its participation pathway identifies seven stages in a player's development as they transition from junior through youth to adult football (see Figure 9.2) (Meylan et al. 2011). Each stage is based on a player-centric approach, with clear guidelines provided for coaches and administrators about each stage to meet player needs, including: the apportionment of training time to spend on general movement, football technique, football coordination and small-sided games; and game day organisation in terms of format, player numbers, field, goal and ball size, and match duration and frequency.

The first three junior stages focus on creating a positive football experience, having fun and learning FMS and football specific skills through playing a progression of small-sided games. The two youth stages are where players begin to specialise in football, play conventional 11-a-side matches, and learn the physical, technical, tactical and mental skills to transition into adult football. The two adult stages provide opportunities for players to perfect and stabilise their performance. Across all the stages is superimposed a 'football for life' philosophy. This encourages players at any stage, regardless of age or ability, to play community football for enjoyment, fitness and friendship. It promotes "personal success to ensure they remain enthusiastic and choose to stay involved in football" (Meylan et al. 2011: 25), either as players, or to support the game as coaches, referees, and administrators.

STAGE 1: JUNIOR DEVELOPMENT PATHWAYS

Although the national player development pathway formed the centrepiece of the WOFP, it was aligned with similar coach, referee, and administrator pathways to provide players with appropriate support and services (Figure 9.2). When Stage 1 was implemented in 2011, it concentrated primarily on the junior football pathways, including the coaching, refereeing, and capability initiatives needed to cement these in place. This was to ensure that at each stage there was specific support for players, such as competition structures and coaching, tailored to meet their needs and stage of development (Herdman 2010). Two detailed instructional manuals were published to support coaches organise and run the first three stages of the community pathway and its recreational pathway holiday programmes (Herdman, Priestman, Koutstaal, Eaddy, Readings, and Meylan 2011a, 2011b).

The decision to focus on junior football was based on the premise to grow the game, and NZF first needed to strengthen its base. The initial emphasis was to expand the opportunities and experiences offered to junior players, by enhancing the quality and range of football initiatives and services, to increase recruitment and retention. To accomplish this, three distinct but interconnected recreation, participation, and emerging talent pathways were designed for junior players overlain with age-related, game format and competition initiatives; serviced by better qualified junior coaches/referees; and clubs with capability systems and procedures to support their consistent delivery. These coaching and capability requirements were provided by the introduction of: two coach development pathways to improve the quality of junior coaches and coaching in junior clubs; Quality Marks for clubs, schools, and private providers to raise standards and ensure consistency in the delivery of junior football; an online programme (Goal Net) for clubs to improve their administrative processes; and specific 'females in football' opportunities to allow more girls to experience and participate in football (Herdman 2010).

Most important of these was coach development and coaching because they were critical to player development. This required NZF to train and support sufficient coaches with the requisite knowledge and skills to meet the needs of junior players. Previously, football did not have a coordinated or aligned national coach development programme.

NZF's goal was to create a 'culture of coaching excellence' within junior clubs (Herdman 2010). Under the WOFP, clubs were placed at the centre of the coach development process and empowered to have their own club-based coach educators trained to deliver courses within their club. This allowed clubs more flexibility in when and where they ran their courses, and removed barriers, like cost, travel, and the expectation inexperienced volunteers, often with limited confidence and football competence, would attend centralised courses to become junior coaches.

REVIEW QUESTIONS

1. What was the national player development framework and where did it sit in the WOFP?
   - How many pathways did the framework offer players, and what was the intent of each pathway?
2. Why did NZF decide to begin with junior football when implementing its WOFP?
3. Why was coach development considered so important, and how did NZF propose to improve its delivery?

IMPLEMENTING THE PLAN: THE FOOTBALL DEVELOPMENT NETWORK

In late 2010, in preparation for introducing the WOFP, NZF persuaded its Federations to restructure their existing coaching and development delivery networks by recruiting a highly capable workforce with the expertise and skills to implement the WOFP's strategies and initiatives. Each Federation advertised for a FDM and FDOs to establish their RFDUs. Finding the right people was not easy, as the role was focused on development not coaching. They were to be field operatives working with parents, teachers, and volunteers in schools and clubs, enthusing youngsters about football's opportunities, and assisting schools and clubs make the changes necessary to adopt and deliver the new initiatives, especially the junior pathways and coach development.

By early 2011, most Federations had engaged a FDM and FDOs, many with experiences of football in England and Scotland. In preparation for implementing the WOFP's first stage, NZF's director of football and NFDU staff, conducted a nine-day national induction workshop in Auckland for these newly appointed personnel. The intent of the workshop was to educate and inform them about the WOFP, its purpose, strategies, and initiatives, and their critical role, responsibilities, and likely challenges as regional change agents in its implementation (Astle 2011b, 2011c) (see Pause and ponder 9.2). Practical sessions were also used to improve their understanding of the principles underpinning the WOFP and demonstrate how to communicate and consistently present the various football initiatives within schools and clubs to ensure the quality of the football experience for junior players.

PAUSE and PONDER 9.2

WOFP implementation: change messages

1. **Change must be tested** – with initiatives piloted, and amended as appropriate, before being launched.
2. **Change is a slow process** – especially when it involves diffusing new ideas within volunteer-led schools and clubs. It takes time to adapt and adopt them as the norm.
3. **Change must be integrated** – to be effective, with player and coach development aligned and operating in tandem. More and better players need to be supported and serviced by better and more coaches.
4. **Change is incremental** – like building a pyramid, first a strong foundation must be laid, adding one block at a time (i.e. manageable amounts for an organisation's capability and capacity versus its available resources). WOFP initiatives must be prioritised and built from the bottom up.
5. **Change must be communicated ('sell change')** – with FDMs and FDOs having an in-depth knowledge and understanding of the WOFP, its purpose and principles, and the objectives, organisation, and outcomes of each of its initiatives, to inform and persuade volunteers, parents, and teachers in schools and clubs of their value and benefits.
6. **Change is about standing in someone else's shoes** – to understand the obstacles facing volunteers in schools and clubs in adopting new initiatives, and parents registering children in them. Encouragement, support, and guidance must be provided to overcome these.
7. **Change raises questions of how many (quantity) versus how good (quality)** – and the need to balance these in terms of recruitment versus retention, and growth versus sustainability.
8. **Change will be resisted** – status quo versus value added, conservatism versus innovation – new initiatives must have a value proposition for schools and clubs that benefits them and their participants.

Regional change agents such as FDMs and FDOs must understand these messages about the change process and realise that "sports development cannot be an overnight panacea; to be effective it will take time" (Watt 2003: 72).

Source: Astle (2012).

Questions

1. Why is introducing change into community sport a challenging process?
2. Select a change introduced into a sport of your choice, and indicate which of the above messages were evident in its adoption?

To ensure the Federations and their RFDUs were on track and aligned with the WOFP's strategic objectives and funding, a system of accountabilities including planning, SLAs, agreed outcomes with a portion of 'at risk' funding, and reporting procedures were introduced by NZF. Each Federation was required to create a regional football development plan and annual business plan, with the latter replicated by individual business plans by FDMs and FDOs to align and guide their annual schedule of work. Regular reviews of Federation, FDM and FDO business plans were undertaken. FDOs were required to record appropriate school and club data to measure WOFP outcomes, which FDMs collated and reported monthly to NZF to assess the effectiveness and impact of specific WOFP initiatives on participation. Unfortunately, NZF had no accurate participation data, so during stage 1 they had to establish procedures to collect data to create baselines against which outcomes and progress could be measured (Herdman 2010). After the WOFP's first season of operation, a review was undertaken by Snowling (2011) to gauge its impact on community football (see Case study 9.1).

CASE STUDY 9.1
WOFP review

Neil Snowling, Senior Advisor – Monitoring and Performance, Sport New Zealand, Wellington, New Zealand

In late 2011, the NZF Federation CEOs were interviewed to ascertain the WOFP's impact on junior football after its first season of implementation. Overall, they were very positive about the WOFP in terms of the principles, research, and best practice on which it was based; the financial support, quality resources, and overall guidance provided by NZF; and its ability to grow the game. It created significant alignment across the game and was given the highest priority by the Federations in their business plans. It also improved the Federations' relationships with schools, clubs, local councils, RSTs, and each other, and ensured their staff involved with schools and clubs delivered beneficial initiatives, not arbitrary activities for the sake of it.

The Federations were pleased with their RFDU staff structures, and technical capabilities of their FDMs and FDOs. The junior participation pathway initiatives had been prioritised as they were considered critical to changing "the 'fabric' of how football is delivered in New Zealand" (Snowling 2011: 1). The full range of WOFP initiatives expected to be delivered in stage 1, however, had not occurred because: there were too many for the FDOs to effectively implement and volunteers in schools and clubs to cope with at once; the late timing of the release of some initiatives by NZF; and the interest and receptiveness of schools and clubs to be involved. So in season one, the junior participation pathway and recreational pathway school holiday festivals were successful. The talented pathway and girls football received limited attention, and the recreational pathway ASB Fun Football Centres were halted because of conflict with similar club revenue raising activities. Coach development although seen as critical did not occur at a rate sufficient to support junior player growth.

Despite the satisfaction with the WOFP's early impact, several challenges were identified to be subsequently addressed:

1. Timeliness and planning of implementation raised concerns about the late receipt of initiatives from NZF, and the speed, volume, and expectations of initiatives to be delivered. Disquiet was expressed about the sustainability of future planned implementation, and how it would affect delivery quality and need to prioritise some initiatives over others. It was felt better NZF planning was required to ensure the WOFP roll out was achievable, without sacrificing quality by delivering too much too quickly, and within acceptable time frames in which current and future work were balanced.
2. Resources and capability were stretched putting pressure on Federations who had difficulty recruiting the right people for their FDO positions, and on their FDOs to deliver the various initiatives. The problem was some FDOs lacked the skills and capability to deal with the scope of their role. While they had strong technical/coaching capabilities, they did not have a background in administering, managing, strategic thinking, or planning.
3. Geographical spread of some Federations made it difficult to service more remote areas with available staff, because distances and cost of travel limited the time FDOs could spend delivering the WOFP.
4. Understanding the WOFP and communicating the change process required more extensive consultation and communication by NZF with school and club volunteers and parents, to understand their needs and expectations, and educate them about the WOFP, its purpose, individual initiatives and principles to reduce resistance to change, and get better acceptance and buy-in.
5. Lack of facilities put considerable pressure on existing facilities.
6. Recreational pathway initiatives created conflict with similar initiatives usually delivered by clubs and private providers to raise revenue. NZF needs to assess the viability of these national initiatives.
7. Differences in funder requirements consumed considerable FDM and FDO time, because of no alignment between different funders' expectations around delivery and reporting.

The Federations agreed the WOFP was moving the game forward, improving alignment across the sport, and changing the game's content with its age and stage appropriate formats. However, they also felt some challenges had arisen because the WOFP required "a change in culture in the whole football community and generally NZF underestimated this change process and what is required to achieve this" (Snowling 2011: 6).

Questions

1. List the positive impacts of the WOFP implementation.
2. What challenges were experienced, and why were some initiatives prioritised over others?
3. Which two challenges do you consider the most significant, and what key messages would you relay to a sport considering implementing a sport development plan?

THE ONGOING IMPACT

In early 2012, NZF organised a second national workshop for its FDMs and FDOs to review the WOFP's progress. The success of the junior participation pathway initiatives in their first year was acknowledged, and issues raised by Snowling's review discussed, especially the pace and volume of implementation, why some initiatives were prioritised over others, and the lack of specific competencies among the FDMs and FDOs to plan, deliver, administer, and monitor the full range of initiatives. It was determined for 2012 the initiatives prioritised in 2011 would continue to be expanded, but more attention must be given to coach development and launching the junior talented-perform pathway. To take pressure off the FDMs and FDOs, NZF secured additional Sport NZ sport development and targeted KiwiSport investment to expand its Federation RFDUs, with part-time football development coaches, and full-time women's development officers and futsal development officers to implement the junior recreational pathway, girls' football and futsal initiatives respectively (NZF 2012).

The resignations of NZF's inaugural director of football in late 2011, who masterminded the WOFP, and had seniority at NZF and respect from the Federations, followed in the next 18 months by its CoachForce director and the replacement director of football strongly impacted the WOFP's phased implementation. The WOFP drifted, with limited NZF direction, and reduced focus on the WOFP's guiding principles and initiatives. Fortunately, the experience and knowledge within the Federation RFDUs kept the programme on track, albeit with less guidance, support, and pace.

In 2014, NZF appointed a community football director with considerable experience of the WOFP process as a Federation CEO, the confidence of the Federations, and leadership and planning capabilities to refocus them on the WOFP, but with a revised timetable. While the WOFP blueprint remained, more emphasis was placed on clubs to improve their management (Quality Mark), administration (Goal Net), services (coach and referee development), and infrastructure (facilities) to ensure the quality of their delivery of community football (Mitchell 2017). To accomplish this, and refine existing or design new WOFP initiatives, NZF's NFDU specialist staff was expanded to cover operations, competitions, growth, and technical development. More regular meeting opportunities were scheduled for NFDU and RFDU staff to interact, be updated and exchange ideas; and all new staff to attend national inductions.

While the WOFP's staged implementation has slowed since 2012, it has continued to increase the quality of player experiences through appropriate playing opportunities and higher standards of coaching. Junior player numbers have grown, with total participation reaching 117,000 (90,000 males and 27,000 females) by 2016. This growth has been supported by Quality Mark and Goal Net improvements in clubs; the upskilling of around 5,000 coaches annually through coaching workshops, including over 1,600 new coaches being trained through attending free, introductory football and futsal coach education courses (2016 – 1,895 new coaches); and engagement of referee development officers in each Federation to train and deploy community and talented referees (NZF 2016b).

In addition to participation numbers increasing, since 2014 over 50,000 children have annually sampled football at various community recreational initiative sessions (2016 – 53,988 junior footballers) (NZF 2016b); and the FIFA Live Your Goals Week has increased the awareness of football for females, with over 9,000 girls involved in 100 fun festivals around the country (NZF 2016b). For talented footballers, the talent pathways have been established, from Federation skill centres for junior footballers, through to Federation and national talent centres for youth and adult players. In 2016, the skill centres provided opportunities for nearly 3,000 young players (NZF 2016b).

The most extraordinary growth, however, has occurred in lifestyle football formats, especially futsal (see Facts and figures 9.2). Futsal's popularity arises from its ease of consumption as a sport, being: mainly indoors, small-sided, pay-for-play, flexible, and a non-club experience (NZF 2016a).

FACTS and FIGURES 9.2

Futsal: a rapidly growing sport

Futsal is a modified, five-a-side, indoor variant of football, which originated in South America (Brazil and Uruguay). It is played by two teams of five players, including a goalkeeper, with a smaller, lower-bounce ball than a football, on a hard court surface in a gymnasium or similar indoor arena. Because the game allows rolling substitutions, it is fast-paced, action-packed, with maximum involvement. "A past survey revealed there were over 40 times more touches in futsal than football and its intensity produced a similar heart rate to squash" (Egan 2016: D6).

In NZ, futsal was run by independent operators with minimal national coordination, but in 2010 NZF took control of the sport, and has engaged a national and regional workforce of 14 futsal specialists to oversee its management and development. A futsal-specific coach education programme has been implemented to develop coaches for the sport.

It is now one of the fastest growing sports in NZ, with 21,000 players registered in different leagues. The most talented players represent their Federations in a national domestic competition and NZF has formed NZ men's (Futsal Whites) and women's (Futsal Ferns) teams.

Questions

1. Why is futsal so popular?
2. From your knowledge, what other indoor formats of traditional sports are popular, and are the reasons for their popularity (a) similar or (b) different to futsal?
3. What lessons could traditional organised sports learn from futsal to improve their appeal?

In 2016, NZF formulated a long-term strategic plan for 2016–2025, 'Shaping Football in New Zealand' (NZF 2016a). The plan operates in three-year cycles to allow priorities to be regularly reviewed and refreshed. It is underpinned by its two operational plans: the WOFP (Herdman 2011, updated NZF 2017) (community football) and 'Beyond Football Plan' (NZF 2014) (high performance), whose future key outcomes are respectively "More New Zealanders playing and loving football" and "Our elite teams winning at global pinnacle events" (NZF 2016a: 4). To ensure the former's participation outcomes, NZF has reiterated its commitment that "the needs of our players must remain at the core of our thinking and doing" (NZF 2016b: 36). To do this, it recognises that critical to stage 2 of the WOFP is the need to address the issue of retention, as the current junior 'participation bulge' transfers into youth football. Presently, in this transfer player numbers drop from 54,000 junior footballers down to 26,000 youth players (NZF 2016a). The challenge to counter this faces NZF and its Federations as they embark on implementing the WOFP's youth initiatives.

REVIEW QUESTIONS

1. In implementing the WOFP, how did NZF underestimate the change process and what were the effects?
   - Consider Pause and ponder 9.2, and suggest how NZF might have prevented some of the challenges that arose from the WOFP's implementation.
2. What has been the impact of the WOFP on community football numbers?

CONCLUSION

This chapter has explored the struggles facing football in NZ as a minority sport to gain acceptance. This was not helped by a NSO that at times was dysfunctional, over-focused on searching for talent and international recognition, and lacked the capability and financial viability to lead and develop football as a sport. The latter was left to the uncoordinated but passionate efforts of volunteers in clubs, and later schools. There was no common approach, attitudes were focused on talent, winning, and 11-a-side football for all, with the resultant variances in players' football experiences contributing to a high dropout rate, especially of youth footballers.

In the first decade of the twenty-first century, a confluence of factors, including the appointment of a transformational director of football, supported by a restructured NSO with a new CEO, board and awareness of the need to adopt a more holistic view of football, saw the creation of a series of plans, that were collated into one comprehensive WOFP to develop football from bottom to top, with the object of growing and strengthening football's community base. The WOFP represented not only a significant change in NZF's philosophy of football, but also provided an exemplar for SPARC of the whole-of-sport process, and how it creates a context for community sport development, which other sports could use to revitalise and grow their sports. It was participant-centric, with multiple pathways that recognised player development as non-linear and flexible, and provided opportunities, but more importantly experiences for players to satisfy their needs, realise their potential, and enjoy the game for life. For this to occur, matching coach, referee, and administrator pathways were wrapped around the player pathways to provide the necessary support, services, capability, and infrastructure to enable players to fulfil their football desires.

Because the WOFP was three years in the making, it was launched as a package of strategies and initiatives at each stage to be implemented simultaneously. The volume and speed of implementation, coupled with the expectations of NZF, however, were greater than the competencies of many FDMs and FDOs, and capability of volunteers to absorb, adopt, and effectively deliver these in schools and clubs. This caused some early 'teething' issues, as did the resignation of key national personnel, but the subsequent slowing of the pace of change, consolidating implemented initiatives, addressing identified key areas of concern, especially coach development, and increasing the RFDUs with specialist staff to deal with the junior recreational initiatives, girls' football and futsal, has allowed the junior stage to be consolidated prior to commencing the second stage of youth football. The health of community football is in good shape, player, coach, and referee numbers have grown, opportunities and experiences have diversified, and NZF has also recorded more consistent international success in both men's and women's football.

ACKNOWLEDGEMENT

Thank you to Cameron Mitchell, former Community Football Director, Football New Zealand, current Chief Executive, Cricket Wellington, for contributing to the 'The ongoing impact' section in this chapter.

REFERENCES

Astle, A. M. (2011a). *Community sport implementation plan: Collaborative delivery and outcomes.* Planning document. Sport and Recreation New Zealand, Wellington.

Astle, A. M. (2011b). *Whole-of-football plan: A SPARC perspective.* Powerpoint presentation New Zealand Football First Training and Support Workshop, Auckland Sport and Recreation New Zealand, Wellington.

Astle, A. M. (2011c). *Fundamental principles of community sport development.* Powerpoint presentation New Zealand Football First Training and Support Workshop, Auckland. Sport and Recreation New Zealand, Wellington.

Astle, A. M. (2012). *Community sport development: A major change process.* Powerpoint presentation New Zealand Football Second Training and Support Workshop, Auckland. Sport and Recreation New Zealand, Wellington.

Astle, A. M. (2014). *Sport development – Plan, programme, and practice: A case study of the planned intervention by New Zealand Cricket into cricket in New Zealand.* Unpublished PhD thesis, Massey University, Palmerston North, New Zealand.

Balyi, I. (2001). Sport system building and long-term athlete development in British Columbia. *Coaches Report, 8*(1), 22–28.

Balyi, I. (2002). Long-term athlete development: The system and solutions. *Faster, Higher, Stronger, 14,* 6–9.

Egan, B. (2016, Saturday, December 17). Futsal latest boom sport in New Zealand. *The Press,* p. D6.

Gryphon Governance Consultants. (2011). *Organisational change in seven selected sports: What can be learnt and applied?* Sport and Recreation New Zealand, Wellington.

Herdman, J. (2009). *National football development plan.* New Zealand Football, Auckland.

Herdman, J. (2010). *Whole of football plan: Business plan.* New Zealand Football, Auckland.

Herdman, J. (2011). *Whole of football plan: One game, one team.* Auckland: New Zealand Football.

Herdman, J., Priestman, B., Koutstaal, J., Eaddy, S., Readings, T., & Meylan, C. (Eds.). (2011a). *Junior framework: Love the game.* Auckland: New Zealand Football.

Herdman, J., Priestman, B., Koutstaal, J., Eaddy, S., Readings, T., & Meylan, C. (2011b). *ASB fun football centres: Keeping our children active and healthy.* Auckland: New Zealand Football.

Hillary Commission. (1988). *KiwiSport: Play it cool.* Activities Manual. Wellington: Hillary Commission for Recreation and Sport.

Hilton, T. (1991). *An association with soccer: The NZFA celebrates its first 100 years.* Auckland: New Zealand Football Association.

Kilgallon, S. (2010, August 29). Focus shifts to fun for kids: Game a bucket with a hole in it. Backgrounder, *Sunday Star Times*, p. B9.

Meylan, C., Koutstaal, J., Priestman, B., Eaddy, S., Rumpf, M., & Herdman, J. (2011). *National player development framework: Players first*. Auckland: New Zealand Football.

Mitchell, C. (2017). *Federation investment schedule 2017–2020*. Planning document. New Zealand Football, Auckland.

Murray, B. (1994). *Football: A history of the world game*. Aldershot: Scolar Press.

New Zealand Football. (2008). *Strategic plan 2009–2011*. Auckland: New Zealand Football.

New Zealand Football. (2012). *SPARC investment overview*. Investment Application Commentary. New Zealand Football, Auckland.

New Zealand Football. (2014). *Beyond football: Winning at FIFA World Cups*. Auckland: New Zealand Football.

New Zealand Football. (2016a). *Strategic plan: Shaping football in New Zealand 2016–2025*. Auckland: New Zealand Football.

New Zealand Football. (2016b). *New Zealand Football: Annual report 2016*. Auckland: New Zealand Football.

New Zealand Football. (2017). *Whole of football plan*. Auckland: New Zealand Football.

Parent, M., O'Brien, D., & Slack, T. (2012). Organisational theory and sport management. In L. Trenberth & D. Hassan (Eds.), *Managing sport business: An introduction* (pp. 99–120). London and New York: Routledge.

Ronay, B. (2016). *Football, fire and ice: The inside story of Iceland's remarkable rise*. Retrieved from www.theguardian.com/football/2016/jun/08/iceland-stunning-rise-euro-2016-gylfi-sigurdsson-lars-lagerback website.

Small, J. (2003). *Canterbury soccer 1903–2003*. Christchurch: Mainland Soccer.

Snowling, N. (2011). *Interview findings for New Zealand Football Federation CEOs*. Programme review. Sport and Recreation New Zealand, Wellington.

SPARC. (2006). *Coach development framework*. Wellington: Astra Print.

SPARC. (2009a). *Sport and recreation – Everyone. Everyday. Sport and Recreation New Zealand's strategic plan 2009–2015*. Wellington: Sport and Recreation New Zealand.

SPARC. (2009b). *Sport and recreation pathway*. Unpublished document. Sport and Recreation New Zealand, Wellington.

SPARC. (2009c). *NZ sport and recreation pathway*. Unpublished presentation. Sport and Recreation New Zealand, Wellington.

SPARC. (2010a). *Community sport strategy: 2010–2015*. Planning document. Sport and Recreation New Zealand, Wellington.

SPARC. (2010b). *Future NSO community sport investment*. SPARC Board paper. Sport and Recreation New Zealand, Wellington.

Walters, S. (2011). *Whose game are we playing? A study of the effects of adult involvement on children participating in organised team sports*. PhD, Auckland University of Technology, Auckland.

Watt, D. C. (2003). *Sports management and administration* (2nd ed.). London: Routledge.

Worth, G. H. (2010). *Drivers and impediments for grassroots participation in football in New Zealand*. MBA, Massey University, Palmerston North.

PART IV

Reflections on sport development in practice

Practitioners' perspectives on the 'development of sport' in a community setting

The 'development of sport' is about innovation and change. It is about organised community sport, and its predominant volunteer-based club and school structure, adapting to the challenges of change arising from the diversification of sport and shifts in social attitudes and lifestyle choices, making individuals more discerning about not only 'what' sports they want to play, but increasingly 'when', 'where', and 'how' they want to play (see Chapter 2). It is about proactive NSOs with the leadership, capability, and resources planning innovative programmes and initiatives, and implementing these, often through networks of SDOs, to support volunteers in clubs and schools adjust to these changes. For community sport to remain contemporary and meaningful, it needs to be accessible, affordable, and appealing to participants. It is about providing a range of flexible and adaptable opportunities and quality experiences that satisfy the differing needs and expectations of participants of various ages, abilities, interests, and genders. Increasingly, how sport delivers these opportunities, in terms of the experiences these afford, are becoming more important for participants if they are to start and stay in sport.

Are these contentions about the 'development of sport' consistent with how it is perceived by other sport development practitioners and administrators? There is a paucity of research on SDOs, especially those in sport-specific roles within organised sport. Apart from studies by Bloyce, Smith, Mead, and Morris (2008) and Bloyce and Green (2011) of generic SDOs working for local authorities in the UK, there is little information on the views of sport development practitioners about the 'development of sport' process, its objective, and its value for both the sake of sport and its participants.

This chapter will:

1. Ascertain from NZC's CCCs, as sport-specific practitioners, their views and experiences of the 'development of sport' process, and how these align with their understanding of the objectives of NZC's programme.
2. Discern from other sport development practitioners and administrators working in various capacities in different sports bodies and countries their understanding of the 'development of sport' process, its focus, and how it aligns with their current role.
3. Compare the latter's broader perspectives of the process with those of the CCCs focused on developing cricket in NZ, and consider the increasing consciousness in the development process of participants' experiences of sport, and its potential impact on their social and interpersonal skills.

THE PERSPECTIVES OF NZC'S COMMUNITY CRICKET COORDINATORS

To understand the 'development of sport' in practice, Astle (2015) undertook a survey of sport-specific SDOs in NZ to get their in-field perspectives of 'doing' sport development. A sample of 14 of NZC's full-time CCCs, instrumental in implementing its NDP (Astle 1999, 2009) was used to seek their views of the 'development of sport' process, and how these aligned with their understanding of the objectives of NZC's programme. While the CCC sample was relatively small, they were representative of 14 different urban and rural-based associations distributed throughout NZ. They had been employed as CCCs for between two and 15 years, with five engaged for less than three years, and the remaining nine for at least four years, of which four had over 10 years experience. This number and spread of CCCs was similar to the 16 generic SDOs, employed in 10 different local authorities in the UK, studied by Bloyce et al. (2008) and Bloyce and Green (2011). The survey was confidential, so neither individual CCCs nor their association were revealed, instead individual CCCs were identified using an alphabet letter (i.e. CCC 'A').

Similar to Bloyce et al's. (2008) findings, the CCCs' views of sport development were consistent in their universal acceptance of the 'development of sport' interpretation of the value of sport and nature of sport development within community sport. They were unanimous sport development included: the promotion of sport to encourage participation; the provision of relevant sporting opportunities and positive experiences to attract and retain participants of all ages, abilities and interests, but especially children and young people; and the availability of intrinsic benefits from sport participation for both individuals (e.g. fun, skill development) and future sustainability of sport (e.g. growth in participation, more capable volunteers, clubs and schools) (see Figure 10.1).

Typical of their views was sport development is about "the promotion of sport . . . at a community level" (CCC 'A'); "offering playing opportunities, programmes and competitions that allow participants to enjoy sport and improve within it" (CCC 'B'); and "increasing numbers playing the game and improving the skill level of participants at all levels" (CCC 'C'). They believed this required them as CCCs to provide the leadership and support to achieve these objectives and put "in place the necessary tools for the sport to grow" (CCC 'D'), such as: developing and maintaining pathways of opportunities for players and coaches, improving facilities, and building capability within clubs and schools to effectively deliver sport. The identification and development of talent, particularly age-group representative players (9–18 years of age) was mentioned by three CCCs. They expressed concern about the availability of quality coaching for young talented players, and as full-time employees, felt it their responsibility to nurture these players to both retain them in the game and expand the talent pool, despite this not being within the remit of their role. Three other CCCs indicated participation offered more than just opportunities to play sport. They perceived it afforded learning experiences to acquire life skills and values (see Case study 10.2).

NZC's NDP sought to achieve two key objectives. First, growth, by increasing participation in grassroots cricket, and second, sustainability, by ensuring this increase in participation was maintained over time (Astle 2014). The CCCs' views of the 'development of sport' were consistent with their understanding of the process in practice. They realised to achieve the programme's objectives they had to promote the game at all levels to actively encourage more people to play cricket, especially boys and girls, to grow its player base. As CCC 'B' stated,

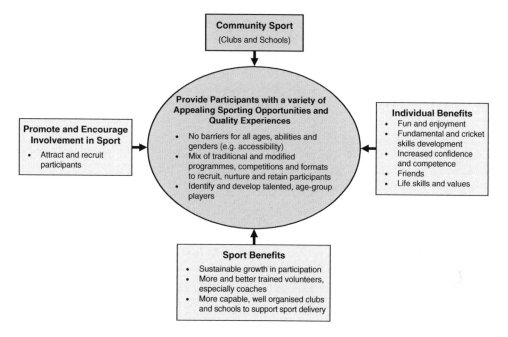

FIGURE 10.1 Summary of the CCCs' views of sport development

Source: Astle (2015: 15).

"I still work on a pyramid model believing that the more kids we get playing the game and having a positive experience the better health the game will be in." This was reinforced by similar comments from other CCCs about ensuring participants attracted to cricket were offered more diverse, meaningful opportunities and high-quality experiences that were fun, enhanced their skills, provided competitive challenges, and allowed them to realise their potential, including representative honours.

To achieve NZC's objectives required the CCCs to market the programme, enthuse and educate volunteers in clubs and schools, especially parents and teachers, for them to understand its objectives, its structured framework of aligned player and coach development pathways, and its progression of initiatives offering a diversity of opportunities to participate, contribute, and build the capability of the game, its people and its organisation. This necessitated the CCCs have a strong "community engagement with schools, clubs, teachers and parents" (CCC 'C') and be able to create an "awareness about the game of cricket and passionately pass on its positive messages so others may benefit from its values and enjoyment" (CCC 'F'). To capture this interest and actively recruit participants, the CCCs used NZC's programme to establish and maintain in their communities a "transparent pathway for players with programmes/opportunities available at each stage of the players' development/ age . . . [in order] . . . to provide an organised, progressive and fun experience of the sport" (CCC 'D').

To enable this to occur the CCCs implemented a series of retention measures. These included: building and managing strong relationships with volunteers, particularly coaches; providing the latter, with a pathway of coach education opportunities to upskill them commensurate with the age, ability, and interest of the players they coach; strengthening the administration and delivery of the game in clubs and schools, and linkages between them to allow improved player transition; and creating and maintaining partnerships with local councils and community funders to provide quality facilities and funding support for clubs and schools. The importance of attracting, improving the capability, and retaining volunteers was seen as paramount by the CCCs to ensure players start, succeed and stay in the game, and cricket has a sustainable future. As CCC 'B' indicated:

> cricket needs quality coaches and good volunteers . . . We need to be putting processes in place to allow these people to come forward and then reward them for their time and effort to retain them with us. Without them the sport does not function.

Since 2010, changes in NZC's leadership, funding model and priorities have detrimentally impacted its NDP and CCCs (see Chapter 5 and Case study 7.1). The CCCs have witnessed the programme being allowed to drift and deteriorate, sponsors being lost, and themselves being forced to operate with less guidance, funding, and resource support. A breakdown in the alignment of the programme's pathways and initiatives, and its accountability systems and procedures, through a lack of understanding of their importance and contribution of the programme, has required individual CCCs to become more self-reliant, resorting to their own resources, local initiatives, and funding sources (Astle 2015). NZC's associations have also taken advantage of NZC's loss of focus and direction, reducing their CCC numbers to reallocate their funding elsewhere, often to the professional game, or lessen their effectiveness by cluttering their role with coaching and administration tasks (Astle 2015; Astle, Dellaca, and Pithey 2013; Astle and Hill 2017). Fortunately, since 2016 NZC through its 'One Cricket' review is attempting to resurrect the NDP, by providing direction and accountability, building effective partnerships, and clarifying and supporting the CCC roles (Snedden 2017a, 2017b) (see Case study 7.1).

In summary, the CCCs were very clear about the 'development of sport' focus of their role and understood the process in practice with respect to their implementation of NZC's programme in clubs and schools. This entailed promoting cricket as a sport, attracting and retaining participants through providing appropriate and attractive opportunities and experiences to increase player satisfaction and numbers, and ensuring growth was maintained through retention measures, such as club and school capability, game format diversification, coach availability and competence, and facility provision.

REVIEW QUESTIONS

1. List three prerequisites the CCCs considered were essential for the 'development of sport' in practice.
2. What were NZC's programme objectives, and how did they align with the CCCs' view of the 'development of sport' process?
3. What are retention measures and their purpose? Give two examples.
4. What has occurred to distort the CCCs role and how have they responded?

THE PERSPECTIVES OF OTHER SPORT DEVELOPMENT PRACTITIONERS AND ADMINISTRATORS

During 2017, six sport development practitioners (SDPs) (Anna Walker, Kieran McMillan, Ian Sandbrook, Michael Peacock, Stuart Leighton, and Lindsay Calton) and four sport development administrators (SDAs) (Peter Miskimmin, Tony Gill, Peter Clinton, and Trafford Wilson), all of whom are active in leading, managing, delivering, or influencing the development of community sport, were asked their views of the meaning of 'sport development' in a community sport context, their understanding of the main focus of the process, and how this aligned with the primary purpose of their role. Each of these practitioners and administrators had over 10 years experience working in the sport development field across a range of settings: schools, clubs, RSOs, NSOs, national sport agencies, and international sport federations; with knowledge of sports as diverse as athletics, basketball, cricket, football, hockey, inline skating, rugby, skateboarding, snowsports, squash and surfing; and sports systems in Australia, England, NZ, Scotland, and East Asia and the Pacific.

WHAT DOES THE TERM 'SPORT DEVELOPMENT' MEAN IN THE CONTEXT OF COMMUNITY SPORT?

In Chapter 1, the complexities of the term 'sport development', its multifaceted assumptions and implications, and its different interpretations and their shifting emphasis over time and settings, are articulated. The subtle changes in emphasis within a 'development of sport' context are encapsulated in Walker's reflections:

> taking on my first 'sport development' role . . . I understood sport development to be an all-encompassing and ill-defined term that, in short, captured everything occurring outside the realm of high performance. Certainly, that was the essence of the job description I inherited! Efforts related more to the preservation of the sport than the participant . . . Over my 14 years working in the field in various countries, the label attributed to this area of the sporting profession was refined in different settings. 'Community sport' (New Zealand) and 'sport participation' (Australia) emerged as new descriptors of the area previously known as 'sport development'. At the same time, there was a more defined awareness and a greater articulation of the benefits of sport for the individual and society distinct from the achievement of elite success.

The shift in emphasis within the 'development of sport' identified by Walker, from traditionally being everything outside high performance, to primarily preserving organised community sport in the face of the challenges of change, and now realising this is not achievable just through providing more relevant opportunities for participants, but increasingly depends upon the quality and mix of experiences these offered participants, was also identified by the CCCs and SDPs/SDAs, and is a recurring theme throughout this book. In other words, the benefits derived from the 'development of sport' which were initially more sport-focused, where increased opportunities for participants equated to growth, have progressively become more participant-focused, because to sustain growth, opportunities must provide experiences that satisfy participant needs and expectations to retain their interest and ongoing involvement. There is also a mounting recognition of the value of such experiences in both sport and beyond in the lives of participants and their communities (see Figure 10.1).

This evolving appreciation of the 'development of sport' as providing both relevant opportunities and meaningful experiences, and why and how this has occurred is reflected in the SDPs/SDAs' responses. Both groups understand the change challenges facing community sport, and the mechanics of the 'development of sport' process required to ensure organised sport remains relevant and thrives. As Miskimmin indicated "our world is changing. Our society is increasingly diverse. So the challenge and opportunity is for sports to maintain relevance." Because sport is competing with sophisticated entertainment and sport competitors (e.g. eSports, more individual fitness options) "for people's discretionary time and money . . . It needs to be easy to join, be based on what people want and when they want it" (McMillan). To do this, and more effectively provide for the changing needs of clubs and schools at a community level, NSOs have had to self-review to ensure their development programmes match these wider community needs (Clinton). In the process, sports have sought to become more collaborative and connected, with "pathways and support offered from NSOs, through RSOs and onto clubs and schools. Within that there has been a focus on how sport is organised and governed, and the quality of opportunities for all involved – including players, coaches and officials" (Miskimmin), and on "engineering the strategies and priorities to assist making the sporting experience the most enjoyable and beneficial it can be for participants" (Clinton).

To achieve this, has required NSOs to have the leadership, capability, and resources to intervene into community sport, and introduce the following improvements, identified by both the SDPs/SDAs and CCCs, to attract and grow the number of players and volunteers engaging in sport in clubs and schools, namely:

- Quality programmes based on research and insight, underpinned by integrated and aligned pathways for players, coaches, officials, and administrators, incorporating game formats that cater for players across all the ages and stages of their life, and development and training opportunities for coaches and officials.
- Promotional campaigns that have simple, but impactful messages to attract players and volunteers.
- Effective programme delivery with quality coaching and officiating, and well organised, capable clubs and schools with welcoming and inclusive environments, and technology (e.g. website, social media) to profile programmes and communicate with players and volunteers.
- Meaningful partnerships with community supporters (e.g. local councils) and funders to improve and support the infrastructure and services provided by clubs and schools.

These were seen as prerequisites to sport providing appealing opportunities that are more appropriate, fun, and most importantly accessible, through the offer of formats that remove barriers to participation (e.g. cost, geography, time), making sport easier to enter and more inclusive (e.g. for disabled participants) (see Case study 10.1). This has enabled sport to not only attract increasing numbers of participants, but also provide "them with fantastic experiences that instil a lifelong love of sports" (McMillan), as well as use "sport for social good . . . to positively impact on . . . [participants and their] . . . communities" (Sandbrook).

CASE STUDY 10.1

Becoming inclusive: cricket for children and adults with disabilities

James Carr, former part-time Learning Difficulty/Physical Disability Cricket Development Officer, Lancashire Cricket Board, England

Disabled sports or parasports are played by persons with a disability, including physical and intellectual disabilities. Many disabled sports are based on existing able-bodied formats, modified to meet disabled people's needs.

The move to make sport more inclusive and attractive for disabled people to play is illustrated by the Paralympic Games. Started after the Second World War, and overseen by the International Paralympic Committee (IPC), these games, which have summer and winter versions, are now major international, multi-sport events, involving athletes with a range of disabilities. In 2016, the Paralympic Games which followed the Olympic Games in Rio de Janeiro catered for 4,342 athletes from over 150 countries.

The profile of disability sport in the UK has increased in the last two decades, because of the involvement of the British government national sport agency, Sport England (Kitchin and Howe 2014). Since 2004, Sport England has charged NSOs to mainstream the provision of sporting opportunities for disabled people and invested over £170 million in NSOs to achieve a more inclusive sporting system.

In 2007, the England and Wales Cricket Board (ECB) launched its 'One Game' strategy to create a more inclusive game, with a pathway of cricket opportunities for all, regardless of ability, gender, or race, and integral to this was its appointment of a national disability manager (Kitchin and Howe 2014). In 2009, the ECB signed a memorandum of understanding with four disability sport development organisations to unify the approach to providing disability cricket for deaf and hearing-impaired players, players with learning disabilities, blind players, and players with physical disabilities.

To offer an all-inclusive game, the ECB's 39 county cricket boards engaged paid or volunteer disability cricket development officers (CDOs) to implement the strategy in their counties. For example, the Lancashire Cricket Board funds a Learning Difficulty/Physical Disability (LD/PD) cricket programme for children and adults with disabilities that mirrors mainstream cricket. A LD/PD CDO facilitates the delivery of opportunities from 'have-a-go' fundamentals and enjoying playing cricket recreationally, to competing for county and international representative teams.

The LD/PD CDO visits specialist schools or units and runs six-week blocks of sessions to signpost disabled participants to focus clubs that cater for disability. Spread around the county, these clubs host fortnightly LD/PD cricket sessions on Saturday mornings.

As the part-time LD/PD CDO, I attended a Sports Coach UK workshop for coaching disabled people. Subsequently, I adopted a philosophy of coaching their ability (not disability), and sought guidance from individual players, if modifications were required. Fortunately, I also had access to an ex-England disability international for further advice. My role covered some school visits, but primarily concentrated on providing coaching and development assistance to the LD/PD squads in focus clubs, and for those selected into county squads to play in inter-county competitions. This required running winter and summer training modules and overseeing match-day programmes.

Disabled players chosen to play inter-county matches are also eligible to be selected for England. In 2015, an England team competed in the first disability World Cup in Bangladesh, which was heavily subsidised by the International Red Cross. The ECB hope, with ICC support, to stage a physical disability T20 World Championship in England in 2019, to coincide with the Cricket World Cup.

NZC does not have a disability strategy, although it seeks to be inclusive. Deaf cricket and blind cricket are played in NZ, under the auspices of their own organisations. For example, blind cricket, which has been played for over 30 years, has a regular summer competition organised by the New Zealand Blind Cricket Association. From this, a national team, known as the 'BlindCaps', is selected to compete in T20 Blind Cricket World Cup tournaments.

Questions

1. Why have sports become more inclusive and who often has instigated this?
2. How are disabled athletes catered for in sport?
3. What approach has the ECB adopted to become more inclusive and how is this delivered in their counties?
4. What training did the LP/PD CDO receive, and how did it influence his coaching of disabled cricketers?

REVIEW QUESTIONS

1. List three differences between the CCCs and SDPs/SDAs influencing their views of sport development.
2. According to Walker how has the focus of sport development changed over time?
3. What is the difference for participants between an 'opportunity' and an 'experience'? Give an example of each. Why is the latter becoming increasingly important for sports to attract and retain participants?
4. What prerequisites were considered necessary for NSOs to achieve their sport development objectives?

WHAT DO YOU SEE AS THE MAIN FOCUS OF 'SPORT DEVELOPMENT'?

Is the main focus of 'sport development' in community sport – growth, sustainability, talent development, a combination of these, or do these outcomes of sport first need to recognise and satisfy participant needs and motivations through access to relevant sporting opportunities and quality experiences? As Clinton noted, "there are many competing priorities . . . any one 'main' focus will ultimately be determined by the current and future needs of the community (participants), as well as the current capability of the sport itself". Among the SDPs/SDAs' views, the consensus focus was on participant needs, and their satisfaction through the meaningful experiences afforded by access to appropriate sporting opportunities, and how these were organised, presented, and serviced by clubs and schools. This was clearly articulated by Miskimmin:

> Putting the needs of the participant first – including their social, emotional, spiritual, cognitive as well as their physical needs – and creating a lifelong love of sport and activity through quality experiences . . . For young people getting their first sporting experiences at school or clubs, it needs to be fun so that they want to take part and through this develop the skills and confidence to remain in sport and active recreation throughout their life.

This provision of variously described 'good', 'amazing', 'fantastic', 'quality' sport experiences, was acknowledged as being dependent upon the capability and capacity of sports, especially their volunteer-led clubs and schools, to tailor appealing opportunities and successfully deliver these to meet the changing needs and demands of participants. In other words, it was perceived as an integrated "sporting package" designed and offered by sports and delivered and serviced by clubs and schools (Leighton and Calton). The prime driver for sports to achieve this has been their need "to grow the number of people engaging in . . . sport" (Sandbrook) to ensure their future sustainability. There was only one mention of this also contributing to the "talent pool for high performance sport" (Peacock). The sustainable growth in participation was seen as requiring the provision of opportunities that are "accessible, structured, age/stage appropriate, well-resourced and guided by quality instruction" (Wilson). However, sports must be aware that:

> because our population is changing, the local end of the traditional sport development pathway is increasingly diverse. For sports to tailor to the changing needs of the participant, local matters most. The traditional pathway is still critical, but what happens at national and regional levels needs to allow for local needs to be meet – and recognise that these vary.
>
> (Miskimmin)

Therefore, to be impactful the 'development of sport' must be integrated across a sport organisation – nationally led, regionally managed, and locally delivered – with variances in the latter encouraging innovative solutions and insightful lessons to be shared (see Chapter 7). If this is "done right, sport development allows players, coaches and officials to have a good experience which hopefully leads to a lifelong involvement in sport" (Wilson), and can also "contribute to community identity, serving as a focal point for engagement, pride and achievement" (Peacock), as well as "over time, make a meaningful difference to a community" (Gill).

HOW DOES THIS ALIGN WITH THE FOCUS OF YOUR CURRENT ROLE?

The focus of SDPs/SDAs roles, while aligned with their understanding of the main purpose of sport development, varied in accordance with their position within a sport or sport partner and how this influenced their outlook. In other words, their focus reflected whether they were leading, managing, delivering, or supporting the sport development process. This is evident in the following views.

I. From SDAs as national and regional CEOs of sports or sports partners leading and investing in sport development programmes:

> My role is to lead an organisation that is putting sport in a new context, helping our partners adjust to the changing New Zealand and respond to what's happening at a local level. (Miskimmin)

II. Through SDPs as national or regional SDMs planning and managing these programmes:

> In my role we provide national cricket federations with the direction, guidance and tools that they in turn need to provide their communities with in order to sustainably grow participation. Predominantly we do this through development of an appropriate long-term strategy and annual plans, financial investment and influencing the establishment/maintenance of a culture within these federations (especially board and senior management) that prioritises the grassroots game. And never forgetting that cricket will only be successful in growing if it delivers on its promise to participants of being fun, family/community oriented and contributing to an active and healthy lifestyle. (McMillan)

> This is absolutely aligned to the focus of my current role. My headline target is a '20% increase in committed participants' by the end of 2019. I will be judged on this at the end of the cycle. How I go about achieving this target is where it gets a little interesting as I believe positioning the sport as a primary contributor to positive social/community development will be the main driver in achieving this target. Essentially, we need to target the 95% of people in Scotland that don't follow cricket and don't have an affinity to it, and the best way to achieve this and access these people is by creating meaning and impact that isn't just about the sport. (Sandbrook)

III. To SDPs as regional SDOs and local volunteers at the coalface delivering these programmes in clubs and schools:

> My role in a nutshell is to get as many children as possible playing cricket. In my role I am constantly promoting cricket throughout New South Wales communities, the programmes I am promoting are at a foundation level appealing to 5–12-year-olds. The programmes are aligned to appeal most importantly to the children, where they can acquire the skills to progress through the junior pathway into traditional club cricket, but also be an enjoyable experience so they fall in love with the sport as both a player and a fan. (Peacock)

This 'top-down' cross-section of perspectives of the 'development of sport' process, begins with the recognition by sport leaders of change and need for community sport to respond and adapt; is followed by the planning and resourcing of programmes to provide national direction, initiatives and targets to revitalise, grow, and sustain community sport by sport managers; and finally, the implementation of these programmes by SDOs, and their delivery by volunteers in clubs and schools to recruit and retain as many participants as possible. They all concur that if sport is to counter the effects of change and achieve its participation targets, it needs to be a fun, meaningful experience that instils a lifelong love for and involvement in sport.

There was also universal acceptance that increasingly this was best accomplished by sport not just seeking to develop itself for its own ends of growth and sustainability, but also to develop the personal skills and values of participants, and the latter extending beyond sport to influence the lives and lifestyles of participants and their communities. It was contended that promoting sport solely for the sake of sport was limiting if it did not recognise and promote the benefits of the participatory experiences it offered, especially in team sports, for personal (e.g. life skills, positive social values) and community (e.g. engagement, identity, and cohesion) development (see Case study 1.1). For these reasons, sports are increasingly shifting from a sport-centric to a participant-centric approach, by embracing a broader vision of the 'development of sport' to realise more of sport's potential to inculcate 'sport and development' character-building lessons for life, and in so doing contribute to alleviating social welfare and community issues in developed countries ('development through sport') (see Case study 10.2); and engaging underprivileged participants in developing countries to improve their education and life skills ('sport for development') (see Case study 10.3). This is apparent in Walker's holistic vision of sport and sport development:

> in the journey that I find myself still in the midst of as a professional in the Australian sporting landscape today. I am driven by a passion to help evolve the 'sport development' mindset, to help sports – from community to national levels – to develop a greater awareness of, and ability to capture and tell the story of their impact – their genuine place in the world – to audiences both within and outside of the sports industry.

CASE STUDY 10.2
Building community through rugby

Ige Egal, Executive Director, Toronto Inner-City Rugby Foundation,
Toronto, Canada

Rugby is a minority sport in Canada with 27,500 club rugby registrants. Like all team sports, rugby provides opportunities to participate, develop skills, compete, enjoy, and succeed in sport, and through this experience have fun, make friendships, create a sense of belonging, learn to communicate, understand teamwork, and build character and resilience. The Toronto Inner-City Rugby Foundation (TIRF), founded in 2011, is a rugby-centred community development organisation, which engages in and combines the benefits of 'development of sport' and 'development through sport' to fulfil their vision of young people growing up as healthy, educated, community-minded citizens to become champions in both rugby and life. To achieve this, TIRF has sought to remove barriers to participation for young people to rugby in neighbourhoods underserved by sport in central Toronto, a city of 2.8 million. It has introduced rugby programmes and competitions; improved the sport's capability and infrastructure; provided equipment; reduced membership fees; and trained volunteer coaches and referees to service the game. At the same time, it has used rugby as a tool for social good emphasising the acquisition of the above intrinsic values from participating in sport, increasing access to leadership and mentoring experiences, and offering career and educational opportunities for participants to transform their lives beyond rugby.

TIRF with its partners, Rugby Canada, Rugby Ontario, school boards in Toronto, and Toronto city itself, has established a programme embracing a package of initiatives to allow young people to sample, play and progress in rugby, and receive support beyond the game. To introduce children (6–12 years) to rugby, TIRF has set up a flag rugby demonstration programme in schools and community groups, so children can improve their physical literacy having fun learning and practising basic rugby skills and playing games in neighbourhood leagues. In 2017, TIRF hired 53 part-time local SDOs, who visited over 200 schools and community groups, reached 27,438 students, and hosted 12 neighbourhood leagues and five festivals.

For young people (14–18 years), TIRF arranges access to playing opportunities in clubs and tournaments; and for the most talented, provides financial and logistical support for them to attend development clinics, and progress on the high-performance pathway to regional and national representative teams. For those aged 14–22 years, a range of beyond rugby opportunities are available to acquire leadership skills, receive mentoring, experience careers through trade-related apprenticeships and obtain scholarships for further education. To build the capacity, infrastructure, and services to create an environment where rugby is available and accessible, TIRF with its partners has supplied rugby equipment and apparel to high school teams, subsidised coaching qualifications for teachers and youth workers, and matched these volunteer coaches with teams.

TIRF's programme is not without challenges, including: declining sport participation in Canada; low investment in sport by school boards and governments; limited availability, accessibility, and affordability of community sport, which often lacks infrastructure and support services; and little societal understanding of the value and benefits of sport. On top of this, TIRF has chosen rugby, a minority sport, as the focus of its development programme in underserved inner-city communities. To meet these challenges, TIRF has established a coherent plan with clear objectives, and created partnerships to resource its programme which blends access to rugby skill development and playing initiatives with social and educational experiences. The key message of TIRF's programme is that it is more than rugby, and rugby is more than just sport, in that it provides opportunities to play as well as build life skills, which are impactful on individuals and their communities.

Questions

1. What is the TIRF and what opportunities did rugby offer it to realise their vision?
2. Where has the TIRF used rugby to remove barriers to participation, how has it done this and for what reasons?

3. How does the TIRF programme illustrate how their programme is more than rugby, and rugby is more than just sport?
4. Is this philosophy evident in a sport you are familiar with, and what influence has it had on participants?

CASE STUDY 10.3
Life through cricket in Sri Lanka

Alex Reese, Chairman and Founder, Cricket Live Foundation, Christchurch, New Zealand

Launched in 2014, Cricket Live Foundation operates a 'sport for development' programme 'Life Through Cricket' in four centres Sri Lanka.

The idea for the Cricket Live Foundation emerged, when as an 18-year-old I spent a gap year after leaving secondary school living in Mumbai. I became aware of children living in marginalised slum areas who had an incredible enthusiasm for life, a blindingly obvious love for cricket, as did the rest of the nation, but a total lack of motivation to go to school and learn. This is where the seed for the programme was sown. It began in Sri Lanka because of a funding partnership with the MJF Foundation, the charitable arm of Dilmah Tea.

The programme's objective is to leverage the shared values of cricket and life to enrich the lives of underprivileged children from these marginalised communities to develop education and life skills: respect for friends and family, self-discipline, teamwork, nutrition and healthy living, and punctuality and time management.

It runs in three-year cycles to give children the maximum exposure to environments that promote learning and life skills development. It has a 'bottom-up' approach to selecting children who need the most support: orphans, children from single parent homes and communities with domestic violence, drug and alcohol abuse, and sexual violence.

'Life Through Cricket' uses local staff who understand local social issues and provide consistent support to the children. These staff are trained twice a year by coaches and teachers from NZ, Australia, and/or South Africa. This involves two-week courses focusing on cricket coaching and the use of cricket and its values to develop good people.

There are currently 500 children in the programme, 400 boys and 100 girls, supported by 18 staff. A typical week for the children is two days of structured cricket training (two hours per day), one day of life skills development sessions (e.g. teamwork, public speaking, community work), and one day of formal tuition run by staff. This runs for 40 weeks each year, for three years.

Challenges to the programme have shaped our success. The biggest challenge was the selection of local coaches. The belief in Sri Lanka was to be a good coach you had to be at least a first-class player. The programme's view was good people make the best coaches, and so shortlisted potential coaches from similar backgrounds to the children, who understood the programme's purpose and problems, and most importantly, were trustworthy and respectful. The cricket we could teach; personality and attitude we could not. After the programme's first year, people were less critical because it upskilled and employed local people, and positively impacted the children involved.

This impact was measured by school attendance, behavioural shifts and community development. School attendance was a prerequisite to developing children's academic performance. Cricket was the incentive to get them to school, so attendance was well above the national average.

To gauge behavioural shifts quarterly interviews were conducted with school principals, teachers, parents, and coaches. Evidence indicated boys were more proactive in doing household tasks (e.g. cleaning, washing); children were more sharing (e.g. food, clothes); and there was greater gender equality with boys and girls interacting positively together.

These factors have contributed to overall community development. Locals are proud to see the children walk through town in their cricket gear, they attend events and matches, and parental support for their children at programme cricket tournaments and events, has increased from 20% up to 80%.

Questions

1. Why did 'Life Through Cricket' select cricket to headline its programme, and for what other purposes does it use cricket?
2. Why is it critical to use local staff to run the programme?
3. What challenges does the programme face that differ from those in a sport of your choice?
4. How was the impact of the programme measured? What effect is it having on children, their parents, and local communities?

While the CCCs and SDPs/SDAs agreed on the meaning of sport development and its main focus in community sport, the wider and more diverse experiences of the SDPs/SDAs revealed their broader awareness of the scope of the 'development of sport' process in terms of its potential benefits and impact. Although its prime objective is to grow and sustain community sport by creating a more varied menu of relevant sporting opportunities for participants, there is an increasing recognition that what influences, attracts, and maintains participant involvement, are the sporting and social experiences they receive from the diversity and quality of these opportunities, and how these are delivered by clubs and schools, that have a positive and beneficial impact on their involvement in sport, their lives beyond sport, and often their communities (see Case studies 10.2 and 10.3).

This wider perspective of the intrinsic value and impact of sport experiences could be considered a response by sports to satisfy the objectives of funding partners (e.g. corporate sponsors, national sport agencies, Gaming Trusts). Their traditional interest and investment in sport and its development, has in many cases widened from funding infrastructure and coaching, to now seeking more extrinsic social, personal, and community outcomes from sport, to enhance their brand appeal or justify their investment or function (see Case studies 2.3 and 2.6). The latter is influenced by central government investment, where changes in governments and Sport Ministers sees fluidity and short-termism in their policies and programmes, moving the outcome goalposts for NSOs. However, it may be seen as sport itself increasingly realising the potential value of the opportunities and experiences it provides individuals and communities to engage and grow in sport (Shilbury, Sotiriadou, and Green 2008), and the possibilities these intrinsic outcomes have to enhance sport's future appeal, growth, and sustainability.

Whatever the reason, although different interpretations of sport development are differentiated in Chapter 1 for ease of understanding and study, in reality they are not mutually exclusive, but are more often mutually reinforcing, despite the differences in their primary objectives and outcomes. This reflects the views of the SDPs/SDAs, and supports Bowers and Green's (2016: 15) contention that:

> there is no inherent reason that development cannot occur *in* and *through* sport synergistically. This is particularly, but not exclusively, the case for youth sport. Why wouldn't you want to develop children's sport skills and abilities while at the same time developing their social and interpersonal skills?

Many initiatives and their support resources produced by sports increasingly emphasise this synergy. For example, it is acknowledged in NZC's MILO Have-A-Go Cricket coaching manual, in the statement: "Coaches are central to the sport. They have the satisfying challenge of not only teaching players individual skills and the requirements of the game, but also instilling in them appropriate values and attitudes" (Astle 2000: 6). "Almost without exception, everyone who has been involved in sport can recall instances where people they have coached have developed greater confidence in themselves and learned how to get along with others" (email correspondence with Geoff Watson, 8 January 2018). Furthermore, most:

> practitioners like to see benefits beyond the purely sporting . . . it is often individual stories of people's lives being improved through sport that are the most rewarding – seeing someone/a group grow in confidence is often every bit as rewarding as seeing numbers of participants increase . . . One trait many practitioners seem to share is the desire to make a positive difference to people and seeing people smile is a significant reward.
>
> (Email correspondence with Geoff Watson, 18 January 2018)

While there is an increasing emphasis on sport's contribution to the social and personal skills and values of participants, and community engagement, identity, and cohesion in the 'development of sport' process, the purpose and focus of its practitioners is principally on growing and sustaining community sport, they are not explicitly seeking to use sport to address broader social issues. To try and stretch the capability, capacity, and resources of NSOs and their practitioners beyond this is counterproductive, being neither practical nor effective. Where it has been tried there has been a relative neglect by practitioners of their hands-on delivery of sport-specific outcomes (Bloyce and Green 2011; Bloyce et al. 2008).

REVIEW QUESTIONS

1. What was the main focus of the 'development of sport' according to the SDPs/SDAs?
2. Why has the emphasis shifted more to participant experiences, and for what reasons?
3. What are intrinsic benefits for (a) sport and (b) participants? Give two examples of each.
4. From your experience of participating in any sport, list the main sporting and non-sporting benefits for you personally and for your community.
   • Are these benefits by-products of participation in sport, or are they outcomes of conscious efforts of clubs and schools to develop participants for sport and beyond sport, or a combination of both?

CONCLUSION

While there is limited coverage of the role and experiences of generic SDOs, very little is available on sport-specific practitioners. In this chapter, the in-field perspectives of the latter are examined to establish their understanding of the purpose, focus, and importance in their roles of the 'development of sport' process.

As an example of sport-specific SDOs, NZC's regional CCCs were surveyed to ascertain their views and experiences of the 'development of sport' process, acquiring from implementing its NDP within cricket clubs and schools. Their perspective of the process was consistent with the 'development of sport' interpretation in Chapter 1, but also with how their role aligned with NZC's objectives to grow and sustain participation in community cricket. The CCCs used the programme's initiatives to promote cricket's opportunities and experiences, and assist clubs and schools deliver these to recruit and retain participants. This was perceived as beneficial for the sport's revitalisation and growth, and its participants' quality and depth of experiences.

In comparison, the insights of a more diverse group of SDPs/SDAs were also sought. Although their perspectives were broader, being based on more in-depth and varied experiences of the 'development of sport' in different sports and countries, they concurred with the CCCs' understanding of the purpose and focus of the process. However, they were more specific about the demands of the process, and its increasing emphasis on the experiential dimensions of participants involvement in sport to achieve sport's objectives, satisfy participants sporting needs and expectations, and develop skills and values that impact their lives beyond sport. The intent of the latter, is about sport and its practitioners recognising and emphasising the benefits of participating in sport. This involves encouraging clubs and schools to have greater engagement in their communities and deliver sport programmes that acknowledge the importance of developing participants' sporting and social skills and values (see Case studies 1.1, 2.3 and 4.4), rather than "using sport as a tool to achieve broader aims that are most often outside the scope of . . . sport itself" (Schulenkorf, Sherry, and Phillips 2016: 6).

REFERENCES

Astle, A. M. (1999). *New Zealand Cricket: National development plan*. Planning document. New Zealand Cricket, Christchurch.

Astle, A. M. (2000). *MILO Have-A-Go cricket coaching manual for children 6–8 years*. Christchurch: New Zealand Cricket.

Astle, A. M. (2009). *New Zealand Cricket: National development plan and programme*. Planning document. New Zealand Cricket, Christchurch.

Astle, A. M. (2014). *Sport development – Plan, programme and practice: A case study of the planned intervention by New Zealand Cricket into cricket in New Zealand*. PhD, Massey University, Palmerston North, New Zealand.

Astle, A. M. (2015). *Development of sport in practice: Sport development officers – New Zealand Cricket's community cricket coordinators*. Unpublished survey.

Astle, A. M., Dellaca, K., & Pithey, R. (2013). *Canterbury Cricket Association: District reviews* (Report). Christchurch: Canterbury Cricket Association.

Astle, A. M., & Hill, S. (2017). *Otago Cricket Association: District reviews*. Auckland: New Zealand Cricket.

Bloyce, D., & Green, K. (2011). Sports development officers on sport development. In B. Houlihan & M. Green (Eds.), *Routledge handbook of sports development* (pp. 477–486). London and New York: Routledge.

Bloyce, D., Smith, A., Mead, R., & Morris, J. (2008). 'Playing the game (plan)': A figurational analysis of organisational change in sports development in England. *European Sport Management Quarterly, 8*(4), 359–378.

Bowers, M. T., & Green, B. C. (2016). Theory of development of and through sport. In E. Sherry, N. Schulenkorf, & P. Phillips (Eds.), *Managing sport development: An international approach* (pp. 12–27). London and New York: Routledge.

Kitchin, P. J., & Howe, P. D. (2014). The mainstreaming of disability cricket in England and Wales: Integration 'One Game' at a time. *Sport Management Review, 17*(1), 65–77.

Schulenkorf, N., Sherry, E., & Phillips, P. (2016). What is sport development? In E. Sherry, N. Schulenkorf, & P. Phillips (Eds.), *Managing sport development: An international approach* (pp. 3–11). London and New York: Routledge.

Shilbury, D., Sotiriadou, K., & Green, B. C. (2008). Sport development. Systems, policies and pathways: An introduction to the special issue. *Sport Management Review, 11*(3), 217–223.

Snedden, M. (2017a). *Positioning cricket for the future*. Unpublished One Cricket Project Report. New Zealand Cricket, Auckland.

Snedden, M. (2017b). *Positioning cricket for the future: Interim report on 'support for the delivery of community cricket'*. Unpublished One Cricket Project Report. New Zealand Cricket, Auckland.

CHAPTER 11

Closing the innings
Development lessons to be shared

From the experience of instigating the 'development of sport' process in cricket in NZ, and subsequently consulting on the design of a similar process within football, hockey, and tennis, valuable lessons were learned. These are substantiated by the case studies of different sports in various countries interspersed throughout this book. Their applicability to other NSOs seeking to develop and enhance the appeal of their sport and improve its delivery in clubs and schools are outlined in this chapter. To adopt these lessons, NSOs need the leadership and vision to promote innovation and change, and the capability and commitment of resources long term to implement them. Eady's (1993: 76) reference to this still resonates:

> The main requirement for success is strong management commitment, preferably explicitly stated in the form of a . . . sports development strategy along with financial support to ensure that delivery is achievable.

From these lessons 10 steps are identified as key to developing community sport. They represent a systematic approach to creating the building blocks necessary to plan and implement a 'development of sport' programme to revitalise, grow, and sustain community sport in clubs and schools.
   This chapter will:

1. Examine the advantages of an integrated 'development of sport' programme with pathways of sequential initiatives compared to stand-alone or 'one-off' initiatives, especially those targeted as legacy projects for major world sporting events.
2. Identify and discuss the steps NSOs need to address to create and manage an effective development plan, programme, and practice to grow and sustain community sport.

PLANS, PATHWAYS, AND PARTICIPATION

The lessons learned from the experience of cricket, football, hockey, and tennis in NZ are transferable across different sized and structured sports. But to communicate and implement these can be as Snedden (2018: 1) states a "hard slog because it involves constantly chipping away at established mindsets and behaviours, to get leaders at the coalface of community . . . [sport] . . . being prepared to look at things differently".
   NSOs with a national SDM and SDO staff have the distinct advantage of being able to focus fully on 'why', 'what', and 'how' they intend to influence the development of their

sport. Those also with regional SDO networks are further advantaged by being able to facilitate this with volunteers in clubs and schools. NSOs who have insufficient resources to fund SDOs, however, are not precluded from shaping the development and delivery of their sports. Proactive NSOs of small to medium sports (500–15,000 participants) in NZ have effectively introduced initiatives to revitalise and grow their sports (MacFarlane 2016). For example, Australian Football League New Zealand introduced AFL KiwiKick to engage children aged 5–12 years in their sport and teach them its FMS of kicking, catching, passing, and bouncing (www.aflnz.co.nz/afl-kiwikick/). A decade on, their elementary pathway now extends through the sport into youth and adult levels. NSOs of smaller sports, because of their size, are also often more closely connected with their stakeholders, so face fewer obstacles to disseminating change.

Over the past 20 years, a number of mainly larger sports in NZ have introduced integrated community sport development programmes with frameworks of aligned pathways and sequential initiatives. These cater to both the recreational and competitive needs of participants, allowing them to move up and/or across multiple, aligned pathways to define their individual development pathways depending on age, ability, interest, and gender.

Other NSOs have opted to create stand-alone or 'one-off' initiatives to address 'gaps' in their community sports. In NZ, tennis initially introduced a stand-alone initiative, Grasshoppers, to meet the needs of a specific segment of their market (i.e. children) to increase participant numbers (SPARC 2009d) (see Case study 8.3). This, however, was "a programme in isolation", not part of "an integrated participation pathway" with an obvious progression of opportunities (Tong 2012: 3). For this reason, it did not transfer young players into regular tennis participation. It was therefore superseded by Tennis Hot Shots, an integrated package of modified school and club initiatives for 5–10-year-olds, to learn tennis skills and register in local clubs (see Case study 8.4).

The tenuous impact of 'one-off' initiatives on participation is also evident in the legacy projects associated with major world sporting events. For example, the 2012 London Olympic Games made extravagant claims and provided substantial investment to create a long-lasting impact on participation in the UK (Girginov and Hills 2008; Green, K. 2012). These claims were questioned by the likes of Draper (2003, quoted in Charlton 2010: 358) who stated "it is no good having a great Olympics in 2012 and inspiring many people to take up sport if we don't have facilities, coaching and infrastructures to get them involved and keep them in sport". After the Olympics, others confirmed Draper's concerns. Shephard (2013) indicating insufficient grassroots coaches were recruited and trained to sustain any excitement spike in participation generated by the Olympics. The latter, Macrae (2017) suggested, required localised strategies to be introduced prior to the event to improve the capability and capacity of clubs and their volunteers, including coaching and facilities. Similar reasons have been identified for the lack of participation legacies from other major sporting events (Mutter and Pawlowski 2014; Veal, Toohey, and Frawley 2012). Many legacy projects as well as being 'one-off', are also often short-term. Because they are not integrated into the pathways and initiatives of sports, they fail to sustain an impact on participation, for when they cease so does participant involvement.

To be effective, the 'development of sport' requires a planned and systematic approach that is long-term, and integrates all the elements of player, game, coach, provider, and facility development (see Figure 2.1) within a collaborative community sport development and delivery system (see Figure 11.1). A framework of aligned development pathways across this

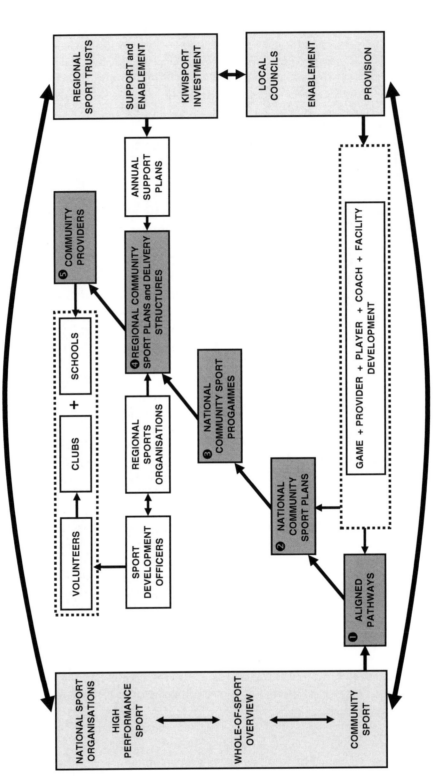

FIGURE 11.1 Collaborative community sport development model in New Zealand

Source: Astle (2011: 19).

system, integrated by sequences of appealing opportunities, allows players attracted to a sport to be nurtured and retained within community sport, because of the mix of experiences and services offered to satisfy their changing needs. The practicality of these pathways to practitioners is succinctly stated by a SDO (quoted in Kitchin and Howe 2014: 72), "I don't like to be doing things that are just a one-off, you've got to have the relevance to the pathway."

REVIEW QUESTIONS

1. What are the prerequisites needed for NSOs to intervene in developing community sport?
2. What are the advantages of NSO's programmes with aligned pathways of sequential initiatives?
   - Why have some NSOs opted for 'one-off' initiatives? What are their disadvantages?
   - What other factors contribute to the failure of 'one-off' initiatives, especially those promoted as legacy projects, to impact on community sport participation?

STEPS IN THE PROCESS

On the basis of the experience Astle gained from designing and implementing NZC's development plan, programme, and practice; his subsequent longitudinal research of its impact on community cricket (Astle 2014); and knowledge acquired from working closely with other NSOs, particularly football, hockey, and tennis; the value of taking logical steps to introduce the innovation and change necessary to develop community sport became apparent if NSO interventions were to be successful. The steps identified by Astle (2014), whose order in the sequence is interchangeable, are implicit in the responses in the change model in Chapter 6 (see Figure 6.1). These require NSOs (and/or RSOs) to:

1. **Have or acquire the prerequisite leadership, vision, and capability to consider their sport holistically in order to adopt a balanced and integrated approach to the development of their sport** (see Chapter 3), instead of NSOs focusing almost totally on high performance, as many with professional arms do; this requires them to take a 'big picture' view of their sport that recognises the interdependence of high-performance and community sport, and the importance and value of community sport participation (see Figure 11.2). Maintaining this whole-of-sport view requires ongoing reinforcement and commitment, as changes in NSO leadership and priorities often sees the re-emergence of a competitive, pathway logic which considers community sport simply as a function of high-performance sport, with little awareness of the needs and expectations of the 97% of participants who are not part of this pathway (see Facts and figures 1.1).

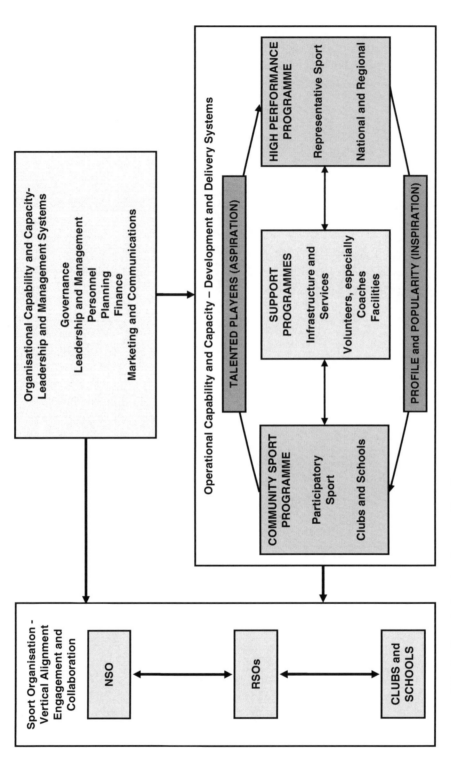

FIGURE 11.2 Whole-of-sport planning: key considerations

Source: Astle (2011: 7).

Experience working for SPARC and Sport NZ showed there was little value providing community sport investment to NSOs who lacked proactive leadership and capability. Such NSOs could often not account for this investment, which was often diverted into other areas of their business (Astle 2014; Snedden 2017a). This was illustrated in 2012, when several provincial softball associations expressed disquiet about the capability of Softball New Zealand (SNZ), its risk of losing Sport NZ funding, and the precarious position of their sport in terms of its dwindling profile and growth (Smith 2012a, 2012b). To tackle these issues they stressed the critical need to address four areas of concern: "a lack of a clear vision, a lack of strong and objective leadership at the top, a lack of dynamic delivery at both SNZ and regional level and a lack of any innovative recruitment/growth strategies" (Smith 2012a: B15). They were adamant progress would require a whole-of-sport focus, which concentrated on "softball in New Zealand not Softball New Zealand" (Smith 2012a: B15).

For community sport development programmes to be effective, NSOs must be capable, and willing and ready to intervene in the development of their sport. For SPARC (2009a: 6) this required NSOs to be "'investment-fit' and able to get on with the job". In addition to rugby, cricket, and netball, the other NSOs initially targeted by SPARC to develop their sports at a community level (football, hockey, gymsports, rugby league) had all benefited from previous SPARC funded and guided capability building prior to their selection (Astle 2011; Gryphon Governance Consultants 2011).

2. **Appoint a SDM or equivalent with the seniority to lead, make strategic decisions, plan, manage, and strongly advocate for the 'development of sport' process** (see Chapter 5). It is imperative the appointee is a senior manager, so they are in a position to inform, educate, and promote the importance, value, and needs of developing community sport throughout their sport organisation, and influence the decision-making of the NSO's CEO and board and its regional CEOs, not an easy task when many leaders are engrossed in high performance and winning. Without such seniority, as illustrated in Case study 7.1 (cricket) and Chapter 9 (football), where SDM positions were relegated to middle management after both sports had inaugural transformative managers with seniority, they struggled to influence decisions about the direction of their programmes, or demand a fair share of investment to support their implementation in clubs and schools, which diluted their programmes and diminished their impact.

For smaller sports, NSOs may need to contract an experienced consultant, or utilise the knowledge of an influential volunteer or volunteers from within their sport to kick-start and oversee steps 3–5. NSOs must be aware that to identify and select a suitably qualified person as a SDM is not an easy task, given the newness of sport development, and diverse skills and capabilities required in the role (see Chapter 5).

3. **Create a 'whole-of-sport' overview** (see Figures 2.2, 11.2, and 11.3). The Sport and Recreation Pathway (see Chapter 2 and Figure 2.4) provides a theoretical guide to help NSOs identify their sequence of aligned and integrated pathways spanning their operations from community sport to high-performance sport (SPARC 2009b, 2009c). HNZ and NZF both used this as the basis for creating their whole-of-sport overviews (see Figures 3.2 and 9.2). The pathway identifies five stages in the process of player development in sport. The first three stages (Explore, Learn, and Participate) occupy most players' sporting life span. The latter two stages (Perform and Excel) cover regional to international high-performance opportunities for the few talented young people and adults.

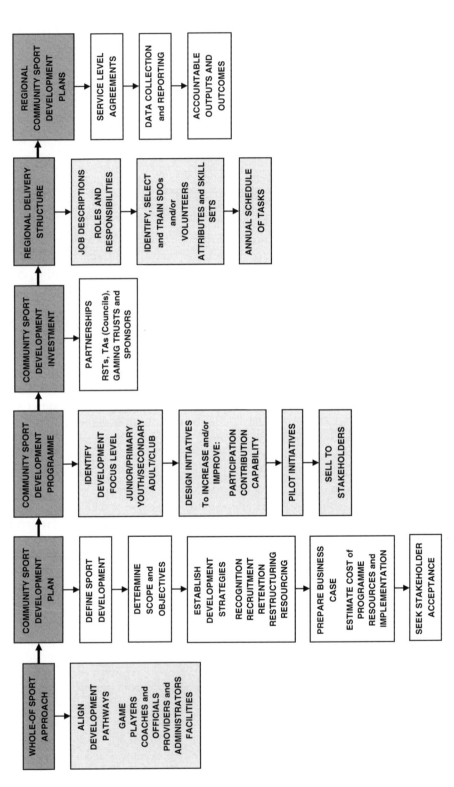

FIGURE 11.3 Designing and implementing a community sport development plan, programme, and regional delivery structure: key considerations

Source: Astle (2014: 259).

The design of a whole-of-sport overview is not complicated, but research and consultation with key stakeholders is vital in its formulation. It can be presented diagrammatically as a framework that underpins the planning process and binds a sport together. It acts as a blueprint for ease of presentation, explanation, and a ready source of reference to gauge progress.

It is best devised by first identifying the bottom-to-top sequence of existing and proposed playing opportunities from entry level to elite within its player development pathways (see Figure 4.1 – cricket). The Sport and Recreation Pathway's 'Learn' and 'Participate' stages in a sport's player development pathways are evident in its multi-strands of conventional or 'competitive' playing options and recreational or 'social' opportunities (see Figures 3.2 and 9.2). It is essential sports accommodate these different pathways. The modification of sports with various formats, player numbers, scheduling, durations, equipment, and playing surface dimensions, while more reflective of the recreational pathway, is increasingly straddling all pathways (e.g. T20 in cricket) (see Chapter 4).

Once the player development pathways have been determined, they can be surrounded by comparable integrated pathways of development opportunities for coaches, referees/umpires, and administrators, that align to each other and the player pathways. At each step in these support pathways the opportunities for recipients, many of whom are volunteers in clubs and schools, must be appropriate to the stage of development of players. This ensures they are equipped with the necessary knowledge, skills, and resources to service and satisfy player needs. For example, the entry-level MILO Have-A-Go Cricket initiative for children was matched by a similar coach education course for parents and teachers to train as MILO coaches (see Chapter 4). This provided them with the know-how and resources to run the programme, teach their children basic skills of the game, and provide a fun first experience of cricket for players, parents, and teachers (Astle 2000a).

4. **Define the meaning of 'sport development' and determine its scope** (see Figure 11.3). This was key to the success of NZC's NDP. For this reason, NSOs need to decide the purpose and objectives of sport development, and how much of their whole-of-sport overview will be subject to achieving these. They may be to attract new participants (Grow), support and motivate existing participants to keep playing (Sustain), and/or provide enhanced opportunities to nurture talented performers (Talent Development) (Bloyce, Smith, Mead, and Morris 2008).

For NZC, the purpose of its programme was to grow and sustain 'participation', and its scope was 'community cricket' delivered mainly by clubs and schools. This equated to the Sport and Recreation Pathway's 'Learn' and 'Participate' stages. It was not about developing talented players, which was the domain of high performance, which encompassed the 'Perform' and 'Excel' stages. HNZ and NZF, however, included responsibility for the 'Learn' and 'Participate' stages, and most or all of the 'Perform' stage in their community sport programmes, leaving only 'Excel' for high performance (see Figures 3.2 and 9.2). Unfortunately, the inclusion of the 'Perform' stage of regional representative teams within community sport, often burdens SDOs' core development work. Even despite the tighter scope of cricket's programme, this intrusion has still happened, where it has hampered the effective operation of its CCCs (see Chapter 5).

In cricket, high performance has gradually retreated from the 'Perform' stage to focus only on 'Excel'. This has left the former to increasingly be absorbed within its development programme. This lack of responsibility by high performance for the talent pathway through the 'Perform' stage is a major fracture point in the delivery of many sports. Schools and clubs produce quality players and coaches, but NSOs because of limited resources, expertise, and their frequent over-focus of attention and investment on their elite/professional arm (Walker 2017), are reluctant to invest time, funding, and educative guidelines into the 'Perform' stage of their pathways. This results in poorly defined and supported pathways for them reaching the top echelons of their sports. In NZ, this is exacerbated by Sport NZ's investment model which earmarks funding primarily for community sport (i.e. 'Learn' and 'Participate') and the 'Excel' pinnacle of high performance. The 'Perform' gap is considered NSOs' domain, but frequently is not filled by them, leaving SDOs and volunteers to ensure sports' best young players are not lost. Their retention and development places unreasonable demands on SDOs and volunteers, with the former often not completing their negotiated community sport development tasks (see Chapter 5).

To try and address this 'Perform' stage, High Performance Sport NZ's (2013) 'Pathway to Podium' programme since 2013 has targeted the development of a limited number of young, talented athletes across a range of sports. In the UK, to alleviate this situation, Sport England adopted an investment strategy with its NSOs which emphasised both participation and talent (Sport England 2008). This apportioned investment to increase participation ('Grow' – 15%), maintain participation ('Sustain' – 60%), and nurture talent so more move to elite programmes ('Excel' – 25%) (Charlton 2010; Sport England 2009). While this funded both the sport development work of SDOs and legitimised their involvement in talent development, it often compromised the former.

REVIEW QUESTIONS

1. Why do SDMs need seniority in a NSO to effectively lead a 'development of sport' process?
2. What is a whole-of-sport overview?
   - How did the Sport and Recreation Pathway provide NSOs with a simple theoretical guide to construct their whole-of-sport pathways?
3. Why is it critical to define sport development and how does this influence the scope of a sport's development programme?
   - What was the scope of NZC's programme? How did it differ from football and hockey?
   - How has cricket's scope been compromised and what impact has it had on its CCCs? How did Sport England try and circumvent this?

5. **Formulate a national sport development plan** (see Figure 11.3 and Chapter 3). This should be centred on the whole-of-sport framework of aligned development pathways and identified sequences of initiatives. It should incorporate the objectives and strategies

that underpin these initiatives, a proposed regional delivery structure, and business case estimating its likely design and implementation costs. An account of this step and sequence of phases within the planning process are detailed in Chapter 3. In preparing and presenting a sport development plan it is essential to seek input and feedback on the change and innovation it proposes for the development and delivery of community sport. Consultation with key stakeholders (e.g. board, staff, RSOs, clubs, schools and potential supporters, such as national sport agencies), and their broad acceptance of the plan is necessary before starting the next step of programme design. Although this may lead to some revision of the plan, this should be minimal if a NSO is well integrated with its RSOs, and the sport development message has been regularly, widely, and clearly communicated throughout the sport.

6. **Design a coordinated national development programme with a progression of initiatives that meet the plan's objectives and strategies** (see Figure 11.3 and Chapter 4). Programme design must take account of what opportunities and experiences should be packaged in the different types of initiatives within sport's pathways, and what level in the sport and target audience these initiatives should be directed. There needs to be a balance between providing competitive and recreational pathway initiatives, and decisions made if partnerships with outside providers are necessary to offer alternative action initiatives, and whether to blend these into their pathways (see Figure 4.1). For example, Cricket Scotland has partnered with Last Man Stands to deliver its very popular alternative social initiative, which Walker (2017: 58) describes as "post-work, eight-a-side, 20 five-ball overs, get changed under a tree" cricket (see Case study 4.4).

The quality of the experiences offered to participants is increasingly becoming the key determinant in their attraction and retention in a sport. No longer is it just about sports providing opportunities to participate, these now need to be not only relevant and appealing but also well organised within a supportive and welcoming environment that offers the services and infrastructure to satisfy the varied needs and expectations of participants (and at entry level, their parents). The emphasis for participants is therefore increasingly on the quality of the experience sport affords them, and for sports, on understanding and offering these experiences to generate among participants a lifelong love of sport ('sport for life').

Most NSO programmes begin by targeting the primary/junior level of their sports with entry-level initiatives to attract and recruit 5–7-year-old children. Chapter 4 outlines how the early emphasis of NZC's NDP was on its MILO initiatives aimed at the primary/junior level, followed later by the Community Cricket initiatives directed at the secondary/youth and club/adult levels. It is essential initiatives and their support resources are not only designed mindful of the opportunities and experiences they present to satisfy the needs of both participants and the sport but are tested for their appropriateness and ease of delivery prior to their sport-wide introduction. This provides valuable feedback on their effectiveness and the best approach to implement these.

For example, NZF piloted its Junior Framework in 100 of its 500 clubs to understand the impact it would have on junior football, how the delivery worked within clubs, and what fine-tuning was needed before the national roll-out (Herdman 2011). Piloting reduces the risk of widely implementing a poorly conceived initiative, and its possible negative effect on investment, SDO confidence, and stakeholder acceptance of change. The feedback received from a pilot is crucial for SDO training and provides them with valuable insights in how to effectively market an initiative in clubs and schools. It also furnishes evidence of the value and applicability of an initiative when approaching funders for support to assist their delivery (see Chapter 4). The sourcing and forming of such partnerships is vital for NSOs to establish and maintain an effective regional delivery network (see Case studies 2.4 and 2.6). The size and reach of which is ultimately dependent upon the level of funding acquired (see Chapters 2 and 5).

7. **Establish a regional delivery structure** (see Figure 11.3 and Chapter 5). Central to this step is the appointment of a nationwide team of SDOs to facilitate the implementation of a NSO's development programme. Their role is to market the programme and its initiatives, enthuse and attract individuals to participate in these, and motivate and train volunteers to deliver them in clubs and schools. It is ultimately the SDOs who bring the programme alive and translate it into practice. For NSOs to identify and appoint suitably qualified personnel is not easy, and often hinders the effective and consistent delivery of their programmes (see Chapter 5). For example, the introduction of NZF's WOFP was hampered by some of its FDMs and FDOs, who had adequate technical and coaching skills but lacked the necessary management, administration, strategic thinking, and planning skills required in their roles (Snowling 2011). This meant they were in development roles they were not capable of doing (see Case study 9.1).

Most NSOs of small- and medium-sized sports have insufficient resources to engage SDOs. For them to influence the direction of their grassroots sport, they must create a shared understanding with volunteers of a vision for the development and delivery of their sport. This requires change and consensus on a national pathway of sporting opportunities and experiences and their mode of delivery. For many such sports, however, their volunteer-driven initiatives are often locally or regionally focused, with variations in delivery making it difficult to agree on a unified national pathway of opportunities.

For NSOs of larger sports looking to establish a professional delivery network, they must have a clear understanding of the skills and capabilities, and role and responsibilities they require of their SDOs (see Appendix 5.1). These should be incorporated into position specifications and job descriptions and circulated to their RSOs (see Appendices 5.2 and 5.3). They then must ensure appointed SDOs understand their responsibilities, expectations and role as 'ambassadors' of their sport, NSO, RSO, and programme partners; and are trained appropriately to fully comprehend the objectives, strategies, and initiatives of their development programmes, so they can confidently communicate these to stakeholders.

8. **Instigate a system of procedures and accountabilities to guide the operation of the delivery network and measure its effectiveness and wider impact of their programme and its various initiatives** (see Figure 11.3 and Chapter 6). This involves establishing an integrated, hierarchical system of planning, procedures, and accountabilities that align a sport organisation's operation from NSO, through RSOs, to clubs and schools. This requires RSOs to formulate regional development plans which reflect the objectives, strategies, and outcomes espoused in their NSO's national development plan. Subsequently, for national outcomes, KPIs are set, and targets negotiated with each RSO, and incorporated into their annual operational plans, and then SLAs signed off specifying NSO and RSO roles and responsibilities, and RSO accountabilities for national development investment. This investment needs to be 'tagged' against agreed community sport outcomes, and 'at risk' if they are not achieved, because there are numerous examples of NSOs and RSOs diverting this funding for other purposes, such as administration and high performance (see Case study 7.1). In turn, RSOs need to establish a similar system of partnership agreements and accountabilities for the

trickledown of development investment and delivery of agreed outcomes with clubs and schools (see Figure 6.3).

Within this system, SDOs should assist formulate these regional plans and local partnership agreements, and record and report against their outcomes. To do this effectively, SDOs together with club and school volunteers, must clearly understand the objectives and strategies of a national programme, and know how to effectively deliver its various initiatives. This requires NSOs to provide, and train them, to use standardised procedures, templates, resources, and systems of delivery, including data collection and reporting. In the case of cricket, this involved the initial training of personnel, ongoing induction of new CCCs (see Appendix 5.3), and professional development opportunities and updates through regular association meetings and annual national forums and conferences (see Chapters 5 and 7). Each CCC was supplied with operating handbooks (Astle 2000c, 2001), coaching manuals (Astle 2000a, 2000b) and a toolkit of development resources. NZC also established expectations for its CCCs' professional appearance and presentation as ambassadors of the sport in the community.

It's important SDOs receive clear direction from their NSOs about their work programmes, and system of accountability for their performance, based on planning, SLAs, and regular recording and reporting of progress against agreed targets. Otherwise, as Eady (1993: 76–77) notes:

> the frequent absence of stated policies and the lack of . . . strategy containing aims and clearly defined objectives often mean that the effectiveness of SDOs . . . [is compromised by a wide range of differing responsibilities that limits their prime function of ensuring the] planned, active and progressive provision of sporting opportunity . . . to people of all ages at all levels of ability.

9. **Regularly monitor, evaluate, and continuously improve all aspects of the programme** (see Chapter 7). NSOs should not only monitor, receive feedback, and evaluate the effectiveness of their programmes and SDOs, but also provide progress reports to their boards, sponsors, and supporters, such as national sport agencies. Regular reporting and reviewing by RSO-based SDOs against agreed targets, as part of routine monitoring required for SLAs, should be used to gather data on participation, contribution, and capability. This can be used to assess the local impact of a national programme, its specific initiatives, and effectiveness of its SDOs in delivering these. Annual data collection and collation methods, such as a sport-wide census of participation (and possibly contribution); yearly national meetings of SDOs to network, exchange ideas, and provide feedback (see Case study 7.4); and regular in-house or external reviews by independent consultants (see Case studies 7.1, 7.2, and 9.1) all provide evidence of trends, impact, and overall success (or otherwise) of a NSO's programme and/or specific initiatives. The ongoing monitoring of the performance of programmes against their designated objectives, and effectiveness of individual initiatives and SDOs, is necessary for the continuous improvement of current initiatives and resources, design of new ones, and their effective delivery (Sport England 2009). SDOs also need to be appraised at least once annually by their RSOs and/or regional SDM against their regional plans, competencies, and position descriptions. The achievement of agreed targets and key stakeholders feedback should also be used to evaluate their capabilities and performance, and identify possible professional development opportunities.

REVIEW QUESTIONS

1. What key elements need to be included in a sport development plan?
   - How important is consultation, with whom, and why?
2. Why should NSOs pilot initiatives?
3. How do SDOs bring a sport's development programme alive and translate it into practice?
   - Why is it essential SDOs are well trained and have appropriate systems to guide their operations?
4. What are the benefits for NSOs in monitoring and evaluating their programmes and SDOs?

10. **Commit for the long term, to ensure the sustainability of sport development programmes, and enable meaningful evidence to be collected to demonstrate their positive impact on community sport.** Evidence suggests that national sport agencies, NSOs, RSOs, and their sport development practitioners and consultants need to understand the 'development of sport' is a long-term process, and to be effective requires an ongoing commitment of approach and investment to ensure it is sustainable.

'Long term' and 'sustainable' are complementary. They imply the 'development of sport' process must be enduring if it is to innovate and maintain an appealing, accessible, and affordable diet of relevant sporting opportunities and experiences a sport can offer to attract, develop, and retain participants; plus support their ongoing provision and quality, and improve the capability of clubs, schools, and their volunteers to create a conducive environment with the appropriate infrastructure and services.

The longitudinal study by Astle (2014) of the impact of NZC's planned intervention into cricket in NZ showed sufficient time is required not only to design a national plan and programme, establish a delivery structure and implement the programme, but also consistently achieve an agreed set of outcomes to substantiate the plan's objectives. It is suggested that at least 10 years be allocated by a NSO before it has enough longitudinal data to assess the effectiveness and impact of its programme. This is because it takes time, acceptance, collaborative effort, patience, and commitment to successfully influence volunteer delivery systems at a community level.

Unfortunately, evidence from countries such as England (Keech 2011) and NZ (Collins, S. 2011) shows 'development of sport' policies and programmes have played second fiddle to high-performance interests, stretched resources, fluctuated in emphasis, and been short-term (Houlihan 2011a, 2011b; Nicholson, Hoye, and Houlihan 2011). This is despite the frequent statements by central governments, their sporting agencies, and NSOs about the necessity of intervening into community sport, particularly to increase participation.

When considering community sport development programmes, short-term means they are not given enough time to demonstrate their impact. Nicholson et al. (2011b) claim on average this is often only three to four years but can be as short as one year. Sport

England (2007) and Gryphon Governance Consultants (2011) both recommend a minimum of five years be given to implement, embed, and gauge a programme's impact. Short-termism leads to a lack of continuity in programmes which have insufficient time to prove themselves or affect change; dissatisfied and disenfranchised participants; and uncertainty of employment for SDOs.

For many NSOs, the short-term nature of their programmes can be linked to poor monitoring and data collection systems, so they have insufficient longitudinal data to demonstrate their effectiveness (Nicholson et al. 2011b). It can also be attributed to changes in NSO leadership and boards, shifting their strategic priorities and investment, with no thought to its impact on their community sport programmes (see Case study 7.1). This frequently occurs because NSOs reprioritise high-performance, especially professional sport. Hence, they either overload their development programmes with everything other than the 'Excel' component of high performance, or seek shorter-term, 'one-off', quick-fix solutions, often to attract targeted audiences based on age and/or ethnicity to grow their sport, without thinking about maintaining an integrated mainstream programme capable of ensuring their long-term involvement. The encroachment of the professional game and its overconsumption of resources has adversely affected community sport, drawing considerable funding away from its development, and creating considerable tensions within sports (Hunt 2014; Napier 2014; Snedden 2017b; Walker 2017).

It took NZC two years, following the appointment of its inaugural NDM, to research, consult with stakeholders, identify the key elements in a community cricket development and delivery system, and crystallise these into a national development plan (Astle 1999, 2009) (see Table 11.1). This set the platform for incremental innovation and change, as part of its evolving NDP, which pervaded community cricket over subsequent years, as initiatives and resources were designed and phased in at different levels of the game – primary/junior, secondary/youth, and club/adult. This gradually added to the CCCs' toolkit, and allowed time for them to be understood, accepted and diffused into clubs and schools.

NZF were advantaged by being targeted by SPARC/Sport NZ to receive investment and assistance to support its director of football and national development staff to formulate their WOFP over three years (Herdman 2010), and then over the next year pilot their first set of initiatives and resources aimed at the junior level (see Chapter 9). The intention was to subsequently implement the WOFP in three stages over six years, commencing with junior development, followed by youth and finally senior development, and at each stage introduce a complete set of national initiatives that straddled its recreational, competitive, and talented pathways. Despite the planning, financial support, resources, time taken to educate stakeholders, appoint and train FDMs and FDOs, and positive response to its introduction, there were still some implementation challenges.

These related to the immensity of the task of trying to implement seven new junior initiatives concurrently. This tested the skills and capability of the FDMs and FDOs to effectively communicate their benefits, receive buy-in from clubs and schools, successfully deliver all the initiatives, as well as undertake the administration, monitoring, and reporting necessary for NZF and its funding partners. As a consequence, the plan's roll-out was much slower than expected, competitive initiatives were

TABLE 11.1 Community cricket development and delivery system: key elements

Elements	Processes	Pathways	Resources	Partnerships
People (participants and volunteers)	• Recognising (attracting) • Recruiting • Retaining	• Development pathways • Opportunities • Experiences	• Access to CDO network • Coaching and development manuals • Plan, programme and, information booklets	• MAs, DAs, clubs, schools, RSTs • Gaming Trusts and sponsors
Plans	• Researching and planning • Determining scope and objectives • Defining strategies • Preparing a business case	• Aligned player and coach pathways and initiatives • Integrated delivery structure	• National development plan • Implementation procedures and support documents	• NZC, Sport NZ, and sponsors
Programmes	• Researching • Innovative designing of initiatives • Piloting initiatives	• Coordinated, progressive, flexible and adaptable initiatives • Range of relevant competitions, formats and tournaments • Multi-stranded opportunities • Age/stage, ability, interest, and gender experiences	• National development programme • Coaching manuals and DVDs • School Support and Club Assist information booklets • Administration handbooks	• NZC, Sport NZ, and sponsors
Structures (a) Providers (clubs and schools)	• Integrating community cricket • Improving organisational capability, infrastructure, and services • Restructuring • Resourcing	• Vertical integration of sport organisation (national to local) • School-club links	• Health checks • CCC advice, guidance, assistance, and funding • Information booklets • Service level or partnership agreements	• Volunteers • MAs, DAs, sponsors, Gaming Trusts and RSTs
(b) Delivery network (CCCs)	• Identifying and selecting • Employing • Training	• Position descriptions • Annual schedule of tasks • Career options	• Branded clothing • Instructional manuals • Office space, laptops, mobiles and vehicles	• NZC, sponsors, MAs, DAs, clubs, Gaming Trust and RST funding • MA, DA, club and RST office provision
Facilities and equipment	• Designing • Constructing • Improving	• Age/stage appropriate facilities • Modified equipment	• Funding • Information booklets • Equipment donations	• NZC • Gaming Trusts and sponsors
Monitoring and evaluation	• Recording • Reporting • Reviewing	• Standardised sequence of procedures • Agreed accountabilities and targets (outputs and outcomes)	• MA monthly and summative reports • Annual NZC Census • Annual national development conference • Review documents	• NZC and NZ Cricket Foundation **Impact**

prioritised over others, and coach development was not synchronised with player recruitment. Concerns were also expressed about the sustainability of the planned implementation in terms of available staffing and funding, and speed of the roll-out to "ensure quality is achieved through consolidation rather than delivering too much too quickly" (Snowling 2011: 6).

NZF's experience illustrates programme implementation needs to be phased and managed so that NSO expectations match the capability and capacity of SDOs and volunteers to understand, accept, and deliver these. It takes time and perseverance by SDOs to ensure the programme's initiatives are adopted and effectively introduced by volunteers into clubs and schools. Some take longer than others to be convinced of the value of change and innovation over the status quo (see Chapter 6). Too often NSOs want to impose their own demanding agendas and time frames on community sport without considering the existing rhythms, abilities, and commitments of its volunteer base. As NZF found in trying to implement frame breaking change across the football community, it "underestimated this change process and what is required to achieve this" (Snowling 2011: 6).

The 'development of sport' process also must be sustainable if it is to be effective. Lindsey (2008) suggests the terms 'sustainable' and 'sustainability' are used very liberally in the context of sport development with little guidance as to how they should be achieved. 'Sustainable'' is defined in this book as to retain, maintain, continue, keep going, or prolong. It implies continuity and the importance of a long-term time frame. Some apply 'sustainability' to the capability of NSOs to continuously deliver agreed outcomes, others to funding their development initiatives to ensure they have a lasting impact on the sport.

NZC perceived 'sustainability' as an embracing, multi-dimensional, dynamic concept. It referred to the capability and capacity of both its NDP to create and maintain relevant opportunities and experiences, and individuals, clubs, and schools to adopt these to change, retain, and build on these improvements (Charlton 2010). In other words, sustainability in cricket was seen as an outcome of the planned and ongoing integration of the key elements (game, player, coach (volunteer), provider, and facility development) that comprise the 'development of sport' process (see Figure 2.1).

The interconnectedness of these elements was critical to the long-term sustainability of NZC's programme, so too was NZC's guarantee of funding to support the regional delivery network (see Chapter 5). While at times during the first decade of the programme the funding flow was less than expected, which slowed its implementation, its overall steady increase gave confidence to the RSOs and their CCCs that NZC valued and supported the programme. Indeed, the continued investment by NZC and impact of its programme encouraged additional funding support from local and regional partners. This contrasted with the second decade of the programme, where funding, guidance, and support were reduced by NZC, as it reprioritised high performance, especially its professional arm. The integrity and sustainability of other sports' development programmes have also been affected by overdependence on, and variability of, funding sources. Indeed, NZF's Federations expressed concern about the sustainability of their FDMs and FDOs, and future effective delivery of the WOFP because of "the risk of relying on grants and risk of key stakeholders . . . withdrawing funding" (Snowling 2011: 8).

REVIEW QUESTIONS

1. What two important considerations are highlighted for NSOs intervening in community sport?
2. What length of time is considered necessary to design, implement, and measure the impact of a community sport programme, and why?
   - What are the side-effects for sports compressing the time frame and introducing too many initiatives concurrently?
3. What does 'sustainability' mean in terms of a community sport development programme?
   - Is it about funding or creating enduring innovation and change within community sport, or both?

CONCLUSION

Reflecting on the lessons learned over the past two decades from NZC's intervention to grow and sustain community cricket, similar development experiences observed in football, hockey, and tennis, and insights of other practitioners working in different sports and countries, this chapter has identified 10 bespoke steps required to create, implement, and monitor a 'development of sport' plan, programme, and practice. These steps, while interchangeable in sequence, are founded on a whole-of-sport blueprint, within which community sport must be defined and delineated, before a sport development plan is researched and prepared, a programme designed and tested, and then implemented and monitored in practice in clubs and schools. The plan and derived programme are participant-centred, being structured around multiple player pathways and initiatives, bounded and serviced by aligned pathways and initiatives which engage and progress coaches, officials, and administrators. The translation of the programme into practice by a regional delivery network, requires the selection of SDOs with the capability and skills to facilitate its implementation, by persuading and training volunteers to deliver its initiatives which cater for the diverse needs of participants at all levels. To assist SDOs and ensure the effectiveness of the programme and its initiatives, standardised systems of planning, procedures, and accountabilities need to underpin their delivery, and regular recording and reporting of outcomes undertaken and evaluated to measure their effectiveness and impact.

To successfully introduce these steps and maintain the vitality and integrity of the underlying programme, NSOs must commit to a long-term strategy and judiciously phased and managed implementation, not a short-term, or 'one-off', quick-fix. Sufficient resources and time must be allocated to achieve its community sport objectives of growth and sustainability. Each step must be addressed by NSOs and sport development practitioners, if they intend to influence their sport within clubs and schools, especially to challenge what's happening now, and putting in place strategies and initiatives to introduce new ways of presenting and delivering their codes. Pause and ponder 11.1 offers a checklist for practitioners, based on the lessons learned, of prerequisites for community sport interventions.

PAUSE and PONDER 11.1

Key do's for development of community sport interventions

- **DO** ensure NSOs and/or RSOs undertake appropriate research and stakeholder consultation as a basis for drafting a whole-of-sport overview, defining development and its scope, and formulating an integrated community sport development plan and programme.
- **DO** understand that it is no longer just about the provision of relevant opportunities, but how they are packaged and presented to meet participants' needs and the overall quality of their sporting experience.
- **DO** allocate sufficient, sustainable funding to establish and maintain the intervention, then 'ring-fence' it specifically for the development of community sport, do not bulk fund it so its purpose is not apparent.
- **DO** set specific accountabilities for this funding, not vague outcomes, with clear evidence required of it being used to fund SDO salaries, implement specific initiatives, and achieve agreed targets.
- **DO** undertake regular monitoring and evaluation of the performance of NSOs and/or RSOs and their adherence to the development programme.
- **DO** appoint a SDM with the seniority to advocate for, and influence NSO and/or RSO boards and senior leaders, as without seniority and access to decision-making, SDMs are left to the vagaries of changing sport policy and funding priorities.
- **DO** establish SDOs job specifications and position descriptions that clearly focus on their 'development of sport' role to revitalise and grow community sport, not coaching, and ensure it is not overburdened with tasks outside its remit, such as administration and facility management.
- **DO** ensure SDOs have the depth of capability, knowledge, and experience to fulfil their full role, not just aspects of it.
- **DO** appraise SDOs regularly, and ensure they receive strong support, encouragement, and guidance from their NSO and/or RSOs.
- **DO** fund SDOs adequately, ensure they are trained properly to undertake their role, and receive regular networking and professional development opportunities.
- **DO** encourage tertiary institutions to offer courses or modules in sport-related courses on sport development, especially the 'development of sport', and the requirements of working in, and introducing change and innovation into, a volunteer environment, to get buy-in and acceptance, and build trust and credibility.
- **DO** concentrate initially on areas of strength in community sport and ensure they are stable and functioning effectively, before moving to more challenging targets. Too often this is done in reverse, that is, instead of working to sustain strong clubs and schools, the tendency is to try and reactivate subsistence-type clubs and schools, or try and get inactive people active, with limited effect. It is important in development to start in the centre and work outwards.

- **DO** discourage NSOs and RSOs building office-chair empires of highly paid SDMs and administrators, with few, less well-paid SDOs trying to deliver programmes. Development is about being in the field, face-to-face with volunteers, players, parents and teachers, meeting challenges head-on, devising practical solutions, not pontificating from afar. SDMs need to be in the trenches with their soldiers, not watching the action from a safe distance.
- **DO** be aware of diverting scarce funding into other regional bodies that sit outside the direct sport delivery system, many building their own empires, and as such resented by the sports at a regional and local level for consuming valuable community resources but do little to support their function.
- **DO** undertake research to establish more precise definitions of participation and improve systems for collecting and collating 'development of sport' statistics, especially for participation. Don't use exposure or sampling figures to inflate participation numbers.
- **DO** engage with local government for them to partner in the provision of spaces and facilities for community sport.
- **DO** ensure a greater connect, not disconnect, between national sport agencies, NSOs, and communities. Too often decisions are made at the first two levels about legacy projects and 'development of sport' change and innovation, but without any consultation or buy-in from community volunteers. It is just assumed they will do it! There is a lack of understanding of the role and importance of volunteers and their needs. If they are required to deliver new initiatives, they must be (a) made aware of these, (b) buy into their value and benefits, and (c) have the capability, capacity, infrastructure, and services within their clubs and schools to adopt and effectively deliver these.
- **DO** ensure funding and programmes are both sustainable and long-term. Little is achieved, apart from alienation and distrust, when programmes are changed, with little chance to see if they are effective, or if funding is withdrawn, because it is to be placed elsewhere.
- **DO** understand that change at a community level is slow and incremental, it requires patience and perseverance, it must be communicated continuously, because of volunteer turnover, training is essential, as is consistency in purpose and focus, and long-term commitment.

REFERENCES

Astle, A. M. (1999). *New Zealand Cricket: National development plan*. Planning document. New Zealand Cricket, Christchurch.

Astle, A. M (2000a). *MILO Have-A-Go cricket coaching manual for children 6–8 years*. Christchurch: New Zealand Cricket.

Astle, A. M. (2000b). *MILO Kiwi cricket coaching manual for children 7–10 years*. Christchurch: New Zealand Cricket.

Astle, A. M. (2000c). *MILO initiatives: Guidelines for MILO Summer Squad cricket development officers*. Instruction manual. New Zealand Cricket, Christchurch.

Astle, A. M. (2001). *Community Cricket initiatives: Community cricket coordinators' manual*. Instruction manual. New Zealand Cricket, Christchurch.

Astle, A. M. (2009). *New Zealand Cricket: National development plan and programme*. Planning document. New Zealand Cricket, Christchurch.

Astle, A. M. (2011). *Community sport implementation plan: Collaborative Delivery and outcomes*. Planning document. Sport and Recreation New Zealand, Wellington.

Astle, A. M. (2014). *Sport development – Plan, programme and practice: A case study of the planned intervention by New Zealand Cricket into cricket in New Zealand*. PhD, Massey University, Palmerston North, New Zealand.

Bloyce, D., Smith, A., Mead, R., & Morris, J. (2008). 'Playing the game (plan)': A figurational analysis of organisational change in sports development in England. *European Sport Management Quarterly, 8*(4), 359–378.

Collins, S. (2011). Sport development and adult participation in New Zealand. In B. Houlihan & M. Green (Eds.), *Routledge handbook of sports development* (pp. 231–242). London and New York: Routledge.

Charlton, T. (2010). 'Grow and sustain': The role of community sports provision in promoting a participation legacy for the 2012 Olympic Games. *International Journal of Sport Policy, 2*(3), 347–366.

Eady, J. (1993). *Practical sports development*. Harlow: Longman.

Girginov, V., & Hills, L. (2008). A sustainable sports legacy: Creating a link between the London Olympics and sports participation. *The International Journal of the History of Sport, 25*(14), 2091–2116.

Green, K. (2012). London 2012 and sports participation: The myths of legacy. *Significance, 9*(3), 13–16.

Gryphon Governance Consultants. (2011). *Organisational change in seven selected sports: What can be learnt and applied?* Sport and Recreation New Zealand, Wellington.

Herdman, J. (2010). *Whole of football plan*. Business plan. New Zealand Football, Auckland.

Herdman, J. (2011). *Whole of football pilot ready to take flight*. Retrieved from http://nzfootball.co.nz website.

High Performance Sport New Zealand. (2013). *Sports talent development programme announced*. Retrieved from http://hpsnz.org.nz/news-events/sports-talent-development-programme-announced website.

Houlihan, B. (2011a). Sports development and adult mass participation. Introduction: The neglect of adult participation. In B. Houlihan & M. Green (Eds.), *Routledge handbook of sports development* (pp. 213–215). London and New York: Routledge.

Houlihan, B. (2011b). England. In M. Nicholson, R. Hoye, & B. Houlihan (Eds.), *Participation in sport: International policy perspectives* (pp. 10–24). London and New York: Routledge.

Hunt, T. (2014, September 13). Sevens boss says he chose to resign. *The Dominion Post*, p. A3.

Keech, M. (2011). Sport and adult mass participation in England. In B. Houlihan & M. Green (Eds.), *Routledge handbook of sports development* (pp. 217–230). London and New York: Routledge.

Kitchin, P. J., & Howe, P. D. (2014). The mainstreaming of disability cricket in England and Wales: Integration 'One Game' at a time. *Sport Management Review, 17*(1), 65–77.

Lindsey, I. (2008). Conceptualising sustainability in sports development. *Leisure Studies, 27*(3), 279–294.

Macrae, E. (2017). Delivering sports participation legacies at the grassroots level: The voluntary sports clubs of Glasgow 2014. *Journal of Sport Management, 31*(1), 15–26.

MacFarlane, C. (2016). *Sport New Zealand smaller NSOs*. Powerpoint presentation to Tier 4 and 5 NSOs' Forum. Sport New Zealand, Wellington.

Mutter, F., & Pawlowski, T. (2014). Role models in sports – Can success in professional sports increase the demand for amateur sport participation? *Sport Management Review, 17*(3), 324–336.

Napier, L. (2014, September 14). The fight for netball's dollars. *Sunday Star Times*, p. B6.

Nicholson, M., Hoye, R., & Houlihan, B. (2011). Conclusion. In M. Nicholson, R. Hoye, & B. Houlihan (Eds.), *Participation in sport: International policy perspectives* (pp. 294–308). London and New York: Routledge.

Shephard, S. (2013, July 26). 2012 Olympic legacy: Built to last? *Sport*, pp. 24–26.

Smith, T. (2012a, November 13). SNZ president backs crisis meeting over sport's direction. *The Press*, p. B15.

Smith, T. (2012b, December 15). Softball NZ's serious crisis needs real resolution. *The Press*, p. D4.

Snedden, M. (2017a). *Positioning cricket for the future*. Unpublished One Cricket Project Report. New Zealand Cricket, Auckland.

Snedden, M. (2017b). *Positioning cricket for the future: Interim report on 'Support for the delivery of community cricket'*. Unpublished One Cricket Project Report. New Zealand Cricket, Auckland.

Snedden, M. (2018). *One cricket – Community cricket*. Unpublished NZC Board Report. New Zealand Cricket, Auckland.

Snowling, N. (2011). *Interview findings for New Zealand Football Federation CEOs*. Programme review. Sport and Recreation New Zealand, Wellington.

SPARC. (2009a). *Sport and recreation – Everyone. Everyday. Sport and Recreation New Zealand's strategic plan 2009–2015*. Wellington: Sport and Recreation New Zealand.

SPARC. (2009b). *Sport and recreation pathway*. Planning document. Wellington: Sport and Recreation New Zealand.

SPARC. (2009c). *NZ sport and recreation pathway*. Powerpoint presentation. Sport and Recreation New Zealand, Wellington.

SPARC. (2009d). *Powering participation: Successful initiatives to boost sports participation and club membership*. Wellington: Sport and Recreation New Zealand.

Sport England. (2007). *Impact in 3D: A learning guide for practitioners in community sport*. Retrieved from www.sportengland.org/research/evaluating_impact.aspx website.

Sport England. (2008). *Grow, sustain, excel: Strategy 2008–11*. London: Sport England.

Sport England. (2009). *Secondary offer: Measuring the impact of interventions*. London: Sport England.

Tong, J. (2012). *A review of the Grasshoppers program and its impact on junior club membership in New Zealand*. Programme review. Tennis New Zealand, Auckland.

Veal, A. J., Toohey, K., & Frawley, S. (2012). The sport participation legacy of the Sydney 2000 Olympic Games and other international sporting events hosted in Australia. *Journal of Policy Research in Tourism, Leisure and Events, 4*(2), 155–184.

Walker, P. (2017). Cricket's battle for the working classes: Breaking the grass ceiling. In L. Booth (Ed.), *Wisden cricketers' almanack* (154th ed., pp. 55–61). London: John Wisden & Co.

Website

www.aflnz.co.nz/afl-kiwikick/

Index